Human Capital
2002

The PricewaterhouseCoopers Endowment for
The Business of Government

THE PRICEWATERHOUSECOOPERS ENDOWMENT SERIES ON THE BUSINESS OF GOVERNMENT

Series Editors: Mark A. Abramson and Paul R. Lawrence

The PricewaterhouseCoopers Endowment Series on The Business of Government explores new approaches to improving the effectiveness of government at the federal, state, and local levels. The Series is aimed at providing cutting-edge knowledge to government leaders, academics, and students about the management of government in the 21st century.

Publications in the series include:

2001
Transforming Organizations, *edited by Mark A. Abramson and Paul R. Lawrence*
E-Government 2001, *edited by Mark A. Abramson and Grady E. Means*
Managing for Results 2002, *edited by Mark A. Abramson and John M. Kamensky*
Memos to the President: Management Advice from the Nation's Top Public Administrators, *edited by Mark A. Abramson*

2002
Innovation, *edited by Mark A. Abramson and Ian D. Littman*
E-Government 2002, *edited by Mark A. Abramson and Grady E. Means*

Human Capital 2002

EDITED BY

MARK A. ABRAMSON
THE PRICEWATERHOUSECOOPERS ENDOWMENT
FOR THE BUSINESS OF GOVERNMENT
and
NICOLE WILLENZ GARDNER
PRICEWATERHOUSECOOPERS

ROWMAN & LITTLEFIELD PUBLISHERS, INC.
Lanham • Boulder • New York • Oxford

ROWMAN & LITTLEFIELD PUBLISHERS, INC.

Published in the United States of America
by Rowman & Littlefield Publishers, Inc.
4720 Boston Way, Lanham, Maryland 20706
www.rowmanlittlefield.com

12 Hid's Copse Road
Cumnor Hill, Oxford OX2 9JJ, England

British Library Cataloguing in Publication Information Available

Library of Congress Cataloging-in-Publication Data Available

0-7425-2276-8 (alk. paper)
0-7425-2277-6 (pbk.: alk. paper)

Printed in the United States of America

⊖™ The paper used in this publication meets the minimum requirements of American National Standard for Information Sciences—Permanence of Paper for Printed Library Materials, ANSI/NISO Z39.48-1992.

To

Bruce and Judy Abramson

Chris Gardner

TABLE OF CONTENTS

PART I

The Human Capital Challenge

CHAPTER ONE

The Human Capital Challenge

Mark A. Abramson
Executive Director, The PricewaterhouseCoopers
Endowment for The Business of Government

Ruby B. DeMesme
Director
PwC Consulting

Nicole Willenz Gardner
Partner
PwC Consulting

Introduction

The federal workforce and federal workplace are changing. There has been change in agency missions, change in the nature of work, change in performance requirements, and change in the demographics and expectations of the new workforce. It is often said that the only thing that has been constant in the past decade has been change.

While change can be viewed as both stressful and unpleasant, it can also be viewed as an exciting challenge and an opportunity for improvement. The federal government now faces two major challenges:

- The people challenge
- The workplace challenge

And government needs to respond effectively to both challenges if it is to continue to perform the ever changing and more complex missions and activities assigned to the federal workforce.

The need to respond to both the people and workplace challenge is driven by a vision of the 21st century workforce as one that is agile, highly skilled, adequately compensated, and appropriately assigned. In addition, the work environment must be safe, healthy, and productive, offering flexible

---

Change Drivers

There is now a confluence of events that has created powerful drivers to transform the federal workforce and workplace. The drivers are:

- **Shifting Demographics:** The workforce is changing in both complexion and responsibilities. These changes allow for new and diverse skills and talents to enter the workforce and the opportunity to restructure agencies to become more citizen-centric and results-oriented.
- **Budget Constraints:** When funds are limited, agencies must focus on improving employee productivity and the capability of the entire workforce.
- **Market Force Demands:** As part of the "now" generation, the government workforce will be held accountable for becoming leaner, more flexible, and more responsive and timely in delivering services. By attracting and retaining the best and brightest minds, who bring new ideas with them, innovations in performance will be more likely to occur.
- **New Technology Requirements:** Gaining access to and applying today's technology to recruitment, records management, systems integration, and employee services will provide the tools needed to better respond to workforce and customer demands.

policies and modernized systems. To meet this vision, the government must undergo a transformation. The first step in achieving that transformation is to change the way it has traditionally viewed people. Instead of taking them for granted, people are now being recognized as "human capital"—the key to an organization's success or failure. This change in attitude toward employees is a key step in the transformation that is under way throughout government.

The People Challenge

The new conventional wisdom is that all sectors of society are engaged in a "war for talent." While the "supply and demand" of talent tends to fluctuate with changes in the national economy, the key point is that talent can no longer be taken for granted and that all organizations must now engage in competition for the best and brightest in the nation's workforce. The "war for talent" has many components: how organizations recruit, retain, and develop their people.

The "war for talent," however, starts with recruiting. In their book *The War for Talent*, Ed Michaels, Helen Handfield-Jones, and Beth Axelrod write, "The recruiting game has changed dramatically. It's no longer about selecting the best person from a long line of candidates; it's about going out and finding great candidates." (Michaels et al., 13) Another "war" book, *Winning the Talent Wars* by Bruce Tulgan, also emphasizes the importance of recruitment. He writes, "Your human resources department can no longer be on the sidelines for the talent wars. They must become strategic staffing war rooms, central to the daily scramble." (Tulgan, 74)

A prime recruiting ground for government continues to be schools of public policy and public administration. In chapter two of this book, "Winning the Best and the Brightest," Carol Chetkovich presents findings from her research on public policy student attitudes toward public service. She found, somewhat surprisingly, that even students who had chosen to obtain a master's degree in public policy were now leaning toward seeking employment in the nonprofit or private sectors rather than the public sector. The students, however, continue to voice support for the concept of public service.

If the trend is to be reversed, Chetkovich concludes that a series of actions are needed on both the part of public policy school themselves and the government. In the area of recruiting, Chetkovich recommends that the government:
- Recruit earlier, more energetically, and proactively.
- Streamline and increase flexibility in hiring processes.
- Open up more lateral hiring options.

The Chetkovich recommendations for aggressive recruiting and lateral hiring are strongly supported by the "war for talent" literature. Michaels, Handfield-Jones, and Axelrod write, "We believe that companies must fundamentally rethink and rebuild their recruiting strategies. They should hire at all levels—middle and senior as well as entry levels—which is a powerful way to inject new skills and new perspectives." (Michaels et al., 13)

Like the private sector, the government has traditionally been characterized by lifelong careers in the same organization. "For several generations, the corporate ladder was the dominant image for the way people move through companies. People entered at the bottom, and if they were successful, climbed to the top," write Michaels, Handfield-Jones, and Axelrod. (Michaels et al., 71) They argue, as do many others, that the old paradigm has now been shattered. It began to break in the early 1990s, report Michaels, Handfield-Jones, and Axelrod, "when companies realized that they didn't have enough talented managers in their ranks to pursue all the opportunities and challenges they were facing.... By the end of the decade, promoting exclusively from within, the cultural model that had existed since the beginning of the Industrial Revolution, was disappearing." (Michaels et al., 71)

Over the last several years, both the executive branch and the United States Congress also came to the realization that the federal government might not have all the talent it needed to respond to the increasingly complex tasks that it was being asked to undertake. In response to the perceived need for additional talent from the outside, Congress gave four federal agencies special authorities for hiring professionals from the outside. The special authorities also included increased flexibility in setting their pay and recruiting outside candidates. In chapter three, "A Weapon in the War for Talent," Hal Rainey presents case studies of how the Federal Aviation Administration, the U.S. Patent and Trademark Office, the Office of Student Financial Assistance, and the Internal Revenue Service have used their special authorities to recruit new, experienced talent into the federal government.

The use of special authorities has proven to be controversial in the federal government. There have been complaints from some senior career civil servants that the new special authority executives are receiving a higher level of pay than members of the career Senior Executive Service. But Rainey concludes that special recruiting authorities have proven to be a valuable addition to an agency's hiring portfolio. It can be argued that in the "war for talent" era, the federal government needs a broader set of hiring "tools" than have traditionally been available in the past. Just as the private sector concluded that it may no longer have all the necessary talent within its own organizations to meet future business challenges, the federal government may also sometimes need to go outside of its own organization to recruit new talent. Rainey quotes from IRS testimony to Congress, "Our critical pay

Organizational Checklist—Responding to the People Challenge

One of the key elements in organizations moving forward is for each to review where they currently are and where they want to go in the future. Organizations should ask themselves the following questions:

- How successful are your recruiting efforts?
- Do your workers' present skills match your future position requirements?
- Are your employees being developed for today's—and tomorrow's—mission?
- Are your employees agile and mobile?
- Do you have a succession-planning program in place?
- How well prepared are you for pending retirements in your organization?
- Are you fully using the flexible recruiting and retention tools currently available?
- Do you have a human resource strategic plan in place?
- Do you have an adequate training budget?
- Do you offer employee education advancement options?
- Do you have a formal employee recognition program?

executives bring external experience, practices, and knowledge not currently available within the organization."

Another major theme of the "war for talent" is the need to develop and nurture talent already in the organization through a variety of executive development activities. The conventional wisdom now is that special attention and increased resources need to be devoted to developing employees in order both to enhance their ability to achieve their organization's mission and to serve as a major retention tool. Nearly 60 percent of managers who intend to leave their current employer within the next two years cite insufficient development and learning opportunities as critical or very important reasons for their leaving. (Michaels et al., 98)

In chapter four, "Organizations Growing Leaders," Ray Blunt describes how five organizations in the federal government—the Pension Benefit Guaranty Corporation, the United States Coast Guard, the Western Area Power Administration, the Veterans Benefits Administration, and the Social Security Administration—each created effective executive development programs. While there are common elements in all the programs, one is impressed by the variety of techniques and approaches used in the various programs. Blunt writes, "There are few consistent practices used by all of the exemplary organizations. The use of senior mentors, the identification of behavioral leader competencies for development ... the use of well targeted internal training courses, and the use of self-development study or reading are all consistent practices. In addition, exposure to the strategic agenda and to officials of the organization and the use of individualized development plans are widely used."

In chapter five, "Leaders Growing Leaders," Blunt shifts his focus to the importance of individual leaders developing their successors. Blunt describes four roles that current executives can play in developing future leaders: as exemplars, mentors, coaches, and teachers. In support of Blunt's emphasis on the importance of mentoring and coaching, the "talent" literature views coaching as both an important retention and development tool. Bruce Tulgan writes, "It takes time to build an unstoppable groundswell, but the need for coaching is immediate." (Tulgan, 114) He reports that many organizations are turning to dedicated insiders or outside professionals to be coaches to employees throughout the ranks.

There is clear evidence that public policy students are eager for both developmental activities and the opportunity to be mentored and coached. In chapter two, Chetkovich recommends that government support professional development and make advancement opportunities clear as effective recruiting tools. She writes, "Entry-level professionals are very concerned about the possibilities opened up or closed down by their first position, particularly given the expected fluidity of their careers. Even if advancement in the traditional sense of promotions on a career ladder is not available, the opportunity to learn, to develop new skills, and to be exposed both to new substantive areas and to other institutions and actors are all extremely valuable and appealing aspects of the job."

In chapter four, Blunt states that the "use of challenging job-based experiences" as a development strategy is a key principle of excellent organizations. While "job-based experiences" are clearly viewed as a major factor in an individual's personal development as a leader and manager, the reality is that mobility continues to be limited in the federal government. With the exception of temporary assignments as part of agency executive development programs, such as those described by Blunt in chapter four, individuals are pretty much left to their own devices to find new positions and challenges in government.

In chapter six, "Reflections on Mobility," Michael Serlin presents case studies of six individuals who achieved high mobility and moved across the federal landscape during their careers. Serlin argues that such mobility is good for both the individual moving from agency to agency and the organizations receiving them. "All of the individuals featured," writes Serlin, "introduced approaches in the agencies they joined by building on past managerial experiences and knowledge." In many ways, these individuals became living "knowledge transfer" agents by bringing their experience from one organization to another.

Serlin recommends that the federal government become more aggressive and active in encouraging mobility within the federal government. He advocates more cross-training across government and the creation of both a web-based database of senior executives and a well-staffed and knowledgeable executive search office in government to assist agencies in filling key senior career positions. In a related theme to Chetkovich's call for an increase in lateral hiring, Serlin recommends the development of incentives to encourage executives who leave federal service to return later in their careers.

By effectively responding to the various aspects of the people challenge, such as recruiting and development, the federal government will come a long way to preparing itself for the next decade and beyond. But if it does not also effectively meet the second challenge, the workplace challenge, any success in meeting the people challenge will have gone to waste. Responding effectively to the workplace challenge is potentially government's greatest retention tool. Employees will continue to work for their present employer as long as they are being engaged, challenged, and stimulated in a pleasant, congenial work environment. Nearly 60 percent of managers report that "interesting, challenging work" is the critical factor in their decision to join and stay with an organization. (Michaels et al., 45) Thus, it can be argued that the "work" and the "workplace" are keys to retention and productivity in the office.

The Workplace Challenge

This second challenge can be characterized as the challenge to create a workplace in which individuals find fulfillment and satisfaction, and achieve their personal—and the organization's—goals. The workplace challenge is multifaceted and must be viewed from several vantage points. First, it deals with the environment, both physical and emotional. It includes the treatment of people and the application of guidelines and processes, and it encompasses the infrastructure from which transformation takes place. The environment is generally measured by the "climate" in the workplace: the way people feel about their work, their leaders, and their co-workers. The goal is to make the climate highly conducive to ensuring employees' personal and professional growth. Emphasis should be placed on making the workplace pleasant from both a visual and comfort standpoint.

Just as the "war for talent" has spawned a growing literature, so too has the "workplace" issue, with a focus on both positive and negative trends surrounding the workplace. In *White-Collar Sweatshop*, Jill Andresky Fraser describes the trend toward longer hours, declining rewards, and increased pressure in the private sector. She writes: "Workloads have gotten so heavy that free time really does seem an unimaginable luxury for men and women in all kinds of jobs and industries across the United States. Cell phones, laptops, and other workplace technologies loom as inescapable, since without them white-collar staffers cannot hope to meet the '24/7' demands of their employers. As layoffs, benefit cutbacks, and subtle forms of age discrimination have become ever more pervasive throughout the business world, long-term security for many people now seems to hang on the whims of the stock market, rather than on the strength of their careers." (Fraser, 200)

On the "positive" side of the workplace literature, Don Cohen and Laurence Prusak's *In Good Company* describe how organizations are now using "social capital" to improve life in the workplace and to make organizations more effective. Cohen and Prusak define social capital as consisting of "the stock of active connections among people: the trust, mutual understanding, and shared values that bind the members of human networks and communities and make cooperative action possible." (Cohen and Prusak, 4) Their picture of organizations is much more positive than that of Fraser. Cohen and Prusak describe corporations that are working hard to increase trust and communication within their organization.

In chapter seven, "A Learning-Based Approach to Leading Change," Barry Sugarman describes a new organizational model—the learning organization. Building on the work of Peter Senge, Sugarman contrasts the new learning organization with the traditional model of the bureaucracy. The new learning organization is more informal, more creative, more participatory, and more flexible than the traditional bureaucracy. Sugarman presents three case studies of federal organizations that attempted to move toward a learning organizational model. He also describes how a learning-based change model differs from the traditional change model.

While the learning organization model has not yet spread to many other organizations in government, it is precisely this model that Chetkovich argues will be more appealing to the new generation of students entering the workplace. To attract more public policy students, she recommends in chapter two that government:
- Offer work that makes use of the candidate's skills and interest in policy.
- Restructure workplaces away from hierarchy and toward interaction.

Chetkovich writes, "Numerous scholars and consultants have argued that the successful 'organization of the future' will be fluid and interactive rather than rigid and hierarchical. Communication and coordination arrangements will shift according to the nature of the task, and accountability will be based more on results than rules; it will also be mutual rather than top-down.... Just as flexibility and autonomy can be satisfying, a rule-bound hierarchical environment can be disheartening to employees and discouraging to prospective candidates."

Organizational Checklist—Responding to the Workplace Challenge

Just as organizations should ask questions related to meeting the people challenge, there are also questions that should be asked in regard to the workplace challenge:

- Do workers have adequate office space, use of computers, and safe working space?
- Are enterprise portal systems available to employees?
- Is there a strategic plan that addresses separate program planning for Equal Employment Opportunity and diversity programs?
- Is there a partnership council with scheduled meetings (at least quarterly) with the unions?
- Do you provide alternative work schedules?
- Is flexi-place work scheduling available?
- Do you provide transportation subsidies?
- Do you offer child-care services on the premises or provide subsidies?
- Do you have separate Equal Employment Opportunity and diversity programs?
- Are meals, or access to kitchens, readily available?

A major defining characteristic of the new workplace will be the concept of collaborative management. In chapter eight, "Labor-Management Partnerships," Barry Rubin and Richard Rubin describe the collaboration that took place in Indianapolis, Indiana, between labor and management. They present a case study of how Mayor Stephen Goldsmith forged an effective working partnership with the American Federation of State, County and Municipal Employees (AFSCME).

Another key characteristic of the organization of the future is that it will be a more diverse workplace than it has been historically. In chapter nine, "A Changing Workforce," Katherine C. Naff and J. Edward Kellough explore the concept of diversity and its implication for the workplace of the future. Naff and Kellough support the concept of diversity set forth by the National Aeronautics and Space Administration (NASA), which says that employees are diverse because "they bring a variety of different backgrounds, customs, beliefs, religions, languages, knowledge, superstitions, values, social characteristics ... with them to the workplace." In addition to racial and ethnic cultural groups, NASA also states that there are class cultures, age cultures, gender cultures, and regional cultures.

Naff and Kellough explore the differences between diversity and the traditional equal employment opportunity/affirmative action approach. They describe the diversity literature, which argues that diversity must be "managed" in the future if organizations are to effectively create workplaces in which employees work together in a cooperative, productive manner. Without increased attention to differences and how individuals from different backgrounds work together, there is danger that productivity and organizational effectiveness will suffer in the years ahead. Rather than being about legal and social requirements as has been historically the case with EEO/affirmative action, Naff and Kellough support the argument that managing diversity is about "productivity, efficiency, and quality."

Clearly, the multiple dimensions of the people and workplace challenges discussed in this chapter present senior leadership in the federal government with a daunting task. Office of Personnel Management Director Kay Coles James has expressed a vision for a future federal workforce that is "world-class" and against which the private sector will benchmark for best practices. We present this volume to spark debate and discussion about how this lofty vision can become a reality.

Bibliography

Cohen, Don and Laurence Prusak. 2001. *In Good Company: How Social Capital Makes Organizations Work*. Boston: Harvard Business School Press.

Fraser, Jill Andresky. 2001. *White-Collar Sweatshop: The Deterioration of Work and Its Rewards in Corporate America*. New York: W. W. Norton & Company.

Michaels, Ed, Helen Handfield-Jones, and Beth Aexlrod. 2001. *The War for Talent*. Boston: Harvard Business School Press.

Tulgan, Bruce. 2001. *Winning the Talent Wars*. New York: W. W. Norton & Company.

Recommended Reading

In addition to the books listed in the bibliography, the following are also recommended:

Cappelli, Peter. 1999. *The New Deal at Work: Managing the Market-Driven Workforce*. Boston: Harvard Business School Press.

Ciulla, Joanne B. 2000. *The Working Life: The Promise and Betrayal of Modern Work*. New York: Times Books.

Donkin, Donald. 2001. *Blood Sweat & Tears: The Evolution of Work*. New York: Texere.

Drucker, Peter. 1999. *Management Challenges for the 21st Century*. New York: Harper Business.

Leadbeater, Charles. 2000. *The Weightless Society*. New York: Texere.

Pink, Daniel H. 2001. *Free Agent Nation: How America's New Independent Workers Are Transforming the Way We Live*. New York: Warner Books.

Rayman, Paula M. 2001. *Beyond the Bottom Line: The Search for Dignity at Work*. New York: Palgrave.

Reich, Robert B. 2001. *The Future of Success*. New York: Alfred A. Knopf.

PART II

The People Challenge

CHAPTER TWO

Winning the Best and Brightest: Increasing the Attraction of Public Service

Carol Chetkovich
Assistant Professor of Public Policy
John F. Kennedy School of Government
Harvard University

This report was originally published in July 2001.

Introduction[1]

All employers today are engaged in an intense competition for good people. The economic growth of the 1990s, the increasing fluidity of professional careers, a declining supply of workers in the executive pipeline, and the high skill-demands of a knowledge-based economy have resulted in a "war for talent" waged by those who understand that human resources represent an organization's primary competitive advantage (Chambers, et al., 1998; Tulgan, 2001). In this context, government's decades-long struggle to attract and retain qualified personnel takes on even greater urgency (GAO, 2000; Garland, et al., 1989; Volcker, 1988; Conant, 2000). Both college-student interest in government careers and graduate enrollment in public administration programs, after peaking in the mid- to late-1970s, declined steeply in the 1980s (Conant, 2000) and college graduates of the 1990s have been found to hold negative views of federal government employment (GAO, 1994).

In the current climate, even graduates of public policy and administration programs are moving in increasing numbers away from government employment and into the private sector. Smaller proportions of these students are entering the public sector at graduation, and among those who do, increasing numbers leave eventually for other sectors. In some cases the shift reflects a choice to work in the nonprofit world, but the proportion entering the private (for-profit) sector is also growing. A recent survey of graduates from several public policy and administration programs found that 76 percent of those in the Class of 1974 entered the public sector at graduation, but among the Class of 1993, the proportion was only 49 percent; in addition, at the time of the survey (1998), only 50 percent of the earlier group and 41 percent of the later one were still working in government (Light, 1999). At Harvard's Kennedy School of Government the Master in Public Policy (M.P.P.) Class of 2000 sent more students into the private sector on graduation than into government (42 percent versus 34 percent).

What is puzzling is not that some proportion of graduates from public policy and administration programs enter the private sector, but that the magnitude of the shift away from government is so large. These are students who chose to enter schools of government, not law or business. For so many of them to shun government employment—at a time when the public-sector talent pool, particularly at the federal level is diminishing—raises concerns about the future of government and questions about the role of institutions designed to train public leaders.

How should we understand the private-sector employment of policy graduates? Is it a different form of public-interest work, a short-term opportunity for new skill development to be followed by public-sector employment, or a decisive turn away from public-service careers? Do students enter these programs with a lesser commitment to public service than in the past, or rather with a different notion of it—one that de-emphasizes government? Given the motivations and expectations of today's students, what can government do to compete more effectively for their talent? And what can graduate schools do to help ensure that government remains a viable option in the "new public service" (Light, 1999)?

Data to address these kinds of questions are available from an ongoing, in-depth study of public policy training and socialization being conducted at the Kennedy School of Government (KSG) and University of California, Berkeley's Goldman School of Public Policy (GSPP). Master of Public Policy students in KSG's Class of 2000 and GSPP's Class of 2001 are participating in a series of five surveys and—for a subset of each class—semistructured interviews. Surveys and interviews are being conducted at entry, the end of the first year, the beginning and end of the second year, and several months after graduation. The data-collection plan permits comparison of the responses of individual students at different points in time as well as an opportunity to explore through interviews the meaning of closed-ended survey responses. Because the KSG students have completed their graduation-round of surveys and interviews, while GSPP students in the study have not yet graduated, the analysis here is based on the Harvard group. Details on sample sizes and response rates may be found in Appendix I.

The report looks first at the students' work-sector plans reported at different points in time, using data from the surveys and the school's Career Services office. These quantitative data are followed by a closer focus on the motivations and expectations expressed in initial interviews, which reveal the ambivalence and fluidity in student career intentions. The next section considers how the standard policy training process may interact with student attitudes to weaken rather than solidify a public-sector career orientation. A blend of interview and survey data are then used to explore the question of what draws policy students to the private versus public sector, and whether students who choose the former are doing so with the expectation of engaging in a different form of public service.

A summary of key findings is accompanied by recommendations to government on how it can compete more effectively for these candidates, and to public policy schools on how to strengthen the public-service orientation of their students and support the placement of graduates in public-sector jobs.

The View from the Students

From Entry to Graduation: Changes in Student Work-Sector Plans

KSG students were asked at three different points in time in which sector they planned primarily to work; options included various levels of government in the United States and internationally, domestic nonprofits and international non-governmental organizations (NGOs), domestic and international for-profits, "other sector" and "don't know." In the first two surveys, respondents were asked to give only one answer, and in the fourth survey those who had accepted a job were asked for one answer (about that job), but others were free to give multiple answers.

A relatively small proportion of students indicated planning for private-sector careers at entry, but a nearly equal number were undecided, and government's share was less than half of the total. A comparison of those answering the question in both the first and second surveys shows a very slight net shift toward the private sector (see Table 2.1).

Figures from the fourth survey (at the end of the program) and data from the school's Career Services office reveal a more decided shift toward the private sector. Table 2.2 shows the figures for those answering the work-sector question on both second and fourth surveys. (Numbers change for second survey respondents from Table 2.1 because not all responded to the fourth survey.) Because the fourth survey allowed multiple responses from those not yet employed, the proportions indicating government among their possibilities is relatively high (45 percent versus figures of 42 percent for nonprofits and 35 percent for the private sector), but among those choosing

Table 2.1: Planned Work Sector at First and Second Surveys
(Students responding to both first and second surveys, N = 100)

Planned Primary Sector	First Survey (at entry)	Second Survey (end of first year)
Government	39%	37%
Nonprofit	26%	24%
Private	15%	19%
Other	6%	6%
Don't know	14%	14%

Table 2.2: Planned Work Sector(s) at Second and Fourth Surveys
(Students responding to both second and fourth surveys, N = 81)

	Second Survey (end of first year)	Fourth Survey (near graduation)	
Government	41%	26%	government-only
		16%	government or nonprofit
		1%	government or private
		2%	any sector
Nonprofit	22%	19%	nonprofit-only
		16%	nonprofit or government
		5%	nonprofit or private
		2%	any sector
Private	17%	27%	private-only
		5%	private or nonprofit
		1%	private or government
		2%	any sector
Other/Don't know	20%	4%	

a single sector, the proportion selecting the private sector is as large as the proportion favoring the public sector. Furthermore, data published by KSG's Career Services on job placement for this class show changes in the same direction but even more pronounced. Career Services reported that as of September 2000, 42 percent of their respondents had taken private-sector jobs, versus 34 percent in government and 24 percent in nonprofits (Kennedy School of Government Career Services, *Placement Report 2000*).

How should we understand these apparent changes over time among students in KSG's M.P.P. program? Are students being pulled away from government toward others sectors? What happens to those who are uncertain? Individual-level analysis and correlations reveal that orientation remains consistent for some students in each sector, but that there is also considerable movement in all directions, including students becoming both less and more uncertain. Additionally, though the private-sector proportion is larger at the end of the training than at the beginning, even at entry there is a non-negligible proportion that is either private-oriented, has mixed aims, or is very uncertain about sectoral direction. And, finally, as the next section illustrates, even those students who express public-sector intent on a survey don't necessarily have in mind a traditional career-long commitment to government.

A Closer Look: In-Depth Discussions with Entering Students

A look only at survey responses and their change over time suggests that many students shift their career orientations from the public and/or nonprofit sectors toward the private sector by the time they graduate. But initial interview comments reveal a greater mix of motivations at the outset, and less clarity of direction than closed-ended survey responses might suggest, particularly among those whose responses indicate public-sector plans.

The distribution of intended work sectors among those interviewed differed slightly from the survey respondents as a whole, with a higher proportion of interviewees planning nonprofit careers, a lower proportion planning government, and a higher proportion in the uncertain or "other sector" categories. The proportion looking to predominantly private-sector careers was identical to the private-sector proportion among survey respondents as a whole.

Among the 26 initial interviewees were seven students whose survey responses indicated an intent to work primarily in the public sector, two at the federal level and five at the state or local level. But interview comments revealed expectations for something very different from a traditional public service career, particularly for the two men aiming at the federal level. Both of them anticipated movement between public and private sectors, and both sought high-level advisory roles in government. As Kevin[2] explained:

> I think that I do want to work in the policy sector—I do want to work for the government at some point and that's an absolute. But I think to do that really effectively it's very important to know about the private sector.... I think I want to do international policy in working for the government ... but I don't anticipate something like that happening right out—after I get out of the Kennedy School... I don't anticipate myself being a bureaucrat from the day I get out of the Kennedy School until I retire.

One desirable scenario, he said, would be to work in a consulting firm or a bank for a couple of years and then "when someone gets pulled out of one of those to go work in Washington—you know, they get the tap on the shoulder" he would find himself going along. It would be "a very secondary role, but at least switching into a direct advising to someone who's been appointed to something a little higher up. Sort of like the short-cut method of getting into government." When he said he wanted to work for the government, he meant "something very meaningful in a policy-advising role ... not just ... reading articles and summarizing them."

Marlon insisted that "I want to spend the majority of my life in the *public* sector, rather than the private sector." He went on to explain that "something I'd like to do at one point is be chief of staff for a congressperson, something [like] that." But at the same time, he believed he probably would work in the private sector for a time "because I need the experience and I probably need the money to pay back for college." He noted that one of his professors had commented on how "later in our lives the distinction between whether we will spend the majority of our lives in either sector will become blurred. And people will move from one to the other. So I guess being able to have the sets of skills that will allow me to move from one to the other [is important]." He was thinking also about attending law school, but said he didn't think he wanted to go into corporate practice.

> ... I don't want to do that, I mean that's not what I think I want to do, but also I think part of why I don't want to do that is 'cause I've never had the exposure to the private sector.... I haven't given myself the opportunity to be seduced by the private sector.... [For me, it's more] the elements involved in a job than necessarily the job itself. So I could be a paid lobbyist by a law firm, or work with representatives, stuff like that. That'd be fine with me and I'd [be] able to have the financial satisfaction and ... the satisfaction of the job.

Though Marlon said he wanted a career primarily in "public service," it wasn't clear from these kinds of comments what that meant for him; when he was asked directly, the answer he gave reflected a very broad notion defined more by what the work *isn't* than what it *is* (see "Struggling to Define 'Public Service'"). Neither Marlon nor Kevin included the federal government among their sector options on the graduation survey.

The five other interviewees whose survey responses favored public sector careers (in state or local government), though perhaps clearer in their definitions of public service than Marlon, nevertheless did not express particularly strong commitments to the public sector and in some cases reported decidedly mixed feelings. Geoff had worked in state government and was interested in continuing to work on social issues but was gravitating away from social service programs and toward economic development. In part this reflected the feeling that "government programs I'm increasingly not sold on, and I'm increasingly becoming frustrated with, and find them actually less interesting ... [in] the problems that they confront over and over again." Although he had found his state government work satisfying, he also found his public-sector colleagues far less dynamic and entrepreneurial than those with whom he had worked in the nonprofit sector. Arthur reported a very similar experience in which he had found an opportunity to work on discrimination issues at the state level very meaningful, but found coworker performance somewhat unprofessional: "I think it exacerbated some of my stereotypes of state workers a little."

Victor and Alicia also reported an interest primarily in state and local government, but both described their plans in a way that very much left

---

Struggling to Define "Public Service"

Carol: What does the phrase "public service" mean to you?

Marlon: That's a very good question. One would say the lines are blurring. Well, you know public service when you see it because it's no pay or low pay. That'd be the first clue. To me, public service means not being beholden—the monetary interest being the height of—the goal is not to make a profit. So any organization ... or entity ... whose goal is not to make money ... That's how I sort of define it, and I realize like—at one point I was really bad about saying, "Oh, that's 'public sector', 'private sector'" and making the division between the two. But now I'm a little bit less so because I mean one can call a profit industry who's not doing its job and making a profit a "nonprofit," you know, to some extent. .... A nonprofit can act just like a profit, it just, it's in the mission of the organization.

---

open the possibility of working outside government. Alicia's orientation was driven by a deep commitment to educational equity coupled with a desire to see the immediate impact of her work in her own community. She didn't imagine she'd stay with one employer for an extended period, and "ultimately if it worked out ... I'd probably want to do something that was independent-contracting oriented, in terms of tackling these issues, even if what I did by and large was still work with government agencies." Victor offered strikingly similar comments, saying he'd like to work as a liaison to federal or state agencies on behalf of local community needs, "whether that came through a consulting role—I don't know how it would be formulated ... I wasn't thinking private, at all. But again, who knows how it will turn out." The remaining respondent whose survey indicated a preference for the public sector was Anna, whose aim was to work with Native American tribes to strengthen their administrative and judicial capacities. Her commitment to public-sector work seemed the most definitive, though she also might consider self-employment consulting to tribal clients. In summary, even those expressing a preference for pre-dominantly public-sector careers at entry reflected ambivalence and uncertainty in their interviews.

Those who were either unclear about sector or inclined toward non-profits at the outset (half of the original sample, two-thirds of those partici-pating in all interviews) often spoke of the public sector in disparaging terms. Maria was "kind of disillusioned with government." Susan said when a college advisor suggested she think about KSG, "I heard 'government,' and I was like no, I don't want to go into government." And Leo noted that "I'm interested in government and public service [but] I don't want to be some mid-level bureaucrat in a cabinet department of something." Melanie's friends had questioned her coming to KSG because, as they put it, "'It's a school of government. Do you really want to work for the government—you [who] have problems with the government?'" In response, she said, "I think if you want to change anything, you gotta know what the problem is. Or the source of it .... I think the biggest [hardest] thing for *me* is gonna be taking a job in the government, more so than taking a job with the private sector." Asked to be more specific about what she called her "fear of government," she explained, "I don't want to be a part—right now—of decisions that I feel like could backfire, or I don't want to be a part of something ... I can't influence yet .... And I feel like I would be more effective if you know, five or 10 years down the line I joined the government with more experience, where I can wield that experience and say, look, listen to me!" Those who—like Flynn and Beryl—wanted to bring about social change through political mobilization thought primarily in terms of the nonprofit sector rather than government.

Some students were relatively indifferent to sector or explicitly planned multi-sector careers, usually beginning outside government. Jenna said simply, "I think that I will move around a lot between sectors ... I'm interested in so many things, and I think that, that I'm *good* at different things, and I think I'd like to test my skills in a bunch of different areas." Her entry survey indicated she didn't know what sector she planned to work in; at the end of the first year, she said state or local government, but at graduation had taken a consulting job.

Shelly and Peter both entered with a strongly expressed commitment to public service but simultaneously felt private-sector work initially was a strong possibility. Having worked in a hunger program, Shelly felt that she "really had the people in my mind and in my heart" and wanted to do social policy work, but at the same time "felt like going into nonprofits is very limiting.... I'm actually interested in going into management consulting for a few years ... and then *hopefully* that will train me better as a public servant—that's my hope and dream, to go back into policy service, whether it's at the government level or in community-based organizations...."

Peter grew up in a working-class family, took advantage of opportunities for upward mobility, and "felt compelled to ... give back." He had worked in nonprofit organizations and aimed eventually for "city government/politics" or "the nonprofit foundation track" but said that "short term, I'm considering options like consulting."

Diana was initially thinking in terms of the nonprofit world but wasn't committed to it: "I guess I'm not *averse* to going into the private sector, but ... I think it has to fulfill a larger agenda of public service and I don't think that would be well enough thought out if I were just sort of pursuing it because it was lucrative, because everybody else was doing it, whatever."

In Veronica's case, a desire to work in policy-related journalism meant that she was likely to locate in the private sector even with a public-interest orientation. Darian had changed from a private-sector technical career "because I want my work to be more in line with my passion," but he had very little idea what that might mean in terms of sector or even the kind of work he would do.

In summary, few of these students expected on entering policy school that they would pursue lifelong careers in the public sector. Not only did they anticipate crossing sectors, but many saw serious drawbacks to a government career, based on their lack of confidence in government's ability to perform well, low expectations for both the intellectual challenge and influence they would have, and the assumption that—relative to the private sector—there would be less innovation, fewer opportunities and support for learning, and fewer resources. Those interested in nonprofits recognized the resource constraints of this sector but also believed it would offer greater potential than government for exercising influence and creativity. Such opportunities are particularly important to KSG students, many of whom explicitly aspire to the role of "leader," which they define in agentic terms. According to their survey responses, almost all would say a good leader is interested in innovation as opposed to preservation (91 percent versus 9 percent) and has a results orientation rather than a process orientation (77 percent versus 23 percent). Their interview comments suggest that the public-sector roles they associate with leadership are primarily those at the very top, usually elected or appointed.

In this discussion of the uncertainty and fluidity of student career expectations, it is also relevant that a startling proportion of entering KSG students are either pursuing concurrent degrees or are thinking about obtaining another graduate degree later. Among the interview respondents at entry, seven either possessed such a degree or were pursuing one, and another eight were seriously contemplating doing so; in other words, less than half of the interviewees clearly saw the M.P.P. as their only postgraduate degree. Among survey respondents, the pattern was similar: 10 percent were in a joint or concurrent program, and of the remaining group, 57 percent were thinking about pursuing another degree in the future—most commonly law or business, and occasionally a Ph.D.

The Interaction of Public Policy Training and Student Expectations

Data from the second-round interviews and survey responses suggest that the first-year school experience does little to enhance students' public- or nonprofit-sector orientation. As noted earlier, among those responding to the relevant questions on both surveys, expectations regarding primary work sector shifted very slightly toward the private, for-profit domain, and away from the public and nonprofit sectors. Within the same sample, nearly an additional one-fifth in each survey were uncertain or planning mixed careers. More detailed information gathered in second-round interviews underscores the survey findings. Among the interviewees, half came from public or nonprofit work; at the end of the year, two-thirds of this group were uncertain or looking to a mixed career, while one-third planned (uneasily) to continue in the government or nonprofit sectors. Among the interviewees who had come from private or mixed experience, none planned to move entirely into the public or nonprofit sector; almost all expected mixed careers or were uncertain about future direction.

It is not so much the case that strongly public-oriented students change their views, then, but that students with rather ambiguous inclinations at entry seem to have their misgivings about government work confirmed or at least not countered in their first year of training. Why might a public policy program have this effect? Interview comments and survey responses suggest some possible answers.

Lessons Learned

In the first year of their training, public policy students are exposed to a variety of formal and informal influences through their core curriculum and extracurricular activities. At KSG, as in most policy programs, the first-year core curriculum includes a variety of methodologically oriented courses with a strong emphasis on analytic training in statistics and economics (referred to by Fleishman [1990:739] as "the overarching intellectual framework of public policy" and by De Soto et al. [1999:82] as "the central socializing tool" of public policy programs). Taken together, the curriculum is designed to equip students for policy analysis and action by fostering strategic thinking in politics and management, developing ethical reasoning skills, sharpening critical capacity, and sensitizing students to the complexities of policy making. The effect is—not altogether unintentionally—to make students more cautious about governmental intervention (De Soto et al., 1999). In microeconomics particularly, students are often exposed for the first time to the difficult trade-offs entailed in policy choices and the potential for public policies to introduce major inefficiencies and other undesirable consequences into the economy; the benefits of the market are made even clearer. Other elements of the core curriculum highlight the vagaries of political decision making and the challenges of public management—and increasingly, the ways in which the public sector looks to the private sector for effective techniques (De Soto et al., 1999; Brown, 2000).

When students were asked on their second survey to state the "main lesson" they had learned in their first year, quite a few of the responses

First-Year Students Speak Out

Following are some of the responses offered in answer to the question, *What would you say is the main lesson you've learned in your first year of policy school?*:

"It's very easy to criticize policy, very hard to change it."

"How to identify better the kinds of convoluted objections different people/groups will have to different policies or policy approaches."

"Don't take for granted that you're doing something that delivers value."

"It is always wise to remember how little I know."

"The different constraints in policy implementation and analysis."

"1. The devil's in the detail. 2. The danger of bumper sticker politics. 3. It's all about externalities."

"Systematic change is slow. 'Playing the game' is hard."

"Conviction despite discouragement."

"Public policy is much more complex/multifaceted than I had realized."

"I don't want to be a bureaucrat—which appears to be what the M.P.P. is training me to be."

"Really, there are no easy answers to any policy problems. There will always be winners and losers. Several factors depend on who's where. Leadership plays a large role in this."

"Public policy problems are harder than they appear."

"It's all who you know."

"There isn't a right answer. Persuasion is the art that carries the day."

reported either negative reactions to public-sector work or cautions about policy making.

In final comments on the first year, a few students commented directly on what they saw as a programmatic bias toward the private sector, saying, for example, that there was "not enough overt encouragement for public service (an underlying 'private is best' trend)," or that the school should be renamed the "John F. Kennedy School of Management Consulting. Not all of us are here to learn how to be consultants—some were lured by the term 'government' in the title." Consistent with the hypothesis that the first year has a conservatizing effect is the very slight shift toward the right in reported political views from entry to second survey.

Students are learning useful lessons when they take cautions about policy making to heart, but if an important feature of their public-service motivation has to do with "changing the world to make it a better place," they may also be disheartened by these lessons. On the first survey, students were presented a long list of possible skills they might be seeking to develop and asked to select the five most important. "Policy design" was the most commonly selected area, but at the second survey, well under half of the students said they had developed skill in this area; most of the reported skill development was in the areas of economics and statistics. Clearly, statistics and economics are relevant to policy design, but the students' responses may reflect a belief that these tools are more easily used to critique interventions than to craft solutions.

Construction of a Professional Identity

At the same time as they are receiving messages about the difficulties of designing effective policies and implementing successful programs, the students also take the analytic orientation of their training as an unsatisfying indication of the narrowness of the roles for which they are being prepared. "While the publicity material put emphasis on becoming the 'leaders of tomorrow'," wrote one student, "much of the core curriculum seems to gear us toward being the 'analysts' and 'policy wonks' of the future. Many of our assignments ask us to role-play at a graduating career position, instead of further down the line (i.e., 'write a memo as a newly hired policy analyst to the assistant secretary of HHS.')." Said another, "I ... find the focus on providing analysis rather than or at the expense of providing leadership disconcerting." And a third commented, "The mission of KSG is to develop leaders for the future; skill-learning is necessary, but insufficient toward this, and KSG should seek to help those who need it to find their focus, their passion.... [KSG could] provide passionate people not only with *tools* but also with vision, guidance, confidence. That is how to build *leaders*. Today KSG is satisfied with mass-producing analysts, while trusting that some will become leaders."

Some students are particularly disturbed by the message they read into the school's "Spring Exercise," a required component of the core in which students role-play government staff members working under tight deadlines on a current policy problem. They are given material on the problem, asked to synthesize it, write memos, and brief a high-level official on issues and recommendations. Though many students find the experience energizing, it is also not uncommon for some to feel uncomfortable with the constrained role they play. The following survey comment was typical of concerns raised by students uncomfortable with the exercise: "Much of the [first year's] work has been challenging and engaging. However, the Spring Exercise really allowed me to 'see behind the curtains' and glimpse the administration's expectations of the majority of M.P.P. graduates—not to engage in long-term problem solving/strategy generation, but to study issues on a superficial level and summarize them for other decision makers." When student assessments of the value of different courses were compared by planned work sector, it was found that those planning—at graduation—a public-sector career were considerably more likely than those planning either a nonprofit or private-sector career to identify Spring Exercise as one of the most valuable courses.

Asked on the second survey whether or not they were beginning to get a sense of a professional identity (how policy professionals were expected to think and act), about two-thirds of the respondents said they were. Of this group, though, almost half reported feeling some tension between this mainstream professional identity and their own personal values. Judging from explanatory comments, this conflict reflected the issues cited above—that is, a dissatisfaction with the incrementalism emphasized in policy training; disillusionment over the policy-making process and worry over tensions between policy goals and political or organizational realities; and a rejection of the narrow, analytically focused role associated with policy professionals. The picture that emerges from the comments is one of an activist-oriented group coming up against the constraints of policy training. It is noteworthy that those reporting a tension between professional and personal identities were significantly more liberal than those saying they felt no such conflict. Though negative comments were also offered by more conservative students, it is not surprising that liberals would be more vulnerable to disillusionment, as they are more likely to enter with high hopes for public-sector activism.

"Some personal values conflict with the 'game' of politics (when it involves deceptive strategizing, etc.)," wrote one student. "Also the central role of economics conflicts with my beliefs when the distributive failures are not addressed. Finally, I don't believe in many 'U.S. national interest' arguments." Another commented, "I struggle with idealism versus reality. The entire [politics] curriculum deals with reality ... when do we think about ideals?" The following represent a sampling of comments on perceived values conflicts:

- "I feel I am less willing to actively bargain with or trade support as required for a political professional. I remain interested in other policy professional opportunities."
- "I don't know how well I'll deal with the partisan gaming that many policy professionals must deal with."

- "I expect to have difficulty working within professional policy organizations with which I do not share a basic sense of mission."
- "Policy professionals are expected to be 1) politically moderate, 2) generalists. I am neither—I am unapologetically liberal, interested in civil rights."
- "Conformity seems necessary, lack of strong political opinions seems the norm ... these conflict with my fundamental values."

Some students were particularly unhappy with what they believed to be an elitist and/or incrementalist view of policy making. Their comments:

- "I am anti-elitist. KSG teaches to a policy elite with training that isolates policy professionals from the electorate. I think this is un-democratic."
- "I am not comfortable with the idea of expertise and the role of hierarchy in this culture. Yet policy professionals are expected to perpetuate this system."
- "KSG represents the elite and their needs and does not care about the majority or the needs of the disadvantaged. KSG focuses more on what is and how to perpetuate a dominant capitalist structure that inevitably relegates the less powerful into poverty."
- "Many of my beliefs are in changes to the system that are probably too broad to be undertaken at one time."

"I want to lead, not analyze and assist" was another common explanation for the tension between professional identity and personal dreams, as the following comments illustrate:

- "I am more interested in politics and activism."
- "I am unhappy that I am being taught to be a bureaucrat at the expense of leadership skills. I feel the two should both be emphasized at KSG."
- "I don't see myself in the 'policy professional' role that is projected—memo-writing intensive, overly earnest—basically the idea that one way is the only way."
- "The identity of a policy professional suggested at KSG seems to be one where the professional does lots of analysis but takes few stands, makes few judgments, does not lead."
- "The Kennedy School has given me the impression that policy professionals are highly process-oriented. I am results-oriented and felt frustrated all year. I also don't want to worry about money my whole life."

Inspiration and Motivation

At the same time, most students said they had encountered inspiring examples of public service in extracurricular events and coursework (88 percent of the survey respondents had done so), and that their own career thinking had been influenced as a result (77 percent of those who had been inspired said it affected their career thinking). The list of people mentioned as inspiring is quite varied, including high-level elected officials, agency heads, protagonists in teaching cases and other readings, faculty members and fellow students who have devoted time to community service. The proportion of students identifying "ability to make a social contribution" as a highly important feature of work rises over the year (from 54 percent in the first survey to 62 percent in the second). In addition, almost three-quarters of the second-survey respondents indicated they felt they could "make a difference" in terms of policy or practice, and another 22 percent said they might be able to do so. About 31 percent said their belief in their own capacity to make a difference had grown, and another 52 percent said it had remained unchanged over the year. It seems that the students do not lack inspiration, nor do they emerge from their first year feeling unable to have an impact. But this inspiration and confidence do not link to public-sector career plans.

Motivations and Expectations Related to Choice of Sector

The growing movement of public policy and administration graduates away from government careers undoubtedly reduces the public-sector talent pool. But we are in a time of smaller government, a growing nonprofit sector, and increasing public-private partnerships or contracting arrangements in which private firms take on more of the work of the public sector. Perhaps the loss of these graduates to the public sector is offset by a rise in the number of public-spirited professionals in the private sector. Some scholars make this argument, suggesting that the entry of policy students into the private sector can provide important social benefits, as graduates bring with them a commitment to the public interest, a language that supports dialogue across sectors, and a set of analytical tools that highlight public concerns (Fleishman, 1990; Light, 1999; Stokes, 1996). Furthermore, the lines between sectors are blurry; philanthropic jobs do exist in private firms, and some of the work of the private sector supports public sector performance (such as private consulting to government).

With respect to the study respondents it is too early to know what kind of work will characterize their careers, but it is possible to ask what draws them to private- versus public-sector employment at this time. The answers may suggest both what it would take for government to make a stronger appeal to more students and how much students entering the private sector look like those who enter the public sector.

In interviews, students did sometimes allude to the private sector as a way to produce public value—for example, in community and economic development projects, socially oriented private enterprises, or offering technical assistance to government. And in the fourth survey, a slight majority of those who included private-sector options in their planned work sector(s) said they expected that work to have a substantial public-sector component. More commonly, though, in both interviews and survey responses students explained their interest in the private sector in terms of the greater professional opportunities they felt it offered: professional development; skill acquisition; an innovative, fast-paced, and flexible environment; and of course, more money (a particularly significant factor given high debt burdens). In addition, because many students expect to work in multiple sectors *and* believe that it is more difficult to enter the private sector from the public sector than vice versa, they fear that beginning in the public sector will unnecessarily foreclose their options. For the most part, they believe their private-sector employment will be short term (perhaps two to four years), and that it will allow them to enter public or nonprofit work with enhanced skills, greater credibility, and better financial security.

In the fall of their second year students begin to think seriously about jobs and often struggle with the question of career direction. Interviews conducted at this time revealed considerable ambivalence about choices, and a very common sense of conflict between the policy orientation that had brought students to KSG and the powerful lure of the private sector. The accompanying interview excerpts illustrate the strong feeling of some students that private-sector experience is not only desirable but necessary (see "Second-Year Students Talk about Career Direction" in Appendix II). They do not necessarily think of most of these jobs as a form of public service, but rather as a (hopefully) short-term venture that they believe will "jump-start" their careers.

The argument that policy professionals should understand the market and appreciate it for what it accomplishes is perfectly reasonable. But the admiration for the private sector that is conveyed in these comments is accompanied by a disdain for the public sector, almost an inferiority complex, that is worrisome. Furthermore, though these students contemplate entering private employment with the expectation of eventually entering public service, even now they recognize that this move may never happen.

Survey responses provide an additional perspective on how motivations and expectations are related to choice of sector. At the time of the fourth survey (near graduation), over half of the respondents had either accepted a job or were considering offers. All students were asked in which sector their job—if they had one—was located, or if still looking, in which sector or combination of sectors they planned to work. Of the 92 students who responded to this survey, 23 (25 percent) checked only public-sector options, another 23 (25 percent) checked only private-sector options, 17 (18 percent) checked only nonprofit options, 26 (28 percent) checked more than one sector (primarily a combination of government and nonprofit options), and 3 (3 percent) were uncertain. (Though the substantial proportion favoring public and/or nonprofit sectors at this point is heartening, note that the actual distribution of jobs as reported by KSG Career Services was more heavily tilted toward the private sector.) What is potentially interesting for this discussion is a comparison of those answering government-only (hereafter, the "public-sector group") to those answering for-profit-only (the "private-sector group") on the fourth survey. Though the numbers are small and the comparison more suggestive than conclusive, the responses of the two groups to other questions may add to our understanding of the meaning of the private- versus public-sector choice.

One striking comparison is in the reasons students gave for sector choice in response to an open-ended question. Among those favoring the private-sector, the most common reasons, by frequency of mention, were: financial rewards/security; skill development; challenge/pace/creativity; a desire for private-sector experience; and advancement opportunities. For the public-sector choice, the most common reason was a desire to make a social contribution (expressed as "serving the public," bringing about "social change," "making a difference"), and the next most common reason was interest in a particular policy area or program. Comments from non-profit-oriented students also mentioned the element of service and desire to make a difference (by far the most commonly mentioned reason), but in contrast to the public-sector group, cited as well opportunities for innovation and entrepreneurship.

These remarks are consistent with a number of other survey responses. For example, the public-sector students were more likely than the private-sector group to have entered KSG with a strong idea of a substantive area in which they would like to work (73 percent versus 57 percent), and to have had a particular issue of concern (82 percent versus 60 percent), a difference that was also evident at the end of the first year. In addition, at the second survey 70 percent of the public-sector group versus 48 percent of the private group anticipated working in a particular policy area. In terms of desirable work roles, initially slight differences grew over the first year, at the end of which the private-sector group was considerably more likely than the public-sector group to desire management (55 percent versus 25 percent) and much less likely to desire advocacy (5 percent versus 20 percent).

The public and nonprofit groups' desire to have a social impact were also evident in the fourth-survey responses to a question about the student's confidence in his/her ability to "make a difference" in terms of improving policy or practice. Though at the end of the first year, the private-sector students had been slightly more confident of their ability to "make a difference" than were the public-sector students, in the fourth survey the pattern was reversed. At graduation, public-sector students were much more likely to say yes, they could make a difference (65 percent versus 32 percent of the private-sector group) and the private-sector group was more likely to say "maybe" (50 percent versus 26 percent of the public-sector group). Those headed for nonprofits were most confident: 94 percent of them said yes, they believed they could make a difference.

These patterns are quite similar to some of Light's (1999:97) findings, in which graduates taking their first job in government were much more likely than their private-sector colleagues to value the opportunity to have an impact on national or local issues.

The relative importance of salary and expectations for higher salary also distinguished the two groups from the outset. The government-oriented students had lower salary expectations at entry than did the private-sector group (23 percent of the former versus 59 percent of the latter had initially expected annual salaries under $45,000). Though neither group cited high salary as among the most important qualities in a job, the private sector group did assign this feature greater importance than did the public-sector group (2.18 versus 3 on a scale of 1 = very important to 5 = very unimportant; $p < .0004$). In addition, the public-sector group was much more likely at entry to list salary among the three *least* important features of a job (73 percent did so, compared to 32 percent of the other group; $p < .0058$), though this distinction had greatly diminished by the end of the first year, perhaps reflecting rising concern about debt repayment among public-sector students. Conversely, a job's "opportunity to make a social contribution" was valued by both groups at entry but was more likely to be cited by the government-oriented than private-oriented students as among the most important job qualities at both the beginning and end of the first year (64 percent versus 36 percent put it among the top three factors in the first survey, and 56 percent versus 33 percent in the second).

The education-debt burden is a very real concern for most students, and the significantly higher salaries offered in the private sector are unquestionably an important consideration in the decision- making process, though it is not clear that debt burden predicts career choice. It is true that a higher proportion of the private-sector group cited financial obligations as among the potentially significant constraints on their job choices (68 percent versus 41 percent), but this difference does not appear to be reflective of their M.P.P.-related debt. The average proportion of financial support coming from non-family loans is approximately 41 percent for both groups, and responses on other sources of financial support do not vary significantly.

In conclusion, public policy students enter the private sector hoping to gain skills, credibility, and experience; to make enough money to pay off debts and live comfortably; and to enjoy the resource-rich and fast-paced environment of the private sector. Though some see themselves serving the public interest through a private-sector job, more common is an expectation that their major public contribution will come later, when they leave the private sector for government or perhaps the nonprofit world. Some undoubtedly will do this, but research indicates that the move from private- to public-sector employment among public policy and administration graduates is not common (Light, 1999).

Findings and Recommendations

Findings

Public policy students, whose training is intended to produce skillful managers, advocates, and analysts for public programs, are increasingly likely to enter other sector employment on graduation and less likely than their predecessors to plan long-term careers in government. Though some cross-fertilization between sectors is not only inevitable but desirable—particularly as we move into an era of smaller government and greater public-private integration—the scale of the shift in this particular population—together with the attitudes uncovered in this study, make the trend problematic. In thinking about how to promote more interest in the public sector, the following key findings from this study are relevant:

- Most policy students do not enter their programs planning for non-public-sector careers, but neither do they have a strong orientation toward the public sector. In fact, disparaging attitudes toward government employment are not unusual.
- Though some students remain consistent in their plans to work in a particular sector, many are uncertain at entry and there is evidence of considerable fluctuation in plans throughout their time in graduate school.
- Compounding their uncertainty over the direction of their careers is the common student expectation that they will move between sectors or at least feel that they should be prepared to do so. At the same time, many believe that it will be easier to move from the private to the public sector than the reverse. In this context, it seems much wiser to start in the private sector.
- The policy training process does little to promote a stronger public-sector orientation among students, and may even confirm misgivings about government among those who enter with ambivalent attitudes. Second-year interview comments revealed a particularly strong curiosity about and admiration for the private sector that was at times coupled with a troubling disdain for government.
- Some policy students seek private-sector jobs with a public orientation, such as consulting to government. Others, however, choose the sector because they expect it to offer much stronger opportunities for professional development, intellectual challenge, advancement (even in subsequent public-sector employment), and financial security. Many of these students believe that the only government jobs open to them at this stage would be routine and narrow in scope, with no room for influence or autonomy.

- Large debt burdens coupled with significant salary differences between sectors are also important factors. Though salary is not by any means the only consideration, it clearly enters into the students' decision-making process and is frequently cited as a major reason for choosing the private sector.
- For those who do pursue public-sector work, probably the strongest drawing card is the possibility of "making a difference"—particularly of having an impact in a policy area of interest. Students headed for the public sector are much more likely than their private-sector counterparts to expect to be able to make a difference and often cite this as a reason for their choice of work sector.

What can be done to counteract the trend of policy students away from government employment? The findings summarized above suggest a number of possible actions that can be taken by government to compete more effectively for policy school graduates and by policy schools to support government in its effort to recruit the best and brightest. In particular, the following areas need to be addressed:

- enhancing the appeal of public-sector work and respect for government;
- addressing financial concerns;
- improving career guidance, linkages, and ease of entry into government.

In each of these areas action is needed by both government and policy schools. In some, independent actions will be mutually reinforcing; in others, more cooperative efforts are needed. Specific recommendations are described below.

Recommendations

Enhancing the Appeal of Public-Sector Work and Respect for Government

Though some students do enter policy school with a private-sector orientation, most come from policy and service-oriented positions in the public or nonprofit sectors, and their plans for the future are generally quite open. The choice of policy school is motivated both by a hope that it will supply career-enhancing skills and by a desire to serve an interest greater than a single firm's bottom line. The first of these motives—career ambitions—inclines students toward the private sector insofar as they perceive it to offer greater opportunities for professional development than does government. This is an issue government must address through the design of work and careers as well as how these are communicated to prospective candidates. The second motive—a public-interest orientation—is one to which government can successfully appeal, but which the schools must work to preserve, strengthen, and clarify.

Government Actions

Offer work that makes use of the candidate's skills and interest in policy.

The policy students who choose government do so in large part because of their desire to have an impact. Simultaneously, those who avoid government do so because they believe they will have no influence, and their time will be spent on circumscribed, routine tasks offering no professional growth. New graduates are not necessarily aspiring to decision-making roles, but they are looking for positions in which they can think about programs or policy, offer advice that will be taken into account, and feel that they are making a contribution commensurate with their skills.

The good news is that policy-oriented government jobs that include such opportunities can be very attractive and satisfying, but of course jobs that do not can be quite frustrating. In an interview several months after graduation, one of the students in this study expressed great satisfaction with her work as a Presidential Management Intern (PMI)—despite its low pay—but observed that a friend working as a PMI in another agency was so disheartened she was on the verge of leaving. One important different was the interns' degree of involvement in office decision making: The first student had a supervisor who sought her ideas and took them seriously; the second student was more often ignored. In the latter case, government effectively neglected its most important advantage in the competition for talent: the chance to be involved in programs and policy making.

Support professional development and make advancement opportunities clear.

Entry-level professionals are very concerned about the possibilities opened up or closed down by their first position, particularly given the expected fluidity of their careers. Even if advancement in the traditional sense of promotions on a career ladder is not available, the opportunity to learn, to develop new skills, and to be exposed both to new substantive areas and to other institutions and actors are all extremely valuable and appealing aspects of a job. Challenging first assignments are a particularly critical element of effective human resource management: They let the new entrant demonstrate and develop skills, send her the message that she is taken seriously by the organization, and give the manager information about how well the new employee performs.

When the Presidential Management Intern (PMI) program works as intended, it serves these kinds of functions well and remains an effective recruiting device, but insufficient attention to development and limited rotational opportunities (as well as extremely low pay) can greatly diminish its value. Similarly, summer internships are potentially an excellent opportunity to recruit good candidates, but the opportunity is wasted if the internship is not well structured. For agencies that are serious about recruiting talent, the most important feature of the internship is an opportunity to learn; this means providing assignments that use and stretch the student's capacity, coupled with training and support from other members of the work group. An internship that involves no development is actually counter-productive because it signals to the student that this is probably not a learning environment.

Restructure workplaces away from hierarchy and toward interaction.
    Numerous scholars and consultants have argued that the successful "organization of the future" (Hesselbein, et al., 1997) will be fluid and interactive rather than rigid and hierarchical. Communication and coordination arrangements will shift according to the nature of the task, and accountability will be based more on results than rules; it will also be mutual rather than top-down. Changes of this sort are believed to enhance both organizational performance and employee commitment in private, public, and nonprofit sectors (Ackoff, 1994; Heckscher and Donnellon, 1994; Ostroff, 1999).
    Just as flexibility and autonomy can be satisfying, a rule-bound, hierarchical environment can be disheartening to employees and discouraging to prospective candidates. One KSG graduate who had joined a private-sector consulting firm found herself staffing a project for a public-sector client in which some of her classmates worked.

> When asked if she would rather be in their position or hers, she said, "It's not difficult. I'd rather be where I am." In explaining, she alluded to having not only greater opportunities for professional development, but also "a level of access to the top leaders in the state agencies that we were working with that they didn't have. I could call the deputy commissioner of the Department of Revenue up and say, 'You know, I know you want two things for [this program]; you're not going to get this one. This is the one you should go for ... [and here's why].' And they couldn't make that call.... And that's one of the frustrations that people have, with working in the public sector, is it's so hierarchical that a deputy commissioner wouldn't have a reason to talk to an analyst in ... this division.... Whereas anyone from the outside coming in ... [could have that access].... It's totally dysfunctional.... [From the outside] you definitely feel like you're making an impact, and you can see the results when you sit in a meeting with the governor, and someone is going through an analysis that you did and using it to make a decision about x million number of dollars...."

It should be noted that the ability of federal agencies to respond to these kinds of recommendations is partially constrained by conditions over which agencies have no control, such as the heavy layer of political appointments at the upper levels of government, civil service regulations, and other legal requirements. A discussion of such issues is beyond the scope of this report, but the findings of this study provide additional evidence of the need for reform (see National Commission on the Public Service, 1989). To the extent that public managers do have discretion in human resource management, however, they should be explicitly accountable for their performance in this area.

Policy School Actions

Focus on substance as a way to sustain passion.
Public policy students often complain during the first year about losing their sense of commitment and "passion"; they have trouble connecting the reasons that brought them to policy school with the largely analytical work they do in their classes. The methodologically focused core of policy schools is intended to train students to approach problems analytically, and to serve both generalists and specialists. It may be effective in these aims, but it is generally not very helpful in strengthening public-service motivations. End-of-year comments from students are instructive in this regard:

- "It is very easy to get wrapped up in the core classes and lose track of your career goals..."
- "I've definitely been frustrated with the constant focus on domestic policy issues in my core courses ... These things have absolutely no relevance to my intended career, but have nevertheless dominated my academic experience thus far."
- "I have enjoyed my first year ... I feel some of my greatest skills acquired have been personal skills around time management, working with people, etc. I am very confident that I have improved my ability to do work and have improved 'how' I work. I am less confident that I have learned 'what' I need to know.... There has been less substance available on issues that I care about than I had initially anticipated."
- "Core curriculum is very rigid. Ability to critically engage in real, thoughtful policy analysis is limited .... [KSG is] training consultants and bureaucrats, not thinkers!"

These comments are consistent with study survey data suggesting a correlation between an interest in particular policy areas or issues and a public-sector orientation. A strong motivating factor for many students is their concern about particular policy areas, and though they need to be trained to think about these in a structured way, that training should not lower their enthusiasm. In their regular reviews of core curricula, policy schools ought to look seriously at the question of how the curriculum can be refined or revised to support public-interest motivations in their students. Though the particulars of the reforms would vary by institution, it can be said that enhanced attention to substantive areas of interest—in as many contexts as possible—is probably a major component.

Teach students to be analytical and critical without denigrating government or public programs.

For the many change-oriented students who come to policy school, probably the most powerful lessons of the core curriculum have to do with the difficulty of effecting change and the negative unintended consequences that can come from major public interventions. Because so many students enter without a strong sense of the workings and benefits of the market, it makes sense that their training heighten this understanding and awareness. But a balance must be struck, so that students leave these programs with a realistic but respectful view of government.

In interviews, students often commented on the positive lessons they were learning about the private sector, but rarely talked about how they had a better appreciation for government. This effect came through particularly powerfully in an impromptu interview with a student who wanted to talk about his transition from a nonprofit to a private-sector work orientation.

It was clear that he had come to see much more value in the private sector than he had initially. When asked if he had an idea about how this shift had come about, he hesitated for a moment, and then in a rush began to speak about a number of classes that had shown him a different view of the market. "It was great to kind of see the world through economic theories.... And that was important to me ... to forming my ideas." He mentioned a class on the reform of political economies, and how "that was very interesting—looking at it from a macro perspective, and you know, what different countries are doing to reform their economies and structure safety nets and kind of the trade-off between efficiency and ... having a more equal system in terms of the distribution of wealth, but not being very efficient.... What a simple, but striking—such a revealing concept. So that was revolutionary to me. It was just—it really said something about what I believed in.... And whereas I do think that some things are, you know ... the government's role is to provide some basic things to everyone, other things I don't believe government should have a role in. And that was very revealing for me because I just never came to that conclusion."

A broadening of perspective is essential, but in many students' comments there is a sense of the pendulum simply swinging in the opposite direction. Rather than coming to a position in which they think, "Now with this stronger understanding of the private sector, I can help to make and implement better policies," they seem to move away from the public (and in this case, nonprofit) sector altogether. Policy schools should look care-fully at the lessons embedded in their curricula and strive for a better bal-ance, with a stronger link back to the important role of the public sector.

The task is not impossible, and it may be helpful here to quote a stu-dent whose view was less critical and more hopeful than most. She wrote on her final survey:

> As one of the few who are lucky to get an education, as a Muslim, a woman and a Bangladeshi, I feel a great responsibility toward people all over the world, but especially towards the common Muslims in general as they are oppressed by their own as well as other governments. As my edu-cation continues, I have grown from caring about Bangladeshis to caring about all people. I have come to understand that building political power for and unifying Muslims is important in creating a voice for us. The Kennedy School of Government has helped tremendously by giving me the tools to start building my career in this respect. The school has also opened doors for me in an area of concentration that I would never have thought of choosing had I not come to this school—public management. Countries can never do without governments; and governments can never do with-out public management!

Provide models of successful governmental programs/agencies and pro-active governmental careers.

Even before coming to graduate school, and certainly in their activities outside the school, policy students are exposed to a general social environ-ment that disparages government and reveres the private sector, particularly during economic boom times. Acknowledging the effect this environment has on their students, policy schools may need to work harder to promote a more positive view of government.

Policy programs do make some effort to inspire students with successful examples, but more could be done, and more thought could be given to the types of role models that are promoted. Many of the lessons embedded in both curricular content and extracurricular activities focus on public-sector officials at the highest levels, usually appointed or elected positions (Chetkovich and Kirp, 2001). Again, a better balance is needed. Today's stu-dents are looking for entrepreneurial opportunities within the policy context, and are uninterested in work that consists entirely of carrying out someone else's orders. In visiting speakers as well as case protagonists, they need to see innovative career public servants who work proactively on policies and programs of social significance.

In addition, schools should think about the messages conveyed by professional exercises such as KSG's Spring Exercise (which is described to

the students as being to policy students what moot court is to law students).
These kinds of exercises are strong carriers of cultural as well as technical
lessons, and if students come away disheartened by the qualities of the role
they've been asked to play, the message about public-sector careers is a
negative one.

Government and Policy Schools in Partnership

Work together to improve public-sector effectiveness and reputation.

High-visibility partnerships between schools and government agencies,
along with special efforts to identify and publicize public-sector success
(such as the Ford Foundation-funded "Innovations" program at KSG, but
also including academic research projects) could contribute to a better balance in attitudes. A related point is the need to improve government performance. Low confidence in government isn't entirely groundless, and
some students speak from direct experience when they express doubts
about the public-sector workforce. Improving public-agency effectiveness
should be a high priority in the research, consulting, and community-serv-
ice activities of policy schools. On the government side, public leaders
should reach out to university partners to support their own efforts to
enhance performance.

Addressing Concerns about the Debt Burden

Salaries are not the only appealing element of private-sector careers or
even necessarily the most important. At the same time, the enormous gap
between public- and private-sector salaries—particularly in postgraduate
entry positions—coupled with the major debt burden carried by graduates
of private institutions, must factor heavily into student career decisions. In
KSG's M.P.P. Class of 2000, the median salary for private-sector jobs in the
United States other than consulting to the public sector was $95,000-
$100,000. Median salaries for government jobs in the United States were
$40,000 for federal jobs, $43,000 for state jobs, and $50,000 for regional
or local jobs. The median salary of the Harvard Business School's M.B.A.
Class of 2000 was $100,000 plus $30,000 in signing bonuses, tuition reim-
bursement, and guaranteed year-end bonuses.

Government Actions

Address the wage gap.

Government agencies do not have to pay the same salaries as the most
lucrative private-sector firms to recruit talent, but they must narrow the gap.

Capable graduates of public policy programs starting in private-sector employment can earn up to three or four times a PMI's salary, not including other benefits. Though the PMI includes some loan forgiveness, the amount does not come close to balancing the scales, and the salary gap is both a practical constraint and a source of hard feelings. Public managers who want to hire and retain good people must do what they can to see that employees are fairly compensated and rewarded for performance, including taking advantage of the special pay authorities available to them. One potentially useful option is the authorization to repay student loans, as detailed in Office of Personnel Management regulations implementing PL 101-510. Although the regulations (at 5 CFR Part 537) stipulate maximum yearly and total repayment amounts as well as a minimum service requirement, the agencies have some flexibility in design. Most importantly, they have the option of offering payment increases or renewals without requiring new service agreements, which can make the payment-to-service ratio much more generous.

The program provides flexibility in payment, but not additional funding to implementing agencies, so it is of limited value where resources are already very scarce. The problem of inadequate pay scales and budgets is larger than any single agency and requires broader administrative and legislative attention.

Policy School Actions

Increase loan-forgiveness programs and redirect financial support.

On the schools' side, more needs to be done in the way of loan forgiveness and scholarship support for those entering public service. The Kennedy School recognizes the magnitude of the problem and is taking important steps to address it more effectively, including raising its cap on salaries eligible for loan forgiveness and refocusing need-based financial aid from need-at-entry to need-at-exit. In other words, the objective will be to support needy students entering low-paid public and nonprofit jobs at graduation rather than those who take a highly paid consulting position, regardless of prior socio-economic status.

Improving Career Guidance, Linkages, and Ease of Entry into Government

Interviews with policy students revealed a great deal of uncertainty and confusion about career direction, and many students expressed a wish for stronger guidance as they wrestled with the questions of how to think about their careers and even—perhaps especially—what to do next. Many may enter the private sector because it's an obvious, attractive short-term option that they believe will open rather than close off later opportunities. Anxious about their futures, they feel reluctant to pass up appealing private-sector offers that come early in their second year. To the extent that other options are viable and even preferable, the students must be helped to identify them.

Government Actions

Recruit earlier, more energetically, and proactively.

Private-sector firms put a great deal of energy and resources into recruiting activities. Consulting firms, for example, send representatives to campus early in the fall to pitch their firms to students, answer questions, and begin a highly structured but engaging series of screening procedures. Through proactive recruitment techniques and early employment offers, they maximize their ability to choose from among the best possible candidates. The relative absence of government recruiters—especially early in the year—their less dynamic presentations, and the slow pace of screening procedures result in a decreased pool of candidates for public sector jobs. Of respondents in this study who reported having accepted a job offer as of the final-semester survey, a higher proportion were entering the private sector than government.

Successful private-sector firms are also good at knowing what kind of talent they need and going after it. Strategic human resource management starts with an identification of the qualities and capacities the organization needs for high performance; then a recruitment program is designed specifically to find and attract people with those qualities (Chambers et al., 1998). Every stage of the process supports the selection of the right people, including targeting, presentation, and selection procedures. Public agencies need to be just as thoughtful about all of these steps.

Streamline and increase flexibility in hiring processes.

More than one student commented in an interview about the daunting paperwork, narrow requirements, and lengthy screening processes for federal government positions. One exceptionally talented candidate accepted a PMI offer at a particular agency, then waited so long for a security clearance that he feared his PMI would expire before he could use it. The agency's response was to suggest that perhaps he should consider other PMI offers, which he had already rejected in the interest of taking this position. He re-activated his job search and eventually took a position in the private sector. In a competitive labor market, with candidates who are anxious to return to work, delays and other procedural barriers to employment are quite costly. They also confirm the impression of government employment as excessively bureaucratic.

Open up more lateral hiring options.

Enhancing the appeal of entry-level professional jobs may help to stem the tide of graduates turning to the private sector for postgraduate employment. But if present trends toward multisector careers persist and students continue to look to the private sector for a "jump start," it will be necessary for government to increase options for lateral entry into career positions.

Policy School Actions

Strengthen institutional linkages to good public-sector employment opportunities.

As noted, private-sector firms conduct earlier and more aggressive outreach than public or nonprofit employers, and for students worried about postgraduate employment, it can be hard to defer a decision until other options have been considered (particularly when they may be difficult to unearth). Schools need to work with each other and with public and nonprofit employers or networks of employers to facilitate the matching of students with jobs in these sectors. Some effort is being made in this direction at KSG and other policy schools, particularly with U.S. federal government agencies. But there are also many good opportunities in state and local government or with nonprofit organizations (domestically and internationally) that students tend not to see. With today's information technology it should be possible for schools to connect with networks of smaller and more distant employers in a way that makes students aware of these opportunities.

Provide students with better and earlier financial guidance.

Two years ago a group of M.P.P. students at KSG constructed a "quilt" of poster cards on which all members of the KSG community were invited to offer their feelings about "Why we are here." In colorful, sometimes elaborately decorated squares, people told family stories, stated their "commitment to give back" or wrote simple things like "Justice," "Real Freedom for All," or "Public Service and Leadership." Dean Joseph Nye's square read, "Our mission is to train public leaders!" Immediately to its right hung a square from an M.P.P. student that read, "Ten minutes ago the financial aid office told me that I must earn $103,174 next year in order to repay my loans on schedule. I don't want to work for McKinsey, Dean Nye. Please show me the public service job that pays this much and I'll take it." To this student, public-sector employment seemed totally out of the question.

Some of the students interviewed for this study had little or no idea that it might be possible for them to live on the salaries they could earn in public-sector positions. In some cases they seemed to overestimate their immediate needs and to underestimate both the starting salaries they might obtain (for example, in state government) and the potential for earnings increases. Without misleading students, it should be possible to provide them with information that would help them think about public-sector work as a realistic possibility. It would also be wise to counsel students earlier on to ensure that they have adequate time to think through financial concerns.

Teach "survival skills" for public-sector employment and provide long-range career guidance that supports those who want to start work in the public or nonprofit sectors.

Just as there are techniques for succeeding in private-sector settings, there are lessons to be learned from successful public servants on how to find and make the most of opportunities in government. Policy schools could assist students by linking them with effective public managers and government positions offering the greatest promise of professional development. Schools could also ensure that their students receive training and advice relevant to government careers—a kind of "insider's orientation to public sector employment." Such advice might include information about working conditions in particular agencies, suggestions about things to look for and questions to ask of prospective government employers, and strategies for managing careers in the public sector.

In addition, students need better long-term career counseling. It is an unusual student who has a clear idea of his or her career options and direction and feels able to make sensible choices without much guidance. When Kevin (see "Second-Year Students Talk about Career Direction" in Appendix II) said, "What am I going to do for a career search when ... the ideas I have for what I want to do are five or 10 years down the road?", he was not alone. It is hard for students to conceptualize what a satisfying government *career* might look like—where it would start and how it could develop—or to see that starting in government wouldn't necessarily hamper one's later choices. In a vacuum of alternatives, private-sector options are particularly appealing, and a stronger case needs to be made for government as a reasonable starting point and for public service as a viable long-term choice.

Making the case for government means making it clearer to students how they can develop professionally in the public sector and what starting opportunities are available to them. Faculty members who have ties to government can be particularly valuable sources of information for students, and connections to alumni are another resource. But even advisors who don't have useful contacts can still encourage and support students' public-service orientation by reminding them of the sector's value, challenge, and possibilities.

Dennis's comments highlight the confusion experienced by many students. He noted that "part of the difficulty being here ... part of the wonderful thing and the difficult thing is you're not channeled into a path. And so you have a hard time measuring yourself against other people or other benchmarks ... where do I stand up ... maybe I need to do this [private job] to prove myself.... But at the same time, that's the wonderful thing about being here because your opportunities are so much more vast. But that can be scary at a time when you're feeling very anxious and confused." Perhaps no additional advising or support would have changed Dennis's choice of a postgraduate position in consulting, but it could have helped him think more clearly about it. And for some, thinking more clearly might enable them to choose public service.

Postscript

This chapter was originally prepared in the spring of 2001 and focused on the attitudes and choices of the Kennedy School's MPP Class of 2000. Though the employment goals and outcomes of this group reflected a longer-term trend among public policy and administration students, this particular class did graduate into an unusually strong economy. Since then, the economy has softened and private-sector employment opportunities have diminished, a fact bound to have some effect on student choices. In addition, the events and aftermath of September 11, 2001, appear to have affected the public's attitudes toward government and young people's interest in public-sector employment, though it remains to be seen how deep or long-lasting this effect will be.

In terms of the employment destinations of subsequent Kennedy School graduates, the most recent data available relate to the MPP class graduating in June 2001. This data, collected by KSG's Career Services from May through August 2001, indicate some shift from the previous year, but still a sizable private-sector proportion. Among those graduating in June 2001 who provided responses: 40.5 percent went to the public sector, 38.7 percent to the private sector, and 20.7 percent to nonprofits (Kennedy School of Government Career Services Office, 2001).

More generally, anecdotal reports indicate increased interest in government employment and in public-service education (Clements, 2002; BusinessWeek Online, 2002), but there are no comprehensive data that would indicate clear-cut trends. Government may face a window of opportunity now in terms of attracting talent, but changes in recruitment and human resource management may still be necessary for the government to be successful in the long term.

Appendix I:
Study Methods

A longitudinal study is being conducted at two graduate schools of public policy—the Kennedy School of Government at Harvard and the Goldman School of Public Policy at the University of California (UC), Berkeley. The study design includes repeated surveys of a particular M.P.P. class in each institution along with repeated interviews with a subset of the class, so that individual responses can be compared across time.

The first KSG survey was distributed to the 164 students in the M.P.P. Class of 2000 at their orientation in fall 1998. Subsequent surveys were distributed only to those students who responded to the first survey and were still in the M.P.P. program at the time of the later survey; some students who are pursuing concurrent degrees have yet to complete the program and therefore have not participated in all surveys. As a result, the total number receiving surveys diminished with each round. Questionnaires were coded with a unique identifying number, but students were instructed not to put their names on the surveys, and the names of respondents were known only to the researcher and her assistants, none of whom were students from the school. Table 2.3 shows the timing of the surveys, the total number of students receiving each survey, the number responding, and the response rate. Respondents to the initial survey varied from the class as a whole in having a higher proportion of women, whites, and U.S. students, and having on average slightly more work experience.

In addition, from among 90 volunteers at KSG, a purposive sample of 26 students was chosen for interviews. Criteria for selection included vari-

Table 2.3: Response Rates and Timing of KSG Surveys

KSG Surveys	Number surveyed	Number responding	Response rate
First survey, Fall 1998	164	126	77%
Second survey, Spring 1999	125	104	83%
Third Survey, Fall 1999	122	95	78%
Fourth survey, Spring 2000	108	92	85%
Fifth survey, Spring 2001	n/a	n/a	n/a

ation by sex, race/ethnicity, socioeconomic class, and political perspective; of the initial group of 26, 14 were women (seven self-reported as white, seven as members of other racial/ethnic categories) and 12 were men (five self-reported as white, seven as members of other racial/ethnic categories). Though the survey included international students, all interview respondents were U.S. nationals. All interviewees who have continued in the program have been re-interviewed on the same schedule as that used for the surveys. One interview respondent (a woman) dropped out after the first year and four others (two women, two men) have pursued concurrent degrees, deferring their final year in the M.P.P. program and consequently their second-year interviews. As a result, the full series of four interviews (to date) has been conducted with 21 members of the original interview sample. As shown in Table 2.4, the interview respondents included disproportionately more people of color and lower-socioeconomic-class students, and slightly more women than the respondent group as a whole. Political views were similar between the two groups both in terms of the distribution and the average.

A similar set of procedures is being used at UC Berkeley, where the class is much smaller. An entering class of 44 received the initial survey and 10 individuals were selected for interviews. Respondents are being followed in the same manner as at KSG.

Table 2.4: Selected Characteristics of Interviewees and Survey Respondents at KSG

	Initial Interview Sample N = 26	Initial Survey Respondents N = 126
Sex	46% male	51% male
Race/Ethnicity	46% white	64% white
Average Political View (on scale of 1 = most liberal to 7 = most conservative)	3.08	3.08
Socioeconomic Class	27% lower/lower-middle 27% middle 46% upper/upper-middle	10% lower/lower-middle 40% middle 50% upper/upper-middle

Appendix II:
Second-Year Students
Talk about Career Direction

Kevin

Kevin worked over the summer for an economic development project in a developing country, where he saw firsthand the potential value of organizing and supporting local microenterprises. "I talked to [an acquaintance] about his village .... it basically has a bunch of people working together to produce these crafts, and ... there are these exporters that come in and buy all this stuff up at—I'm sure—cents-on-the-dollar, and then take it back and export it. And I was thinking, you know, there's so much possibility there for these people to self-generate and grow at an individual level." He said one career choice for himself would be to work for an international nonprofit in microlending, but another alternative "at the practical level" would be a consulting firm.

I also—when I think career—think very much in stages. Right now one of the things I know is that there's not one single career that I think will satisfy me and keep me interested and keep me energized enough to actually contribute for the next 40 years. So, with that in mind, I also know that there are certain skills that I can gain from doing consulting to a private-sector organization."

His puzzle now is, "What am I going to do for a career search when ... the ideas that I have for what I want to do are sort of five or 10 years down the road, not next year.... And if I don't know what I'm going to do next year, is something like consulting, where I can get the skills and I can get the money, valuable? ... And one of the things I'm very confident of is if I get a job with a top-tier consulting firm or a top-tier I-Bank, I would get skills. My concern ... is would I make sure to get out?" He thought friends would help him hold to his long-range public-service commitment, but then acknowledged that some of them were in the same bind. A colleague whose own background was entirely in nonprofits was looking into private consulting, and Kevin said, "I really understand that and I actually would *recommend* that, cause I think I learned a lot, just in the private-sector environment I was in ... I think there is a language to learn and a mentality to understand that you learn better if you're in it.... But it's amazing to see how people justify these things. I mean I hear myself doing it..."

Dennis

Dennis's long-range desire to work in city government or local politics was affirmed in his internship with a city office. "I do think that that's a place where I want to invest some of my time in my career, at some point, in the near future …. I enjoyed … knowing that the work I was doing had some immediate impact for the community that was outside the door …. There was a sense of local politics and commitment there that inspires me …. I was working with people who were very inspired and committed and smart."

When asked what he was thinking about for the near term, he said, "That's what I'm struggling with. I mean I feel very confused about what I want to do next, in some ways. I feel like it would be a mistake to go right into city government. And I feel like I might do it, but as a last resort …. Part of the anxiety I'm experiencing this couple of weeks is the loan situation, which has just put a panic on me … I don't know if city government will pay me well enough—although I think it has the potential … part of me feels like (.) I want to—I don't know, I'm confused, I'm very confused about it. The thing I'm thinking a lot about right now is management consulting. And I'm applying for those jobs and I'm starting to prepare myself for the interviews, and I feel like I've rationalized it in a way that makes a lot of sense. And one is the loans, but that's not the primary reason, the other reason is that I feel like I'll gain some of the tools and the frameworks and some real hard skills there that I might be able to use, that I *will* be able to use back in city government." He had worked with someone who had moved from consulting into local government and he appreciated her capabilities: "There was just a way of approaching these problems that I really appreciated, and part of me thought maybe that training is something I will be able to use in a way that'll make me a better city employee or public policy person or public leader. And then the other piece of it is more strategic. I think coming from that world, the management consulting/private-sector world, I might have higher entry points into city government.... I'm thinking maybe I will get further and I'll be able to do more if I start that way versus coming in at some other level from here."

When asked why he was "struggling" as opposed to simply deciding to pursue consulting with the idea of switching later, he said, "Well, part of it's the switching tracks, and I worry about it, although I think I trust myself enough that that [staying in the private sector] hopefully won't happen." He also acknowledged that he wasn't sure he was prepared to do the management consulting work and wanted to find out. "I'm being persuaded by the Career Services office to look at really hard-core private-sector management consulting, whereas I originally wanted to do management consulting that was public sector, and they said, 'Well, if you're going to go for this, go for the very hard-core private stuff,' 'cause they said that'll get you further …. And so now I'm revisiting that. I mean I'm still going to apply for both, and I think I have a better shot at the public-sector stuff for obvious reasons, but it doesn't pay as well, it doesn't give you as much credibility. I mean there's a lot of downsides to that, too. And part of me now is feeling like, well, maybe I need this challenge to, like, prove myself. Can I *do* this private-sector stuff? I want to see, you know.... And part of me is intrigued, taking a class at the Business School, that the quality of response and thoughtfulness is high [there]. There's a level of engagement there that doesn't happen here in the classroom in the same way. And I'm intrigued by that. I'm really intrigued to see why is that. And I want to understand that in a way that maybe I *could* bring it into the public or nonprofit sector."

He drew an analogy between his comparison of the business-school and policy-school cultures to the difference he'd seen when he interviewed for internships at OMB [the Office of Management and Budget] and then a private consulting firm. "There was just clearly a difference in culture, in approach, in the way people even composed themselves ... And I realized that I want to know why that is so—is it just this thing called 'profit' or is it something else? And if it is just profit, then we need to find a way to make the nonprofit and the government sector get the same out of people and attract the same kinds of people."

When pressed to explain in more detail the differences he saw between business and policy classrooms, he said, "How I've tried to understand what's going on in the business school is I think there's a certain set of assumptions about human behavior and incentives there that are built off of the private sector. And that's what they're teaching, right? There's a certain way of structuring an environment to get people to respond the way you want them to.... And I think the people who go there in some ways ... buy into those assumptions, or aren't as willing to challenge them, and I think that makes the place run really smoothly ... sort of like a machine. It's getting people to think on their feet and respond quickly and make judgments and be assertive about it, and not question themselves in the same way. And I feel like here ... people come at this from all different perspectives, which is what makes this place so amazing, but then when you put them all in the classroom, I think it doesn't work in the same way, it doesn't run as efficiently or as smoothly. And I think people here ... question authority, they question structures and process more, which again is what makes this place interesting, but at the same time ... it takes a different kind of facilitation here to make that run well."

If he entered the private-oriented firm he was thinking about, he would have no expectation of doing public-sector work, "and that wouldn't be the selling point to hire me." He wasn't terribly excited by the firm's recruiting presentation, but what did attract him was "the way they put out their philosophy or their mission, which is, one is giving the client the best product and the other is really retaining, recruiting, and developing the best consultants.... And that really attracts me. I'd like to have an environment where I actually think about my own professional development and am supported to do that, when I leave here. And I don't see that happening in a government or nonprofit job."

Jenna

Jenna had gone into the Career Services office in her first year with "this idea that I was interested in the private sector, primarily driven by my concern about my debt burden but also in a real way driven by an understanding that I really needed to know what goes on on both sides of the coin in order to be able to be effective in either place. And the only option that was presented to me there was Big Six management consultants. And I had gone in thinking public relations, government relations, marketing in general, any number of things that I completely forgot about when I was presented with this, 'OK, you have to prepare for case interviews.'" Over the summer she worked in a firm that consulted to public-sector clients, an option she was open to pursuing again at graduation. But she had also been thinking about "the strengths, the opportunities that would be offered by straight private-sector consulting."

At the time of our third interview she had started leaning against the latter, in part because the selection process suggested to her that she might not enjoy the work or fit well in those firms. "So I have to kind of rethink all of that. And I also think that one thing that I'm doing is really kind of questioning, do I really have to be in the private sector? What does it do to me if I extend the time that it takes to pay things off or really push for—it's probably possible to do better than I think financially ... in a government job or in a [nonprofit]—and I haven't really looked at that.... So I'm trying to figure it out, all the while knowing that my hunch is that I may end up in a private firm that does public work but really kinda hoping that there are other options. But also, I recognize that my career would get a really—I mean, what a great jump start, to start in an interesting private-sector job and then cross over. And am I like giving up more than just the money ... there's a whole idea that it's easier to cross from private to public...."

Asked what she would choose to do if the debt worry could be resolved, she answered quietly, "I don't know. I mean that's funny, you'd think that I'd have an answer, like that," she said, snapping her fingers. "I think that I'm really drawn to the idea of having a position that allows me to interact with the public, in a way that's appropriate to my skill level. I mean I'm not ready to be representing an agency yet, but maybe representing an agency to a segment of the public, whether it's doing legislative liaison work for a public agency or whether it's doing client and consumer and community relations ... I like being a mouthpiece for something I believe in. Or on the other hand, doing policy planning and program design.... But it's all creative. And the problem with that in the public sector is that there are so often limits and you know, I don't think always, but ... I'm interested in ... really understanding whether or not I think this is true ... you know, is bureaucracy really limiting—as limiting as we like to think it is or as we're *taught* to think it is, here?

I mean so much of what I'm interested in is, so we're given a sea of administrative mandates, how can we cut through them? How can we change them? So I'm not, I'm not convinced that that's a barrier to the creative process, so ... maybe if I still think I can do that and be satisfied, in a public [agency]—I would prefer ... to tell my mother I'm working for DSS [Department of Social Services] in Massachusetts rather than some company that provides cable services." She chuckled. "But, you know, I also at this point don't want to close my mind and my search to anything."

Endnotes

1.   The author gratefully acknowledges the assistance of the Kennedy School of Government and the Goldman School of Public Policy, the financial support provided by The PricewaterhouseCoopers Endowment for The Business of Government, and the participation of the students who shared their views and experiences.

2   All students names are pseudonyms. Transcript conventions include the following: ellipses indicate omitted text; comments in brackets are not the speaker's words but are inserted to make sense of a passage.

Bibliography

Ackoff, Russell. *The Democratic Corporation: A Radical Prescription for Recreating Corporate America and Rediscovering Success.* New York: Oxford University Press. 1994.

Brown, Peter G. "The Legitimacy Crisis and the New Progressivism." In *Public Service: Callings, Commitments, and Contributions,* ed. M. Holzer. Boulder, Colorado: Westview Press. 2000.

BusinessWeek Online. "Uncle Sam Wants You, and You, and You..." January 31, 2002. www.businessweek.com.

Chambers, Elizabeth G.; Foulon, Mark; Handfield-Jones, Helen; Hankin, Steven; and Michaels, Edward G. "The War for Talent." *The McKinsey Quarterly.* 1998 (3): 44-57.

Chetkovich, Carol, and Kirp, David L. "Cases and Controversies: How Novitiates Are Trained to Be Masters of the Public Policy Universe." *Journal of Policy Analysis and Management.* Forthcoming Spring 2001.

Clements, Barbara. "Public Sector's Job Security Looks Attractive to Upcoming Oregon Graduates." *The News Tribune.* February 4, 2002.

Conant, James K. "Universities and the Future of the Public Service." In *Public Service: Callings, Commitments, and Contributions,* ed. M. Holzer. Boulder, Colorado: Westview Press. 2000.

Crewson, Philip E. "Are the Best and the Brightest Fleeing Public Sector Employment? Evidence from the National Longitudinal Survey of Youth." In *Public Service: Callings, Commitments, and Contributions,* ed. M. Holzer. Boulder, Colorado: Westview Press. 2000.

De Soo, William; Opheim, Cynthia; and Tajalli, Hassan. "Apples and Oranges? Comparing the Attitudes of Public Policy Versus Public Administration Students." *American Review of Public Administration.* 29 (1): 77-91. March 1999.

Fleishman, Joel L. "A New Framework for Integration: Policy Analysis and Public Management." *American Behavioral Scientist.* 33 (6): 733-754. July/August 1990.

Garland, Susan B.; Cahan, Vicky; Yang, Catherine; and Dwyer, Paula. "Why Civil Servants Are Making Tracks." *Business Week.* January 23, 1989: 60-61.

Heckscher, Charles, and Donnellon, Anne (Eds). *The Post-Bureaucratic Organization: New Perspectives on Organizational Change.* Thousand Oaks, California: Sage Publications. 1994.

Hesselbein, Frances; Goldsmith, Marshall; Beckhard, Richard. *The Organization of the Future.* San Francisco: Jossey-Bass Publishers. 1997.

Kennedy School of Government Career Services Office. *Placement Report 2001.*

Kennedy School of Government Career Services Office. *Placement Report 2000.*

Light, Paul C. *The New Public Service.* Washington, D.C.: Brookings Institution Press. 1999.

The National Commission on the Public Service. *Leadership for America: Rebuilding the Public Service.* Washington, D.C. 1989.

Ostroff, Frank. *The Horizontal Organization: What the Organization of the Future Looks Like and How It Delivers Value to Its Customers.* New York: Oxford University Press. 1999.

Stokes, Donald E. " 'Presidential' Address: The Changing Environment of Education for Public Service." *Journal of Policy Analysis and Management.* 15(2):158-170. 1996.

Tulgan, Bruce. *Winning the Talent Wars: How to Manage and Compete in the High-Tech, High-Speed, Knowledge-Based, Superfluid Economy.* New York: W.W. Norton. 2001

U.S. Government Accounting Office (GAO). *Federal Employment: How Government Jobs are Viewed on Some College Campuses.* Report No. GAO/GGD-94-181. Washington, D.C.: GAO. 1994.

U.S. Government Accounting Office (GAO). *Human Capital: Managing Human Capital in the 21st Century.* Statement of David M. Walker, Comptroller General. Report No. GAO/T-GGD-00-77. Washington, D.C.: GAO. 2000.

CHAPTER THREE

A Weapon in the War for Talent:
Using Special Authorities
to Recruit Crucial Personnel

Hal G. Rainey
Alumni Foundation Distinguished Professor
School of Public and International Affairs
The University of Georgia

This report was originally published in December 2001.

Introduction

Public Management Challenges and Dilemmas

In recent years, Congress has provided certain federal agencies with special authorities for hiring professionals and executives to help the agencies compete for talented people in highly competitive job markets. Current and classic challenges in governmental management served as driving forces behind these initiatives:

- *The need for skill sets that are new, hard to attain, or both.* Government faces a pressing need for highly educated and experienced people to help federal agencies meet such immediate challenges as developing their computer, information, and communication systems amid the rapid changes in those technologies. This challenge involves finding not just technically proficient people, but also finding people who combine such knowledge with executive leadership ability or particularly valuable perspectives and backgrounds.

- *A competitive economy and market for such people.* The same imperatives drive business and nonprofit organizations to compete for these talented individuals. The constraints in government on pay levels and other incentives, and on the processes of recruiting and hiring, impede government agencies in this competition.

- *Impending retirements in the federal service.* Large numbers of executives, managers, and professionals in the federal service are becoming eligible for retirement, raising the challenge of replacing them.

- *The "human capital crisis" in government.* Officials and observers regard these conditions as building to a point of crisis in the federal civil service personnel system because of the intense competition and constraints in replacing and maintaining talent in positions of great importance to the nation.

- *The challenge of streamlining and improving government.* These challenges relate more generally to the long-standing concern over making government agencies more streamlined, flexible, responsive, and less bound by red tape and rigidity. The pursuit of flexibility in organizations and their management has been a central challenge across the last century that will intensify in the new century as organizations struggle to adapt to rapid change and increasing complexity.[1]

- *Improving the business of government.* Similarly, reforms have also sought to make government more "businesslike" and to improve governmental performance by drawing on resources from business and other nongovernmental sources, and by introducing conditions in governmental management that resemble conditions in the business sector.

The use of special hiring authorities attempts to provide government with forms of flexibility available in business.

- *Balancing the need for decentralization to provide flexibility and adaptability, against the need for accountability, consistency, and equity.* This is a classic problem in all administrations, but especially in public administration. As agencies receive more authority to do the hiring they want to do, it raises the challenge of wide variation and fragmentation of the federal personnel system, and the challenge of assuring accountability for appropriate use of these new authorities. Later sections will describe how the Internal Revenue Service (IRS) and other agencies have successfully responded to the need to justify and carefully use their new authority.

These and many other current and classic issues are in play in these recent developments in the federal system. Finding out how the federal agencies handle these new authorities and opportunities becomes essential when considering their future application to other agencies.

The "War for Talent"

Demand for more highly trained and skilled employees is increasing, and demand for less-skilled employees is going down.

Organizations must compete for the more highly skilled people in what authors are calling the "war for talent."[2] A report by McKinsey & Company coined this term in concluding from a study that "the most important corporate resource over the next 20 years will be talent," and that that talent will also be the resource in shortest supply.[3] An obvious example of this pressure comes from the breathtaking pace of development in computing, information, and communications technology, including the incredible rise of Internet activities. As organizations press to respond to these developments, they have to search for knowledgeable people who can help them do so, driving up demand for such people.

Computer technology firms have been competing for talent not just on the basis of salary and tangible benefits, but also with promises of a high quality of working life, support for family and other personal issues, meaningful work, and educational and developmental opportunities. The websites of most successful business firms are now crowded with descriptions of such opportunities and arrangements for prospective employees. The website for IBM contains a good example of such efforts. General Electric's website announces that the company spends over $1 billion per year on leadership and personal development, and describes the opportunities for leadership and professional development programs.[4]

In this competition, government faces severe challenges. Even as the importance of "human capital" becomes more widely accepted in government circles, other reports announce an impending crisis in human capital.[5] Downsizing in federal agencies, impending retirements of baby-boomers, uncompetitive compensation packages for highly qualified people, and the complexities of the federal personnel system all hinder government in the competition for talent.[6]

The History of Federal Hiring Trends

The challenges for federal agencies may be worsening, but they are by no means new. Managers in government have complained for decades about the rigidities and red tape of governmental personnel systems. Many federal managers say that the web of rules and procedures has created impediments to hiring particularly desirable candidates because of such requirements as having the central personnel agency rate and rank candidates. If the candidate does not come out in the top three in the ranking process, the agency cannot hire the person. In addition, this process takes time. Even after the rankings, there are often long delays before the person can actually be hired. Then, of course, government must compete for top talent against private firms with more opportunities to fashion attractive compensation packages, including stock options that government cannot offer. Actually, as described, the federal personnel system currently allows a variety of flexibilities and has many special categories and arrangements, but generally the system is not well designed to provide rapid, flexible, and competitive strategies for hiring top talent.

The Trend Toward Decentralization of Human Resource Management Authority

These characteristics of our federal system and similar concerns in other nations have given rise to an international trend toward decentralization of personnel authority and other responsibilities in government. (See Table 3.1.) In the United States and many other countries, reformers have sought to make government more businesslike in many ways, and have sought to decentralize and simplify many of the administrative procedures of government.

Much of this activity has focused on the purportedly excessive rules and procedures for personnel administration and for procurement and purchasing. Experts and federal executives and managers have been expressing these concerns for a long time. In a book published several decades ago, John Macy, the highly respected former head of the U.S. Civil Service Commission (the predecessor of the current Office of Personnel Management [OPM]) mentioned the frequency of such complaints from federal adminis-

Table 3.1: A Brief History of Federal Hiring with Emphasis on Professional and Administrative Jobs: Centralization and Decentralization

Centralization and Decentralization	Since the 1880s, there have been periods when the government's hiring system has been centralized and periods when it has been decentralized. Historically, a centralized system has been seen as more expert and incorruptible, while a decentralized system has been seen as less bureaucratic and more conducive to expedited decision making (1999, 1).
Centralization: from 1880s	From its establishments in the 1880s, until the early 1940s, the Civil Service Commission (CSC) applied a highly centralized examining system to fill positions in the competitive service (2000, Appendix 3).
Decentralization after WWII	However, decentralized examining continued after World War II, because centralized examining proved incapable of meeting the demands for new employees as the civil service expanded. In 1949, the first Hoover Commission recommended giving primary responsibility for recruiting and examining federal employees to the agencies (Ibid).
Centralization during 1950s–1970s	In 1954, the CSC resumed its earlier heavy reliance on centralized examining with the introduction of the Federal Service Entrance Examination (FSEE), replaced by the PACE in 1974, an entry-level examination for most professional federal jobs (Ibid).
Decentralization in 1980s	Among the goals of the Civil Service Reform Act (CSRA) of 1978 was the decentralizing or delegation of many personnel authorities. The CSRA has affected the increase of agencies' staffing authority and the increase of the use of "direct hire" authority for hard-to-fill vacancies (1994). Due to the Luevano consent decree in 1981, the Office of Personnel Management (OPM) announced the establishment of a new Schedule B-PAC hiring authority. Schedule B-PAC is used for hiring into positions for which it is not practicable to hold a competitive examination. It made the federal hiring process completely decentralized (2000).
Trends in 1990s and Current Situation	As a result of legal challenge, OPM eventually abolished the Schedule B-PAC authority and introduced a centralized examination (ACWA), which was first administered in 1990. But the test was abandoned in 1994 because of a slowdown in hiring and the structural disadvantages of centralized examining (Ibid). In 1996, OPM delegated to agencies the authority to examine applicants for virtually every position in the competitive civil service. Agencies may perform the staffing work themselves or may contract the work with OPM (1999, vi).

Sources:
U.S. Merit Systems Protection Board, "Restoring Merit to Federal Hiring: Why Two Special Hiring Programs Should be Ended." 2000, Appendix 3.
U.S. Merit Systems Protection Board, "The Role of Delegated Examining Units: Hiring New Employees in a Decentralized Civil Service." 1999.
U.S. Merit Systems Protection Board, "Entering Professional Positions in the Federal Government." 1994.
U.S. Office of Personnel Management, "Deregulation and Delegation of Human Resources Management Authority in the Federal Government." 1998.

trators.[7] In 1986, the National Academy of Public Administration published a report lamenting the excessive constraints on federal managers, including the constraints on human resource management decisions.[8] The cover of the report featured an illustration of Gulliver tied down by the thousands of tiny ropes with which the Lilliputians had bound him. As one of many parts of the new trend, in the U.S. federal government many personnel procedures and authorities, including those for hiring, have been decentralized and delegated from OPM to the operating agencies.

In the 1990s, the Clinton administration and the National Performance Review (NPR) redoubled the efforts to loosen some of the rules and constraints. NPR reports called for substantial deregulation and decentralization of authority over personnel matters to the operating agencies. As Table 3.2 illustrates, the proposals did have significant effects, including considerable decentralization to agencies of hiring procedures. Yet this decentralization usually involved having the agencies take over from OPM the complex process of examining, ranking, and listing candidates for jobs in an "agency certificate" process that replaced the "OPM certificate" process. Although this decentralized hiring procedures, the process remains elaborate and rule-intensive. In addition, agencies have varied a great deal in the degree of authority actually distributed within the agency. The federal reports describe mixed opinions among federal managers and personnel specialists over just how much decentralization and deregulation has actually occurred and how much things have changed.[9] While they tend to report that they feel the agency certificates and other decentralized procedures speed up the hiring process, many federal executives and managers still see the hiring process as slow and cumbersome.

Because of these constraints, and usually in relation to major reform efforts, Congress has given certain agencies special authorities for hiring key people. Legislation mandating a major overhaul of the Internal Revenue Service (IRS) included the provision of a variety of special flexibilities in personnel administration. These flexibilities include the authority to hire up to 40 people for four-year terms at salaries not to exceed that of the Vice President of the United States. Congress also passed legislation making the Office of Student Financial Assistance (SFA) in the Department of Education, which channels $54 billion per year in financial aid to students, a Performance-Based Organization (PBO).[10] (See Table 3.3 for a description of the PBO concept.) As part of this legislation, Congress gave the agency authority to hire 25 people for important technical and professional responsibilities without regard to the standard limits and rules for salaries for such employees. Congress also designated the U.S. Patent and Trademark Office (USPTO) as a PBO, and gave the agency independence from its parent agency, the Department of Commerce, in decisions about the designation of executive positions in USPTO. In 1996, Congress gave the Federal Aviation Administration (FAA) authority to establish its own personnel system independent of the federal personnel system and the Office of Personnel Management. Many of these changes are quite recent and still developing, and in only two of these cases did Congress provide authority for flexible hiring of specific numbers of positions at specifically designated pay levels.

Actually, Congress provided a complex array of flexibilities for these four agencies, as described in the sections that follow, and the situation for each agency is unique. This raises an issue that will come up again later in this chapter—the issue of wide variation among agencies in the patterns of flexibility provided. As an additional complication, the federal personnel system itself has many variations, special provisions, and flexibilities within it. Thus it becomes important to try to understand the character of the current system to see how the special authorities differ from it.

Table 3.2: Recent Decentralization of Hiring Authorities

Congress and the Clinton Administration	Congress and the Clinton administration required OPM to delegate nearly all of its hiring-related authorities to agencies (MSPB, 1999, 2).
	The administration's budget proposal for FY 1996 significantly reduced the amount of money for OPM's division that handled competitive examining. The FY 1996 appropriation, which decreased OPM's budget by approximately $40 million, reflected that reduction (Ibid).
	Congress also amended Section 1104 of Title 5 to remove most restrictions on OPM's ability to delegate examining authority to agencies and to authorize OPM to provide staffing assistance on a reimbursable basis through the revolving fund to agencies exercising delegated examining authorities (Ibid).
National Performance Review and Responses of Office of Personnel Management	Decentralization of the federal personnel system and the accompanying widespread delegation of personnel authorities to federal agencies have been stimulated by the NPR initiatives (MSPB, 2000, 5).
	The NPR's 1993 report, *From Red Tape to Results: Creating a Government that Works Better & Costs Less,* calls for fundamental changes in the federal staffing process: "Give all departments and agencies authority to conduct their own recruiting and examining for all positions, and abolish all central registers and standard application forms" (cited in MSPB, 1994, vii).

continued on next page

Table 3.2: Recent Decentralization of Hiring Authorities *(continued)*

National Performance Review and Responses of Office of Personnel Management	In addition, the report calls for actions in the federal HR system such as (1) simplifying the General Schedule system to give agencies more flexibility in classification and pay; (2) allowing agencies to design their own performance management and reward systems; and (3) improving the system for dealing with poor performers (OPM, 1998).
	In accordance with these recommendations, since 1994 OPM has taken actions such as (1) abolishing the Federal Personnel Manual (FRM); (2) eliminating mandatory centralized registers; and (3) delegating hiring authority for virtually all federal positions to the agencies, although less progress has been made in classification and dealing with poor performers due to the lack of legislative action (OPM, 1998).
	Putting personnel authorities in the hands of agency managers has focused attention on the need for ways to hold them directly accountable for the results of their personnel decisions. In this regard, the NPR included a new emphasis on accountability (MSPB, 2000, 5).
Government Performance and Results Act of 1993	The Government Performance and Results Act (GPRA) and other "good government" laws further expanded the emphasis on accountability of managers for results and mandated ways to measure performance and hold each level of an organization accountable for its successes and failures (MSPB, 2000, 5).
	Consequently, federal agencies now are legally required to define their mission in terms of outcomes and develop strategic plans to accomplish their missions with improved effectiveness and efficiency. A key element in those strategic plans is the development of performance indicators for all important tasks. Hiring is such a task; consequently, the stage has been set for the normal processes and machinery of government to hold managers accountable for matters such as their hiring decisions (MSPB, 2000, 5).

Sources:
    U.S. Merit Systems Protection Board, "Restoring Merit to Federal Hiring: Why Two Special Hiring Programs Should be Ended." 2000, Appendix 3.
    U.S. Merit Systems Protection Board, "The Role of Delegated Examining Units: Hiring New Employees in a Decentralized Civil Service." 1999.
    U.S. Merit Systems Protection Board, "Entering Professional Positions in the Federal Government." 1994.
    U.S. Office of Personnel Management, "Deregulation and Delegation of Human Resources Management Authority in the Federal Government." 1998.

Table 3.3: PBOs—Performance-Based Organizations

National Performance Review's Criteria for PBOs	a. clear mission with broad support from stakeholders b. focus on ends (and customers) rather than means c. operations separated from policy making and regulatory activities d. appropriate awards (compensation at market rates) or sanctions for the chief executive e. ability to raise revenues (proposed by the NAPA 1996 report as an additional criteria)
Foreign Experience	1. United Kingdom • The model of "Executive Agency"—that is, the PBO Framework—was included in the "Next Steps" program launched in 1988. More than 100 government programs have been transformed into performance-driven organizations as part of Next Steps. • Each agency operates under a "framework document" that defines its duties, establishes annual performance goals, and confers freedom from specified government-wide requirements respecting procurement, budgeting, and personnel. Chief executives are accountable for achieving the performance goals, are appointed competitively from among candidates in the civil service and the private sector, and report directly to the ministers. 2. Canada • The Increased Ministerial Authority and Accountability (IMAA) initiatives as well as the introduction of Special Operating Agencies (SOAs) have launched efforts to conduct government operations in a more businesslike manner. • The IMAA initiatives require departments to agree, through a Memorandum of Understanding (MOU) with the Treasury Board (TB), to changes in its planning, monitoring, control, internal audit, and program evaluation functions in return for increased operational flexibility. 3. New Zealand • Reform efforts are based on a number of principles including: departmental functions should be clearly specified; their policy and operations functions should be separated; and departmental managers should be fully accountable for running their organizations efficiently. • Key features of this new system include appointment of departmental chief executives on a limited term; performance-based contracts; annual agreements between ministers and chief executives specifying performance expectations; annual assessment of chief executive performance against these agreements; and the near total delegation of input control to chief executives.

continued on next page

Table 3.3: PBOs—Performance-Based Organizations *(continued)*

Initial Proposal for PBOs	The Vice President's Initial Proposal for PBOs includes a cost recovery criterion (ability to raise revenues). Based on this criterion, the initial proposal includes three agencies in the Department of Commerce: Patent and Trademark Office (PTO), the seafood inspection service of the National Oceanic and Atmospheric Administration (NOAA), and the National Technical Information Service (NTIS).
PBO or Other Statutory Authority	In establishing PBOs, agencies have the option of fully exercising existing personnel authorities and flexibilities, and of seeking the right to use the Demonstration Project authority. Within such authority, agencies can design their own personnel system, as was done in the Navy's China Lake project. However, some agencies have been able to replicate such "demonstrations" only with express statutory authority. The General Accounting Office (GAO) and the National Institute of Standards and Technology received such authority in separate statutes; NTIS and PTO are seeking legislative authority as well. On the other hand, OPM is encouraging agencies to seek demonstration authority.
Office of Personal Management's. Initial "Template" about PBO Proposal	OPM has been working with the Office of Management and Budget (OMB) and the NPR in developing policies and practices proposed for the activation and functioning of PBOs. OPM has created a "template," dated March 1996, setting forth personnel authorities already available to federal agencies. This is intended to permit PBO initiatives to begin quickly without needing to seek new legislative authority.

Sources:

   Alasdair Roberts, *"Performance-Based Organizations: Assessing the Gore Plan," PAR Nov./Dec. 1997, Vol. 57, No. 6.*

   James Thompson, *"Quasi Markets and Strategic Change in Public Organizations,"* in Jeffrey L. Brudney, Laurence J. O'Toole and Hal G. Rainey, (Eds.), *Advancing Public Management: New Developments in Theory, Methods, and Practice,* Washington, D.C.: Georgetown University Press, 2000.

   National Academy of Public Administration, *"A Performance Based Organization for Nautical Charting and Geodesy."* 1996.

   National Performance Review, *"Performance-Based Organizations: A Conversion Guide."* November, 1997.

The Federal Personnel System: The Complex Context

Anyone can see why managers might want more freedom and flexibility within the federal personnel system. A large system that has emphasized accountability, equity, and fairness within and across agencies, the federal system for hiring, pay, and other human resource requirements involves elaborate rules, procedures, and categories. Title 5 of the U.S. Code delineates much of the elaborate federal personnel system. Federal managers and professionals discussing the system constantly refer to "Title 5" when they talk about its characteristics ("... under Title 5 we have to ...") and about such matters as whether an agency, a group of employees, or a procedure is under Title 5 or exempt from it. Such discussions arise not only because Title 5's definitions and rules include many special situations, but also because federal legislation has set up special situations that involve exemption from Title 5.

For example, Table 3.4 provides a summary of the pay structure of the federal civil service. It shows a variety of pay categories, including numerous different categories and plans for higher-level professionals and administrators in different agencies. This elaborate system also shows that the federal personnel system has done a lot to provide for variation, special situations, and special needs, and hence has responded to the complexity of its environment and tasks. At the same time, however, the system includes many rules and constraints on executives and managers trying to carry out the work of their programs and agencies. For example, the system involves a set of schedules or defined categories of pay level, with upper limits on them. Obviously, while the system may have its merits, the basic schedules impose limits on executives' ability simply to decide on the pay to offer a person they want to hire as an executive or high-level professional.

In addition, Table 3.4 shows that Title 5 does have provisions for special salary rates and other variations, but executives often point out that they still involve complicated procedures and constraints. For example, one executive interviewed for this report pointed out that Title 5 provides for special pay for a critically needed type of employee in a highly competitive occupation. To use it, he said, "... you have to get approval from OPM and OMB, and there are so many strings attached that it is really hard to use this authority...."[11] So, as pay levels and other forms of compensation for highly educated and talented people in the private sector go up, those in government trying to hire people at that level feel more and more constrained.

Similarly, Title 5 and the federal personnel system provide a complicated set of methods and authorities for hiring people, as summarized in Table 3.5.

Table 3.4: Pay Structure of the Federal Civil Service and Special Pay Plans: Types of Federal Pay Systems

Basic Statistics	Total Employment: 1,671,438 (as of March 31, 2000) There are three categories: (1) General Schedule, 72.8%; (2) Federal Wage System, 12.3%; and (3) Other Pay Systems under Other Acts and Administrative Determination, 15.0% Average Salary for Full-time Employees: $50,429 (GS, $49,428; FWS, $37,082; Other, $66,248)
General Schedule (GS)	According to chapter 53 of Title 5, the GS pay system covers most "white-collar" positions in the executive branch and certain legislative branch agencies.
Federal Wage System (FWS)	The FWS covers trade, craft, and labor occupations ("blue-collar occupations") in the federal government (chapter 53 of Title 5).
Other Pay Systems under Other Acts and Administrative Determination	1. Similar to General Schedule: covers some employees in Departments of Defense, Commerce, Nuclear Regulatory Commission, Treasury, State, and FAA (27,600). 2. Administratively Determined (pay plan AD): covers some employees in Departments of Defense, Justice, Health and Human Services, Veterans Affairs, and other Departments. Congress authorizes agency heads to set salaries for those in these systems. 3. Veterans Health Administration: provides unique pay plans for employees like doctors, dentists, nurses, and assistants (pay plan VM, VN, VP). 4. Foreign Service (pay plan FO, FP): established under the Foreign Service Act of 1980. 5. Executive Schedule (pay plan EX): established by Congress to cover top officials in the executive branch. 6. Senior Executive Service (pay plan ES): covers most managerial, supervisory, and policy positions in the executive branch which are classified above GS-15 and do not require Senate confirmation. 7. Other Senior Level Pay Plans: (a) Specially Qualified Scientific and Professional Personnel (pay plan ST, authorized under section 3104 of Title 5); (b) Statutory Rates not Elsewhere Classified (pay plan SR)—nonsupervisory and nonmangerial employees classified above grade 15 of the GS; (c) Administratively Determined (Senior) Pay Plans—the AD pay plan described above contains some highly paid employees; (d) Administrative Law Judges (AL) and Contract Appeals Board Judges (CA); (e) Senior Foreign Service (FE) and Ambassadors (FA). 8. Other: includes special systems such as those for the Tennessee Valley Authority (TVA), the Federal Reserve Bank, The Canal Zone, and pay plans established under both the Financial Institutions Reform, Recovery and Enforcement Act of 1989, and the Federal Employees Pay Comparability Act of 1990. Also includes Demonstration Authority pay plans.

continued on next page

Table 3.4: Pay Structure of the Federal Civil Service and Special Pay Plans: Types of Federal Pay Systems *(continued)*

Special Salary Rates	The OPM has the authority to establish special rates of pay under section 5305 of Title 5 and has oversight authority for certain special rates authorized under Title 38 for GS and GM employees.
	Special salary rates can be set for white-collar positions where federal agencies have difficulty recruiting and/or retaining qualified personnel in certain occupations. Under Title 5, minimum special rate salaries may be no more than 30 percent above the GS step 10 salary for each particular grade.
	As of March 2000, there were 138,455 white-collar workers being paid special rate salaries (117,940 Title 5 and 20,515 Title 38). The white-collar special pay rate work-force was distributed as follows: Professional (35.6%), Administrative (6.5%), Technical (24.2%), Clerical (18.0%), and Other (15.7%).

Source: U.S. Office of Personnel Management, "Pay Structure of the Federal Civil Service." 2000.

While the system has defenders who make a strong case for it, some federal executives and managers, and some expert observers, have been critical. They have focused their complaints in particular on the basic system of competitive hiring through "OPM certificates," whereby the Office of Personnel Management certifies the most qualified candidates, and on the application of the "rule of three." Under this procedure, when an agency wants to hire someone, OPM plays a central role in ranking the candidates according to a set of criteria. It then provides the agency with a list of the top three candidates from which the agency can choose the person to hire. This process obviously takes some control out of the hands of the agency. Critics of the system point out that criteria used in the rankings—such as "veterans preference," under which candidates get points for being a military veteran—may not really reflect the best qualifications for the job. The process is also lengthy. Even after agency officials choose someone to whom they will make an offer, they may have an additional wait before the person can actually start work. Good candidates typically have other opportunities and frequently take other jobs rather than wait for the entire process to be completed.

Concerns about this process, as well as efforts to reform the personnel system in general, have produced other alternatives, such as "agency certificates."[12] Under this procedure, OPM delegates to a federal agency the authority for examining and ranking candidates for a position the agency needs to fill. OPM regulates this process, which often closely resembles the OPM certificate process except that it does not have to go through OPM. For example, a federal manager or professional with a specific expertise, such as a federal scientist, may describe a process for hiring in her agency

Table 3.5: Typology of Federal Hiring Methods for Professional and Administrative Occupations: Six Types of Federal Hiring Methods

Competitive Hiring	Characterized by (a) rating candidates; (b) ranking candidates; and (c) referring candidates in rank order, which is subject to (d) veterans preference rules and "rule of three."
Cooperative Education Program	Allowing students enrolled in two- or four-year college programs to work for federal agencies. Upon completion of academic program, they may—without competition—be converted to a competitive service appointment at the discretion of the agency. Neither veterans preference nor the rule of three applies.
Veterans Readjustment Appointments	Permitting agencies to hire qualified veterans into the competitive service without competition. Veterans are eligible for these appointments for specified time periods following their separation from the armed forces.
The Outstanding Scholar Hiring Authority	Procedures established by court order in 1982; using baccalaureate GPA or class standing as eligibility criteria for appointment; allowing candidates who meet the eligibility criteria to be directly hired without competition to determine who are the best qualified among the eligible candidates. Veterans preference and the rule of three do not apply.
The Bilingual/ Bicultural Hiring Authority	Used when a job requires proficiency in Spanish and English; in such situations this authority permits the appointments of individuals who achieve merely passing scores on an appropriate examination.
Special Appointing Authorities (Residual Category)	Includes special authorities established by statute, executive order, or civil service rule. Some of these authorities permit noncompetitive appointments into the competitive service. No single authority in this category represents a large number of appointments, but collectively they do account for a relatively large number of hires each year.

Source: U.S. Merit Systems Protection Board, "Restoring Merit to Federal Hiring: Why Two Special Hiring Programs Should be Ended." 2000, Appendix 3.

as first involving the preparation of a position description that specifies qualifications and requirements for the job. The agency then advertises the position, and candidates fill out standard forms in addition to addressing questions about how their qualifications suit them for the job. A committee consisting of professionals, personnel specialists, and other appropriate people ranks the candidates. The agency brings in the top six people for an interview. After the interviews, the executive who has to make the final decision receives a list of the candidates regarded by the committee as the best qualified. The executive, who has also participated in the candidate interviews, makes the final choice.

Such a procedure has many good qualities, such as fairness, openness, participation, and professionalism. It can still involve a lot of time, however, and still involves a degree of passiveness on the part of the recruiters, that is, compared to a situation in a private firm where a group of executives targets a talented person they want and goes after him or her. This is a more formalized and elaborate procedure.

Because of the drive to give operating agencies more control over their own hiring, still other methods and authorities have developed.[13] These alternatives have included, for example, "direct hires." The percentage of people hired under OPM certificates and agency certificates went down during the 1980s and early 1990s, and hiring by other methods such as direct hires went up. Significantly, however, by the late 1990s the percentage of newly hired people brought in under competitive hiring methods (like the certificate methods) was going up and hiring by the other methods going down.

Existing Flexibilities: The Three R's

Efforts to reform and improve the system have provided many flexibilities for agencies under current Title 5 and other laws and rules (see Table 3.6). For example, most federal managers know of the "Three R's," which refers to provisions for recruitment, retention, and relocation. These provisions permit bonuses or extra payments of up to 25 percent of base salary for recruiting, retaining, or relocating an employee. Title 5 also includes various provisions for "critical pay" for critically needed job candidates who are hard to obtain, and other arrangements for paying special amounts to critical or special employees. Many agencies have made use of the existing flexibilities under Title 5.

Exemptions from Title 5

In addition to the available flexibilities, a variety of organizations and organizational units in the federal government are exempt from Title 5. Government corporations, independent establishments, and some ordinary agencies have received congressional approval for exemption from Title 5 and for creation of their own personnel systems, or for partial exemptions. OPM issued a report based on a study of 18 organizations that are exempt from Title 5 and found that this exemption provided increased flexibility and independence in their human resource management (HRM) practices (see Appendix). In such agencies, HRM staff became more involved in designing and experimenting with new alternatives, and tended to be more closely integrated into management decision making in the agency. At the same

Table 3.6: Hiring Innovations and Flexibilities within Existing Laws (Best Practices)

While the NPR advocated decentralization and substantially increased delegation of authority that requires comprehensive civil-service reform legislation, such legislation has not been passed. On the other hand, many agencies took actions to reform HRM within the structure of the current system. Many of these innovations and flexibilities are stimulated by the agencies' efforts to compete for human resources with the private sector and other governmental agencies.

Agencies	Innovations and Flexibilities
Department of Commerce, Census Bureau	The bureau competes for highly trained experts in survey design and data analysis directly with the rapidly growing high-technology segments of the private sector. The bureau has found it difficult to fill the positions of statisticians and computer specialists. The difficulties in hiring are not from a lack of delegated authority but rather the **inability to offer a competitive salary** comparable to what private sector companies can offer. Thus, the bureau has developed some innovations to deal with this problem. • **The Electronic Hiring System:** an online hiring process permits individuals to log on to its hiring system; expert applicants can apply online for a position; applications are processed and applicant referrals are made within two or three days. • **COOL (Commerce Opportunities Online):** an interactive, automated, and web-based merit promotion vacancy announcement and application system. • **Using Temporal Appointments:** term appointments provide the bureau with a flexible work-force possessing the necessary skills for the work to be accomplished. • **Using a Contractor to Staff Data Capture Operations.** • **Highlighting the Bureau Quality-of-Life Programs** as a way to entice potential employees. • **Emphasizing Continuous Learning Programs,** such as the Census Corporate University, as a way to attract potential employees.
U.S. Department of Agriculture, Forest Service	• **Centralized Online Application Processing:** the use of open, continuous announcements, categorical grouping, and alternative delegated examining unit procedures make it possible for the agency to maintain lists of names for ready referral; managers submit requests to fill positions online and are referred candidates using an online certificate referral system. • **Excepted Appointment Authorities:** used for professional hard-to-fill occupations. • **Pay Bonuses and Relocation Packages to New Recruits:** the recruiters have the delegated authorities to hire and offer both pay bonuses and relocation packages in order to compete with the private sector for similar pools of candidates. • **Using Co-ops to recruit Co-ops.**

continued on next page

Table 3.6: Hiring Innovations and Flexibilities within Existing Laws (Best Practices)
(continued)

Agencies	Innovations and Flexibilities
U.S. Department of Agriculture, Agricultural Research Service	• **Categorical Groupings:** the USDA Demonstration Project, a joint effort of the Agricultural Research Service (ARS) and the U.S. Forest Service, tested a comprehensive simplification of the hiring system for both white-collar and blue-collar jobs. The demonstration project procedures have since been made permanent under separate legislation obtained by the department (Omnibus Reconciliation Act of 1998). The procedures provide for "Categorical Ranking" (quality groupings), a three-year probationary period for scientific positions, an alternative referral system for veterans, and an alternative to the rule of three. Under this process, candidates are ranked into the three possible groups (quality group, single group, and quality group plus eligible group). There is no further rating required, and the highest group is then referred to the selecting official to begin the selection process. • Agencies may use modified quality grouping procedures in rating candidates, especially in situations where large numbers of applicants are anticipated.
U.S. Department of Agriculture, Animal & Plant Health Inspection Service	• **Coordinated College Recruitment:** selection authority has been delegated to the respective first-line supervisors. The agency maintains a permanent staff who maintain the ongoing contact needed to remain in the forefront on college campuses. In the recruiter network, the 90 to 100 recruiters with collateral duty assignments from the scientific and mission support areas enhance the agency recruitment effort.
Department of Defense, Defense Finance and Accounting Service	• To compete effectively with the private sector in the "war" for accounting and financial talent, the service uses automated internal and external recruitment. • **Automated Staffing System:** it is almost completely automated in its staffing function using RESUMIX or PERSACTION (electronic application systems providing a paperless process).

Sources:
National Academy of Public Administration, "Innovative Agency Employment Practices." 2001.
National Academy of Public Administration, "The Case for Transforming Public Sector Human Resource Management." 2000.

time, however, the study found less difference between these agencies and those covered by Title 5 than the researchers originally expected, apparently for several reasons. Exempt agencies still try to adhere to merit system principles. They have to develop and defend their new systems and often draw on existing practice to do so. They often have to deal with unions that place constraints on flexibility in managing human resources. The greatest differences between the exempt agencies and those still covered by Title 5 tended to be in areas such as position classification and compensation, with fewer differences in such areas as recruitment. The study showed that exemptions from Title 5 make a difference, but not necessarily a huge difference, and called for continued attention to exemptions to understand their effects.

All of these variations and flexibilities show that the personnel system of the U.S. government has responded to pressures for more decentralization, deregulation, and increased flexibility and adaptability. It is a gross oversimplification to claim that the system involves a monolithic, strictly structured lattice of bureaucratic constraints. However, its variations and complexity appear to be part of the reason that federal managers want more independence from it. Some managers and experts say that the confusing array of authorities and special provisions makes it difficult to compete for talent while having to wend your way through the system. In addition, many of the flexibilities and special provisions available under Title 5 still have many strings attached. OPM regulates them, and procedures such as agency certificates often require steps at the agency level similar to those required for OPM certificates. To use many of the provisions and authorities, the agency must get approvals from OPM and sometimes other authorities. For example, as mentioned earlier, to use the "critical pay" provisions under Title 5, the agency has to get approval from both OPM and OMB.

For these reasons, executives, managers, and personnel administrators in federal agencies often continue to look for independence from many of the personnel rules and procedures centralized under OPM by Title 5. This makes it important to monitor the uses that agencies are making of some of the flexibilities recently granted to them, as in the cases of the four agencies covered in this report.

Case Studies of Special Recruiting Authorities

Federal Aviation Administration: A New Personnel System

The Federal Aviation Administration (FAA) received the most general grant of flexible authority of any of the four agencies. In 1996, Congress authorized the FAA administrator, in consultation with employees and experts, to "… implement a personnel management system for the FAA that addresses the unique demands on the agency's workforce …" and that provides "for a greater flexibility in the hiring, training, compensation, and location of personnel." With the exception of several provisions, the new system was to be exempt from Title 5. Also in 1996, the agency issued the FAA Personnel Management System (PMS). The PMS gives the heads of FAA's "line of business" and staff organizations the authority to determine the number and types of employees in their organizations, based on the amount of funds allocated to them. The system gives the administrator authority over the selection of persons to fill any vacant positions, and gives the heads of staff and business units authority over selection for any vacant executive or senior professional position in their units, subject to the approval of the administrator. Table 3.7 provides additional details about the authority granted to FAA.

The PMS also established the FAA Executive System, with provisions for performance bonuses and other features similar to the Senior Executive Service, but with more emphasis on linking compensation to performance and increasing accountability for management. The system streamlines executive disciplinary actions to allow prompt removal of poor performers.

The new system also streamlines hiring through authority for "on-the-spot" hiring for special needs and hard-to-fill positions. It provides for recruitment bonuses, for reducing the number of hiring authorities to be considered, and for reducing other rules to allow faster hiring. A Centralized Applicant System provides managers with applicant lists and ratings much faster than before. An automated system places job vacancy announcements on the Internet, reducing the time required to advertise vacancies by 80 percent. The PMS also decentralizes, to the line of business units, the decisions and funding for employee training, and includes new provisions for labor relations.

A Focus on Mission

Personnel officers at FAA express strong convictions about the benefits of the new flexibility and authority. They feel that the new PMS enhances FAA's ability to focus its human resources management on mission accomplishment. One of FAA's human resources administrators said, "We are much better able to focus on the mission and how you try to accomplish it through the people part of the equation. We have made tremendous strides in how we attract, hire, and retain the right people; and other agencies are trying to duplicate what this agency is doing." They are making strides, he and others say, through the new performance incentive programs and new position description and classification procedures that link individual objectives to FAA's strategic objectives. Table 3.8 provides details about a number of the developments at FAA.

In addition, FAA human resource officers say the new freedom has provided people there with the incentive and opportunity to develop innovative

78 Hal G. Rainey

Table 3.7: Department of Transportation—Federal Aviation Administration (FAA)

Legislation
The special authority for hiring and pay of the FAA is granted by Section 347 of the 1996 Department of Transportation and Related Agencies Appropriations Act (P.L. 104-50; 49 USC 106 note) and by Section 253 of the Federal Aviation Reauthorization Act of 1996 (P.L. 104-264; 49 USC 40122).
According to Section 347 of the law, in consultation with employees of the FAA and such non-governmental experts in personnel management systems as he may employ, and notwithstanding Title 5 and other federal personnel laws, the administrator of the FAA shall develop and implement a personnel management system for the FAA that addresses the unique demands on the agency's workforce. Such a system shall provide for a greater flexibility in the hiring, training, compensation, and location of personnel. The provision of Title 5 shall not apply to the new personnel system, with the exception of whistle-blower protection (Sec. 2302); veterans preference (Sec. 3308-3220); limitations on the right to strike (Sec. 7116); anti-discrimination (Sec. 7204); suitability, security, and conduct (Chapter 73); compensation for work injury (Chapter 81); retirement, unemployment compensation, and insurance coverage (Chapter 83-85, 87 and 89).
According to Section 40122 of the Federal Aviation Reauthorization Act of 1996, the administrator shall negotiate with the exclusive bargaining representative of employees of the administration; and no officer or employee of the administration may receive an annual rate of basic pay in excess of the annual rate of basic pay payable to the administrator.

Flexibilities
The FAA Personnel Management System (PMS), signed by the administrator in March 1996, is intended to make the personnel management system for the FAA more efficient and to provide greater flexibility in the hiring, training, compensation, and location of FAA personnel. The new system is exempt from substantially all of Title 5. Key characteristics of the FAA's hiring and pay system include:

a. **General Authority to Employ:** Each head of a line of business or staff organization is authorized to determine the number of employees for their organization based on the amount of funds allocated to the line of business or staff organization by the administrator.
b. **Types of Employees:** Each line of business and staff organization is authorized to hire any type of category of employee.
c. **Selection of Employees:** No vacant position shall be filled by any means other than selection and approval by the administrator; and no vacant Executive or Senior Professional position shall be filled by any means other than selection by the head of the line of business or staff organization in which the position is located, and approval by the administrator.
d. **Classification of Positions:** Each head of a line of business or staff organization shall conduct a classification review of all positions in their organization; the number of position descriptions shall be consolidated and reduced to the maximum extent feasible.
e. **Executive System Performance Incentive Plan:** The administrator or the head of a line of business or staff organization may pay a performance incentive to an employee in the Executive System in accordance with the criteria that were in effect for Senior Executive Service employees; the total amount available to a line of business or staff organization to pay incentives to employees in the Executive System shall be determined solely by the administrator.
f. **The President appoints the Administrator of the FAA.** There is not special authority, which is without regard to Title 5, to pay the administrator.

Table 3.8: Additional Information about the Federal Aviation Administration (FAA)

Title 5 Exemption and Merit Principles Major	• It is an excepted service agency based on its own statutory authority, like GAO and FDIC (NAPA, 1996). • The 1996 legislation granting the agency authority to create its own responsive HRM system exempted the organization from most Title 5 requirements, including the Merit Principles; it no longer operates under the umbrella of the Department of Transportation's personnel structure. • However, the agency has declared that its newly emerging HRM system should be consistent with those principles. For FAA, merit policies and practices require a balance between fairness and the flexibility to achieve organizational results.
Characteristics of HR Changes	• Replacing its Senior Executive Service (SES) with a new FAA Executive System. This executive system links compensation to performance with increasing accountability for management; decreases the average days for executive disciplinary and performance actions to allow prompt removal of poor performers (NAPA, 1996). • Hiring practices are being streamlined by relaxing or eliminating some OPM regulations, giving managers increasing authority for on-the-spot hiring in special cases, authorizing recruitment bonuses and other incentives, and decreasing the time it takes to hire external and internal candidates (NAPA, 1996).
Recently Introduced Tools to Improve the Hiring Process	• The use of a Centralized Applicant System, which provides automatic consideration for applicants and the opportunity for managers to hire without announcing a vacancy. This system will review qualifications and assign ratings and rankings, enabling managers to get referral lists over 90 percent faster. • "On-the-spot" hires for special program needs and hard-to-fill positions. • Elimination of time-in-grade, other than qualification requirements, for promotions. • Use of the Internet for job applications. In its automated staffing system, Selections Within Faster Times (SWIFT), vacancy announcements are placed on the Internet and automated tools are available for creating, copying, and storing vacancy announcements. The agency states that this had reduced the time required to advertise vacancies by more than 80 percent and provides greater assurance that employees and outside applicants have timely access to vacancy announcements. • Noncompetitive conversion from temporary to permanent status if competition is held initially for the temporary position. • Standard position descriptions that reduce the time for creating a job by more than 90 percent. • Reduction in the number of hiring authorities to three (permanent, temporary with time limit, and temporary without time limit).

continued on next page

Table 3.8: Additional Information about the Federal Aviation Administration (FAA)
(continued)

Classification & Compensation System	• Has developed its own classification system to meet competitive needs and to move from seniority-based pay systems to perform-ance-based alternatives.
Workforce Development and Training	• Has decentralized and deregulated training funding and decision making; each organizational "line of business" will identify its needs and develop a training plan; each will have more flexibility to make decisions about employee training.
Labor Relations	• Established the National Employee's forum (representatives of employee association and special emphasis groups) to serve as one point of check and balance to ensure appropriate representa-tion and protection for employees against undesirable practices. • Has initiated a new appeals process called Guaranteed Fair Treat-ment. A three-member panel consisting of one advocate chosen by each side in a dispute and a neutral arbitrator resolves appealed actions. This process replaces the MSPB appeals process and greatly reduces time frames for resolving disputes.

Sources:
   National Academy of Public Administration, "A Performance Based Organization for Nautical Charting and Geodesy." 1996.
   U.S. Office of Personnel Management, "HRM Policies and Practices in Title 5-Exempt Organizations." 1998.

executive and professional recruiting processes. The heads of the line of business units make the decisions about the positions needed in their units and the types of people to fill them, and the human resource officers report that they now work harder at playing the role of partner with administrators in supporting these decisions. They say they now strive to work collabora-tively with the executives to determine their needs, engaging in discussions of what they want to see happen, how a position will relate to accomplish-ing strategic objectives, and the key skills and foci of the position.

FAA representatives say they also make more effective use of recruiting firms to target appropriate people for positions—a point that people in the other agencies with flexibilities emphasize. They say before they got the new authority and flexibility, there was not much sense in trying to use such firms. Since job candidates had to go through ranking processes and other proce-dures through the OPM, an individual they might want to hire might not end up on the list of candidates from which they could choose. Even if they got to choose the person they wanted, the process took a lot of time, and there were often additional long waits before the person could actually start. Good candidates would be gone. Under the old system, there was a tendency to put out an announcement and hope for applicants. Now, they say, they are much better able to bring recruiting firms into the process to help locate the type of people FAA executives and human resource professionals have decided to recruit. They feel they have also learned to make more creative use of advertising. Of course, the streamlining and automating of their own procedures helps, too. "Now," says one FAA administrator, "we can choose the right person for the right job. We can find the best person."

FAA spokespersons see significant progress in acquiring sophistication in how to search. They have brought in more people from outside the agency, with new and necessary skills and perspectives. They are better able to introduce considerations of leadership ability into their recruiting, as well as an emphasis on experience in working collaboratively with customers, clients, and partners. This latter emphasis supports the effort to make FAA more collaborative with customers, to move away from serving as "police officers" and toward talking with customers and citizens about alternatives, possibilities, and how FAA can help them do their jobs.

They report a sense of increasing success in recruiting the people they want and need. "In information technology, we have been able to attract people at the top of the game in the federal government and the private sector," asserts an FAA human resource official.

Pressed for evidence of this success, FAA representatives report that 17 percent of newly hired executives have come from outside the agency. As for senior executive positions in such areas as research and development, 90 percent have come from outside the agency. Concerning the new PMS in general, they point out that there has been no major lawsuit or other major complaint nor an increase in grievances.

U.S. Patent and Trademark Office: USPTO as a PBO

The U.S. Patent and Trademark Office (USPTO) represents a more limited version of providing an agency with flexibilities in recruiting and hiring. USPTO takes in over a billion dollars in revenues per year as fees for reviewing patent and trademark applications and for issuing them. In part because of this businesslike revenue-generating characteristic, Congress designated USPTO a "performance-based organization." The concept of a PBO had been implemented in the United Kingdom as part of reform efforts there. It made its way across the Atlantic during the Clinton administration when the National Performance Review began to promote the idea (see Table 3.3). Establishing an agency as a PBO usually involves hiring the head of the agency on a contract for a certain number of years, with a performance contract or agreement establishing annual performance objectives that the agency must meet. Meeting and exceeding these objectives can win a performance bonus for the top executive. Often executives at the second level in the agency are hired under performance contracts as well, and the agency typically receives independence from many of the rules and requirements imposed on typical government agencies. The idea is to allow the agency to perform like a business.

As has been the case with government corporations and authorities, the legislative branch tends to apply the PBO concept in varying ways, specific to individual agencies.[14] For USPTO, for example, unions representing personnel in the agency strongly opposed proposals to exempt USPTO from federal personnel policies and rules. Thus, USPTO ended up remaining under Title 5. Representatives of USPTO suggest that USPTO employees and union members, who tend to be highly professional and highly educated, wanted to retain the due process protections under Title 5 that provide employees rights to due process in decisions about firing and disciplinary action. As a result, most of the employees and managers in USPTO remain under the personnel rules of the federal government that apply to other agencies. See Table 3.9 for a more detailed description of the provisions for USPTO.

Table 3.9: Department of Commerce—United States Patent and Trademark Office (USPTO)

Legislation
In November 1999, the President signed into law the Patent and Trademark Office Efficiency Act (P.L. 106-133, Appendix, Section 4701, that amends 35 USC 1). This act re-established the PTO as the USPTO, a Performance-Based Organization. The USPTO retains responsibility for decisions regarding the management and administration of operations, and exercises independent control of budget allocations and expenditures, personnel decisions and processes, procurement, and other administrative and management functions.

Flexibilities
a. **Head of the Agency:** The USPTO is headed by an Under Secretary of Commerce for Intellectual Property and Director of the USPTO, appointed by the President and confirmed by the Senate, in order to provide policy direction and management supervision for the USPTO.
b. **Appointment of COO:** The Secretary of Commerce appoints a commissioner for patents and a commissioner for trademarks to serve as chief operating officers (COO) for the respective units. The commissioners have five-year terms and will be responsible for all aspects of the activities of the USPTO.
c. **Compensation of COO:** The commissioners enter into annual performance agreements with the Secretary and are eligible for 50 percent bonuses based on their performance under those agreements.
d. **Personnel Management:** Officers and employees of the USPTO continue to be subject to Title 5.
e. **Public Advisory Committees:** The law establishes Public Advisory Committees for Patents and Trademarks, each with nine members appointed by the Secretary for three-year periods, to review and report on the policies, goals, performance, and user fees of the USPTO.

USPTO representatives point to one very significant change, however, that they regard as important in the quest for executive talent. The PBO legislation gave USPTO certain grants of independence from the parent agency, the Department of Commerce, in personnel matters. Prior to this, when the USPTO's Executive Resources Board determined there was a need for a new SES level executive, they had to compete with other agencies in the Department of Commerce. Commerce had a fixed number of SES positions that were allocated among the department's agencies, such as USPTO and the National Oceanic and Atmospheric Administration. But now, if USPTO executives decide they want to create a new executive position, they have more freedom. They can work directly with OPM on creating the position without going through Commerce. USPTO representatives feel that this flexibility provides them with significant opportunities to determine their own configuration of executive resources.

The situation at USPTO brings up the important point that the special authorities and flexibilities Congress may grant to agencies can be highly politicized. For USPTO, an exemption from Title 5 did not come about because a major professional association, a union, opposed the exemption. Unions can mount significant opposition to situations that give managers more discretion and authority. Generally, the design of the grants of authority often involves various forms of lobbying and selling to Congress by agency representatives and representatives of other groups. The situation at USPTO is still developing, and possible flexibilities in human resource management may yet be worked out between USPTO and OPM in a "memorandum of understanding." Table 3.10 provides additional information about the transformation of USPTO to a Performance-Based Organization.

Office of Student Financial Assistance: A PBO with Special Positions

In another alternative for providing an agency with flexibility in fighting the war for talent, Congress has given some agencies a specific number of special positions for use in attracting the "hard to attract." In another variation on the PBO idea, Congress made the Department of Education's Office of Student Financial Assistance (SFA) into a Performance Based Organization through legislation that granted SFA several forms of "personnel flexibility."

- The new PBO would not be subject to ceilings on the number and grade of employees. (Previously, the agency was subject to ceilings based on full-time equivalents [FTEs], or hours worked, by employees. Now the agency could make decisions about the number and level of employees within certain dollar amounts).
- The COO would work with OPM on personnel flexibilities in staffing, classification, and pay that meet the needs of the PBO.

Table 3.10: Additional Information about the U.S. Patent and Trademark Office (USPTO)

PTO as a PBO	• Included in the Vice President's 1995 Initial Proposal for PBOs with other agencies, such as NTIS. • Legislation had been proposed by the Clinton administration (H.R. 2533) to grant PTO authority to use commercial business practices and to be permitted waivers from selected government controls in exchange for being accountable for agreed-upon performance goals. • PTO's Human Resource office has been conducting several services to pre-pare PTO for becoming a performance-based organization. These have included benchmarking studies of competency-based systems and reviews of human resource practices and techniques used in several major corporations, such as Texaco. • Human resource management changes for PTO were being developed before the issuance of OPM's template of personnel flexibilities in 1996. They include some proposed flexibilities that go beyond those described by OPM that may be found in other bills such as S. 1458, H.R. 1659, and H.R. 3460. These bills would convert PTO to the Patent and Trademark Corporation, and make it subject to the Government Corporation Control Act. Under H.R. 3460, the corporation would have authority to set pay rates and benefits for its employees, including wages and compensation based on performance.
Efforts to Make PTO a Government Corporation	• In 1989 and 1995, NAPA produced reports related to efforts to make PTO a government corporation at the request of the agency. These reports concluded that the PTO met the criteria for conversion to a wholly owned federal corporation. • These reports emphasized the need for exemption from government-wide regulations about procurement, personnel management, and other administrative systems.
Agency History of PTO	• In 1846, the Patent Office was transferred from the State Department to the new Department of the Interior, where it remained until being moved to the Department of Commerce in 1926. • In 1991, as the result of increases in fees enacted by Congress, the PTO became fully self-supporting from fees and ceased to be dependent upon tax-payer support. • In 1994, fees allocated totaled about $547 million. Of this amount, $25 million was not appropriated to the PTO. Actual operating expenses for the office were $469 million.

Sources:
National Academy of Public Administration, "Designing Outcome Measures at the U.S. Patent and Trademark Office." 1999.

National Academy of Public Administration, "A Performance Based Organization for Nautical Charting and Geodesy." 1996.

National Academy of Public Administration, "Incorporating the Patent and Trademark Office." 1995.

- The COO received authority to appoint up to 25 technical and professional employees to administer the functions of the PBO as members of the "excepted service." These appointments would not be subject to the provisions of Title 5 in their appointments, pay, and classification.

Table 3.11 offers more details. The designation of the special positions as excepted service draws on a long-standing category of employment in the federal service in which a person is exempted, or excepted, from the normal provisions for federal employment such as competitive examinations. While they have often been considered "patronage" positions, these excepted service provisions have more often been used where competitive examinations or other competitive procedures are not practical, and where the positions are not of a policy-making nature.[15] Most federal attorneys, for example, are hired under this category. Designating the SFA positions as excepted service removes them from Title 5 procedures and the supervision of their hiring by OPM.

According to people in SFA, this last authority and other provisions of the legislation could be interpreted in two ways. One interpretation, favored by some SFA people, contends that the act gives SFA authority to hire a reasonable number of senior managers, plus 25 special technical and professional persons. Under the second interpretation, the total of 25 covers senior managers as well as the technical and professional positions. The COO adhered to this second interpretation to avoid any possibility of exceeding the authority granted by the act.

SFA has assigned the senior management positions on the basis of how much supervisory and program management responsibility the position involves. The agency uses the authority for hiring technical and professional people to fill positions requiring technical and professional skills that the agency has difficulty in attracting and for which the SFA has a special need. For example, the agency needed experts in financial management and accounting, and in information technology and other high-tech specialties—positions that typically command substantially higher salaries in the private sector than in government. In addition, the agency recruited people to meet certain strategic priorities, such as a customer service orientation. In its strategic planning and its performance plan, the agency had set goals for improving customer satisfaction, in addition to others such as improving employee satisfaction and improving business operations by reducing unit costs.[16] The COO placed a priority on finding out what "customers" want and need, and as a result, SFA hired some specialists in part on the basis of their unique "ground level" perspective. That is, they have experience dealing with SFA's programs and services at the university or school level.

SFA officials say that the authorities really help them get the people they want and need much faster than before. Previously, they say, it could take up to six months to hire a person due to the rules and requirements for

Table 3.11: Department of Education—Office of Student Financial Assistance (SFA)

Legislation
The personnel flexibilities of the Office of Student Financial Assistance are established by the Higher Education Amendments of 1998 (P.L. 105-244; 20 USC 1018), which created the federal government's first-ever Performance-Based Organization (PBO), a concept promoted by the National Performance Review (NPR). The delivery of federal student aid will be led by an executive with expertise who reports directly to the Secretary of Education and has new administrative flexibility in exchange for increased accountability for results. The PBO will have new flexibility in personnel management, including hiring and evaluating senior managers and recruiting technical personnel.

Flexibilities

a. **Establishment of PBO [Section 141(a)]:** The Office of Student Financial Assistance is established as a PBO in the Department of Education; one of the purposes of the PBO is to provide flexibility in the management of the operational functions of the programs.

b. **Independence [Section 141(b)]:** The PBO shall exercise independent control of its budget allocations and expenditures, personnel decisions and processes, and other administrative and manage-ment functions.

c. **Appointment of chief operating officer (COO) [Section 141(d)]:** The management of the PBO shall be vested in the COO who shall be appointed by the Secretary to a term of not less than three and not more than five years, and compensated without regard to Chapters 33, 51, and 53 of Title 5. The appointment shall be made on the basis of demonstrated management ability and expertise in information technology including experience with financial systems, and without regard to political affiliation or activity.

d. **Compensation of COO [Section 141(d)]:** The COO is authorized to be paid at an annual rate of basic pay not to exceed the maximum rate of basic pay for the Senior Executive Service under Section 5382 of Title 5. In addition, the COO may receive a bonus in the amount that does not exceed 50 per-cent of such annual rate of basic pay. Payment of a bonus may be made to the COO only to the extent that such payment does not cause the COO's total aggregate compensation in a calendar year to equal or exceed the amount of the President's salary.

e. **Senior Management [Section 141(e)]:** The COO may appoint such senior managers as that officer determines necessary without regard to Title 5. The senior managers may be paid without regard to Chapter 51 and 53 of Title 5. A senior manager may be paid at an annual rate of basic pay of not more than the maximum rate of basic pay for the Senior Executive Service under Section 5382 of Title 5. In addition, a senior manager may receive a bonus in an amount such that the manager's total annual compensation does not exceed 125 percent of the maximum rate of basic pay for the SES.

f. **Personnel Flexibilities [Section 141(g)]:** The COO shall work with the OPM to develop and implement personnel flexibilities in staffing, classification, and pay that meets the needs of the PBO, subject to compliance with Title 5. The COO may appoint, without regard to the provisions of Title 5, not more than 25 technical and professional employees to administer the functions of the PBO. These employees may be paid without regard to Chapter 51 and 53 of Title 5.

posting positions. Many good people would not wait that long for a job offer. So one of the benefits of the authorities comes from advantageous timing. In addition, the private sector not only could make a job offer faster, but also could pay more.

SFA representatives say they feel strongly that the authorities have helped them succeed in attracting excellent people in information technology, financial management, and other areas. They report that the agency sometimes identified the persons hired through professional networks in which executives and managers in SFA were involved. In other cases, the networks did not provide the type of people they were looking for, and the agency used recruiting firms with good results. SFA follows no highly systematic way of setting the pay levels of the new excepted service positions, but sets them on the basis of what the person was making in his or her previous position, what the person's supervisor thought was justified and necessary, and the apparent value of the person's skills, credentials, and services.

The noncompetitive and flexible nature of this hiring produced some grumbling from long-term employees, and occasionally some of the new hires might express concern about the level of their salary compared to another recent hire who got more. None of these problems ever became particularly serious, however, and SFA representatives say they never regarded them as cause for major concern or action. Factors that lessen the seriousness of such reactions probably include the very high number of long-term career positions in the agency compared to the small number of excepted service positions. In addition, a lot of employees are likely aware that the excepted service positions have fewer protections against dismissal than career service positions, although they attain similar protections after two years of service.

Because of the different interpretations of the statute providing the 25 positions, the situation at SFA illustrates how important it is that the actual wording of the statutory authority be as clear and unambiguous as possible. It also illustrates a tendency—which was also true at the IRS—for executives who have received these special positions to proceed very carefully in their use. They have obviously considered it very important to demonstrate responsible and well-justified utilization of these special authorities.

Internal Revenue Service: Critical Pay for Critical Positions

The authority granted to the Internal Revenue Service (IRS) involves another variation on providing a specific number of special positions. At IRS, the "critical pay" authorities came as part of major change and reform and play a significant role in those reforms. Years of concern over modern-

ization and performance of the tax system led to the formation of a commission for reform of IRS, which, in turn, led to the Internal Revenue Service
Restructuring and Reform Act (RRA) of 1998. The commission report recommended giving IRS the authority for flexible hiring of key positions.
Among many other provisions, RRA gave IRS authority to hire 40 people in
critical positions. Specifically, the act gives the Secretary of the Treasury
authority for 10 years to hire people to positions that "require expertise of
an extremely high level in an administrative, technical, or professional
field" and that "are critical to the IRS's successful accomplishment of an
important mission." The exercise of the authority must be necessary to
recruit or retain an individual "exceptionally well qualified" for the position. The act limits the appointments of these critical pay personnel to four
years and sets their maximum compensation at the level of the Vice
President of the United States.

RRA provided a number of additional "personnel flexibilities" to IRS as
well. In addition to the critical pay authority, the act provides for the following flexibilities:[17]

- Variation from standard recruitment, retention, and relocation incentives
- Performance awards for senior executives
- Limited appointments to career SES positions
- Streamlined demonstration project authority
- Authority for establishment of a new workforce performance manage-
  ment system that includes, among other provisions, retention standards
  for employees
- Authority for establishing new systems for compensation and staffing,
  including a broad-banding pay system
  See Table 3.12 for additional details.

IRS pursued and received these flexibilities as part of a major overhaul
of the agency. Features of the reforms included a massive structural redesign
to organize the agency into four operating divisions, each serving a set of
taxpayers with similar needs—Wage and Investment, Small Business and
Self-Employed, Large and Mid-Sized Business, and Tax Exempt and
Government Entities. This reorganization reflects an emphasis on enhancing
a customer service orientation in IRS, and on supporting, educating, and
facilitating taxpayers rather than simply demanding their compliance. It
also involved an effort to change the culture of the agency. Assessments of
the agency's culture had indicated the persistence of an enforcement and
compliance mentality among employees. Documents describing the reorganization emphasize the objective of moving the agencies' culture
toward the fundamental assumption that most taxpayers will comply with
the tax laws if they know their responsibilities, and that through communication and education the agency can help citizens comply. In addition, of
course, the reforms were to continue the agency's quest for modernization

Table 3.12: Department of Treasury—Internal Revenue Service (IRS)

Legislation
The special authority for hiring and pay of the IRS is granted by Chapter 95 of Title 5 and the IRS Restructuring and Reform Act (RRA) of 1998 (P.L. 105-206; 5 USC 9501-10).

Flexibilities
Chapter 95 (Section 9501 through 9510) of Title 5 and Section 1201 of IRS's RRA of 1998 are intended to allow IRS managers more flexibility in rewarding good performers and in making employees more accountable for their performance. These provisions give the Secretary of Treasury pay and hiring flexibilities, which are not otherwise available under Title 5. However, the new personnel flexibilities must be exercised consistent with existing provisions of Title 5 relating to merit system principles (Chapter 23), prohibited personnel practices (Chapter 23), preference eligibles, and, except as otherwise specifically provided, relating to the aggregate limitation on pay (Section 5307) and labor-management relations (Chapter 71).

a. **IRS Special Personnel Flexibilities (Sec. 9501):** The new personnel flexibilities granted the Secretary of Treasury must be exercised consistent with existing statutory provisions relating merit system principles and prohibited personnel practices, and to preference eligibles.

b. **Pay Authority for Critical Positions (Sec. 9502):** When the Secretary of Treasury seeks a grant of authority under Section 5377 for pay for critical positions at the IRS, OMB may fix the rate of basic pay, notwithstanding Section 5377 (d)(2), at any rate up to the salary set in accordance with Section 104 of Title III (the rate of pay of the Vice President).

c. **Streamlined Critical Pay Authority (Sec. 9503):** The Secretary of Treasury may establish, fix the compensation of, and appoint individuals to designated critical administrative, technical, and professional positions needed to carry out the functions of the IRS, if the number of such positions does not exceed 40 at any one time.

d. **Recruitment, Retention, Relocation Incentives, and Relocation Expenses (Sec. 9504):** The Secretary of Treasury may pay allowable relocation expenses and allowable travel and transportation expenses for any new appointee to a Section 9502 or 9503 position.

e. **Performance Awards for Senior Executives (Sec. 9505):** IRS senior executives may be paid a performance bonus if the Secretary of Treasury finds such awards warranted based on the executive's performance. The performance bonus may be paid without regard to the limitation in Section 5384 relating to performance awards for SES [Section 9505 (a)], and an award in excess of 20 percent of an executive's rate of basic pay shall be approved by the Secretary. A performance bonus award may not be paid to an executive if the executive's total annual compensation will exceed the maximum amount of total compensation payable to the Vice President [Section 9595 (e)].

f. **Limited Appointments to Career Reserve Senior Executive Service Positions (Sec. 9506).**

g. **Streamlined Demonstration Project Authority (Sec. 9507).**

continued on next page

Table 3.12: Department of Treasury—Internal Revenue Service (IRS) *(continued)*

Flexibilities
h. **General Workforce Performance Management System (Sec. 9508):** The Secretary of Treasury shall establish for the IRS a performance management system.
i. **General Workforce Classification and Pay (Sec. 9509):** The Secretary of Treasury may establish one or more broad-banded systems covering all or any portion of the IRS workforce. The Secretary may, with respect to IRS employees who are covered by a broad-banded system, provide for variations from the provisions of subchapter VI of Chapter 53 relating to grade and pay retention (Section 9509).
j. **General Workforce Staffing (Sec. 9510):** An employee of the IRS may be selected for a permanent appointment in the competitive service in the IRS through internal competitive promotion procedures. Notwithstanding sub-chapter 1 of Chapter 33 relating to examination, selection and placement, the Secretary of the Treasury may establish category-rating systems for evaluating applicants for IRS positions in the competitive service.
k. **IRS Oversight Board:** Section 1101 of the IRS RRA of 1998 establishes the IRS Oversight Board with the Department of Treasury. The Board oversees management of the IRS, recommending to the President candidates for appointment as the commissioner, and, if necessary, recommending the commissioner's removal. The Board also reviews the selection, evaluation, and compensation for certain senior executives in the IRS.
l. **Commissioner of IRS:** Under the Section 1102 of the IRS RRA of 1998, the commissioner will be appointed in renewable five-year terms. The commissioner must consult with the Oversight Board, and the board has review authority over certain operational plans and management matters.
m. **Other Personnel:** Section 1104 of the IRS RRA of 1998 authorizes the commissioner to employ such persons as the commissioner deemed proper for the administration and enforcement of the tax laws, and to issue all necessary directions, instructions, orders, and rules applicable to such persons.

of the tax system, especially through the use of contemporary computing, information, and communication technology.

The Origins of the Critical Pay Authority

According to people at IRS, the idea of pursuing these important objectives through more personnel flexibilities emerged from the deliberations of a committee that Dave Mader, director of operations for IRS, chaired in 1997, as the Commission on Reform was getting under way. Robert Rubin, then secretary of the treasury, and Kay Francis Dolan, deputy assistant secretary for human resources, formed the committee at the suggestion of Mader and others to consider ways to bring about the major reforms that IRS was facing. The committee began to focus on the possibility of gaining some flexibility through independence from the standard constraints and procedures in the federal personnel and procurement systems. This, the committee members contended, would help IRS make the rapid changes and adjustments needed for major reform. Interestingly, then, the ideas emerged from the agency rather than being borrowed or imposed from outside.

It is important to look at how the critical pay authorities have helped IRS to pursue its reform objectives. What has IRS gotten through the use of these positions? People in IRS who have been involved in the program point to many benefits. Ron Sanders, the IRS director of human resources, feels strongly that the critical pay hirees who have come from the private sector and other settings have been crucial in the agency's reform efforts. Besides the high levels of skill and experience they bring, he sees great value in their perspective and attitudes about changes. Sanders describes them as having a "just do it" attitude—a receptive orientation to trying new approaches and taking action.

People hired for the critical pay positions often have a specific challenge, project, or contribution as their focus for the four-year term. Some of the people have assumed these sorts of roles and then moved on. Table 3.13 describes some of those positions.

As for executives and professionals who have been hired and are still with IRS, representatives of the organization make strong claims about their value and quality. In response to questions about these hires posed by the Joint Committee on Taxation, IRS made the following claim:

> The Service has recruited an exceptionally talented and experienced workforce to provide vision, leadership, and guidance which, supplemented by the experience and skills of the career executive corps, has enabled the Service to successfully meet the massive challenges of the complete restructuring mandated by Congress. Our current critical pay executives bring external experiences, practices, and knowledge not currently available within the organization.

Indeed, the agency puts forth a good case for the qualifications of the people hired for critical pay positions and the rationale for bringing them to IRS. They also reported the following information to the Joint Committee:

- The new deputy commissioner for modernization/chief information officer was a top executive in the technology area at Time-Warner.
- Two of the four division commissioners and one of the deputy commissioners are external hires and provide specific industry background and experience, change management experience, and senior leadership.
- All of the senior industry advisors in the Large and Mid-Size Business Division have been recruited from the industries to which they are assigned, making them uniquely suited to providing the most current technical advice to the Service.

Table 3.13: Partial List of Streamlined Critical Pay Executives Who Have Been Recruited by IRS

Position Title	Rate of Pay	Incentives/Bonuses
Chief Financial Officer	$147,500	None
Director, Program Control Information Systems	$130,000	None
Assistant Commissioner (Management and Financial Systems) IS	$135,000	None
Director, Government Program Management Office, IS	$160,000	$15,000 (Recruitment, 11/21/98)
Director, Real Estate and Facilities Management Agency-Wide Shared Services	$176,300	$37,800 (Recruitment, 3/15/00)
National Taxpayer Advocate	$144,800*	$15,000 (Recruitment, 9/1/98) $25,000 (Annual Performance, 1/18/01)
Deputy Commissioner/ Modernization	$155,100*	$25,000 (Recruitment, 9/16/98) $20,000 (Annual Performance, 1/18/01)
Chief Information Officer	$181,400*	$43,600 (Recruitment, 8/11/98) $25,000 (Annual Performance, 1/16/01)

* Salary at departure

- The new national taxpayer advocate had a long and distinguished career in tax advocacy and is well-known in legal circles and in Congress.
- The chief of Criminal Investigations is an attorney with a successful career at Justice and in private law practice.
- The chief of Agency-Wide Shared Services was recruited from a major international corporation and brings to the agency expertise in best practices for commercial service support.
- The associate commissioner for Business Systems Modernization was previously president of the Professional Services Council and joined the Service with a wealth of experience and background in modernizing systems.

- The chief of Information Technology Services was recruited from Marriott International, where he was senior vice president for Information Research Operations and Services.
- The recently hired chief of business strategy and business architecture in the Wage and Investment Division is one of the leading experts in the United States on designing and operating call centers.
- The director of the Stakeholder, Partnership, Education and Communications Office in the Wage and Investment Division came to the Service from Karch International, where he was COO and directed a wide array of successful marketing projects.
- The director of International Operations in the Large and Mid-Size Business Division was formerly the director of E-Business Tax Policy and Practices at a major national consulting firm and had over 15 years of corporate international tax experience.

A Closer Look at Critical Pay Position Holders

A look at some of the individuals hired under the program reveals the reasons for the enthusiastic response to it. For example, Joe Kehoe is now director of the Small Business and Self-Employed Division. People in IRS consider this a strategically important division because of its size—40,000 employees. In addition, there are many important issues about compliance among small business and self-employed taxpayers, and much that can be done in outreach, education, and facilitation for this group of taxpayers. Kehoe was formerly the managing partner of the Washington Consulting Practice of PricewaterhouseCoopers. After retiring from PricewaterhouseCoopers, Commissioner Rossotti recruited him to accept the challenge of taking charge of a 40,000-person division involved with a government activity that touches so many lives. When Kehoe took the job, he says he felt that if he could contribute to improving the programs and activities of IRS, he could contribute to improving working lives and personal lives throughout the nation.

Like many people who move from the private sector into the federal government, Kehoe has a lot of praise for government employees—more specifically, IRS employees. He says he has been impressed with how hard they work and how dedicated they are. He was struck by the large scope of responsibility of many of the executive positions in IRS. After all, he had just assumed leadership of a division of 40,000, at less pay than he had commanded in private business. He also mentions opportunities he sees to bring in new ideas and perspectives from the private sector. For example, he sees possibilities for improving the way IRS examiners conduct their audits, drawing on the most contemporary practices in audits and reviews by private accounting and consulting firms.

Kehoe says he has found many opportunities to encourage IRS employees to move away from a compliance-oriented view of taxpayers toward a view more sensitive to the immense impact that compliance pressures can have on taxpayers. Still, he does not see his role as involving some simple relaxation of requirements for people to fulfill their responsibilities as tax-payers. He says that he has found interesting, in his communications with taxpayers and associations representing taxpayers, the number of people who urge him to make sure that everyone does their fair share. He finds that people do not express strong hostility toward the tax system, but rather the strong desire that the system be made fair and equitable. If some are doing their duty by complying with the tax laws, they want to know that others are required to do so as well.

One of the things Joe Kehoe has done in relation to the critical pay authorities is to use them in pursuit of the priorities of his operating division. For example, the Small Business and Self-Employed Division (SB/SE) hired Tom Dobbins. Dobbins is an example of a younger, less senior acquisition for one of the critical pay positions. He came to IRS with a background in lobbying and public relations work with professional associations; his most recent position before coming to IRS was at a private consulting and public relations firm. Others at IRS point out that Dobbins brought to the organization a background and skills that did not really exist within IRS at the time. With the increased strategic emphasis on outreach, education, and communication with taxpayers, IRS had a strong need for people with knowledge and skills in "marketing." That is, they needed not simply sales-people or public relations people, but people with ideas and experience about how to reach and communicate with key stakeholder groups, such as professional and commercial associations. This connection should enhance the agency's capacity to utilize those groups as channels of communication and education for taxpayers. In such a role at IRS, Dobbins has helped to develop ideas and practices for getting together with those groups to use them as a way to disseminate such technologies as CDs with information about tax responsibilities and procedures for members of such groups.

His perspectives have helped to promote internal communication as well. Dobbins played a key role in planning meetings that brought together large numbers of SB/SE personnel from all over the nation. At the meetings, they heard from the commissioner, the division director, and other leaders, and met with their counterparts from around the nation. Participants in these sessions were so enthusiastic about their value that the meetings may become regularly scheduled activities. Others in IRS credit Dobbins with having an essential influence on these developments by bringing his new perspective and background into the IRS context and raising new possibilities.

Resentment Issues

One potential problem for the critical pay program may come from resentment from long-term IRS career employees over the higher salaries and special treatment of the critical pay hirees. One IRS official mentioned in an interview that he had a good friend, a long-term IRS manager, who deeply resented the critical pay authority because it implied that IRS needed outsiders to come in and fix the agency. When asked whether they have encountered any serious resentment or resistance, people such as Dobbins have little to report. Dobbins says he has noticed an occasional wisecrack about how he is supposed to be "some big expert" that has been brought in, but nothing very serious. Many people in IRS point out that the critical pay hirees may have larger salaries than career managers and professionals, but the careerists tend to realize that they have benefits that the critical pay people do not have. The people in the critical pay positions have four-year contracts and may well be looking for another position outside of IRS in four years. They have often come in from higher-paying jobs or otherwise desirable positions elsewhere. The career people have longer-term career stability and benefits.

Accountability Issues

One of the big issues for critical pay authorities should be obvious to anyone with a background in government or public management. When you give people authority and discretion, it always raises concerns about accountability. How do you give people freedom to make decisions and choices in government agencies without raising such classic problems as cronyism, political string-pulling, or just plain bad choices? The critical pay authorities may work well when IRS has a commissioner with high credibility and competence, with a person such as Dave Mader to shepherd the program along, and other high-caliber people to support and develop it. What happens if you do not have such people involved, and political leaders want to intervene to get poorly qualified friends and allies hired, or the decisions are lax and allow someone with a conflict of interest into an important position?

When asked such questions, people in IRS point to various review procedures and safeguards. For one thing, says Ron Sanders, director of human resources for IRS, the new IRS has an oversight board, and it can play a role in reviewing the use of the critical pay authorities. The General Accounting Office has already produced one report on the implementation of the personnel flexibilities in IRS, and such oversight and review processes can continue as a guard against misuse. The Joint Committee on Taxation has asked IRS to answer questions about the implementation of the critical pay authority and has issued a favorable assessment.

In addition, in its implementation of the critical pay authority, IRS has adhered to many safeguards against its misuse. Deb Nelson and Rhett Leverette, who have responsibility for executive resources and have worked directly with the negotiations and hiring for the critical pay positions, describe an extensive set of reviews and safeguards. Each candidate has to have the standard checks and reports that employment with IRS requires. The candidate has to undergo a criminal background check, a detailed financial disclosure, a reference check, a review of recent tax returns, and other forms of scrutiny. Attorneys from both the Treasury Department and IRS review these checks and disclosures for each candidate. Leverette estimates that the process often takes about as long as standard processes under Title 5. Sometimes candidates being considered for positions express concern about how long the process does take, Leverette says. But the critical pay authorities do provide flexibility in the amount of pay the agency can offer to a person, freedom from controls and checks by some other agencies such as OPM, and the authority to pick out a person they want to hire. The authorities, however, by no means give the agency a release from accountability and checks against misuse.

The Learning Process

As with any innovative program or procedure, the critical pay authorities at IRS have involved a learning process for those involved. Dave Mader reports that people at IRS have found that recruiting firms have come to play a crucial role in enabling IRS to use the authorities successfully. Since the agency now has the flexibility to design and designate positions for particular types of individuals, these firms' knowledge of potential candidates around the nation and the world becomes extremely valuable. The firms can respond to the agency's profile of the person needed and proactively seek out candidates. Tom Dobbins reports that when the recruiting firm first contacted him about the IRS position that he ultimately filled, he thought the recruiter was asking for recommendations and began to name candidates. "I was thinking of you," the recruiter said. Dobbins says he never would have seen himself working for IRS, although he had been thinking he would go into government service at some point. The recruiter convinced him that the position was challenging, interesting, and a good opportunity. He agreed to be put into candidacy for the position and, once in, felt he wanted to present the best candidacy he could. Ultimately he received the offer.

The incident illustrates a point mentioned by people in other agencies as well. Once people in an agency have the flexibility with which they can work, they feel that they can better utilize existing resources and opportunities, such as the availability of recruiting firms. Even though they have had the option of using recruiting firms in recent years, they had little incentive to do so, because if the firm identified a good candidate, the agency still might not have the authority to hire that particular candidate. In addition, the hiring process might take so long that they would lose the person to another job opportunity.

Rhett Leverette, who has worked on the recruiting and "onboarding" of most of the people who have been hired, also describes learning processes from the experiences to date. For example, Leverette and others have been learning more about such issues as fashioning an appropriate compensation offer. They have learned to ask candidates for four years of compensation history, since many of the private sector compensation programs vary substantially from year to year. One needs a sense of the average level in these up and down patterns to develop an appropriately competitive offer. Stock options in private sector compensation packages have been one of the most challenging provisions against which IRS has had to compete. Because IRS cannot offer stock options, it cannot match this aspect of many private sector arrangements. People at IRS, however, are learning that the agency can compete on the basis of other dimensions, such as the challenges and opportunities for significant experience. They are also learning a lot about dealing with such matters as stock options, investments, and ownership arrangements that may require various forms of recusement or divestment by persons hired from the private sector.

Unique Characteristics of the IRS Critical Pay Context

Some special features of the IRS situation that have a bearing on the success of the critical pay program need consideration. In all four of the agencies covered in this report, the personnel flexibilities and special authorities came as part of major reforms and changes at the agencies. The critical pay positions at IRS come as part of a historically significant reform of the agency, which creates very challenging new opportunities for people coming into the organization to participate in changes that, as they put it, can touch the lives of so many citizens.

In addition to the opportunities and challenges of major changes and of work that has an important impact on the public, the IRS provides many positions involving significant scope of authority and responsibility. As an organization with over 100,000 employees, handling millions of tax returns and over a trillion dollars in tax collections per year, the agency offers massive challenges in information technology, executive leadership, public relations and outreach, and many other highly significant and challenging experiences. It appears that the higher pay helps to attract people to the critical pay positions, but that pay alone is by no means their only motivation or even their primary one. This raises the point that the flexibility to design the position and to match the person to the position seems to play an important role in providing the other incentives in addition to pay—challenge, meaningful work, valuable experience, public service—that IRS can offer to candidates for critical pay positions.

Findings and Recommendations

The Challenge of Fragmentation

From the point of view of officials in oversight agencies and bodies such as the Office of Personnel Management and committees of the Congress with responsibility for government operations and the civil service, the spread of special authorities raises a classic issue. People in central personnel offices have tended to emphasize the need for consistency, a coherent policy, and equity throughout a governmental human resource management system within a broad jurisdiction such as the federal government or a state government. As an obvious example, if two people in the system are doing essentially the same work, but one gets paid a lot more, that is unfair. Should one agency have special opportunities and advantages in managing their operations that others do not have? Also, if the system becomes increasingly fragmented and balkanized, the system itself becomes more complex, unwieldy, confusing, and hard to understand and manage.

Representatives of OPM and congressional committees tend to express support for flexibilities in general. They voice concerns, however, about individual agencies going to their authorizing committees in Congress and getting a special arrangement for themselves. From the viewpoint of those concerned with central oversight of the system, one can see why they would see a need for a comprehensive policy concerning flexibilities, so that all agencies might make use of them, rather than just a small set of fortunate ones.

On the other hand, reformers tend to emphasize the value of "tailoring" the system to suit the needs of individual agencies facing particular challenges. They argue that the special authorities of the sort covered in this report show the way toward a broader dissemination of the best practices in flexible hiring and pay provisions. People in the individual agencies point out that they face the challenge to improve now, and cannot afford to wait until some broad, overall policy is developed and adopted.

Findings

Representatives of the agencies given general grants of flexibility report beneficial results. Human resource managers from the FAA say that with their new personnel system, they have improved their recruiting and hiring. They say they now have the incentive and opportunity to behave more proactively in recruiting through such means as search firms. They say they have been successful in recruiting excellent people in such areas as information technology. Human resource management representatives at USPTO note that they did not receive extensive authorities or flexibilities for executive and professional recruiting, since USPTO remained under Title 5. They regard their newly authorized independence from the Department of Commerce in designing and filling executive positions as valuable for executive recruiting, but as of the time of this study they had not used it for filling specific positions with specific recruits.

The two agencies—SFA and IRS—that received authorization for specific numbers of positions with flexibility to recruit critically needed executives and professionals provide evidence of the successful use of these authorities in the form of the impressive profiles and credentials of the persons hired. They also provide evidence of success in the form of agency representatives' positive accounts of the benefits of the new authorities and the people recruited with them.

Agencies that have special authorities for hiring critical and hard-to-recruit personnel tend to approach human resource management differently as a result. Such agencies:

- Devote more time and consideration to conceiving and designing the positions to be filled.
- Have more incentive to invest in position design and recruiting.
- Have more flexibility in deploying resources for recruiting for the special positions. They invest more in recruiting, in the use of executive and professional search firms, and in advertising for the positions. They are more likely to draw on professional and executive networks for finding candidates.
- Have found that success involves much more than just "show me the money." Many of the executives and professionals recruited with special authorities come to government for the challenge and significance of the work. Many of them have made and can make as much money, or much more, in the private sector. While the flexibility in offering more competitive pay levels plays a crucial role in the recruiting of these people, the significance and challenge of the roles offered to them figure just as prominently.
- Report high levels of learning about related matters, including learning about how to locate and recruit candidates, the issues involved in their transition to the organization, and more creative advertising strategies. They report increased and effective use of executive and professional search firms, as well as professional networks. They report learning about how to assess private sector compensation packages and prepare competitive offers, and how to deal with such matters as avoiding even the appearance of a conflict of interest and how to handle matters of stock options available in the private sector but not in government.
- Have high levels of top leadership involvement in position design and recruitment.

- Have attained and used special authorities for critical positions in the context of organizational transformation and reform that has associated the design and recruitment for the new positions with the goals of the transformation and the mission of making the reforms work.
- Devote careful attention to accountability and transparency. They have sought carefully to stay within mandates and to employ checks and reviews to avoid even the appearance of improper procedures or criteria.
- Assign clear responsibility for the successful use of the authorities to executives, managers, and staff members. The implementers have served as sponsors and "champions" of this initiative, and report that they have felt an incentive and a duty to implement it successfully. Other executives and managers in the organizations served as supporters of the initiative.

Recommendations

Recommendation One: Special hiring authorities for executives and professionals have significant value as part of a comprehensive strategy for transforming a federal agency into an organization that better manages for results. Therefore, the use of such authorities should be expanded and extended to other agencies, with careful consideration of recommendation two for key implementation steps.

Among the foremost of these involves the integration of such authorities with a broader strategy for transformation of an agency toward significantly improved results-orientation and mission accomplishment. The pattern of success in the two agencies that received specific numbers of critical pay or excepted service positions makes clear that the effective use of special hiring authorities involves much more than simply handing out to agencies some improved capacity to recruit people they want. It involves a carefully implemented process of empowering executives and managers in an agency to add this resource to a comprehensive strategy. Their strategy must support transformation of their organization toward a greater results orientation and a significant improvement in mission accomplishment.

The many variations and flexibilities described in this report show that the personnel system of the United States government has responded to pressures for more decentralization, deregulation, and increased adaptability to its complex challenges and operating context. It is an oversimplification to claim that the system involves a monolithic, strictly structured lattice of bureaucratic constraints. Indeed, the variation and complexity of the system itself acts as one of the reasons that federal managers want more independence from it. The confusing array of authorities and special provisions makes it difficult for agencies to compete for talent when they have to weave through all the complexities of the system. In addition, many of the flexibilities and special provisions available under Title 5 still have strings attached to them. To use them, an agency must get approvals from OPM and sometimes other authorities. For example, to use the critical pay provisions that already exist under Title 5, an agency has to get approval from both OPM and OMB. For these reasons, executive, managers, and personnel administrators in federal agencies often continue to look for independence from many of the personnel rules and procedures centralized under OPM by Title 5. The success of the special hiring authorities in the agencies on which this report has concentrated suggests the value of implementing them more widely, but with careful attention to recommendations for successful implementation.

Recommendation Two: Organizations granted special authorities should consider the following key implementation steps necessary to effectively use and maximize the impact of these authorities. Key implementation steps include leadership and sponsorship at the top, integration with a comprehensive agency strategy, address critical success factors, clarity of legislative mandate, investments in organizational learning, and maintenance of accountability and transparency.

Leadership and sponsorship at the top. Successful large-scale change requires sustained commitment from top leadership, with additional sponsorship and responsibility from others in the organization. Top executives need to integrate special hiring authorities into comprehensive strategies for organizational transformation and improvement, and to devote attention and resources to their effective utilization. A coalition of executives, managers, and employees needs to have clear assignment of responsibility for the program and to serve as its sponsors and champions.

Integration with comprehensive agency strategy. Special hiring authorities need to be implemented coherently with a more comprehensive vision or strategy for improved performance and results-oriented management. The new positions and people need to be established in a way that aligns them with the agency's strategy for structure, culture, incentive system, and long-term goals.

Address critical success factors. The commitment of leaders and sponsors, and the integration with broader strategies, are necessary because of the need to address critical success factors in the implementation of the hiring authorities. We need to avoid precisely defining these issues or prescribing means of dealing with them in an *a priori* fashion, since implementers in agencies should do much of this work in relation to the needs and circumstances of their agency. Major success factors include:

- *Position design.* Implementers need to devote careful attention to defining the new positions in ways that meet well-developed priorities, and that provide the incentives of significant and challenging responsibility. This crafting of positions and roles becomes doubly important because the person hired may have no entitlement to long-term employment and such benefits as federal retirement programs. These limits also raise such issues as whether the agency should assign the individuals to particular missions or projects that they aim to complete during their tenure.

- *Recruiting.* The implementing officials in the agencies reported increased incentives and opportunities for new recruiting practices. For example, they felt particularly positive about the results they attained through using executive search firms. Implementing officials must invest time and resources in developing new, energetic, and creative recruiting patterns. They must make effective use of new technologies such as the Internet, and of executive and professional search firms.

- *"Onboarding."* While the agencies in this study reported no particular difficulties with bringing the new people "on board," they felt the "onboarding" process to be very important and another part of the commitment to making the initiative work. One explanation for the successful "onboarding" of most of the new people into their new roles and relations with others in the organization came from the unique features of their positions. While one might have expected some resentment from long-term employees of these highly paid newcomers, any such reactions appeared to be ameliorated by the limited tenure and entitlements of the special positions. The long-term employees realized that the new people sacrificed some of the benefits that longer-term employees enjoyed. *Implementing officials need to develop plans and policies for "onboarding" newly hired professionals.*

- *Integration.* Effective position design, of course, also helps with integration of the new people into the organization. For example, both in assignments for critical pay hirees as well as in other instances, the IRS used the approach of putting together a newly hired outsider with a long-term insider. At the top of newly created operating divisions, the IRS leadership teamed an outsider, hired under the critical pay authority, with a career IRS executive. The Large and Mid-Size Business, Small Business/Self-Employed, and the Tax Exempt and Government Entities divisions were all headed by newly hired outsiders with an IRS career executive as deputy. The Wage and Investment Income Division was headed by a careerist with an outsider as deputy.[18] Effectively used, such teaming and partnering of new people and insiders has obvious advantages. It brings in new talents and ideas, but provides for institutional memory. Furthermore, it sends the message to career personnel that their years of work and experience are valued, but does emphasize the need for openness to new perspectives and skills. *Implementing officials should effectively integrate outsiders and insiders as a team.*

Clarity of legislative mandate. The experience to date has also indicated the importance of legislative mandates that assign the new authorities not necessarily with great precision, but at least without significant ambiguities. For example, in one of the agencies the ways in which the new positions could be assigned between executive and professional roles was not clear. Significantly, the chief operating officer chose to interpret the legislation in the way most likely to avoid exceeding legislative intent. *Officials crafting legislation and other implementing mechanisms need to provide reasonable clarity about the authorities provided to the agency.*

Investments in organizational learning. This last example, and others above, illustrate the significant learning that occurs in organizations implementing the special authorities. People in those organizations have tended to share this learning. Their experiences can now inform new initiatives in other agencies. *Officials from the legislative branch, central oversight agencies, and the agencies receiving authorities should engage in communication and share information about the successful use of special hiring authorities, through task forces, advisory groups, consortia, and other arrangements that can contribute to further success.*

Maintenance of accountability and transparency. The attention to accountability is one of the striking features of these initiatives to date. As noted earlier, the executives and managers in the agencies had a strong incentive and sense of duty to make the special hiring provisions succeed. This appears to have spurred them to avoid even the appearance of impropriety. Moreover, they faced serious challenges in bringing people into government with private sector backgrounds that included compensation arrangements that are legal and appropriate in the private sector, but not allowed in government (such as stock ownership in private firms with which the agency does or might do business).

As described above, the chief operating officer in one of the agencies interpreted the legislative mandate in the way least likely to exceed authorization. In IRS, the new recruits still went through all the background checks and reviews applicable to any IRS recruit. The approval process involved consultations back and forth between IRS attorneys and the attorneys of the parent agency, the Department of Treasury. The IRS oversight board can also serve as an oversight authority for these special hiring authorities and their proper use.

Concluding Thoughts

While at first one might think that these special hiring authorities confer on the agencies extensive freedom in hiring—and that this might raise problems of accountability and transparency—the careful attention to such matters so far appears to have avoided such problems. This situation appears ironic at first. Provisions intended to provide more flexibility and authority for recruiting key professionals and executives end up leading the recipients of this authority to show careful concerns for accountability. This actually makes sense, however, in that one would hope that people in public service empowered with authority they regard as valuable to improving their agency's performance will have a strong incentive to use it wisely and effectively. In these agencies, this appears, so far, to be the case.

All officials and authorities involved must maintain the sense that the special hiring authorities confer on the agencies receiving them a major responsibility for effective and accountable utilization of this important resource. This includes making provisions for accountability and transparency, but doing so creatively, so that agencies do not reinstitute the constraints that necessitated these authorities in the first place.

Appendix:
Hiring and Compensation Practices
in Federal Agencies Exempt from Title 5

The Office of Personnel Management (OPM) (1998) concludes that there are no discernable differences in hiring for specialized or shortage category occupations between the non-Title 5 organizations and Title 5-covered organizations despite the greater flexibility generally available to the non-Title 5 agencies. In every organization studied in this report, the merit system principles such as open competition, some form of rating and ranking, classification/compensation systems based on rank or position, and formal due process procedures are incorporated. However, the rule of three and veterans preference are absent in many Title 5-exempt agencies.

This report also finds that there is movement to market-based compensation and pay-for-performance systems that eliminate step increases and general increases and may include broadbanding, variable pay, and linkage of pay systems to organizational goals or performance.

Overall, while Title 5-exempt organizations' practices are similar in many respects to those of Title 5 organizations, they display a capacity to readily respond as a part of the management structure. However, such flexibility raises questions about accountability to the public and the role of central management agencies, such as OPM.

This is a small sampling from the world of Title 5-exempt organizations, which include government corporations, independent establishments, ordinary executive branch agencies with legislative approval to create alternative personnel systems, and other legal entities.

Agencies	Hiring and Compensation Practices
General Accounting Office (GAO)	• Transformed by the General Accounting Office Personnel Act, effective 1980, into an excepted service agency with some authorized exclusions from Title 5. • The act authorized flexibilities in compensation and pay administration. The agency was given authority to operate under the Demonstration Projects provision in Title 5. • Has adopted a pay-banding system that covers evaluator and attorney positions only, with salaries and limitations comparable to the General Schedule pay system; other positions continue to be covered under the GS schedule pay system.

continued on next page

Agencies	Hiring and Compensation Practices
United States Postal Service (USPS)	• Mostly exempt from Title 5; the largest Title 5-exempt organization. • Has introduced structured interviewing to help selecting officials improve their hiring selections. • Has the most formal selection process, which includes the use of national test registers and veterans preference; now considering a new approach to move away from national registers to a testing process that places the responsibility on the applicant to apply for vacancies with score-in-hand rather than waiting on a register. • Has a 90-day probation. • Uses market-based compensation systems; has implemented both a broad band system and merit-based pay for all of its non-bargaining unit positions. Increases in salary are determined solely by performance, and there are no longer any step increases or cost-of-living adjustments.
Tennessee Valley Authority (TVA)	• Mostly exempt from Title 5. • Has a large internship program for targeted areas such as nuclear engineering and offers scholarships to dependents of employees. • Uses a management selection board for some hiring; the selecting official identifies the selection criteria, then the selection board (comprised of the selecting official's peers, customers, etc.) interviews applicants for behavioral competencies while the selecting manager interviews for technical competencies. The board ranks the candidates and the selecting official makes the selection. • Is moving toward market-based compensation systems to be competitive in the newly deregulated utilities industry.
Central Intelligence Agency (CIA)	• Has "rank-in-person" systems where hiring and promotion decisions are based on expert panel reviews of qualifications. In a rank-in-person system an employee is classified according to the skills and achievements he or she brings to the work of the organization, in contrast to the "rank-in-position" approach in the Title 5 classification system, which classifies jobs based on the duties of specific occupations.
Library of Congress	• Not covered by Title 5 but established a formal, merit-based HRM system that mirrors Title 5 staffing regulations. The organization had voluntarily adopted the Title 5 classification and pay systems earlier. It sees a merit-based system as a protection for both the organization and its employees in a highly complex and dynamic environment. • Uses targeted recruitment aimed at specific occupations and skills such as foreign-language competencies.

continued on next page

Agencies	Hiring and Compensation Practices
Library of Congress	• Holds managers accountable for filling positions based on the organization's staffing plan that shows diversity imbalances in the workforce. • Holds managers and HRM staff accountable through the performance system for maintaining the strict time frames embedded in their hiring procedures; a tracking system monitors the status of all vacancies. • Uses a statistically validated scoring scheme to identify the most qualified.
Sallie Mae	• Has simple résumé reviews by selecting officials for rating and ranking procedures.
Federal Deposit Insurance Corporation (FDIC)	• Is an excepted service agency; has a board of directors authorized to make decisions on employee compensation and benefits. It is not required to follow the provisions of Title 5. • Has special hiring authority from OPM to appoint term employees non-competitively to assist in bank closures. • Since its creation, its legislation has been revised, expanding the board's authority.
Smithsonian Institution	• One-third of the workforce is funded and operates under a trust fund, with the remainder covered under the Title 5 system. • Administratively follows Title 5 for classification and compensation because it is easier than establishing their own systems. To promote fairness and equity between the two different groups of employees, it has chosen to manage both sets of employees in essentially the same manner under the same systems.
Nuclear Regulatory Commission (NRC)	• Only partially exempt from Title 5; maintains a highly visible merit staffing system based on the NRC's organizational values and the Merit System principles. • A special Merit Staffing Course, begun in January 1997, instructs supervisors in assuming responsibility for qualifying, rating, selecting, and giving constructive feedback to job applicants. • Places applicants in one of three categories for rating and ranking. • Follows the Title 5 pay structure for ease of pay administration and to sustain inter-agency transfer options for its employees.
Peace Corps	• Holds managers and supervisors responsible for differentiating among candidates and for justifying their selections. • Has a five-year employment rule; employees can have a maximum of two two-and-a-half-year appointments; it reports that this limitation both restricts the hiring pool and reduces performance- and conduct-related actions.

continued on next page

Agencies	Hiring and Compensation Practices
Department of State, Foreign Service	• Only the employees in the Foreign Service are outside of Title 5. • Has rank-in-person systems where hiring and promotion decisions are based on expert panel reviews of qualifications; in a rank-in-person system an employee is classified according to the skills and achievements he or she brings to the work of the organization.
Office of Federal Housing Enterprise Oversight (OFHEO)	• Exempt from Title 5 only for classification and compensation and must adhere to all other provisions such as staffing, performance management, and adverse actions. • To ensure a diverse applicant pool, it uses a Minority Online Information System (MOLIS) that sends vacancy announcements via the Internet to minority institutions. • The authorizing legislation requires that the organization has comparable pay and benefits programs with other federal regulators. The agency uses a broad-band pay system to help recruit for unique and hard-to-fill positions. Examiners and financial analysts at this agency must have a high level of knowledge and expertise related to the banking industry. To attract high-quality candidates, the agency must be able to offer comparable compensation packages, and the broad-band system has given it more flexibility to do so. • However, the agency reported some problems with its broad-band system—that is, problems with employees reaching the top of their pay band too quickly, particularly if the employees are recruited at high points in the pay band. To remedy this situation, it has devised formulas for employees at the top of their pay bands so that some portion or all of their salary increases are granted as cash awards rather than increases to base salary.
Veterans Health Administration (VHA)	• Uses recruitment and relocation bonuses for hard-to-fill occupations for Title 38 employees. Operates a highly publicized Central Placement Service, which is a nationwide automated inventory of applicants for Title 38 positions. • Has rank-in-person systems (Title 38 employees). • Uses an interactive website where candidates can file their applications electronically and get information about the VA.
Office of Thrift Supervision (OTS)	• Fully covered by Title 5 for hiring and staffing. • Has a Fellows Program in which up to 10 Fellows receive 14-month appointments with benefits. • Has implemented pay-for-performance systems and eliminated step increases and annual pay adjustments.
Foreign Agricultural Service (FAS)	• Has rank-in-person systems where hiring and promotion decisions are based on expert panel reviews of qualifications; in a rank-in-person system an employee is classified according to the skills and achievements he or she brings to the work of the organization (Title 22 employees).

Source: *U.S. Office of Personnel Management, "HRM Policies and Practices in Title 5 -Exempt Organizations." 1998.*

Endnotes

1. Organizations have faced increasing complexity and rates of change along most dimensions—technology, human resources, product and service markets, and many others. Leaders and professionals have sought ways to achieve flexibility, adaptability, and innovativeness to cope with the growing flux and complexity. Researchers studying business organizations have coined terms such as "mechanistic" and "organic" to explain the transition that organizations must make. Organizations, they argue, must become less mechanistic or machine-like, and more like living organisms responding and adapting to changing conditions in and around them. T. Burns and G.M. Stalker coined the mechanistic versus organic analogy in The Management of Innovation (London: Tavistock, 1961); scholars and experts on organization and management still regularly use this distinction, and similar ones. For example, see R. L. Daft, Organization Theory and Design (Cincinnati: Southwestern College Publishing, 2001).

Business firms have developed a variety of structures and processes to respond to this imperative for innovation and adaptation. Public and nonprofit organizations have done so, too, but one can hear in many nations a consensus that government organizations need a lot more flexibility and adaptability. In recent decades the U.S. and other nations have undertaken major reforms of their civil service systems. The reformers have emphasized the need to loosen up rules and procedures in those systems to make them more adaptive to the complex and changing conditions in which they have to operate. The reforms have sought to decentralize authority over human resource management from central personnel agencies to operating agencies, to give leaders more authority to control the pay, selection, discipline, and dismissal of their subordinates, and otherwise to reduce central and hierarchical controls over governmental human resource management systems.

2. Bruce Tulgan, Winning the Talent Wars (New York: Norton, 2001). Susannah Zak Figura, "Human Capital: The Missing Link," GovExec.com, March 1, 2000. Susannah Zak Figura, "Fighting for Talent," GovExec.com, April 1, 2001.

3. Ed Michaels, Helen Handfield-Jones, and Beth Axelrod. The War for Talent. Harvard Business School Press, 2001.

4. See http://www.gecareers.com/Career/leadership.cfm and http://www-.ibm.com/employment/whywork

5. See U.S. General Accounting Office, "Managing Human Capital in the 21st Century," Statement of David W. Walker, Comptroller General of the United States, March 9, 2000, GAO/T-GGD-00-77. Also see United States Senate, Committee on Governmental Affairs (2000), "Report to the President: The Crisis in Human Capital," prepared by Senator George V. Voinovich, Chairman of the Subcommittee on Oversight of Government Management, Restructuring, and the District of Columbia. Also see United States Senate, Committee on Governmental Affairs (2000), "Management Challenges Facing the New Administration," prepared by Senator Fred Thompson, Chairman of the Committee on Governmental Affairs.

6. Figura, "Human Capital: The Missing Link" and "Fighting for Talent."

7. John W. Macy, Public Service: The Human Side of Government (New York: HarperCollins, 1971).

8. National Academy of Public Administration, Revitalizing Federal Management (Washington, D.C.: National Academy of Public Administration, 1986).

9. See U.S. Merit Systems Protection Board, "The Role of Delegated Examining Units: Hiring New Employees in a Decentralized Civil Service," 1999; and U.S. Merit Systems Protection Board, "Civil Service Evaluation: The Evolving Role of the OPM," 1998.

10. See Alasdair Roberts, "Performance-Based Organizations: Assessing the Gore Plan," *Public Administration Review,* 57 (6) November/December, 1997, and James Thompson, "Quasi-Markets and Strategic Change in Public Organizations," in Jeffrey L. Brudney, Laurence J. O'Toole, and Hal G. Rainey (Eds.) *Advancing Public Management* (Washington, D.C.: Georgetown University Press, 2000).

11. OPM is the U.S. Office of Personnel Management, the central personnel agency of the federal government. OMB is the U.S. Office of Management and Budget, an office within the Executive Office of the President that has authority over developing and implementing the federal budget.

12. U.S. Merit Systems Protection Board, "Entering Professional Positions in the Federal Government," 1994.

13. Ibid.

14. For a discussion of the variations among government corporations, government enterprises, public authorities, and similar types of organization, see Hal G. Rainey and Barton Wechsler, "Managing Government Corporations and Enterprises," in James L. Perry (Ed.) *Handbook of Public Administration* (San Francisco: Jossey-Bass, 1989).

15. See Kenneth J. Meier, *Politics and the Bureaucracy,* 4th ed. (Fort Worth, Texas: Harcourt College Publishers, 2000), p. 33.

16. U.S. Department of Education, Student Financial Assistance, "Performance Plan, FY 2001," (Washington, D.C.).

17. For more details, see U.S. General Accounting Office, "Tax Administration: IRS's Implementation of the Restructuring Act's Personnel Flexibility Provisions" (Washington, D.C.: U.S. General Accounting Office, April, 2000), GAO/GGD-00-81. Also see U.S. General Accounting Office, "IRS Personnel Flexibilities: An Opportunity to Test New Approaches" (Washington, D.C.: U.S. General Accounting Office, March 12, 1998), GAO/T-GGD-98-78.

18. These ideas and much of the wording is taken from James R. Thompson, "Large Scale Change in Three Federal Agencies: Institutional Alignment as a Precondition for Post-Bureaucratic Reform," a paper presented at the Sixth National Public Management Research Conference, School of Public and Environmental Affairs, Indiana University, Bloomington, Indiana, Oct. 18-20, 2001. Thompson provides an excellent case analysis of ways in which IRS has achieved apparent success in implementing changes in contrast to some less successful change efforts in other agencies.

CHAPTER FOUR

Organizations Growing Leaders:
Best Practices and Principles
in the Public Service

Ray Blunt
Leadership Coach
Council for Excellence in Government
Washington, D.C.

This report was originally published in December 2001.

Introduction

The "Quiet Crisis"

The crisis of human capital may appear to have stealthily crept in by the side door. Some may consider it the latest government fad or flavor of the month. Despite appearances, the human capital crisis is an old stalwart of long vintage. The unfortunate thing is that, "quiet" or not, it is real.

This chapter addresses one key aspect of the quiet crisis—providing for the succession needs of federal organizations. Or, to put it another way, what will it take for the public service to grow the leaders of the future it needs over the next five years?

This is in many ways a sequel to the chapter, Leaders Growing Leaders,[1] which also speaks directly to the critical need to grow the next generation of public service leaders but as a central responsibility *of leaders themselves.* In light of extensive departures expected in the senior ranks in the next five years, chapter five seeks to show how some senior leaders have taken a leadership role to serve the next generation by acting as mentors, coaches, teachers, and exemplars. They are people who understand that leadership growth is best learned from and initiated by senior leaders. They seek to leave a legacy for others by the choices they make.

The key finding of chapter five remains the key finding of this chapter: Leaders beget leaders. Or, as one person said, "To be a leader you must see a leader."

This chapter builds on this initial finding and addresses two new questions: What are the excellent organizations in the public sector doing to grow the next generation of leaders? And, what can we all learn from them? The five organizations profiled are ones that have not simply recognized the need for leadership; they are organizations that have acted.

The Symptoms

The General Accounting Office (GAO) recently referred to government-wide human capital practices as a "high risk" area of concern. This highlights the gravity of the threat to the mission of government agencies if future leader development is not addressed.[2] The neglect of the people side of government has a long genesis, and the culture changes that are needed to resolve this crisis will not yield to short-term commitments.

Take just one cogent example that is indicative of a far wider problem. The Office of Merit Systems Oversight and Effectiveness in the Office of Personnel Management (OPM) recently released its findings on perhaps the most critical part of leader development in any organization, that of first-level supervisors. The results were termed "a wake-up call."

Only four of the 20 agencies surveyed by OPM had formal leadership development initiatives for their beginning supervisors. A relative handful of these individuals received leadership development or supervisory preparation prior to assuming these positions.[3]

Of even more concern, almost half of the selectees for these initial leadership positions were not given these leadership responsibilities because they possessed nascent leadership competencies but because they were the best technical experts.

Currently, leaders at all levels of government are often selected using criteria that are completely at odds with the new leader competencies needed today and in the future—flexibility/adaptability, accountability, strategic thinking/vision, and customer service.[4]

Some Remedies

It is not the purpose of this chapter to lay blame on any one source for the relative inaction of the public service in developing future leaders. Rather, the aim is to highlight the instructive lessons of some selected government organizations that have persevered with foresight and innovation, often out of the limelight, to begin preparing the next generation of leaders.

The purpose is also to again underscore that the strategic response is one that can only be led by senior leaders—leaders who grow leaders—and that it is well within the grasp of a concerted leadership effort by any federal agency given commitment and application of best practices. The exemplary organizations and their leaders examined here have shown the way for the rest of us.

The best practices (or, more precisely, lessons learned or excellent practices) offer learning opportunities for agencies that are beginning to engage the issues surrounding growing future leaders or seeking to revive a flagging effort. These lessons can be both a starting point and a roadmap of ideas and principles from which succession and leader development efforts can greatly profit—the lessons of practical experience.

But first a warning: Simply imitating these practices is not a complete blueprint for healthy leadership growth. Long-term cultural barriers must be identified and overcome.

The Importance of Culture

Change is the central task of the leader.[5] Changing the culture of an organization, even in small ways, is highly difficult. Yet it is the culture of an organization that fundamentally shapes the nature and intensity of such "soft" factors as effective recruitment of excellent young graduates, the climate (non-bureaucratic) for high-energy motivation, and the commitment to service that encourages retention of the top performers. It is such a culture that fundamentally produces consistent and superior results for the American people. This type of culture is shaped primarily by its leaders.[6]

As we will see, the excellent organizations in the private sector have recognized this central truth for many years now; however, it is still an insight not yet widely shared by the public sector. For government, far more reliance is placed on new forms of control systems, enhanced oversight, and the creation of job titles when dealing with organization performance problems. While this chapter will focus on practices and principles, the deeper implications of culture change are also implicit throughout and are briefly discussed in the next section. The importance to success should not be underestimated.

Approach

The following findings on five exemplary organizations have been drawn from interviews with senior organization leaders, succession program managers, and program participants themselves. In each case, I made site visits to the organizations and reviewed existing documentation.

The next section, "Launching a Succession Initiative," is designed as a starting point for organizations considering launching a leader development initiative. Through studying the five organizations, it became clear that for most agencies, succession and leader development is not so much launching a new program as it is transforming an organization culture and its long-held assumptions—managing large-scale change. One of the toughest challenges organizations face is getting off the launch pad. The lessons from their experiences make the case for change: Why they took the first steps they did; why they were able to overcome organizational inertia; why they were able to overcome the current leadership myths embedded in so much of government culture.

"Lessons Learned" is a discussion in some depth of the "what" and the "how"—what each organization is doing and how they are doing it as they seek to provide for the succession of senior leaders. This is a summary of the lessons to be learned from their experiences. It is intended to be practical in nature for use by any organization. It is also consistent with the principles contained in the latest and best research on leader development.

"Making Sense of It All" is a summary containing a comparison of the practices of the five public sector organizations as well as a brief contrast with the practices of the best businesses in America. This is another way to uncover the key success factors and the underlying principles for growing leaders. This analysis results in three key conclusions for action by individual public sector organizations.

The final section, "Recommendations," closes the discussion with broader recommendations for government-wide change to resolve the leadership and succession aspects of the human capital crisis in the next five years.

Launching a Succession Initiative

This section examines two important factors in initiating the programs and practices to be discussed. First, there are barriers to change that exist in almost every federal agency, but most of them are seen here more as myths that the five exemplary organizations have overcome. Second, the reasons are examined regarding why a succession initiative could be successfully launched in these agencies by capitalizing on unique factors of urgency and/or importance.

Overcoming the Myths

For the past several years a number of sources of analysis, thinking, and experience have documented the tepid response of the public sector to the importance of growing leaders for the future. The impact that failure is having on the ability to continue to accomplish the public service mission is now a matter of record. What is not known is the response this knowledge will engender in the next two to three years. But if the past is prologue to the future, there may be unfortunately little reaction. How and why did these five organizations take a different and more successful course?

Past studies by the National Academy of Public Administration (NAPA) and others have identified the reasons behind such levels of inaction. The most frequent response to a 1996 NAPA survey as well as to other inquiries since then can be summarized: "It's the culture."

In his research on world-class organizations, Harvard Business School's John Kotter has identified what he refers to as a "leader-centered culture," an environment supportive of the time and effort to grow leaders. He has concluded from his research that this is the key distinguishing factor in organizations that do an excellent job of leader development.

It would appear from both formal study and my own experience in teaching and coaching young leaders from across government that there is a strong consensus that an opposite type of culture may be a major—if not *the* major—impediment within the federal sector. While lack of funding, small rewards, and lack of political priority are also cited as factors, culture seems to be where it all returns. Is this just an all-purpose cop-out? I don't think so.

Where there are serious gaps between what is said and what is actually done (e.g., "people are our most valued asset," but when the budget knife appears training is cut first), we find clues to the existing people culture in government. These clues are what I refer to here as "myths." These myths are underlying barriers that the five exemplary organizations have had to overcome to engender the organizational energy and the funding for growing leaders as a change initiative. They are widely (and wrongly) accepted arguments that stand against the need for leader development, the need to base it on the factors that really grow leaders, and the possibility that such an investment in developing people will generate real results. These myths are explored in Appendix I.

Initiating Change: The Imperatives

If there are deeply held cultural myths about growing leaders, why were these five exemplary organizations able to overcome these entrenched assumptions? And, why did their agencies make decisions to take such relatively bold steps to initiate an organization-wide response to developing future leaders? The answers are that they tapped into a real, immediate sense of urgency.

In brief, these are the factors—the change-urgent imperatives—which were discovered (either in combination or separately) when examining the launching of leader development initiatives by the five agencies.

1. **The Succession Imperative.** In almost all cases, the strongest imperative for action was the glaring visibility of the number of senior leaders who would likely depart within the next five years and an understanding of the implications that this held.

2. **The Strategic Imperative.** Each organization, in one way or another, made leader development a strategic decision that was reflected in official strategic plans submitted with the annual budget. While not all decisions reflected line-item funding, the substantive presence in the strategic plans did indicate that senior leaders made an intentional decision, which served as a "blocking back" when contrary voices were later raised.

3. **The Performance Imperative.** Environmental factors (e.g., competitive challenges, changing agency roles, industry changes) and current dissatisfaction with organizational performance from external sources (e.g., GAO, Congress, Office of Management and Budget, interest groups) led to a positive response to focus on developing leaders as part of the strategy.

4. **The Competency Imperative.** Closely aligned with the Performance Imperative was the recognition that the changing landscape for performance also required a change in the type of leader being developed. This was consistently seen as a leader with the competencies of the new Executive Core Qualifications (ECQs)—leading change, leading people, results driven, business acumen, and building coalitions. In short, a broader based type of leader with more sophisticated "soft" skills and less emphasis on technical expertise.

5. **The Organization Champion Imperative.** Finally, in almost all instances, there was a clear initiative taken by a senior leader who stood behind the initial impetus for change and allowed leader development to be on the strategic agenda and to be associated with needed strategic change. That key leader also had a strong strategic partnership that developed either with a staff organization or with a specially convened group that developed the initiative for implementation.

Taken together, these offer organizations a beginning point for launching change. It is often the lack of urgency, the absence of what some like to call a "burning platform," that often dooms good ideas for change from getting airborne. Having launched such a change initiative, what practices and underlying principles do these organizations have to pass on to others who are in the early stages of change?

Five Exemplary Organizations: Lessons Learned

Regarding the five organizations discussed in this section, I offer the following framework to give context and meaning to the the "lessons learned."
- An overview of the *Mission Challenge* that each organization faces.
- The *Approach* taken (or strategy for change) once the change imperatives had driven an organizational launch.
- A *Description* of the succession and leader development programs.
- A more detailed look at the *Lessons* that can be learned from the particular efforts of the individual organizations.

Their practices are offered not so much for complete emulation, but to understand that they are based on sound principles that contain certain truths and that they have been adapted to the particular challenges, culture, and realities (e.g., resources) of each of the organizations.

These organizations range in size from large to small. Some are highly technical or engineering organizations, some in the human services business, and some are in the business of law enforcement and national defense.

It is likely that there are instructive lessons for almost any government organization, and that, of course, is the purpose. We begin with one of the smaller organizations.

Pension Benefit Guaranty Corporation (PBGC)

Mission Challenge
PBGC has the mission of protecting participants' pension benefits and supporting a healthy retirement plan system. It employs just over 700 employees and several hundred contract workers, primarily actuaries, accountants, auditors, pension law specialists, and general attorneys. These individuals have highly technical backgrounds and tend to remain within their functional areas for the duration of their careers with PBGC. The corporation falls under the aegis of a board of directors chaired by the secretary of labor, but functions day-to-day as a relatively independent agency.

Early in 1999, the PBGC strategic plan set four corporate strategic goals. While the first three reflected operational, service, and financial long-term priorities, a fourth identified the importance of improving internal management, which included a decision to launch a succession management initiative to respond to projected widespread retirements:

> Working with senior staff, begin to implement a well-regarded Succession Management Program.

It would be more than two years before the pilot program was officially launched.

During interviews, many of the senior leaders articulated the importance not only of replacing so many potentially departing leaders but also of developing new leaders with new leadership skills. These new competencies would include strategic thinking, team skills, customer service focus, and interpersonal competencies.

Approach
Chief Management Officer John Seal assigned the succession management corporation objective to the human resources department under the leadership of Sharon Barbee-Fletcher. She tasked the Training Institute (Karen Lunn, project director, and Dr. Ellen Roderick, institute director), with designing and implementing the succession program. John Seal then championed this initiative for the executive director as the project went from design to implementation.

In turn, a seasoned group of cross-organizational managers served as a work group to develop a succession program based on principles that would best apply to the culture of PBGC. They also used an outside consultant for technical assistance, conducted extensive research, and benchmarked the Social Security Administration (discussed later in this chapter).

The work group members made several presentations to a wider circle of the senior leadership and to potential candidates regarding the succession program's design and scope. That collaborative process took more than one year from inception to the launch of the pilot and included an open invitation to eligible applicants.

The initial response of the eligible pool of managers was quite limited and, in retrospect, reflected that the limitation of eligibility to one component of the organization as a pilot sent a confusing signal. In addition, skepticism about the extent of senior managers' support and the extra work that would ensue for participants were other factors contributing to the initial tepid response. This resulted in a cancellation of the original pilot and some rethinking of strategy before the pilot was reinitiated on a wider scale.

Description

The Leaders Growing Leaders (LGL) succession program is a systematic approach to develop a pool of future leaders that begins with selection of a few participants from a pool of voluntary applicants (over two dozen applied in the first phase). The initial pilot was open to all individuals in the GS 13-15 grades in non-bargaining union positions. A Senior Leader Review Board (SLRB) which represented a broad range of operational and staff disciplines accomplished selection of the seven LGL program candidates.

Once selection was made, each participant selected a senior advisor who would work with the participant to develop an individualized plan for development over the course of the next two years. The individual plans themselves were expected to be based on the candidates' 360-degree Leadership Assessment and reflect six components that the PBGC work group and the SLRB agreed were all essential to future leader development:

- *Action learning.* The team of candidates is expected to work on a "hot" strategic issue as a team and to work with senior leaders to provide a solution for a corporate decision and implementation. The issue is selected by the SLRB from actual strategic issues of the corporation.
- *Challenging work or job assignments.* Short and longer-term assignments outside the candidate's organization experience are used during the two years to broaden learning and are made in conjunction with the SLRB, the supervisors, the participants, and their mentors.
- *Regular interaction with the senior advisor.* Acting as both coach and mentor for the duration of the program, these individuals play a key developmental role. They are selected for being able to provide exposure to the senior-level strategic agendas and decision forums.

- *Leadership training.* Individuals are to identify online, on-site, and external training opportunities as their developmental needs dictate. Funding may be by the sponsoring organization or through the Training Institute or some combination.
- *External programs.* The Council for Excellence in Government (CEG) Fellows Program comprises much of the first developmental year for the candidates. This includes a team action learning results initiative, extensive organizational benchmarking, and exposure to other Fellows and senior leaders across government.
- *Self development.* Consistent with much recent learning about leader development, a strong emphasis has been placed by PBGC on individuals taking responsibility for their own development through, for example, professional reading programs, involvement as a community leader in church or nonprofit organizations, and attendance at professional seminars.

Lessons

There are a few factors that stand out in the approach PBGC has taken that are important for other agencies to consider.

1. Involve senior leaders in leading the initiative.

What particularly stands out in the PBGC example is perhaps the central principle of any excellent succession and leader development initiative—the active involvement of senior leaders in the effort.

That lesson of the importance of the senior leader role came from the less than successful experience in the application process for the initial pilot. Enthusiasm and commitment had not spread beyond the line and staff members of the work group and the chief management officer, and a few others in the Training Institute. With the relaunch of the program under the rubric of Leaders Growing Leaders, a determined effort was made by several senior leaders to encourage the potential candidates. That effort and the widening of the succession program to all non-bargaining unit employees at the GS 13, 14, and 15 levels produced a far wider pool of potential candidates. Then with the successful relaunch, the SLRB was constituted, comprised of six committed senior line leaders, and a group of senior advisors was recruited—one mentor for each candidate.

The PBGC training director then ensured that the board itself received training in its role and in the ideas behind the concepts of the program, and did the same for the senior advisors in separate and joint sessions. This has produced a strong cadre of senior leaders who are already demonstrating that they are in this for the long haul, and not deferring the selection process, candidate assessments, or individual development plan (IDP) development process to a staff. The deep engagement of these senior leaders is a good indicator of longer-term success.

2. Build on existing success.

A second key aspect, perhaps in retrospect, is that PBGC already had some important components in place that had paved the widening of an effort to grow leaders. Rather than jettisoning these, they were incorporated.

For three years, PBGC has had a strong mentoring program pairing several senior leaders with employees who express a desire for mentoring. The corporation has also been using a form of action learning in the composition of what is called a REACH program, using cross-functional teams to solve problems and to learn from their wider involvement in the life of the organization. Another component in place was the existence of a leadership competency model designed for PBGC leaders along with a 360-degree Leadership Assessment linked to the competencies and customized to PBGC leadership situations. All of these were incorporated as key parts of the LGL Program.

3. Make it part of the strategic plan.

It has been vitally important to have the organization's commitment to developing people and to a succession initiative as a strategic plan initiative—particularly when the initial impetus stalled.

That visibility and the alignment of these as strategies that will help drive the mission have given the work group and the organizational champions leverage to make things happen despite initial disappointing results.

4. Emphasize leader learning from challenging experiences.

The commitment to a design that emphasizes challenging, cross-organizational job-based experiences and action learning as the central learning factors is also extremely important as a principle for emulation.

What PBGC anticipates (beginning in this first year and accelerating in the second year of the program) is that candidates will have an opportunity for cross-organizational assignments. That will allow them to do substantive work in other areas of the organization. It will also allow others to step into their shoes for a time and to be similarly stretched—an unanticipated developmental product.

Participants will also be included in task forces, in teams for strategic learning, and in senior forums such as strategic planning meetings and budget reviews. There may be temporary assignments to other agencies, such as the Department of Labor, for wider learning.

The CEG Fellows program is also an opportunity for a team action learning project and for exposure to real experiences in private and public sector organizations through benchmarking and working with a larger team of 25 or so Fellows from different government agencies.

We turn now from an excellent example of an individual succession program to examine a strategic response to leadership at all levels in the Coast Guard.

U.S. Coast Guard

Mission Challenge

The U.S. Coast Guard has been charged with a complex mission—lifesaving and helping to make the coasts both safe and secure. This includes boating safety and search and rescue, aids to navigation, maritime safety, inland bridges, and even lighthouses. The Coast Guard also has responsibility for coastal security and national defense, including the growing need to interdict drugs, monitor for illegal immigration and counteract terrorism. Its domain consists of 95,000 miles of coastline and 3.4 million square miles of ocean and all inland waterways, ports, and harbors. It provides coastal and waterway defense in the event of an attack on the homeland. Finally, its complex portfolio embraces pollution enforcement and prevention as well as inspection of ships for potentially harmful contents and seaworthiness.

Unique within the armed forces, the Coast Guard is located within the Department of Transportation during peacetime but falls under Department of Defense during a declared war. In an otherwise civilian department, the Coast Guard competes for resources and priorities within a different milieu than the other armed services—both an advantage and a disadvantage. Also somewhat unique to the Coast Guard is the presence of an enormous cadre of volunteers, the Coast Guard Auxiliary, with over 35,000 members who primarily reinforce the boating safety mission. The Coast Guard has approximately 35,000 uniformed people and 6,000 civilians augmented by 8,000 Reservists, for a total of nearly 85,000 people.

The Coast Guard has recently received plaudits for its exceptional efforts at defining and achieving results under the Government Performance and Results Act requirements and is generally considered one of the best managed and led organizations in government today. We turn now to the challenges that have impacted its approach to growing leaders for tomorrow.

Approach

The increasing complexity of its mission (and competing resource decisions) was probably the key impetus for a reinvigorated leader development approach. The Workforce Cultural Audit, conducted from 1995 to1997, was a catalyst for identifying a number of changes that were needed in the arena of human capital and leadership development. In addition, a Training Infrastructure Study pointed out how the gaps identified could be closed through a range of improvements and changes.

These factors led to the creation of the Leadership Development Center and, on a broader scale, to an emphasis on people as a top strategic priority for the Coast Guard as expressed in its strategic plan and associated budget. Development of the competencies of all of its people to needed levels, recruiting for a full strength force, and retaining the right levels of knowledge and experience are expressed as priorities second to none.

The Commandant, Admiral James Loy, has also been clear that the Coast Guard can no longer take on all additive missions and that an honest calculation of workload versus resources needs to be a part of the thinking for the future if results are to be retained at current levels. How did this vision for change impact the Coast Guard leader development strategies?

In late 1997, the Coast Guard announced a decision to consolidate all leadership development training into one location as a center for excellence—what was to be called the Leadership Development Center (LDC)—on the grounds of the U.S. Coast Guard Academy in New London, Connecticut. The decision to integrate all leadership development activities and to encourage synergy among leader program planning arose out of the goal to provide leadership and a working environment that enables all people to maximize their full potential and the Coast Guard to maximize mission success.

This strategic decision led to a number of subsequent actions that are now playing out in what the private sector would refer to as a "corporate university" environment—even though a good deal of training is provided off site. The co-location of leader program planning with a good portion of the leader training for officers, civilians, enlisted, cadets, and other officer candidates on site provides an opportunity for generational and experiential cross-fertilization that is rare in government.

Description

The mission at the LDC, currently under the command of Captain Margaret Riley, is threefold:

- Prepare Team Coast Guard (all components of the Coast Guard) to demonstrate leadership competencies and live the Coast Guard core values;
- Support Coast Guard units through service-wide leadership and quality development efforts; and
- Identify future organizational needs and requirements through ongoing research and assessment.

The core values of honor, respect, and devotion to duty and the 21 leadership competencies have been aligned with the new Coast Guard strategic direction as well as to its historical mission of service. This is the central organizing principle that allows integration of each of the programs and courses run at the New London LDC and in leadership courses given on site at various locations around the country. It also allows the LDC to serve as a clearinghouse for information on leadership for the entire Coast Guard and to be a valued research center on new approaches to leader development.

The various leadership programs under the LDC have been designed to be just-in-time, at key transition points in people's careers, when new command challenges lie ahead or when new operational and leadership challenges are anticipated. This is in addition to programs of accession into the Coast Guard such as the Academy.

Thus the leadership programs offered at and through the LDC include separate preparatory courses for rising chief petty officers and chief warrant officers, initial leadership development for mid-grade civilians (GS 12-14), a one-week Leadership and Management School for civilians and military (currently offered 48 times each year at the unit level in the field), and two-week leadership schools for prospective commanding officers and other leaders.[7]

The LDC also provides resources to leaders for growing leaders in the field through an online source of leadership lesson outlines in what is referred to as a "cookbook" approach offering 10 leadership modules. The design is aimed at simplicity so that material is easily taught through a Socratic or coaching approach, discussed among the participants, and integrated with work in real-life applications.

A sample of these modules includes: Followership, Teamwork, Personal Ethics, and Leadership Competencies. For example, a module is included that integrates a viewing of the film *Apollo 13* with a series of questions about how leadership is demonstrated from this real-life historical dramatization.

Another example is an online learning module entitled "So You Want to Be a Mentor (Or Find a Mentor)"—which includes methods of learning for beginning an eight-step mentoring program locally and training for being a mentor or a mentee.

In short, what the Coast Guard has done is to mount both an integrated and a strategic approach to leadership development that is concerned with its cultural distinctives (core values) and essential leader competencies at all levels of the organization.

Lessons

The Coast Guard has distinguished itself among federal organizations in the results it has accomplished and in the overall excellence of its management. But despite good results, the initiative to focus more acutely on the people side of the Coast Guard—and more particularly on growing its leaders—has brought about a number of changes in the last four years that are still being integrated and widened in reshaping not only methods but culture. Lessons learned from the Coast Guard's experience include:

1. Make people and their development a top priority in the strategic plan.

Coast Guard's strategic plan and budget make it very clear that people are the top priority. This starts with Admiral Loy, himself. Despite resource constraints that affect all government organizations, this choice of people (not technology or capital expenditures) has been central over the past several years and continues to be revalidated by the USCG Leadership Council (a high-level committee that supports the Commandant on leadership initiatives).

The groundwork was laid for this in the mid-1990s with the initiative of the Workforce Cultural Audit under the direction of Admiral Loy, who was then the assistant commandant for human resources. The Coast Guard has consistently made people a top priority in a visible way, backing it up with action plans, resources and specific steps over the past five years, including establishing the LDC.

2. Focus on organization socialization as well as individual development.

The establishment of a corporate university approach to leader development offers the potential for what some organizations refer to as "socialization"—an emphasis not entirely on leadership as a skill set, but on leadership as an embodiment of core values in behavior and as a set of aligned competencies that are common and expected for leaders at all levels.

Leader and organizational socialization is about an emphasis on reshaping the organization milieu toward a leader-centered culture. A corporate university also capitalizes on a synergy of effort what the Coast Guard calls "leadership across the curriculum" in all Coast Guard training courses.

In contrast, the dominant form of leadership development in the federal government today is an ad hoc approach that relies upon serendipity for success and on the assumption that leader development consists of attending leadership courses. By consolidating leader development program planning and many of its leader courses under a single organization at one location, the potential exists for the Coast Guard to achieve what they have begun namely, to bring together leaders at all levels, to share a common philosophy (centered on the USCG core values and 21 leadership competencies) of leadership and public service, and to have ongoing involvement of line managers as teachers and contributors to the curriculum.

The Coast Guard also has established a unique opportunity for young people in the process of becoming members of Team Coast Guard to learn from those with experience in an interactive setting. That opportunity for interaction among cadets, officer candidates and line managers is still a work in progress, but it is far beyond what even the best private sector companies are able to offer through such programs as summer internships.

The use of a corporate university model also has allowed the Coast Guard to develop online materials for empowering leaders to grow leaders throughout the Coast Guard.

3. Provide senior leaders tools and the incentives to grow leaders.

The presence of user-friendly online leader development programs provides a means for senior leaders to grow other leaders in the field and on board ships. Similarly, the opportunity to establish formal and informal mentoring programs throughout the Coast Guard has a great potential for shaping a leader-centered culture and is a powerful means of leadership development. The establishment of the Commandant's Leadership Advisory Council (LAC) has been instrumental in spearheading some of these initiatives and in demonstrating the importance and expectations for other leaders.

What is excellent here is the practicality of the leadership development program—conducted by leaders themselves (not trainers or consultants)—for units in the field. Another plus is the way in which the Coast Guard solicits real involvement and input in the evolution of the curriculum by establishing what amounts to a budding community of practice. They have established a web-based compilation of leadership development practices that are currently being used (hence field-tested) and have been placed online for use by others across the Coast Guard. Currently, 27 such "Proven Initiatives" are available under the categories of Leadership, Professional Development, Training, Education, and Other.

The underscoring of expectations for line manager ownership of leader development is an outcome of the formation of the LAC. This group, representing all levels of the USCG, has been charged by the Commandant with gathering leadership development concerns, evaluating the Coast Guard leadership development programs, and disseminating information back to the field. The Proven Initiatives project is one of the innovations under the auspices of the Leadership Development Center.

4. Make self-development a key part of leader development.

The emphasis on self development as a responsibility for all leaders in the Coast Guard has been enhanced by support of the LDC.

The generation of extensive leadership reading lists available to all people online is one tool that has been developed through the LDC. Another leadership self-development activity includes encouraging mentoring and giving practical advice on selecting a mentor. The LDC also sponsors a leadership essay program for individuals to share their practical leadership insights and to reward the sharing of earned wisdom.

The point here is not so much the tools and programs themselves, but the principle that self development is more and more expected of leaders and is not solely an organization or programmatic effort.

The Coast Guard provides an excellent example of a corporate and strategic approach to the challenges of leader development. Organizations with neither the size nor the resources that the Coast Guard possesses nevertheless have ample means at their disposal to tackle this critical need. The Western Area Power Administration is just such an exemplary organization.

Western Area Power Administration (WAPA)

Mission Challenge

The Western Area Power Administration is a business-type organization under the aegis of the Department of Energy. Michael Hacskaylo is the administrator and initiator of the recent emphasis on succession and leader development. WAPA's responsibility is to deliver power for commercial use from federal hydro-generation dams and the 56 power plants of the Bureau of Reclamation, the U.S. Army Corps of Engineers, and the International Boundary Water Commission. As such they own and operate the third largest high-voltage transmission system in the United States. The 17,000 miles of transmission lines span the upper Midwest to the Southwest and out to California in the West (15 states total), delivering electricity to over 600 transmission wholesale customers, primarily for use during peak-hour needs of their millions of customers. They have almost 1,300 employees and 250 contract workers and generate gross operating revenues of almost $900 million.

The mission of WAPA is to market and deliver cost-based hydroelectric power and related services. It has a vision of becoming a premier marketing and transmission organization (their core business functions). Their core values are stated as:

- Treat each other with respect
- Live up to your commitments
- Take pride in what you do
- Work as a team

In an era of reemerging focus on energy and low cost measures, WAPA stands at a strategic point.

Approach

Two factors provided the urgency for and the shape of a change strategy. First was a 26 percent employment downsizing in 1995. This produced not only anxiety but also the realization that an incredible amount of knowledge would be lost. In the process of holding focus groups with employees, the issues of developing the people who remained became more acute.

But WAPA also had a cultural barrier to overcome—assumptions about a past management development program that was viewed as less than successful. With the downsizing and reengineering in 1995 came the elimination of the management development program, which had been seen by many employees as for the "anointed" few as well as simply a career "ticket punch."

Second, there was a change in the nature of the business environment. Energy markets became both more complex and more competitive. WAPA had to become leaner in costs and more mature in their customer service skills. As a result, the strategic plan reflects three major goals around products and services, people, and industry. The people goal is to: ·

> Recruit, develop and retain a safety-focused, highly productive customer-oriented and diverse workforce.

Curiously, even though the succession program is now in its second year, it is mentioned only tangentially in the Strategic Plan and Performance Plan for 2001. The explicit way in which growing leaders is an aligned strategy is not clear yet.

Description

In the wake of downsizing and a competitive business climate for energy, WAPA felt it needed to better understand the organization climate. An organization-wide employee survey and a series of focus groups began to identify the need for leader development, but employees also identified the cultural barrier of anointing the chosen few, as discussed earlier. The insights gleaned from extensive interaction with employees at all levels began to give shape to the succession program design.

The administrator also held a number of sessions with the senior leadership team on the importance of their support for a succession initiative, especially in making available opportunities for details and job rotations for developmental purposes. He made a strong *business case* that would be key to the rationale for this new initiative. This was a critical insight because in a cost-competitive atmosphere, unnecessary overhead costs directly impact customers and WAPA's competitive position.

In October 1999, WAPA publicly launched its Management Succession Program (MSP), identifying a different set of competencies needed in future leaders—skills well beyond the technical qualifications that had previously been considered central. The focus on customer service, and the need to create an organizational climate that would be felicitous for recruiting and retaining the employees needed within a competitive labor market, began to shape the nature of the program design. Included were the Executive Core Qualifications (Leading Change, Leading People, Results Driven, Business Acumen, and Building Coalitions/Communication). In addition, WAPA developed what are referred to as Western-Specific Competencies—Financial/Management Systems, Power Marketing and Operation, Utility Industry, Maintenance, and Safety. It also benchmarked other organizations and did extensive research to understand how best to put a succession program in place for its unique culture.

The Department of Energy was also taking initiative to begin a department-wide succession program, and WAPA staff members participated in these plans and discussions. However, when it became apparent that the department-level initiative was bogging down, WAPA made a decision to move ahead rather than wait for a comprehensive plan to emerge. This was a factor in beginning with a fairly streamlined approach that fit not only the WAPA culture, but also the exigencies of the staffing situation and the need to move ahead with alacrity.

The MSP emerged as a three-year voluntary, primarily self-directed program open to *all* employees who hold a permanent management, supervisory, or team leader position within WAPA. Funding for development and training comes from the individual offices of participants, except for group-wide training that is prorated among all organizations and funded centrally.

Now in its second year, it began with 37 participants from offices around the region with six participants dropping out of the program in the first six months. Since the initiative did not include a selection process, it was able to begin rather quickly after the announcement and application cycle.

While the general thrust is for self development and direction, the program office in the Lakewood, Colorado, headquarters does provide some support as well as overall management of the program. For example, the initial identification of strengths and developmental needs began with a 360-degree feedback process, soliciting feedback from supervisors, peers, and subordinates relevant to the 10 leader competencies. Also, there are group training opportunities approximately once each year for all MSP participants. However, it is the responsibility of individuals to search out advisors, coaches, and mentors on their own.

The development for each individual is set forth in an Individual Progression Plan (IPP) for the three years of the program. Activities are tied to the development of the leader competencies and are subject to supervisory approval. Development activities and challenging job-based experiences are stressed over training, which is viewed as only a supplement, and are focused on gaining new experiences and demonstrating results. In essence this is a "trial by fire," but one that the individual develops. The type of activities that are expected in a good IPP (as outlined in the MSP guidance) would include:

- Details to other parts of the organization
- Temporary assignments and lateral job changes
- Serving as team lead or chair of teams or committees
- Participating on special projects
- Volunteering to act in vacant managerial positions
- Volunteering for leadership in community or church organizations
- Attending off-duty classes
- Professional reading
- Use of videos, CDs, etc.

In addition, the importance of geographic mobility for developmental experiences is stressed and expected.

There are four training courses that are mandatory for each participant, covering diversity, sexual harassment, hiring, and other personnel practices. There is also a mandatory reading list of documents pertaining to WAPA (e.g., the strategic plan).

WAPA also has used a limited team project focused on improving effective project management as an action learning component.

A semi-annual self-evaluation provides accountability for progress against the IPP and is submitted to the supervisor and to the senior manager. Corporate Training Director Ann Capps reviews the accomplishments and progress in development. The WAPA administrator also maintains a review of the development activities of the participants to ensure that senior leaders are supporting mobility and challenging assignments.

Lack of progress by the individual is one criterion for removal from the MSP as is removal from a managerial position. Completion occurs when all of the developmental activities in the IPP are accomplished within a three-year window.

Lessons

While relatively young, WAPA's program has incorporated some unique factors into its MSP design and into its own culture that are noteworthy for a smaller organization considering how best to begin.

1. Initiative by the senior leaders of sub-organizations is important in a large, complex organization.

The initiative and support of the administrator for a succession initiative has been key, as has the decision to proceed ahead of the slower moving initiative of the Department of Energy.

This is a common thread for all excellent succession efforts. For administrations, bureaus, or other types of sub-cabinet organizations, the politics, complexity, and accompanying inertia of a department-wide effort may likely call for initiative such as this when a need clearly exists. Large organizations also should resist the temptation to centralize succession programs where unique cultural factors exist and where individual initiative is moving ahead effectively.

The administrator not only took the lead in launching the leader MSP development and succession initiative, but also has continued to do so. He frequently encourages his senior leaders, ensuring they are fully supportive of cross-functional assignments and engaged in monitoring individual progress. He also conducts conference calls with the program participants during the year and teaches courses in law and congressional relations. Moreover he and many of the senior leaders act as mentors for the participants.

2. Voluntary "selection" can be effective in succession if done wisely.

The voluntary nature of the MSP is a fairly unique approach that offers both strengths and potential weaknesses.

For organizations contemplating launching a succession effort, a "whoever will come" approach makes such a launch occur more quickly and produces a larger talent pool.

In comparison, the PBGC launch of its succession program took longer to get to the starting line because of the time needed to agree on a central program design and because of the concern over any possible perception of favoritism for a particular office. In addition, managing the selection process required time for scheduling, executing, and counseling non-selectees.

The better programs in the private sector take the approach of focusing on the so-called "hi-pos"—high potential candidates—only. Simply because of the effort needed to manage such a program, most for-profit organizations make the practical and cost-beneficial decision to limit the pool being developed to the likely top candidates for future leadership.

The downside of the WAPA approach is that 15 percent of the voluntary participants have already dropped out, which may point to a number of factors that a more rigorous selection would have identified. Even in this streamlined approach to program design, managing over 30 individuals through some of the developmental and assessment activities is time-consuming for a small office and may not pay off for all participants or for the organization. However, the dropouts from the program that WAPA has experienced may be a less painful way to eliminate those lacking the necessary qualities.

3. Self-development is an important component of any succession effort.

The predominance of self development in the WAPA MSP design offers great benefits; however, it does have some risks as well.

By relying on individuals to develop their own program of leader development, WAPA has tapped into the initiative of future leaders. This is one method of sorting out those who are truly potential future leaders and willing to pay a price, from those who may realize that leadership is simply not their calling and at a low organizational cost. This may also prove to be a greater factor in self-motivation than a designed program would produce.

It should also be noted that the WAPA program for succession and leader development is not completely random nor is it subject to whim, but is firmly anchored in challenging job-based experiences and the 10 leader competencies. In short, it employs the research findings on how leaders are best grown.

The approach, however, places greater emphasis on the review process by supervisors and senior managers to understand the gaps in the individual's development and the kinds of experiences best suited to close those gaps. Some senior leaders understand this well; others likely do not, and in those cases the corporate training director is the one tapped to play this role.

4. Accountability is needed for assessing progress.

WAPA has a system of accountability that is reasonably strong and is an important factor in identifying individual progress. Too often, leadership development is simply seen as completion of a program.

The system of accountability is a strong incentive for individuals to make the time to attend to their "important" development agenda in the face of sometimes "urgent" time demands on the job. It also invests supervisors and senior managers in supporting the development of their MSP participants and gives visibility to individual outcomes. While this may somewhat beg the question of the wider organization performance outcomes it nevertheless, has teeth and is an important factor in ensuring success.

The administrator related that he can already see results, with individuals taking on far broader responsibilities, seeking on their own to develop a strategic sense of the business, and working effectively with many stakeholders, including Congress.

5. Job-based challenges must be supported by organizational mobility opportunity.

The emphasis on the importance of job-based experiences and the support for mobility in effecting these developmental experiences is a key WAPA insight and one that borrows from the research and best practices of outstanding organizations.

The Center for Creative Leadership has had a strong influence on the design of most of the better leader development programs in the country. The use of varied, challenging job experiences is the single most important method of developing leaders. This addresses one of the particular needs of WAPA that other organizations may have—a relatively constrained budget for more formal, albeit less effective training.

The fact that real work (challenging, outside the normal experience) is the foundation for leadership learning makes such measures very cost-effective. It does place greater emphasis on the "learning" aspect of such activities by requiring that participants discuss them with experienced leaders or observers to ensure that strengths and weaknesses are identified and that the lessons learned are raised up for future application in future assignments.

We turn now to a larger social service organization—one with a more traditional government role in the processing of claims, counseling clients, and providing financial entitlements—the Veterans Benefits Administration.

Veterans Benefits Administration (VBA)

Mission Challenge

The Veterans Benefits Administration is one of three lines of business (health care, and burial and memorial service being the other two) in the Department of Veterans Affairs. This cabinet department is the second largest department in number of employees. The VBA is responsible for the administration of services in the areas of disability payments to former servicepersons and their families as well as pensions to impoverished former military and their survivors, the guaranty of home loans, the provision of educational assistance, and the management of insurance programs and vocational rehabilitation for those disabled in service. It has approximately 12,000 employees located in 57 regional offices in every state, the headquarters office, and at a dozen military discharge centers. VBA is responsible for a benefits budget of over $30 billion, most of it entitlements. It serves over 3 million former military members and their families (out of a total living veteran population of approximately 24 million).

In recent years, VBA has been the target of several critical congressional hearings fueled by veterans and service organization complaints and by external, independent reports from GAO and the National Academy of Public Administration. These criticisms have targeted VBA's continuing poor levels of service, the slowness of its benefits claims processing, the mounting backlogs of disability claims that have frustrated claimants' needs, and the mismanagement of its automation projects.

All of these sources of concern implied that leadership was in need of significant change. One report found that new automation and reengineering efforts were still likely to fail without significant human capital improvements and far stronger leadership. It was in that climate that in 1995, a well respected career Senior Executive, Joe Thompson, was elevated to the under secretary position from which he sought to transform VBA.

The transformation of VBA has been centered on a grounding in its historic core values, of which VBA had lost sight. A central theme has been rekindling an awareness of the long history of assisting the men and women who fought for this country going back to the Revolutionary War. The leadership development strategy falls within that recommitment.

Approach

The approach to transformation, referred to by former Under Secretary Thompson as "The Roadmap to Excellence," was an emphasis on service to people, streamlining and improving old-line processes with a strong team component, shaping the culture to embed different attitudes and, particularly for our interest, new leadership and technical competencies that will help drive these changes. Thus, succession is one of the key components of the roadmap.

These improvements are characterized most clearly in the vision core values for VBA established three years ago:

> Our **vision** is that the veterans whom we serve will feel that our Nation has kept its commitment to them; employees will feel that they are both recognized for their contribution and are part of something larger than themselves; and taxpayers will feel that we've met the responsibilities they've entrusted to us. Courage, honesty, trust, respect, open communication, and accountability will be reflected in our day-to-day behavior.

VBA used a highly collaborative process in developing a set of 10 core values that would characterize employees interactions with veterans and with each other and which are expected to be modeled by leaders. Four of the **core values** are especially relevant for a discussion of what VBA has taken as a new tack in its leader development and succession initiatives:
- We foster an environment that promotes personal and corporate initiative risk-taking and teamwork.
- We are open to change and flexible in our attitudes.
- Respect, integrity, trust, and fairness are hallmarks of all our interactions.
- We value a culture where everyone is involved, accountable, respected, and appreciated.

The establishment of a function dedicated to the development of people—technical training, general managerial, and leadership development—was a key element of this change. The formation of the Office of Employee Development and Training (ED&T) and the selection of Dr. George Wolohojian as its first director were the first initiatives taken in response to the needs expressed.

VBA also established the Veterans Benefits Academy in Baltimore, which focuses on non-technical and leadership/management training and development, and the Technical Training and Evaluation Staff Office, located in Orlando, which focuses more on technical and computer-based training.

Description

The general thrust of the development efforts by VBA has been toward building a learning organization in response to the climate of change—embedding the notion of continuous learning throughout one's career as a central feature.

The more formal leadership development approach is centered on a competency-based model to meet VBA's leadership succession planning requirements with a consistent set of competencies for both development and assessment of leaders. While the same generic competencies attend at each level of leadership, their expression in leader behaviors is progressive over time. VBA has used the five Executive Core Qualifications (ECQs) as a

The VBA Succession Pyramid

Challenge 2001—While not entirely a leader development program (this would be closer to an organizational socialization initiative), this is intended for the hundreds of recently hired employees as well as others. It aims to foster a deeper awareness of VBA's historical/cultural mission in serving veterans, start to build communities of practice and learning, and begin the practice of continuous learning.

The five leadership development programs are:
- **Leadership Enhancement and Development (LEAD)**—for selected high-potential employees at the GS 9-12 level, providing exposure to the major strategic issues of the organization and using action learning team projects as a centerpiece of leader learning. The 25 selectees meet for a week at a time, three times during the nine-month program.
- **Introduction to Leadership**—includes a basic understanding of human resources policies and practices and a labor relations component for new or potential supervisors.
- **Division Level Management Training Program (DLMT)**—for mid-level employees ready for division supervisory responsibilities.
- **Assistant Director**—(planning stages)
- **SES Candidate Development**—a proactive response to the expected attrition in the VBA SES ranks focusing on the five core Executive Core Qualifications and lasting 12 to18 months.

basic foundation, but added two of their own that apply to their change requirements—Professional and Personal Growth, and Customer Service. (See Appendix II for further discussion.)

The VBA leadership succession program is presently comprised of four (and ultimately five) levels or phases of leadership development, from initial high-potential management candidates to SES development. This approach underscores the importance of continuous and progressive leadership learning. ED&T has developed these programs under the broad direction of the VBA Leadership Steering Group, comprised of senior executives and managers.

Each of the four current leadership development programs features some basic leadership learning principles and methods:
- individual and team action learning projects
- formal classroom training
- cross-functional and shadowing assignments
- mentoring
- stress on self-development actions

In each of these programs, targeted at different stages in a leader's career, individuals prepare a plan for development with their mentors. The plan seeks to capitalize on the application of principles presented in periodic seminars and practiced during the times between seminars, and on the identification of varied, challenging work assignments. A more detailed description of one of these programs —the LEAD Program—will be instructive. (See "The VBA LEAD Program" in Appendix III.)

Lessons

The challenge of transforming an old-line organization whose basic "business" is the processing of claims and applications and interacting with clients, primarily by correspondence and telephone, is a daunting one. The necessity for accuracy, speed, and a human component in customer service has led to a "high-tech, high-touch" response and a strong emphasis on developing leaders throughout their careers. There are three distinctive lessons from the VBA experience:

1. Take a comprehensive approach to develop leaders at all levels.

VBA has invested in a continuous approach to succession and leader development that grows leaders at critical career junctures—at all levels almost from the very beginning of the person's career. It also reflects the need to identify high potential younger leaders and to emphasize development of a broad pool (except incumbent SES members, which is a future developmental agenda item).

The importance of this approach is that it stands a much higher chance of inculcating a leader-centered culture throughout the organization because of the broad nature of the programs themselves; because of the emphasis on engaging leaders to be the mentors, coaches and trainers; and because of the extensive use of action learning team projects at the local office and nationally.

2. Use a competency model as the basis for development of all leaders at all levels and align the behaviors with the strategic direction of change.

A consistent and progressive leader competency model provides a clear understanding of behavioral and skill expectations for leaders—not simply for development but for performance as well. What will be key for VBA is whether the leaders demonstrating these competencies are actually the ones who advance and are rewarded or whether the "old culture" is reinforced by using the old (unwritten) criteria for advancement. The alignment of all components of the human capital system is critical to the success of a competency-based model.

3. The wide use of mentoring is a great enhancement to the potential success of leader development and engages the senior leaders more readily as key actors in the development of the next generation.

The use of mentoring in all of the leadership programs is important because it provides for training and orientation of the mentors and the mentees in certain behaviors that will be useful throughout. VBA has installed an extensive screening process for mentors and mentees that allows for a good match. The requirement to regularly engage each other and the clear description of expectations helps to frame the mentoring component so that it is aligned with the purposes of the leader development activities.

However, the extensive amount of leader development occurring throughout the organization makes it imperative that these mentoring responsibilities are seen as key requirements for senior leaders and not simply as additional duties to be fit in if convenient.

Social Security Administration (SSA)

Mission Challenge

SSA realized several years ago that it faced a turnover in its executive and senior leader ranks that dwarfed the magnitude of the problem in almost any other federal agency. As a result, it also got on top of the problem well before most agencies.

By way of comparison, SSA has a potential retirement-eligible population of 82 percent of the current SES rank leaders, 91 percent of the GS-15 senior managers, and 93 percent of the GS-14 senior managers. That this comes at a time when the workload is spiking with the generational wave of retirement eligibles, the growing ranks of those filing for disability, and the pressures for Social Security reform, makes the necessity for action on succession a strategic imperative.

Approach

SSA is one of the few agencies in government with a clearly developed strategic plan that links its long-term strategy with the development of future leaders. While the key operational thrusts of the agency's strategic plan are to deliver customer-responsive world-class service, promote valued, strong, and responsive programs, and conduct effective policy development and research, the primary goal regarding the people who deliver the services and the programs is:

To be an employer that values and invests in each employee

SSA's strategy to grow leaders has been ongoing for some time and arose out of the transition to becoming an independent agency in 1994. At the time, a GAO report targeted a lack of succession management and leader development as being major issues to tackle for the new organization.

Paul Barnes, one of the key line managers as regional director in Chicago and deputy regional director in Atlanta, has advocated for developing the next generation of leaders. Now, as SSA's associate director for human resources, he leads the four programs that undergird the succession strategy. It is a strategy that includes developmental programs for leaders at all levels.

As one of the more mature leader development programs, they began with a focus on the SES candidates and the more senior leaders at the GS 13-15 levels. This initiative has now progressed to a program for the recruitment and initial development of future leaders and the development of first line supervisors and potential supervisors (GS 9-12). A key objective in all of this has been to break down the career single path developmental stovepipes that have long existed. Interviewees agreed that this paradigm shift has been the toughest cultural challenge to overcome.

Description

Like the VA, SSA has a comprehensive approach to developing leaders over the course of their careers, but it begins with accession into the federal ranks. The following four programs comprise the scope of the national succession and leader development process in SSA:

- Presidential Management Intern Program (PMI) for initial accession, GS 9
- Leadership Development Program (LDP), GS 9-12
- Advanced Leadership Program (ALP), GS 13-15
- SES Candidate Development Program (SESCDP)

These are each national-level programs and are primarily two years in duration. The particular focus of interest is in developing broader based leaders with people and customer service competencies as well as technical competency. In each case, they involve:

- An orientation to the particular career stage and the developmental challenges faced in SSA;
- Core training components geared to the level of need;
- The use of developmental experiences where individuals are taken off their job and placed into challenging assignments for on-the-job leadership learning; and,
- The use of senior mentors for coaching and advice.

There are also some distinctive components to each of the four programs.

PMI Program

Over the past several years, SSA has been recruiting 30-40 PMIs—the top ranking graduate school students who desire a career in public service.

These are truly "the best and the brightest" and SSA has been investing in hiring over 10 percent of the selectees in this flagship OPM recruitment program. SSA says they are particularly looking for individuals with substantive life experience, as well as superior intellectual credentials.

Once at SSA, PMIs are jump-started into mid-level jobs but remain part of a centralized developmental pool where rotational assignments are used to give them varied experiences before being assigned to a permanent position at the end of the two-year program.

LDP and ALP Programs

In keeping with the SSA strategy to begin with the most senior replacement pools, the ALP was launched before the LDP and will take up to four more years to fully implement. The LDP is just emerging from the pilot stage and is on a similar timeline for full implementation. Both programs select applicants in a competitive process that engages senior leaders as selecting officials. The numbers selected are based on replacement projections, flexibility and range of experience and diversity.

Selectees for both of these programs are given temporary promotions and accept new assignments within 90 days of selection. This accomplishes the key developmental task of a new, challenging job-based experience. The added organizational benefit is that their position is also vacated and filled by another person who is also given a job-based development opportunity. The individuals revert to their original position and grade at the end of the two years if they do not find a position at their new, temporary grade.

Both programs also use specially designed structured interviews and self-assessments of the Executive Core Qualifications competencies as a basis for initial selection and later for individual development plans. They also make extensive use of action learning in cluster teams of individuals selected for these programs.

SES Candidates Program

This leader development program is announced government-wide and for selected applicants results in a temporary GS 15 position. The first phase attracted over 400 applicants, 100 finalists and a final class of 35. Senior SSA leaders make the final selections.

Similar to the design for the ALP and LDP, selectees are moved to occupy temporary positions, providing opportunity for a similar "ripple effect" for others assuming temporary positions that have been vacated. For their rotational job assignments, SES Candidates take one temporary position outside of SSA (public or private sector), in operational areas, in the headquarters, and in hands-on jobs serving customers.

There is also an intentional exposure to the most senior executives in SSA and to the strategic agenda and decisions.

Selection into SES positions at the completion of the program is the measure of success used. By all accounts this has been highly successful in accomplishing the initial outcomes. SSA has become a benchmark for several other federal agencies.

Lessons
Given that SSA is further along in addressing succession, there are certain lessons that are highly useful to draw from its experiences:

1. Make a strong business case for leader development.
Too often, anything that sounds like training is relegated into second or third tier priority which cannot withstand competition from operational issues. SSA realized that a massive turnover in its senior leader ranks would ill prepare it for the demographic challenges that all statistical models predicted for its future workload. The political sensitivity of Social Security policy alternatives only enhanced the severity of the challenge. But it was in initially tying the need for leader development to the provision for succession that set the stage for today's success. This priority and the business case made for the strategic plan communicated to decision-makers and supervisors the importance of investing in the development of people at all levels.

2. Get clear senior executive buy-in along with their deep involvement.
SSA chose as its lead champion an experienced operational leader, Paul Barnes, to head the succession initiatives, rather than an HR expert. Barnes had a track record of growing leaders and respect among his peers.[8] As a result, he was better able to engage other senior leaders as mentors and instructors in their various programs. Senior leaders are active participants as mentors and as selecting officials.

3. Use an approach that is grounded in practical research on "best practices" that apply to the public sector.
In this case, SSA grounded its approach in many of the findings from the Center for Human Resources Management at the National Academy of Public Administration. Developed in a series of publications during the 1990s, the research found that there is great value in learning from others in the public sector and private sector and adopting the basic principles and approaches where appropriate to the culture and needs of the organization.

4. Challenging, rotational job assignments are not only the best method of growing leaders, but if properly structured can have a ripple developmental effect.
SSA has a unique and innovative approach to the use of job-based developmental experiences. By temporarily promoting participants and by

centrally controlling their development, they not only can use different experiences as development tools, they open up opportunities for others as well. This may well be the best of the best practices discussed in this chapter.

Making Sense of It All:
Reaching Conclusions for Action

What Does It All Mean?

This is where it gets difficult. Knowing something, even if it is successfully done by others, is no guarantee that we can do it successfully. It's much like riding a bicycle.

To extend the bike metaphor a bit, what we have done in this chapter is simply to describe, in some detail, what it takes to ride a bicycle and how others have done so. But with 10 examples or even 20, we would be no closer to learning how to balance and ride without falling. That takes learning by doing. It's the same way with growing leaders.

At some point, these findings do not make sense until an organization actually begins to do the hard work of finding out what works best for them by taking action. This section is meant to offer additional insights for organizational learning by comparing initiatives in the five public sector organizations and contrasting them with the best lessons and examples in the private sector.

It is hoped that the distilled wisdom will provide actions for organizations to take in developing the next generation of leaders.

We turn now to a brief comparison of what we have seen in the five different public sector organizations.

Key Principles and Best Practices in the Public Sector

Key Principles

The following lessons summarize the exemplary leadership development principles gleaned through the experiences of the five case studies. Embedded within them are several instances of "best practices," implications, and methods that these and other federal agencies have used to produce and to continue to produce excellent results.

Progress with this component of human capital will certainly take time and persistence. The six principles noted here are perhaps better considered "habits"—the underlying truths, if you will, of thought and action in leadership development and succession management that need to be applied

---

Six Principles in Growing Leaders

- It is fundamentally senior leaders themselves who must provide the leadership for a succession initiative aligned with and helping to drive forward the strategic change direction of the organization.

- The framework for an excellent leadership development program is based upon significant, challenging, and varied job-based experiences, intentionally chosen to advance the competencies and to test the character of future leaders.

- Senior leaders must assume responsibility for the development of future leaders as coaches, mentors, teachers—and most of all, as exemplars—within and without leader development programs.

- Strategic partnerships between a cadre of senior leaders and the HR and development organization is key to success in the design of the succession approach, in the selection of future leaders for development experiences, and in the tracking of their progressive development needs.

- Both the competencies needed for the leaders of the future and the outcome measures used to identify success (and accountability) must be aligned with the strategic direction of the organization and must be clearly defined as a "business case."

- Leaders must persistently and patiently lead not simply in the strategic direction but in the change in culture—forming a strategy for cultural change, dispelling the myths, identifying the dislocations between word and action and their underlying assumptions, and championing a long-term investment in every aspect of the area of human capital to which leadership and cultural change are the keys to wider transformation.

---

both consistently and together as a whole. They underscore the findings in "Leaders Growing Leaders."[9]

Best Practices

There seems to be an endless fascination with success and "how to" become like the best companies. This movement probably began with the popular success of Tom Peters and Bob Waterman's *In Search of Excellence: Lessons from America's Best Run Companies*. Unfortunately for the learning enterprise, a decade later many of those companies had gone out of business or were swallowed whole. In truth, what is often posed as "best practices" are more realistically what noted executive educator and author Dave Ulrich calls "interesting practices."

In some ways comparing the practices of the five exemplary public sector organizations with each other can lead to deceptive conclusions—much as contrasting them with exemplary private sector organizations can. This is one reason that I have also tried to examine underlying principles, which are more enduring. So-called best practices can be helpful for insight, but one clear finding is that each organization made decisions about those practices that recognized its own unique circumstances. Size, resources, past experience, change imperatives, and individual culture—each of these has helped to shape the varying approaches taken, and the resulting development and succession initiatives.

It should also be noted that most of these succession programs are relatively new and the lessons of their experience are still being sifted. Even within the same organization (and here I am referring to both private sector and public sector organizations), the existing culture and mission challenges can vary significantly, thus shaping the practices that are adopted.

Observations

There are a few consistent practices used by all of the exemplary organizations. The use of senior mentors, the identification of behavioral leader competencies for development (in some cases keyed to different levels of pending responsibility), the use of well targeted internal training courses, and the use of self-development study or reading are all consistent practices. In addition, exposure to the strategic agenda and to officials of the organization and the use of individualized development plans are widely used.

But beyond these, the practices and their combinations vary widely including the choice of whom to develop for the future leader pool and when development for leadership begins (i.e., at recruitment and at all levels, or only for a selected level of the organization).

Two comments are appropriate here. First, as noted, the mission challenges vary among the organizations, as does the amount of resources available within the organizations. In general, the larger organizations have committed larger amounts of resources to succession and development and tend to have more comprehensive programs for leaders at all levels. This is similar to findings for the private sector.

Second, we also see that these leader programs are still, except for SSA, in the early stages. The reasonable expectation is that given success in meeting the mission challenges through developing future leaders, there will be a widening of the types of practices and the scope of the programs. That remains a speculation, however.

Before positing some conclusions from these comparisons, we turn now to a brief contrast of public sector practices and approaches with those of the private sector. But first, we need to consider one question that hangs over such comparisons: Can the public sector and the private sector be compared?

Table 4.1. Leader Development Practices by Selected Agencies

Development Practice	PBGC	USCG	WAPA	VBA	SSA
Rotational temporary assignments managed by senior leaders	√		√		
Succession/development at all levels		√		√	√
360 feedback	√	√	√		
Action learning team projects	√		√	√	
Exposure to strategic issues agenda	√		√	√	√
Individual development plan framework	√		√	√	√
Use of senior mentors/advisors	√	√	√	√	√
Self development—volunteer church/community leadership	√		√		
External leadership programs	√	√*	√		
Internal training courses	√	√	√	√	√
Development in specific leader competencies	√	√	√	√	√
Self development—readings/ self study	√	√	√	√	√
Observation of senior leaders	√		√	√	
Full-time job rotations managed by senior leaders		√	√		√
Limited selection of high potentials for leader development	√			√**	√
Wide and voluntary participation in succession programs		√	√	√	

*   *Professional military education for senior officers with other military branches.*
**   *In the LEAD Program.*

Uniqueness

What lies behind this question is another question I often hear particularly in benchmarking visits: "The federal government doesn't have a 'bottom line,' so what can we learn from the private sector that can ever be applied to us?"

Admittedly, there are unique factors in the public sector. Many would cite the frequent political turnover at the top of organizations, the number of oversight mechanisms that agencies must contend with, the different types of change challenges that are now occurring, the lack of a Profit & Loss Statement for most agencies, and perhaps a more complex political environment. But the more accurate answer is that the principles and practices of how to grow leaders are not significantly different in organizations. This is borne out by both the research to date and by the results in growing leaders where similar practices have been used by different organizations in the public and private sectors.

Key Principles and Best Practices in the Private Sector

This synopsis of leadership development best practices in the private sector is drawn from a variety of sources.[10]

Key Principles

The following principles are deemed by the private sector as being the most important success factors:

- More than anything, by a factor of 10, development of leaders is based on challenging job experiences.
- The wholehearted support and consistent involvement of senior leaders is the single most important factor abetting development through varied and challenging experiences.
- The intentional encouragement of key relationships between younger candidates and older leaders is fundamental.
- Conducting rigorous and continuous evaluation of outcomes based on sound metrics builds commitment.
- Linking leadership to the strategic direction of the organization and incorporating development of key leadership competencies into the specifics of the strategic plan ensures a compelling business case.
- Involving line managers in the design and overall approach is critical to gaining widespread support and culture adaptation.
- Maximizing the opportunity for feedback at all levels of leadership continues to inject both reality and an understanding of progress, and identifies any gaps in fostering continued development.

What the Private Sector Can Teach About Leadership Development

- Developing leaders can drive the successful strategic direction of an organization.

- Senior leaders' involvement in managing challenging job experiences as a leader development approach in succession is of primary importance.

- Clear organizational measures of leader development success and of senior leader accountability are key to effective alignment.

- Excellent leader development and succession require the commitment of time and thought by senior leaders.

- A self-development ethos is just as critical to success as the support of senior leaders.
- Development to maximize potential is of fundamental importance as a strategy for recruitment and retention of the best employees.

Best Practices

These are the succession and leader development practices that stand out as most consistently employed to good success:
- Action learning
- 360-degree feedback
- Observing senior executives in action
- Involvement in action with the organization's strategic priorities
- Cross-organizational assignments or networking
- Cross-functional rotations
- Individual development plans
- Coaching and mentoring (primarily informal)
- Leveraging internal resources (e.g., in-house leaders) and technology

Observations

What this surface comparison shows is that there are great similarities in the developmental practices between excellent organizations in the public and private sectors. This should not be surprising because, in almost every instance, the design for succession and leader development in each agency examined was preceded by extensive research and benchmarking.

The major difference between the two sectors (at least as of this writing) has been the level of commitment to the strategic importance of people, in general, and of succession and leader development, specifically.[11]

While it is a top priority for the private sector, GAO found in the latest round of strategic and performance plans examined that, for the government, succession remains a work in progress and is not yet a priority for immediate action.[12] Similarly, the U.S. Merit Systems Protection Board recently found that the excellent recruitment program for the best and brightest, the Presidential Management Intern Program, was not using future leadership and management potential as a factor in the candidate selection process.

The highlights from the five selected agencies and the brief comparison with the research on exemplary companies provide the following insights that can help shape public sector actions by an agency whose senior leaders are seriously committed to growing the next generation of leaders. The conclusions from the research lead to the recommendations for action by each organization in government in the next section.

1. Excellent public sector organizations base their practices consistently on the proven principles for growing leaders found both in research and in the best private sector organizations.

The primary principles in evidence are:

- Use challenging job-based experiences, selected by senior leaders, as a development strategy;
- Involve future leaders in a substantial way in the organization's strategic agenda with senior leaders as mentors and through real action learning team projects;
- Use the Executive Core Qualification leader competencies as a template for development—typically using the same competencies by which all senior leaders are selected and held accountable (alignment).

2. Excellent public sector organizations make a business case for succession and leader development.

In fundamental ways, the better organizations have built a foundation for success and for cultural and organizational change linked to their strategic agenda and to results. They understand the need for both programmatic excellence and cultural understanding as a foundation for change.

3. Excellent organizations hold themselves accountable for results in growing leaders and begin by involving senior leaders in significant ways to ensure there is accountability and strategic alignment.

While clear, measurable indication of successful results in growing leaders and their direct link to operational imperatives—e.g., serving customers, providing a great place for employees to work and produce, and achieving important bottom line mission results—are still a work in progress, senior leaders involvement in these organizations is a clear signal that growing leaders is of strategic importance and ensures wider commitment and results.

Recommendations

The following recommendations are targeted to two different audiences: first, individual government organizations and second, organizations with government-wide program or policy responsibility. These are systemic recommendations that are aligned and interrelated.

The focus of this research has been on the practices and principles of growing leaders in excellent public sector organizations. What I would recommend to individual organizations or components of organizations flows directly from these findings. They are recommendations that can be acted upon immediately and certainly within the next two years.

Following these individual organizational recommendations are recommendations that are for government-wide action, based on the basic principles that have been already clearly identified. Several of the more senior leaders have observed in the course of their discussions with me that there are some fundamental policy changes that would be extraordinarily helpful, even essential, for all agencies. For this purpose they are included for consideration, recognizing that government-wide action is notoriously difficult to achieve and they are likely longer term in nature.

Finally, since these six recommendations are ultimately systemic in nature, I recommend that the President's Management Council recruit a cadre of senior career executives (active or retired) to work with them and to help take the lead in energizing both a shared vision and certain action across government as a critical investment in the future of the public service to the American people. This would be a legacy well worth committing to.

For individual government organizations:

(1) Each organization should base their succession and leader development practices consistently on the proven principles for growing leaders:
- Challenging, job-based experiences selected by senior leaders as a development strategy;
- The involvement of future leaders in a substantial way with senior leaders in the organization's strategic agenda, as mentors and through real action learning team projects;
- The use of Executive Core Qualification leader competencies as a template for development—those that are the same competencies by which senior leaders are selected and held accountable (alignment).

It must be noted that the widespread commitment to and use of managing challenging job experiences (not simply "shadowing" for example) as a leader development approach orchestrated by senior leaders themselves is much further along as the *sine qua non* of leader development in the private sector.

As we have seen, the range and extent of practices varies widely depending on the mission challenges each organization faces, their culture, and their current strengths. But the selection of "best practices" themselves may be less important than understanding the fundamental leader learning principles that lie behind them, and that to be a leader a person needs to see real leaders in action.

(2) Make a business case for succession and leader development and ground it in a real imperative that will urge action by senior leaders.

In fundamental ways, we have seen that the better organizations have gone well down the road in building a foundation for success and for cultural and organizational change by linking it to the strategic agenda and to real results. They have built their strategies not as a "good thing to do," but as a driver of the mission. This alignment as a business case is critical to engage senior leaders in spearheading the effort and moving leader development from being an initiative for the HR organization or the trainers and educators to try to sell.

This can be seen in the fact that each of the agencies examined has embarked on the long path of developing their leaders because of strategic mission imperatives and has formed strategies that align with those mission challenges. In other words, they do not simply start succession programs without making the clear business case. This must be the beginning point not only for success but for energetic senior leader involvement all along the way.

(3) Each organization and their senior leaders must hold themselves accountable for results in growing leaders. This begins by involving key senior leaders right from the beginning, but it cannot end there.

The involvement of a few champions of the need to grow future leaders, then a widening circle of senior leaders, is the means to speak volumes to the rest of the organization. That alone fosters accountability for forward movement with excellence. After that, each organization will need to declare clear, measurable indications of successful results—not only in growing leaders, but also identifying the direct and indirect links to operational imperatives—serving customers, providing a great place for employees to work and produce, and achieving important bottom line mission results. These are the ultimate purposes for any investment in growing people as leaders.

The commitment to the development and rigorous use of meaningful measures, and the level of accountability for senior leaders and all employees, are the key factors. Such rigor in meaningful measures of the impact of developing leaders, particularly in holding senior leaders accountable for developing those around them, must be seen not only as a leader's legacy, but as a non-negotiable responsibility.[13]

For government-wide action:

What often causes paralysis in the federal government is the need for wider systemic changes in policy that everyone recognizes must occur. While this doesn't necessarily preclude action by individual organizations with an innovative bent, it is often used as an explanation for inaction when so many priorities compete for attention. The whole area of people is one such issue that has cried out for wider changes for many years, but eluded even the broad reinvention agenda of the last eight years.

To date, the response to this situation has been varied. For example, several organizations have sought individual human resource policy flexibilities. This tack has been used where agencies have either unique challenges or unique political clout. Temporary and demonstration projects are also ways that the "one size fits all" rules are sometimes waived, if only for a time. The organizations profiled in this report have, for the most part, worked around any government-wide impediments without seeking any waivers.

But, government-wide, the response to this need has been a mixed message on leadership, with downsizing of the manager and SES ranks being the most visible message. So far, meaningful changes that benefit people (Civil Service Reform) and allow government to be even minimally competitive with the private sector for the best and brightest (and maybe even that assumption needs reexamination) have languished. There is an apparent lack of policy priority for human capital and succession that is only now beginning to be addressed in policy circles. In short, wider changes are wanted, but it's tough to get agreement on how to do it.

Based on the track record, widespread changes that support the development of leaders are not likely to be realized. That is why the first task of a leader is still to grow other leaders, whether or not the senior leader's own organization or even the federal government is fully supportive—in culture or in policy.

Nevertheless, an optimistic reading of the climate for change in human capital government-wide would lead to at least the following recommendations for action at the federal level. These recommendations emerge directly from the implications of the research on the essential principles and practices for growing leaders. The timing, opportunity, and needs all have coalesced to act on the following initiatives.

For the President's Management Council:

(4) Provide a clear mandate to career Senior Executives to take the lead in growing their successors and incorporate this human capital initiative into a government-wide business case spearheaded by the President's Management Council.

Senior leaders in the career public service often see themselves—and are seen by others—as change implementers rather than change leaders. In other words, they are often seen more in the manager role than the leader role. It is one of the myths of leadership development that is unique to the public sector, where over 3,000 political appointees occupy very senior government leadership positions—and this at a time of downsizing in the career manager ranks. (See Myth 6 in Appendix I.)

And while the new Executive Core Qualifications make it clear that those in the SES ranks and those being developed for senior leadership are expected to lead change, lead and develop people, and focus on results, the reality of senior leaders being responsible for growing their successors has not yet penetrated the culture deeply enough except in rare cases. The change leaders identified in this report—Joe Thompson at VBA, Paul Barnes at SSA, Admiral James Loy in the Coast Guard, John Seal at PBGC, and Mike Hacskaylo at WAPA—are the exceptions still.

As the research and experience show, leaders primarily grow by exposure to challenging job-based experiences and by observing leaders in action. This a long-term proposition, but by the nature of political leadership, there is frequently turnover and often a shorter-run focus on initiating complex policy initiatives within election cycles. This is even truer for those at the assistant secretary or comparable levels than for cabinet secretaries. While the contemporaries of government senior political leaders in the private sector might be responsible for developing their successors, there is no comparable tradition in government. This is one of the factors that makes the challenge of leadership development in the public sector unique.

I need to be clear at this point. There have been and are many extraordinarily good leaders in the political ranks who have done an excellent job of leading change and in growing leaders in the career ranks—James Lee Witt at the Federal Emergency Management Agency (FEMA) and Phil Diehl at the U.S. Mint come immediately to mind. Colin Powell and Paul O'Neill certainly will be included among them as well. They are not only gifted leaders in their own right, they have stayed the course (or, in the case of Powell and O'Neill, likely will) to build the momentum for change over several years and leave a legacy of stronger career leaders after they depart.

While the George W. Bush administration has made a proposal to reduce the number of political positions to approximately 2,000, that will likely not change the culture of expectations for leadership development.

The recommendation here is to establish a clear mandate to Senior Executives that one of their primary tasks in the next three years will be to grow their successors. This is an initiative that can best be taken by the President's Management Council on behalf of the President.

For the Office of Personnel Management:

(5) Make mid-level manager, senior leader and executive mobility a requirement for assumption of future SES leadership responsibility.
This was a proposal that was offered in the last administration for the Senior Executive ranks but was quickly taken off the table. It needs to be re-examined in light of today's reality of how future leaders develop.

Mobility is a key to development of leaders as each of these five organizations has demonstrated in one way or another—intentional moves to new and challenging job-based experiences (not necessarily geographical). It is also a norm among the better private sector organizations we have reviewed. It isn't simply a perk nor is it a means to provide greater variety for managers and executives with an itch to move. It is critical to development and to breaking down the stovepiped barriers of culture that permeate almost every organization in some way. For the effective would-be executive, such opportunity is not a threat but an opportunity. But it takes leadership from the top by OPM and support from Senior Executives themselves as we have seen. Given purposeful policy direction from OPM this becomes a task not for the HR shops, but for the senior leadership of organizations like the five studied.

As we have seen in the leader development path, this opportunity must begin early on with mid-level managers or even with incoming future leaders. Movement from operational field assignments to staff assignments in the headquarters; rotation to other agencies or to other branches or levels of government; exchange assignments with leading private sector organizations—these should be the norm for progression to senior leadership. The days of growing expertise in one functional stovepipe or one agency alone should be drawing to a close.

If pay disparity is to be an issue for senior government leaders, then the career challenge disparity needs to be a gap that is also closed.

(6) Form a volunteer cadre of retiring Senior Executives and those who have already retired to consult back on a part time basis to government organizations as coaches, teachers and mentors of the successor generations.
Many observations have been made about the generation of leaders that is about to pass from the scene or has already departed and the resulting knowledge and leadership gap. Yet, current provisions make it

extremely difficult for these senior leaders to consult back to their organizations on a part time basis—a common practice in the private sector. I have found that many senior people have a great passion for public service and there are likely many who would accept an offer to serve as mentors, coaches, and teachers to help bring along the next generation of leaders.

This, as discussed, is also one of the very best sources for developing future leaders. These experienced leaders are people with the wisdom, the commitment, and the credibility. These are the people who will have the time and inclination to do what their present challenging jobs often deter—grow the next generation. Steps need to be taken now by OPM to revise the policies and to knock down the current barriers. OPM must also lead an effort with individual organizations to recruit those current and former leaders with a bent toward growing others, and to help prepare through selected training sponsored by OPM and the Federal Executive Institute to give back to the next generation from what they have received.

Appendix I:
Leadership Myths and Truths

This material is intended for those who want a more extensive exploration of the "why" issues in leader development. It is framed as a discussion of myth and truth. A bibliography is included for further background reading.

The basic principles or "lessons" for growing leaders and for initiating and managing an excellent program of succession are the antithesis of some well-honed myths about leadership. As we have seen these myths are dispelled by experience and results, which provide the foundation from which these lessons are drawn for others to apply within their own organization's culture.

For each myth there are key lessons of experience that contradict it.

The Six Leadership Myths

Myth 1: Leaders are born, not made.

The research of John Kotter, The Center for Creative Leadership, and others demonstrates that early experiences and even genetic wiring have very little to do with shaping a leader. Other than basic intelligence, few things are predictive of future leadership ability. Leaders can be and are being developed, and much research and experience has demonstrated the falsity of this pervasive myth. But it is still an excuse for doing little or nothing and letting nature take its course.

Myth 2: If leaders can be grown, they develop needed skills by attending leadership development training courses; the more expensive, the better the result.

Leaders are grown—say both the research findings and the applied lessons of that research in hundreds of excellent organizations—by the lessons of challenging and varied experiences, by the relationships they forge with senior leaders, and, most surprisingly, by the hardships of career and life experiences. Training courses (even the ones with the cachet of reputation and good marketing) are more like the teaspoon of salt in the pound of bread dough—a necessary catalyst but a relatively small part that is not tangibly evident in the outcome.

Myth 3: If leaders can be grown, the *best* people to accomplish this task are (a) trainers; (b) consultants; (c) the HR organization; (d) all of the above.

The reason that this is a myth is that the answer is (e) none of the above. The truth is that *the best people to accomplish this task are experienced*

Myths

Myths have always existed in societies as a means of explaining the seemingly unexplainable. When the ancient Greeks and Romans could not adequately understand why things happened, they posited the presence of gods—who watched over mankind and interacted with humans (often capriciously and with similar motives to humans). Both the Greeks and later the Romans were also fascinated with heroic leaders and would ascribe their skills to some form of human connection with the gods. Hence, Achilles was half god and half man, but also an archetype for all leaders.

While modern man tends to denigrate such naiveté, we still have our own myths that upon examination do not hold up any better under scrutiny. The problem is that many believe these myths and then implant them in the very marrow of their organizations—the culture. When applying the lessons of growing leaders to their own situations, senior leaders need to confront the myths that are likely present, if unspoken.

senior leaders, themselves. Experienced leaders have credibility, real life context, and understanding of the culture. They embody the core values and are committed to the core purpose of the organization and of public service. Senior leaders are not only exemplars of good leadership, but they act as coaches, mentors, and even teachers in the process of growing other leaders. That is how the best organizations produce leaders of the future.

It takes leaders to grow other leaders.

To be sure, senior leaders forge strategic partnerships with the HR shop, and use trainers and consultants as well as outside leader development courses. But the key players in all of this are the senior leaders themselves— throughout the organization. (That's one indicator, by the way, of a leader-centered culture).

Myth 4: Leaders are people who have gained expertise and capability in their field. (Its corollary is that there is serious career risk in moving to another functional area, to another agency, or to the field from the headquarters, and vice versa.)

The typical career path of most Senior Executives confirms the existence of this myth in the federal government: advancement to a senior leadership position within one career field and within one organization and often within either a "field" milieu or a "headquarters" milieu.

This myth is disproved rather simply. Get together some future (early to mid-career) leaders and ask them to describe the "great" leaders they have worked for and the "lousy" leaders. Having done this on a number of occasions, I can predict the results.

First, the qualities that people seek in those they will follow voluntarily are not those of capability and expertise in a chosen field, but those of character: integrity, courage, balance, emotional stability, caring and empathy, selfless service, and humility.

The whole subject of how to grow character in leaders is one that deserves separate treatment in far greater length. Suffice it to say that what successful organizations have found is that leaders with depth of character and capability, those with high EQ (emotional quotient), are most likely to be those who have been grown by varied and highly challenging experiences, including learning from life's hardships.

Often these leaders have gained a measure of *humility* by the occasional opportunity to learn something completely outside of their core expertise and to call upon those around them (rather than relying on their own expertise) for assistance in learning. Or perhaps they learn courage when asked to take on a challenge where failure is a real option and staying put offers security. Or they may learn *integrity* in a meaningful way when faced with complex ambiguity in an unfamiliar political or global environment that causes them to fall back upon what lies at the core of themselves and the organization—purpose and values. Or they learn to micromanage their team (among the deadliest of the negatives for "lousy" leaders) and to *trust* their people because they are no longer the resident experts.

In short, most leadership development patterns in government show that growing expertise in a single field has been the road to SES and to (apparent) external success. While it may still be an accurate description of the prevailing milieu today, it also confuses "great" leadership with position and rank and career success and flies in the face of the experience of the best organizations. Leadership excellence is not dependent on rank—it is a deception for some of those aspiring to lead.

Myth 5: Leadership is a "soft" skill that defies the tougher challenges of a performance management orientation and the measurement of hard results. (The corollary to this is that leader development is a task for those in the "soft" functions—HR and training—and not worth the time of senior leaders who engage in the "hard" functions like internal and external budget negotiations.)

The track record of those companies and more recently those federal organizations, that take leadership development seriously and link it to measurable outcomes is far superior to those who don't. What began more than a decade ago as an intuitive response to the need for a different type of leader to transform organizations to meet the challenge of change has now become an established understanding.

Myth 6: Senior Executives are not really the change leaders in their organizations, it is political appointees. If future leaders are to be grown, this is an initiative for the political cadre.

As we have seen, this is one leadership and leader development challenge that is the exclusive province of the public sector (the military and some law enforcement and intelligence agencies aside).

Paul Light has brought a consistent message over the years that the excessive growth in the layers of government with political appointees, Schedule C political support staff, and the use of non-career SES positions to augment political appointments have all worked to the detriment of effective public service in terms of accountability. For growing leaders, this is also true and has two chilling effects related directly to how leaders are grown over time.

One impact is that the initiative for growing leaders passes to those who are least able to invest significant time and energy in what is a long-term proposition. Political leaders have only a short time to implement the policies they wish to enact, and there is little hope of an immediate payoff in growing leaders. And as with every conclusive statement, there are fortunately some good exceptions to the rule—James Lee Witt at FEMA being a most recent example.

A second impact is that the challenging experiences that are so central to growing mature senior career leadership in the SES ranks are often confined primarily to those who are political. This is particularly true where political leaders who are leery of the incumbents do not overcome their initial suspicions of the career bureaucrats and isolate them from substantive discussions, meetings, and policy decision making. Where these responsibilities are seen as those of senior career leaders, the outcome is quite different.

Nevertheless, this is a myth that the public sector must work hard to overcome if the next generation of leaders is to be grown and if Senior Executives are to see this as their task. Senior career leaders must gain a mindset that is similar to that held by most general and flag officers in the military, who clearly see themselves as the stewards of the development of the next generation to follow them and take that role very seriously.

That attitude and mindset is missing among the majority of the career SES ranks. The culture of the bifurcation of leadership between career and political is still a conundrum in many ways. To some extent, the challenge is to draw back on the incoming administration's understanding of the "spoils" due them; to some extent it is to provide more opportunity for leadership by careerists through both better cooperation and better opportunity through reducing the sheer number of political appointees.

Appendix II:
VBA Leader Competencies by Level

Role/Scope	Leading Change	Leading People	Managing for Results	Business Acumen	Building Coalitions, Communications	Professional and Personal Growth	Customer Service
All employees including team leaders	• Creativity and innovation • Flexibility • Resilience • Adaptability	• Conflict management • Cultural awareness • Integrity/honesty • Teamwork • Commitment to people	• Accountability • Decisiveness • Problem solving • Bias for action • Judgement • Technical skills		• Interpersonal skills • Communication	• Willingness to learn • Continuous learning • Personal development	• Commitment to veterans and families • Responsive to veterans
First-Line Managers/Coaches	• Encourages innovation • Creative thinking • Implements change	• Empowers others • Team building • Develops people	• Risk management • Technical credibility • Information-based management	• Personnel management	• Influencing negotiating • Partnering	• Promotes learning • Coaches employees	• Recognizes excellent customer service
Mid-Level Managers (e.g., Division Chiefs)	• Strategic thinking • Establishes direction	• Develops managers/coaches	• Implementing organizational performance goals	• Resource management • Technology management	• Networking	• Provides opportunities for learning	• Empowers others to take action
Directors/Executives	• External awareness • Vision • Bench-marking	• Modeling organization values	• Goal setting • Monitoring organizational performance	• Financial management	• Political awareness	• Creative learning environment	• Breaks down barriers to good service • Establishes customer-oriented culture

Appendix III:
The VBA LEAD Program

This is offered once each year to promising GS 9-12 employees. The first class was comprised of 25 individuals, selected by senior leaders from a pool of over 150 applicants. The application process itself is designed to elicit basic experiential and biographical data and to allow candidates to reflect on various topics such as the strategic challenges facing VBA, their career plans, successes they have experienced, and their interest in future leadership.

Each candidate is expected to do a personal essay reflection on "Is This for Me?" It is a means of encouraging each person to consider whether leadership is what they aspire to and to help them understand the implications for future diverse leadership learning experiences including career geographic and functional moves. This exercise confronts individuals with the need to be honest about both the rewards and the pitfalls of leadership and with their own motives.

The LEAD Program has three weeks of formal training seminars during its nine month duration with 10 separate and varied learning components:

1. **Introduction to other VA organizational elements**—This is done through senior-level speakers from throughout the VA and from site visits to different aspects of VA operations in the field, including hospitals and cemeteries.

2. **Mentor Relationship**—A unique web-based process helps to identify the best pairings combining complementary experiences and the individual's desires. The mentor receives training, as does the mentee, to help gain organizational knowledge, develop a networking system, and to share experiences and advice along the way.

3. **Individual Development Plan (IDP)**—The IDP is based on feedback from personal assessment tools, and input from the mentor and home organization management.

4. **Team-building skills**—Each participant is assigned to work in teams on a variety of assignments, including strategic organizational issues, to help develop or enhance team-building skills, to strengthen leadership and interpersonal skills, and to provide a forum to explore contemporary management issues.

5. **Shadowing assignments**—Each participant selects his or her mentor, plus one of the division chiefs from the home station, preferably in a different division, to shadow for at least one week. The shadowing assignments are designed to give exposure to the challenges of managerial responsibilities and to different approaches to handling them by leaders outside of their normal organization experiences.

6. **Action learning assignments**—Either locally or at another location, office directors coordinate specific team-based assignments to provide work experiences that will strengthen leadership competencies (such as problem solving, conflict management, and written communication) through new challenges.

7. **Presentations**—Throughout the program, there are many opportunities to speak to the group and to senior officials through both spontaneous and planned presentations. As part of the final session of the program, there is a one-hour formal team presentation on the major action learning project.

8. **Management interviews**—Each participant conduct two interviews with senior management officials to gain management insights and knowledge to assist in developing a broader professional understanding.

9. **Assessment tools**—There are several forms of assessment (e.g., 360-degree assessments) used to help provide insights for team learning activities and for preparing the IDP.

10. **Self-study projects**—Several self-study projects are expected including extensive reading assignments and practical learning experiences conducted at the home office.

Endnotes

1. Ray Blunt, "Leaders Growing Leaders: Preparing the Next Generation of Public Service Executives," chapter five.

2. U.S. General Accounting Office, *High Risk: An Update* (GAO-01-263, January 2001).

3. U.S. Office of Personnel Management, *Office of Merit Systems Oversight and Effectiveness, Supervisors in the Federal Government: A Wake-Up Call,* (January 2001).

4. The PricewaterhouseCoopers Endowment for The Business of Government, *Results of the Government Leadership Survey: A 1999 Survey of Federal Executives,* (June 1999), p. 4.

5. John Kotter, *A Force for Change: How Leadership Differs from Management,* (Boston: Harvard Business School Press, 1993).

6. Edgar H. Schein, *Organizational Culture and Leadership, 2nd Edition,* (San Francisco: Jossey-Bass, 1992). These findings have been endorsed for several years by the leading companies in the private sector and help explain the great interest that has been shown in recent years in making the business case for growing leaders.

7. Mid-level and senior Coast Guard officers attend the professional military education senior service schools of the other services (e.g., the National War College, the Navy Command and Staff College).

8. See chapter five, "Leaders Growing Leaders," for a further discussion of Barnes' approach to growing leaders.

9. Blunt, ibid.

10. The following sources have been used as a basis for the research in this section: Cynthia D. McCauley, Russ S. Moxley, and Ellen Van Velsor, eds., *The Center for Creative Leadership Handbook of Leadership Development,* (San Francisco: Jossey-Bass, 1998); Jay A. Conger and Beth Benjamin, *Building Leaders: How Successful Companies Develop the Next Generation,* (San Francisco: Jossey-Bass, 1999); The Corporate Leadership Council, *The Next Generation: Accelerating the Development of Rising Leaders,* (Washington, D.C.: The Advisory Board Company, 1997); David Giber, Louis Carter, and Marshall Goldsmith, eds., *Best Practices in Leadership Development: Case Studies, Instruments, Training,* (Lexington, Mass.: Linkage Press, 1999); "Developing Leaders in the War for Talent," a presentation by McKinsey Company at the Wharton Leadership Conference, June 7, 2001; and the General Accounting Office, *Human Capital: Key Principles from Nine Private Sector Organizations,* (GAO/GGD-00-28, January 2000).

11. See particularly the General Accounting Office, *Human Capital: Key Principles from Nine Private Sector Organizations,* (GAO/GGD-00-28, January 2000) and The National Academy of Public Administration, *Managing Succession and Developing Leadership: Growing the Next Generation of Public Service Leaders,* (September 1997).

12. General Accounting Office, *High-Risk Series: An Update* (GAO-01-263, January 2001).

13. See Larry Bossidy, widely respected CEO of Allied Signal Corporation in his recent article in *Harvard Business Review,* "The One Job a CEO Cannot Delegate."

Bibliography

Conger, Jay A., and Beth Benjamin. *Building Leaders: How Successful Companies Develop the Next Generation.* San Francisco: Jossey-Bass Publishing, 1999.

Covey, Stephen. *Principle Centered Leadership.* New York: Simon and Schuster, 1990.

Giber, David, Louis Carter, and Marshall Goldsmith, eds. *Best Practices in Leadership Development Handbook.* Lexington, Mass.: Linkage Press, 1999.

Kotter, John. *A Force for Change: How Leadership Differs from Management.* New York: The Free Press, 1990.

Kotter, John P., and James L. Heskett. *Corporate Culture and Performance.* New York: The Free Press, 1992.

McCall, Morgan W., Jr., Michael M Lombardo, and Ann M. Morrison. *The Lessons of Experience: How Successful Executives Develop on the Job.* New York: Lexington Books, 1988.

McCall, Morgan W., Jr. *High Flyers: Developing the Next Generation of Leaders.* Boston: Harvard Business School Press, 1998.

McCauley, Cynthia D., Russ S. Moxley, and Ellen Van Velsor, eds. *The Center for Creative Leadership Handbook of Leadership Development.* San Francisco: Jossey-Bass, 1998.

Vicere, Albert A., and Robert M. Fulmer. *Leadership by Design: How Benchmark Companies Sustain Success Through Investment in Continuous Learning.* Boston: Harvard Business School Press, 1997.

Websites:

The Center for Creative Leadership, http://www.ccl.org/

The Council for Excellence in Government, Leadership Development, http://www.excelgov.org/leaddev/index.html

The Peter F. Drucker Foundation for Nonprofit Management, http://www.pfdf.org

The Federal Executive Institute and Management Development Centers, http://www.leadership.opm.gov/fei/index.html

The Wharton Leadership Digest, http://leadership.wharton.upenn.edu/digest/index.shtml

Leaders Growing Leaders: Preparing the Next Generation of Public Service Executives

Ray Blunt
Leadership Coach
Council for Excellence in Government
Washington, D.C.

This report was originally published in May 2000, revised January 2001.

Introduction[1]

"When organizations in every sector of society begin asking the same question at the same time, something is up. The question—raised with increasing frequency by leading public, private and nonprofit organizations—is, How do we develop the leaders our organizations require for an uncertain future?"[2]

Frances Hesselbein

The transformation of the business of government is in progress. It is both a response to the extreme urgency of the changing times in public service and a groundswell in the world of work in general. To navigate these times, and to respond to the forces of transformation, and, above all, to attract and retain the next generation of public servants will require, paradoxically perhaps, today's senior leaders to look far more intentionally to serve the future careers of others.

The legacy of today's senior public service leaders can be to leave behind the people, the culture, the systems, and above all the leadership at all levels—servant leadership—rooted in character and capability, that will ensure that public service truly serves the American people in the next generation. It is the task, likely the predominant task, of senior career leaders, primarily members of the Senior Executive Service (SES), to take the lion's share of the responsibility for building this legacy of future leaders from the ranks of the people with whom they work. There may be no more urgent or important task, but it is one that has gone largely begging for a solution.

This brief examination of the critical issue of the future of public service leadership focuses on how this task can best be accomplished. It points clearly to the following conclusion:

Public service leaders can best be grown through:

- The *examples* of character and capability set by senior leaders' lives;
- Deep and lasting relationships with exemplary senior leaders acting as *mentors*;
- A systematic and strategic combination of challenging and varied job experiences and *coaching* to learn leadership within these on-the-job experiences; and
- Well-crafted and systematic training and development programs that are grounded in practical reality, where leadership is learned through action and through deeply involved senior leaders as their *teachers*.

Understanding the Challenge

"Unlike the possibility of plague or nuclear holocaust, the leadership crisis will probably not become the basis for a best-seller or a blockbuster movie, but in many ways it is the most urgent and dangerous of the threats we face today, if only because it is insufficiently recognized and little understood."[3]

Warren Bennis

Leadership and the development of effective leaders is neither easy nor is it well understood. Growing or developing excellent leaders is not the same thing as producing excellent managers, and it does not occur in the same way. We look to each—managers and leaders —to produce certain outcomes that are essential to their times and to their circumstances.

Good managers produce outcomes that exemplify the very best bureaucracies—predictability, order, efficiency, and consistency. Change comes through gradual improvements. Managers accomplish such consistency through expertise in the functions of planning, budgeting, organizing, staffing, controlling, and problem solving.

Effective leaders produce an outcome of change, often dramatic and highly useful. They take people and organizations through significant change by exercising three important capabilities:

- setting a clear sense of direction with a compelling vision and crafting strategies to reach the vision,
- aligning people around that vision through clear and extensive communication, widespread involvement, and personal example, and
- motivating and inspiring others through satisfying important human needs that builds the energy to overcome barriers they will face.[4]

Character and Capability in Leaders Who Grow Leaders

Mark Huddleston set forth four qualities that senior executives themselves identify as important for leadership success: to have a clear strategic vision, the ability to animate others, an ethic of hard work, and personal integrity.[8]

However, in drilling deeper, the consistent qualities that emerge in the leaders who are not only successful but also grow other leaders would specifically include (in addition to personal integrity):

- An abiding focus on the core purpose of public service
- A deep (and demonstrated) belief in the worth and capabilities of people
- Courage—a willingness to take personal and organizational risks
- Personal caring about people

In a November 1999 study, Mark Huddleston interviewed 21 Distinguished Executive Rank Award winners from the 1997 senior executive class of recipients. He concluded that the current system for developing the next generation of leaders was "largely serendipitous." He cites both complacency and the lack of a coherent approach to developing true leaders (rather than functional experts) as at the heart of the problem.[5]

In 1999, the Ford Foundation, IBM, and the University of Colorado sponsored a national survey of over 600 thought leaders, practitioners, and leadership educators to address the question of future leadership in the public service. The findings were consistent with what other researchers have found in private sector studies—that there is a gap of leadership talent in the public service and that it will almost certainly grow in the next 20 years.

Further, both superior capability and sound character will be essential leadership abilities for public service leaders of the future, but that the latter—the development of character in leaders—is even more important than the former.[6] Their recommendations on how to grow these needed leaders are consistent with the central message of this report.

How Leadership Is Fostered: The Role of Leaders in Shaping Culture

John Kotter's studies of leadership reveal one penetrating finding that can be applied directly to public service. Those organizations that have an earned reputation for attracting and keeping the best talent and for developing a coterie of strong leaders all share something in common—they have a strong culture where *there are consistent shared norms and values concerning the importance of leadership.*

What Kotter concludes is essentially what Edgar Schein concluded nearly a decade before in his classic work *Organizational Culture and Leadership:* The capacity to shape cultural conditions that lead to learning and to the development of leaders that can produce change is the central task of the leader. Kotter's conclusion: "institutionalizing a leadership-centered culture is the ultimate task of leadership."[7]

How Leaders Are Grown: The Lessons of Example and Experience

If growing public service leaders is imperative for tomorrow's changing world, if there is a surfeit of managers and a dearth of public service leaders, if systematic approaches to developing future leaders are rare, and if the task of a leader is to help shape the culture within which leaders develop, what is the best course to take?

By now, it is better understood that, for the most part, leaders are not born—they are made; they are grown. The capabilities that are needed by leaders—the behaviors, skills, mindsets, and attitudes—can be learned; the character qualities of leaders can be shaped within an organization's culture. This puts to rest the most common myth that leaders are born. Both the excellent capabilities and the proven character needed in public service leaders can be "grown" within the organization itself.

These conclusions emerge from probably the best longitudinal body of research on growing leadership available today: the years of study and gathering of data on leaders by the Center for Creative Leadership (CCL) in Greensboro, North Carolina. In studies of leaders in the private sector, the nonprofit world, and the public sector, the findings are highly consistent. Successful leaders grow through particular sets of experiences.[9] CCL's findings place leader learning into four broad categories:

- Challenging job assignments—42%
- Learning from others' examples—22%
- Hardships and setbacks—20%
- Other events—16% (including training and education)

Challenging job assignments are those that stretch the individual. CCL has identified the types of job experiences that produce leadership learning:

- a change in the scope of a job;
- a job that requires a "fix it" opportunity;
- a job that needs to be started from scratch;
- line to staff or staff to line switches (including headquarters to field); and
- projects and task forces that require new skills or learning but where the individual remains on the job.

All of these job-based experiences challenge, stretch, and grow the individual—and produce leader learning. For the leader who wishes to grow leaders, such an understanding is critical. This is, however, a notion that runs counter to the way that government managers typically develop—within their functional, organizational, and geographic "stovepipes," and through training programs attended by individuals—"largely serendipitously."

Leaders Beget Leaders and Leave a Legacy

We see clearly that the task of growing leaders may be as important a task as can be found today in public service and as important a "result." That there are more leaders needed, particularly leaders with new capabilities and solid character, is perhaps intuitively obvious. That leaders develop within a leader-centered culture—one best shaped by leaders themselves—and that leaders develop over time primarily through challenging and diverse experiences is also clear. But, more importantly, what also emerges is that the central role in this drama is not played by leadership training programs alone, though they are important; nor by replicating "best practices," though they are certainly instructive.

Noel Tichy, University of Michigan professor, former head of executive development for General Electric (GE), and long-time consultant to GE and numerous other top organizations, benchmarked many of the best organizations in the world in growing excellent leaders. These included Hewlett-Packard, the U.S. Special Operations Command, Tenneco, AlliedSignal, ServiceMaster, Shell Oil, and the exemplary nonprofit Focus: HOPE, among others. What he found in the very best organizations was highly consistent:

> Winning companies win because they have good leaders that nurture the development of other leaders at all levels of the organization. *The key ability of winning organizations and winning leaders is creating leaders.*[10] (emphasis added)

He saw certain fundamentals demonstrated over and over again despite wide disparity in the types of organizations (including public sector), the leaders, and the cultures. The leaders with a proven track record of successfully growing leaders:

- Assume personal responsibility for developing other leaders.
- Have a "teachable point of view" that they can articulate and show others how to make the organization work effectively, how to grow others, what behaviors are needed, and what values are essential.
- Embody their teachable point of view in "stories" about the past and stories about a visionary future.
- Generate positive energy and encourage other leaders while making tough decisions.
- Devote considerable time to developing other leaders and have approaches that normally involve vulnerability, openness, and a willingness to admit mistakes, thus serving as effective role models.

We now turn to an examination of how these principles can be employed by senior leaders to help grow the next generation of public service leaders—leaders with capability and character who will serve the American people. Then we will take a look at how these principles have been embodied in the lives of three outstanding public service leaders in their roles as exemplar, mentor, coach, and teacher.

Lessons in How to Grow Public Service Leaders

"The ultimate test for a leader is not whether he or she makes smart deci-sions and takes decisive action, but whether he or she teaches others to be leaders and builds an organization that can sustain its success even when he or she is not around."[11]

Noel Tichy

We are accustomed now to the notion of a leader being a lifelong learner and someone who helps build a learning organization. "Teaching," as a generic term, is simply the transmission of personal learning and wis-dom from a leader to others. Exemplary leaders see it as their responsibility and their legacy to grow the next generation. At the end of the day, that is the only way that successful change is sustained.

In that respect, leaders not only learn to be leaders, they learn to be effective "growers"—developers of other leaders able to translate the lessons of their experience into helping others to become leaders. Leaders beget leaders. So where do you begin if this is your objective as a senior leader?

This section focuses on four roles—four areas of action where you can focus your efforts in growing the next generation of public service leaders:
* Growing leaders through personal example—as an *exemplar*
* Growing leaders through significant relationships—as a *mentor*
* Growing leaders through varied experiences—as a *coach*
* Growing leaders through development programs—as a *teacher*

Following this section, three outstanding leaders are profiled. These are public service leaders who have produced significant results and have made a priority of successfully growing other leaders.

Growing Leaders Through Personal Example: As an *Exemplar*

Leadership by example is not a new concept. As Peter Drucker cogently points out, leaders are defined by having followers. Leaders are followed more for who they are as observed by their behavior than for what title they have or how expert they are. In essence, followers choose their leaders. What may be new, however, is the perspective that people learn leadership from you *whether you intend for them to or not*; whether you are an excel-lent leader or not. Simply think about the leaders who have had the great-est influence on you—the ones you want to emulate and the ones you never wanted to be like. Both have helped to shape you. Now think about the people who have worked for you and with you over the years. If they were interviewed about your leadership story, what would they have learned?

The Center for Creative Leadership found that some of the most telling leadership lessons came from simply observing leaders in action. Ironically, the lessons learned came from both good and bad leaders. That knowledge alone should spur leaders to be more aware of the congruency between their talk and action—walk the talk—and to be more conscious of involving younger leaders in their sphere of action. But that can often produce a need to project perfection. Actually the contrary is true.

As Tichy discovered, the best role models were also the ones who were personally vulnerable, open, and honest about their mistakes. As we will see in the lives of the three exemplary leaders identified for this report, it is primarily the personal and character qualities that stand out in people's minds when they discuss leaders they have known. It is those aspects of personal character they exemplify that win them the "right," if you will, to serve others through mentoring, coaching, and teaching. Character and capability in a leader cannot be separated.

While this may be the most important aspect of leaders growing leaders—by their example of character and capability—it is certainly the most elusive to "learn." How can you know if you are setting an example that others want to follow, and how can you become a more effective example?

Many, if not most, who benchmark leadership programs use a method that is designed to get at this issue—360-degree feedback. It is a common best practice to help leaders identify their strengths and weakness; examine the consistency between what they believe about themselves and what others see; and analyze the relationship between "walk" and "talk." Why? Simply because most senior leaders receive less and less feedback the further up the ladder they go. Often their view of their own strengths goes back several years, and those so-called strengths now may be weaknesses.

For example, the self-starting, highly reliable independent thinker may find herself in a situation that calls for significant collaborative relationships and team building. What worked and was valued has now become a hindrance, and a factor that separating her from her colleagues and subordinates. For reasons such as this, many top-flight organizations have identified not only their corporate culture values, but the behaviors that they want to embed in the culture by the example of their leaders. Such feedback from peers and subordinates as well as from superiors—360-degree feedback—combines to provide self awareness and the opportunity to make changes.

Not only is the solicitation of such feedback an opportunity to learn and to change, but it also exhibits an openness and a vulnerability that are important components of exemplary leadership.

Another important place to begin setting an example is in serving rather than seeking to be served.

If our ... organizations are going to live up to their potential, we must find, develop, and encourage more people to lead in the service of others. Without leadership, [organizations] cannot adapt to a fast moving world. But if leaders do not have the hearts of servants, there is only the potential for tyranny.[12]

It was Robert Greenleaf, former head of Management Research for AT&T, who brought the notion of servant leadership into board rooms and executive suites. In his book *Servant Leadership*, he lays out the long known principles and precepts that those who seek to lead must first seek to serve others—to live out a selfless attitude. A motivation of serving others first is one that is particularly appropriate for leaders in the public service, but it goes beyond customer or public service. It includes the sense that a leader is willing to devote his time, attention, and energies to the development of the careers of others—not simply his own. The political culture often subtly affects the already inherent bent that we all have toward self-promotion. Counterintuitively, it is in seeking to serve the development needs of others and their careers that leaders can best set an example that others will emulate and follow.

When the agenda is all about "my needs, my demands, my schedule, my priorities, and my 'face time' with superiors," then it is unlikely that any initiatives to coach, mentor, or teach others will have any more credibility than a formal speech. To get at this, 360-degree feedback may be extremely helpful, but this is also an area that can use some self-reflection. Most of us rarely stop to seriously consider what we are doing with our lives and our time in relationships at work (or outside work, for that matter). The 30-day calendar exercise may be one way to get at this and to begin a systematic plan of serving the next generation of leaders.

Being congruent in action and speech and seeking to serve others before self are two character qualities that distinguish a leader who grows other leaders through example. These qualities also are essential for growing others through mentoring relationships.

Growing Leaders Through Relationships: As a *Mentor*

When Odysseus went off to war, he placed his young son, Telemachus, in the care of an older, wiser man who would advise the young boy and help him to mature should his father not return. By the time Odysseus returned after the war and his long journey home, Telemachus was a man. He had matured not only physically, but in character and wisdom and in war-fighting skill: He was all that his father had dreamed of. Odysseus owed much to the man who helped raise his son. That man's name? Mentor.

To clarify some things about this role, a mentor is not a supervisor, although supervisors can be mentors. A mentor is not a "coach," although coaches can be mentors as well; coaches typically focus on certain skills, not the whole person's potential. (We will discuss the role of leader as coach in the next section.) And a mentor is not a teacher in the strictest sense. While there are clearly aspects of formal teaching in being a mentor, teachers usually work with groups, not individuals. Even within the context of this report, a leader is not necessarily a mentor, but *all leaders should become mentors who help a few others learn to lead*. That is one lesson that Noel Tichy learned from looking at great organizations. And that is a lesson today's public service leaders must heed if the next generation of leaders is to be grown effectively.

Being a mentor is not complex, does not require extensive training, and is not a full-time job. In the best organizations where mentoring occurs, mentoring is not even a formal program, although it can be. All that said, a senior leader can easily become a mentor by keeping a couple of things in mind and then doing just a few key things.

We have already discussed the importance of blocking time on your calendar and reflecting on some of your "stories," which form the basis for others to learn from your experience.

Remember, it's not about you. It is about the people you are mentoring. This is not a power trip or recognition that you know best what is right for another or that you want this person to champion your cause in the organization. At its best, this leader/mentor role is simply servant leadership. Your role is to serve the learning needs of another by building and sustaining a long-term relationship whose objective is to help the other person grow, learn, and reach their potential. To do this you give up some of yourself, including your time, for building toward the future.

You must also keep in mind that the coin of the realm in mentoring is trust, earned trust. Above all, this is a trusting relationship, normally between an older and a younger person. Before you begin mentoring, understand that to effectively build trust there needs to be both mutual honesty and mutual vulnerability laced with deep respect for confidences. A mentor is not to feel like she needs to be a heroine with no visible flaws. Openness to mistakes of the past and learning from them is one of the best "stories" that can be shared. Honesty about fear, doubt, nervousness, and uncertainty are lessons of life that help protégés understand that a leader doesn't always feel inside what is seen from the outside.

So what do you do? First, find a protégé. Look around you at the people who have potential. This is harder than you think. Most of us want to mentor someone just like us—people we are the most comfortable with. But if your interest is in the future of the person and of the organization, you may want to step back and ask yourself if the person you might want as your protégé is really the person with the most potential. You might also want to consider individuals with whom you already have some connection other than a strictly boss to employee situation. Are there people who already ask your advice from time to time? This is a good place to start. Now, what do you do?

In a way, it's like being a good parent—you simply spend some time together in a variety of settings: breakfast, lunch, taking a walk, sitting in your office, at your home, playing racquetball, taking a bike ride—you get the point.

What is the content? Bobb Biehl recommends that you start by asking a couple of questions, and using this simple framework as a point of departure. The questions are: What are your priorities? How can I help you?[13] The easiest topics will likely surround work issues—a problem employee, to stay or not to stay in public service, when to look for a new position elsewhere, how to deal with a pushy congressional staffer, what to do about a boss who won't make a decision.

The key skill you will need is listening—really listening to the words and the tone of voice, and observing the body language. Most leaders find it far easier to simply solve the problem for a person or to tell them what to do. Mentors need to be about helping people make their own way while sharing their experiences and perhaps some options to think about. Similar situations help serve as illustrations, particularly if it is something you struggled with and didn't have a slam-dunk success.

Mentoring, in the sense discussed here, has as its objective not simply helping people to learn, but to learn to become better leaders. That can often mean encouragement to take risks, to break cultural "rules," to get outside the comfort zone or to get out of a career stovepipe. Sometimes it can be helping a person get his or her life into balance when it has become overloaded with work, with no time for "saw sharpening" or decompression, or being with the family, or just having fun. Sometimes it's helping with parenting advice when the burden has become too heavy. So while listening is key, if the objective is leadership, some judicious and caring encouragement (gentle pushing) is often called for as well.

Finally, a good mentor understands the organization culture and the external stakeholders' worlds as well. Introducing your protégés to people and helping them to become exposed to a level of the organization that they will be part of in the future is also an important part of helping them to grow. It's not playing politics; exposure and an opportunity to observe are critical. Let them see you in action if that is not a part of their normal routine and let them give you input. Part of what is learned is "caught" from simply "hanging out" in a work setting with a more experienced person and observing what occurs.

One additional note: If senior leaders take responsibility to mentor two or three others, much like the example of Paul Barnes, at the Social Security

Administration (see page 181 for his profile), this relationship does not depend entirely upon being in a formal position. Certainly experience is the critical commodity, but it is not one that diminishes significantly over time. A mentoring relationship is one that can extend into formal retirement from public service and is a role that more senior leaders should consider establishing—even after they retire. Public service has lost many good senior leaders over the past several years, many to early retirement. They are a scarce resource who still have something to contribute.

Growing Leaders Through Experiences: As a *Coach*

Any senior leader potentially can be a mentor of another whether they are in the same organization or even whether the mentor is actively employed or retired, because the essence of mentoring lies in the relationship. However, being a coach typically requires some form of a leadership role in the organization because here the focus is experiential.

Returning to how leaders are grown, the most significant factors that grow leaders are challenging job-based experiences. A good leadership coach will make it a matter of utmost priority not only to have strong relationships with future leaders at all levels, but also to invest in their growth through intentionally ensuring they get the necessary experiences to become future leaders.

Senior leaders do not "manufacture" other leaders. What you can do, however, is to create the conditions and shape the culture under which people with potential learn and acquire the leadership attributes needed by the organization and public service. You help them to grow in the capabilities and the character which enlarge their capacity to produce change and significant results through others. How would this work? What are some of the things you might do?

Take a look at some of the examples of the three leaders profiled. (The profiles section begins on page 179). Leo Wurschmidt of the Veterans Benefits Administration would take many casual, informal opportunities to talk to people, encouraging them to take new assignments, to take a risk and move to a different type of job or to a different location. Paul Barnes did the same both informally and by reassigning people to work for him in ways that would stretch them. Dr. Janet Woodcock at the Center for Drug Evaluation and Research would spend time with small groups of future leaders, listening to their experiences and offering options. They each made it a point to get younger managers into programs that would allow for developmental assignments and likely job changes.

Each of these individuals created and encouraged developmental opportunities, spent time with both groups and individuals, and had a hand in shaping the infrastructure that supported such leader growth. These examples suggest three actions, that senior leaders in their role as coach can take to help grow other leaders.

Forming individual coaching relationships

Coaching, by its nature, has many elements of individual relationship. In that sense, it is like mentoring. However, the intent of coaching is to create job-based conditions where people learn leadership. This involves:
- challenging others to take initiatives to get out of their comfort zone;
- creating specific opportunities for such stretch work through job changes, job rotation, reassignments, team projects;
- advocating for them to others for such changes; and
- being a "noodge"—helping others to reflect on what they are learning, being a sounding board for problems, and encouraging and even prodding at times to make sure that stagnancy and discouragement don't set in.

Such learning isn't always comfortable. There are organizational cultures where coaching is expected, and cultures where it never occurs. The military, sports, and performing arts are examples of where active coaching for the development of individuals and groups is the norm. Those may be environments that are worthwhile benchmarking for lessons to be applied to certain public service cultures where development is often more passive and individualistic.

"Teaching" how to learn leadership

Here is one place where reflecting on your own leadership and life stories can pay dividends. Many people you will coach do not take the time to reflect on what they are learning or even have a framework for doing so. Typically, early in one's career the habit of simply "churning" at the work for the day is about all that can be managed. By telling others your stories of how you learned from situations similar to the ones they are experiencing, you give them a framework into which their experiences can be fit. You don't have to give them answers; in fact, that doesn't promote learning. Rather, let them use your metaphors and experiences as a means for encouraging their own reflection and learning.

You can also ask questions—a central coaching technique—which helps others learn by reflecting on what is occurring or may occur at work. No lesser light than Socrates pioneered this technique and it remains a good method. Simply asking your protégés questions that cause them to think about what they are seeing or what actions they might take or what they may have missed can be very helpful in leader learning without micromanaging—a deadly leadership sin that takes energy right out of a person.

You can also do periodic organizational "post mortems" after key stages of projects. Putting the entire team in the room and engaging in an honest self critique—senior leaders included—does much to make the point that we are all able to learn from our experiences.

The Army uses such an approach in "after action" debriefings of exercises, where all of the members of a team are quizzed on what happened in a particular scenario, what was going through their minds, why certain decisions were made or certain actions taken, why hesitancy occurred—from colonel on down to second lieutenant. Candid feedback among everyone, without regard to rank, is strongly encouraged as a means to build more openness and enhance the synergy of a team. It is a more active and vulnerable approach to coaching, but one that demonstrates that everyone can learn and profit from each other. You might want to try it out as a coaching technique and as a means of setting an example of openness to constructive criticism.

Active involvement

There are many opportunities for more active involvement—some of which are suggested in the approaches of the three exemplary leaders. These can range from reassigning a promising person to your staff, rotating a high-potential person into a temporary executive assistant or special assistant role, selecting a person to head a special projects team, or intervening with one of your colleagues to transfer a key member of your organization to their area for developmental purposes.

Growing Leaders Through Development Programs: As a *Teacher*

While the culture of public service and the lack of role models are often seen as barriers to growing excellent leaders, so too is the lack of sufficient resources to grow leaders. Translated this means that with the wholesale and often random down-sizing that has been occurring in the last decade, there simply are not the financial resources available for leadership programs.

The options for many organizations are seen as cutting even more people or cutting the margins. The margins are quite often identified as training, travel, and equipment or supplies. Hence, there is a tacit assumption that little can be done to develop leaders if resources are short. While this assumption can easily be challenged on its merits (if people are our top priority, why do we cut people programs first?), among the very best practices for growing leaders are those that are in-house, leader-led, and experiential.

Typically, the role of trainer or facilitator in a leadership development program is considered to be the domain of expert consultants, in-house trainers, or the HR development staff. But, as Tichy found, the very best companies and the very best leaders are themselves the leadership program trainers. This does not mean the token appearance of the "boss" to give the opening remarks in a program or to drop by to see how things are going. Leaders have learned practical lessons, most likely grounded in good theory as well, that only they can pass on in a way that others will want to learn. A "classroom" setting is a good place for such wisdom to be transferred.

Adult learning is centered on what is practical, not simply what is factually true. That is why even the best, most entertaining speakers, trainers, and consultants rarely have a long-term impact. The stories that a leader can tell—often about hard-won experiences, sometimes about failure—are stories that stick and can be applied. (Another good reason to develop your stories.)

GE's former CEO, Jack Welch, the legendary business leader, prided himself on having taught every two weeks at their leadership course in Crotonville, New York, for over 15 years. He actively taught, passed on his stories of change, helped embed the corporate values and "no boundaries" mindset, and served as a coach to participants in these programs. Over the years, he influenced thousands of today's leaders at GE—many that now run the company. But perhaps what GE may be best known for is their use of action learning as a means of developing future leaders. We turn now to what is perhaps one of the best approaches that a leader-teacher can use to grow other leaders.

The effectiveness of action learning and its use in the best organizations[15] builds on the basic understanding of how leaders are grown that was outlined earlier, aspects of which can be seen in the approaches of the three exemplary leaders.

How would it work in your organization? There are seven key elements—each of which can occur as part of a leadership development program without significant expenditure of resources. Such initiatives depend strongly on the direct involvement of senior leaders in the process to produce two things every organization covets: real results and the growth (and testing) of future leaders.

A sponsor

It is important that a senior person sponsor the commissioning of an important project that is essential to the organization—a strategic imperative—and which will take a team to do it successfully. Typically it should be a project that will require out-of-the-box thought, benchmarking of private sector and public sector organizations, and the learning of some new skills. The sponsor both gives the charge to the team and is the person who holds the team accountable for final, well-documented recommendations. The sponsor should also be in a position to make a decision or to get a decision promptly.

A process

This is a leadership learning process. As such, some idea of the approach to be taken needs development. While not complex, it will need to be explained to the team that is formed. Typically it consists of a selected strategic issue; a timeframe for work and bringing recommendations back for decision; the use of experienced coaches who are currently leaders in the organization; and the provision of some form of "just in time" training on team skills, benchmarking, or any technical expertise that will be needed. The key point is to have an approach firmly fixed, and the senior "faculty" and staff identified and briefed.

A team(s)

The team is often composed of individuals from various parts of the organization, selected because of leadership potential for participation in this project. There could also be more than one team to look at various aspects of a problem or vision challenge or to tackle the same project with competing approaches. It is similar to what Dr. Janet Woodcock has done at CDER in using the Council for Excellence in Government Fellows to spearhead special projects and to build their vision and mission. Keep in mind the purpose is twofold: learning leadership through challenging experience and producing a significant change initiative or problem solution.

A project

The sponsor or the senior team identifies the nature of the project. The project team then proceeds to gather data, conduct analyses, and frame findings, conclusions and recommendations for presentation for decision. The primary basis of the learning is in the doing.

A learning of new approaches and applications

Here is where periodic forums such as short skill workshops can be interjected. Other useful resources might include a speaker from an organization that has done something similar, a benchmarking visit to such an organization, bringing in someone from the staff or elsewhere in government with expertise in an area needed, an excellent video presentation, or outside workshop. There might also be time set aside for coaches to tell their leadership stories or for interim check-ins to explore problems or issues.

A presentation

At the point allotted in the project, a formal presentation, often accompanied by a written report, is delivered to the sponsor or the senior team. It is a decision-making forum where tough questions are asked and where professional quality work is expected. A thorough airing of what was done and how and why the recommendations are being made is expected. A decision within a short period of time by the sponsor or the senior team is also part of the agreement. Team members can also be selected for implementing the decision.

A debrief and reflection

The key to embedding the learning is to learn from the experiences of the project. Here is where senior coaching is critical—to help individuals ask themselves the tough questions, to share candid observations about each individual's contributions and areas for learning, to provide opportunity for team feedback to each other. Areas for further individual development and for organizational process improvement are typically identified as a result of this reflection.

Profiles of Three Exemplary Public Service Leaders

To better understand how leaders actually grow leaders, three case studies were developed which show how the following senior executives have worked to develop the next generation of leaders in their organization:

- Leo Wurschmidt, Veterans Benefits Administration, Department of Veterans Affairs
- Paul Barnes, Social Security Administration
- Janet Woodcock, Food and Drug Administration, U.S. Department of Health and Human Services

Growing the Next Generation of Leaders in the Veterans Benefits Administration

The legacy of exemplary senior leaders is not found in plaques or awards, but in the people they have invested time and effort in developing. This is a trait to look for in identifying true servant leaders. In this, Leo Wurschmidt apparently excelled, particularly in the example he set and in the many informal ways in which he coached and encouraged others.

As an Exemplar

Perhaps the outstanding characteristic that people noticed and now seek to emulate is Wurschmidt's abiding belief in the importance of the people of the organization. In a thousand ways he demonstrated this by investing his time and energy in others. He knew the names of hundreds of people who worked for him—their families as well. He took enormous

Leo Wurschmidt
Veterans Benefits Administration,
Department of Veterans Affairs (VA)

Leo Wurschmidt had a long and distinguished career in the VA, holding significant positions of responsibility in all three operational administrations within the VA: those overseeing health care and hospitals; cemeteries and memorials; and the provision of financial and other benefits. He served as an operational field director in San Francisco and Winston-Salem, North Carolina, and he also served in the headquarters as executive assistant to the deputy secretary and as a senior staff official for planning, management, and policy studies.

He served as the southern area director for veterans benefits with responsibility for one of four national regions of the country before health reasons forced him to step down to assume the position of director of the Jackson, VA, regional office.

Wurschmidt attended Columbia and George Washington Universities and graduated with a bachelor of arts degree in political science. He served four years in the U.S. Marine Corps from 1968 to1972.

In 1999 he was named a Meritorious Executive and was also the recipient of the 1999 Leadership VA Alumni Award for superior career leadership. Mr. Wurschmidt passed away in 2001.

---

amounts of time to personally write thank you notes, even for the smallest actions. He was a ubiquitous presence in the office, talking to people informally, and encouraging, questioning, and praising. Everyone interviewed about Wurschmidt mentioned how they make a practice of taking time for others as a result of Leo's example. In his conversations with employees, he often shared his experiences in many different positions and encouraged others to seek new assignments that would allow them to grow.

As a Mentor

He also was known as a willing and open mentor of individuals in the departmental SES Candidate Development Program, sharing an extensive amount of time with these individuals.

What came up most frequently in interviews, however, was not his more formal roles, but the daily time that he took to sit down and talk with people about their future plans and career aspirations. Perhaps because of his own varied career experiences, Wurschmidt was often known to encourage people to seek new experiences in other parts of the organization and outside the organization, and to get into training. He put them on details to widen their knowledge and experience.

He also promoted his people behind the scenes to senior leaders, championing their careers, often in a way that people only found out about much later. It was this selfless use of his time informally mentoring and encouraging people to think about their future that may be his most important legacy.

As a Coach

Wurschmidt made diversity a priority and took action to develop people. He forged a partnership with a historic black university (Jackson State), giving young interns their first experience in public service.

He also was a key person on the Executive Appraisal Team, which established a balanced scorecard combining results and peer assessments of teamwork as a means of developmental feedback for senior executives.

As a Teacher

Wurschmidt was one of the key senior people instrumental in beginning the first Leadership Enhancement and Development Program (LEAD), which was established to identify minorities and women in mid-career at the VA who possess leadership potential and to offer them training and experience. Despite his position as a high-level executive with heavy responsibilities, he also took time to teach at the VBA Development Academy for up and coming employees.

Growing the Next Generation of Leaders in the Social Security Administration

The comments consistently made about Paul Barnes give a clue to one of his most noteworthy qualities—he truly believes that it is critical to invest the time, thought, and effort in bringing forward the next generation of SSA leaders. But the evidence also shows that he deeply understands how to grow leaders, particularly by the example of his life and the quality of his caring investment of time in the lives of others.

As an Exemplar

Barnes's deep commitment to public service and to the people served is perhaps best embodied in the admonition that several people mentioned—"Treat people the way you would want your mother or father to be treated." When he said caring, commitment, and compassion were what public service was about and when he said that the "security" in Social Security is the heart of the mission, those lessons stuck. And they stuck because he walked the talk, which others now emulate. The simple image of older people being someone's mother or father is one that others now use and model in their relationships.

SSA's Leadership Development Strategy[15]

SSA is one of the few agencies in government that has a clearly developed strategic plan that links their long-term strategy with the development of future leaders. This is a "best practice" of the best in business. The more common approach in government is to see leadership development as a program for individuals—with responsibility for it in the HR shop—and as an ad hoc process.

While the key operational thrusts of the agency's strategic plan are:

- To deliver customer-responsive world-class service, and
- To promote valued, strong and responsive programs and conduct effective policy development and research,

the key goal for the people who deliver the service and the programs is:

- To be an employer that values and invests in each employee.

With a potential retirement-eligible population of 82% of the current SES rank leaders, 91% of the GS-15 senior managers, and 93% of the GS-14 senior managers, SSA faces a wave of change in its leadership ranks.

Their strategy to grow the next generation of leaders has been ongoing for some time. Paul Barnes has been one of the key line managers and advocates and is now the overall leader of the HR programs that undergird the strategy. In essence, it is a strategy that includes programs for leaders at all levels:

- SES Candidate Development Program (SESCDP)
- Advanced Leadership Program (ALP)
- Leadership Development Program (LDP)
- Presidential Management Intern Program (PMI) for initial accession

These national-level programs are primarily two years in duration. They involve, in each case, an orientation and some core training; the use of developmental experiences where individuals are taken off their job and placed into challenging assignments for on-the-job leadership learning; and the use of senior mentors for coaching and advice.

By all accounts it is a highly successful model and parallels the "best practices."

The factors that contribute to the success of this approach include:

- Making a business case for leader development that would communicate to decision-makers and supervisors;
- Getting clear executive buy-in and deep involvement; and
- Using the National Academy of Public Administration "best practices" study as a foundation (See Appendix IV under Growing Leaders—"Best Practices" In Organizations).

As a Mentor

Over the years, Barnes was a mentor to countless individuals at SSA who are now, themselves, moving into key positions.

He reached out to many younger persons over the years and remains in contact with them, serving as a source of advice by phone from anywhere in the country. One of his mentoring practices that was cited was the way he exposed his protégés to other senior people. Barnes would take them on trips to the headquarters office or to other regions and championed their careers or their selection into key leader development programs, even though it meant losing these key people for periods of up to two years.

People that he has mentored say that they now practice the same techniques in their leadership roles. They cite such skills as having learned to really listen to both sides. They also try to mimic Barnes's calm practice when dealing with tough issues and people issues. And they are developing others by encouraging them to stretch and grow through new assignments, national leadership programs, and serving as mentors themselves.

As a Coach

Barnes gave people the opportunity to learn and develop as leaders everywhere he went. Consider these comments:

Paul was always interested in bringing along new leaders—he challenged us to try new things outside of our comfort zone.

He appointed me to a new position that challenged and stretched me. He used it as a development opportunity to give a bigger picture of the organization.

Job-based challenges was one practice he used consistently and intentionally. A good example was the "open door coordinator"—a position reporting directly to him as regional commissioner and a communication channel to him with the people of the organization. It was a job that required the utmost of understanding and wisdom in listening to any employee who had a concern with management decisions. The person had to develop a broad understanding of the wider Social Security operations, an exposure to multiple offices, and a range of managerial approaches. Negotiating and listening skills were also central.

The coordinator was able to discuss differing approaches to solutions with Barnes and to draw upon his years of experience. The coordinator also accompanied him on visits to local offices and got to watch firsthand how Barnes worked with local managers and interacted with front-line people, often taking a turn himself interviewing clients or answering phones. Almost without knowing it, the coordinator was getting a crash course in

Paul D. Barnes
Social Security Administration (SSA)

Paul Barnes has served in SSA in a number of highly responsible and visible capacities around the country at all levels for the past 32 years. Currently, Barnes is the deputy commissioner for human resources, a position he has held since March 1997. He is responsible for SSA's people programs for all 65,000 employees, and chairs the National Partnership Council as well.

He has held key leadership roles as director of the Southeastern Program Service Center in Birmingham, Alabama; deputy regional commissioner of the Atlanta region; regional commissioner of the Chicago region; and the assistant deputy commissioner for Social Security operations.

Barnes is the recipient of three Presidential Rank Awards for public service leadership excellence and two "Hammer" awards for significant reinvention initiatives to improve government service for the American people. He has twice received the SSA Commissioner's Citation (the highest award in the Social Security Administration) and has appeared in Outstanding Young Men in America and Who's Who in Black America. In 1997, the Federal Executive Institute Alumni Association selected him as the Federal Executive of the Year.

He is a magna cum laude graduate of Lane College and holds a master's in public administration from the University of Southern California.

leadership on the front lines through involvement and observation. In retrospect, each person who held that position realized that.

In some cases, Barnes would spot a potential leader in a local office and select that person despite an apparent lack of all the credentials. That confidence made a big difference in the way the people perceived themselves.

Barnes also challenged people to be mobile. Perhaps it was his own experiences throughout his career, but he preached the importance of gaining a broader perspective that can only be learned through a variety of situations.

As a Teacher

Paul's own response to the question of the legacy he hoped he would leave behind is most telling about his role as teacher. He immediately said that it was investing in people's lives and helping others understand why that is so important. He felt that the career and leadership development programs in SSA that he helped to launch (see the separate sidebar on the SSA strategy) would live on. Paul Barnes is clearly meeting the central test of leadership; his greatest legacy may be, in the words of one person he has mentored over the years, "written in the lives of the people he has touched."

Growing the Next Generation of Leaders in the Center for Drug Evaluation and Research (CDER)

At the heart of Dr. Janet Woodcock's long-term strategy to change the culture at CDER to one that is outward focused on citizens' needs has been a commitment to developing an entirely new generation of leaders. And at the heart of that strategy has been the use of a leadership development program for the highest potential individuals at the GS-14 and GS-15 levels, primarily through the year-long Council for Excellence in Government Fellows Program. As the director of a very large and publicly visible organization, Dr. Woodcock nonetheless has taken the time to develop others around her and to leave a legacy of a changed culture for the next generation.

As an Exemplar

Courage is an often-overlooked trait in the leader of a non-military organization. Yet to take the people of a large organization through significant cultural change, many of whom are in opposition, requires not only persistence but courage. And courage is as contagious as cowardice. One of the things that Dr. Woodcock seems to have imparted by her example has been the courage of younger managers to become engaged in the Fellows leadership development program and to take on extra results projects that might well cause difficulty with other managers. The very association with such programs was not seen early on in the change process as career enhancing. Dr. Woodcock's own example and willingness to meet often with Fellows and to talk privately in her office despite all of the pressures on her spoke volumes and allowed other managers to emulate her.

As a Mentor

Dr. Woodcock spends enormous amounts of her personal time at lunch with individuals and groups, engaging in small meetings, and having a very open door—particularly to any fellow.

As a Coach

Dr. Woodcock also demonstrates, according to many observers, a sensitivity to coaching—asking questions, drawing out people's thinking, and encouraging people to keep moving forward.

She has placed people into stretch positions and moved people around into new areas of responsibility as a means of both getting new perspectives

Dr. Janet Woodcock
Center for Drug Evaluation
and Research
Food and Drug Administration

Janet Woodcock, M.D., has served as the director of the Center for Drug Evaluation and Research since 1994. Prior to this she was the director of the Office of Therapeutics Research and Review in the Center for Biologics Evaluation and Research (CBER), also part of the FDA. Dr. Woodcock, an internist/rheuma-tologist with prior research experience in immunology joined the FDA in 1985.

She also served as the director of the Division of Biological Investigational New Drugs in CBER from 1988 to1992 and was acting deputy director of the Center from 1991 to 1992.

Dr. Woodcock received her M.D. from Northwestern University Medical School and completed further training and held faculty appointments at Pennsylvania State University and the University of California in San Francisco prior to her public service career.

into different places in the organization and developing individuals with greater breadth and insight.

As a major part of that program, an individual project is identified up front that will produce significant results and serve as a seedbed for developing leadership. These initiatives are discussed at monthly meetings—at which Dr. Woodcock is often present—between all of the fellows and senior leaders. Her approach is to ask questions, to identify issues and barriers, and to keep encouraging individuals in their efforts at change.

Another part of the leader development strategy was to use the Fellows from the first group as a team to initiate a total rethinking of the vision for CDER, its mission, and its values. In the process, the team conducted extensive interviews with all stakeholders. As a result, the real grist for change emerged—saving lives of people by getting drugs to market faster. As might be expected, significant opposition to changes in the status quo were encountered and significant lessons in leadership emerged from real experience—not from textbooks or lectures.

Many of the individuals who have come through this program are now being placed in key leadership positions. They have the vision and values as well as the leadership capabilities and the supporting network to gradually change the nature of the culture at CDER. This is a classic example of a long-term strategic change initiative that has future leader development at its core.

As a Teacher

A key part of that program in the last four years has been the selection of over 70 Fellows for the Council for Excellence in Government year-long leadership development program, and then using these individuals to spearhead change projects and placing them in leadership positions.

In this regard, CDER senior managers have been selecting the best and the brightest potential leaders for this one-year program as a strategic initiative (not an ad hoc effort aimed solely at the individual). They also commissioned a separate leadership program cohort devoted solely to the office and Division director levels. All selections are competitive internally and at the Council, so that those who emerge are recognized as potential future leaders.

Not surprisingly, the most consistent answer given to the question of Dr. Woodcock's legacy was her commitment to growing leaders at all levels of the organization and actually doing it.

Appendix I:
Getting Started

Making It a Priority: Take Stock of Your Time, Then Make the Time

It is quite simply impossible to conceive of a change in any direction, minor or major, that is not preceded by—and then sustained by—major changes, noticeable to all, in the way you spend your time.*

Tichy observes that leaders who grow leaders start by setting an example, blocking time for this important task. Perhaps the greatest message you can give as a leader that you are making it your priority to serve the needs of the next generation is how you use your time.

To start, go back over your calendar for the past 30 days and see how you have spent your time. How much of it was spent on what was most urgent: your "in box," interrupting phone calls or visits, extended meetings about budget issues, correspondence, etc.? How much of your time was spent with your peers or with top executives, Congress, or OMB? If you are like most senior leaders, you will find that, as St. Augustine observed, "the urgent will drive out the important."

It is those very things that are important but not urgent where senior leaders need to focus time—*intentionally* devoting more time to what Stephen Covey refers to as Quadrant II activities.

It may be somewhat shocking to see that there is actually little time spent in intentionally or even unintentionally developing other leaders—mentoring, coaching, teaching, informally interacting. Unless you spend some initial time reflecting honestly on what it is you do with your time, it is unlikely you will make the necessary changes to reorder your time and have it show up on your calendar. That self-awareness is the first step in taking better control over building a leadership legacy.

Finding and Preparing Your Leadership Stories

Effective leaders convey their own learning through stories—the lessons of their experience. In the extensive Center for Creative Leadership research and from Kotter's findings on leaders vs. managers, this is the heart of extending leader learning—teachable experience. Stories wrap the two central facets of leader learning into a package—experience and example—and make it a memorable and practical package.

While there is much that is emerging in research on how the brain works—cognitive science—suffice it to say that we learn and remember information and even plan strategically by ingesting knowledge and storing it in the form of stories. So storytelling should be an integral part of your leadership coaching, mentoring, and teaching. But where do the stories themselves come from? Perhaps you think that you don't have any. Then a first step might be to see what were your own leader learning points.

To start, get a large spiral notebook to use as a journal for notes about what you have learned and want to pass on. On the first page of the journal, draw a horizontal line across the middle. At the top of the upper section write "Highs" in the center. Near the bottom of the page in the lower section, in the center, write "Lows." The horizontal line represents your career or perhaps even your life. The upper portion, the relative "Highs," represents significant challenge, excitement, high achievement, recognition, a great event, or a satisfying accomplishment—personally or professionally. The lower portion, the relative "Lows," represents failure, disappointment, tragedy, a setback, a bad boss, a bad relationship, a dead-end job, boredom, getting fired or demoted, etc.

Once you have identified these key events across the span of your career and personal life, reflect on each one. For each high and each low, begin to draw out the lessons from it that may have informed or reshaped the way you now lead. If it is true that the emotionally impacting events of our lives lead to leader learning —even career setbacks and bad bosses, as CCL has found—then these lessons are critical and constitute the learned wisdom that we each possess about leadership.

Each of these events is a story that can be told to others as an illustration of a key learning in your life. It is a story that links ideas and experiences together with a "moral" or a central learning for others. Not only does this give you insight about how you learned leadership—lessons to pass on—but it gives you ideas about how you might challenge others to learn as well and apply these lessons to their lives.

Writing down these stories does not need to be accomplished at one sitting. Instead, periodically take time to use your Highs-Lows chart to recall what spurred you to learn about leadership. It is a good beginning for developing your own content for ways in which you can help grow other leaders.

* Tom Peters and Nancy Austin, *Thriving on Chaos* (New York: Harper Collins, 1987), p. 498.

Appendix II:
Approach and Methodology

The approach of this report has been to set forth in a cogent way what is known about how to grow public service leaders in an era of great change. The conclusions are drawn from the documented results of research, from the "best practices" of organizations that grow leaders effectively, and from the examples of public service leaders themselves. Many of the insights came from developing a benchmarking report for the National Academy of Public Administration on the subjects of succession management and leadership development. The "filter" however, has been my own, from personal observations from almost 40 years in public service, and from working with the next generation of leaders through the Council for Excellence in Government Fellows and the Leadership Development Academy—the Executive Potential Program and the Women's Executive Leadership Program (WEL).

The need for leadership in the public service is clear; the best practices for growing leaders is evident, if not completely intuitive; and the role of senior leaders in this development process is a well-established approach in the very best organizations—public and private. It is from this foundation that comparative conclusions can be drawn for the public service. But seeing it lived out in the lives of three successful public service leaders and framing it in practical terms gives these findings life and practical application.

In identifying the three leaders profiled, the methodology began, first, with a premise—that where significant change has occurred in a government organization, transformational leadership is behind it. All three organizations in which these individuals are or were leaders—the Veterans Benefits Administration, the Social Security Administration, and the Center for Drug Evaluation and Research—have undergone significant, positive change within the last few years.

Second, it was assumed that there would be some consensus within the organization (and without) that individual leaders, certainly not alone, have been among the key individuals driving change. In that sense, conversations with individuals working in and outside these organizations, many of them future leaders themselves, were conducted.

Third, a more in-depth look at the character and capability of these leaders as examples, coaches, mentors, and teachers was accomplished by interviewing several individuals who have worked for them or are currently working for them, much like a 360-degree feedback process. The primary focus was to identify the practices that selected superior leaders in public service are using in growing the next generation. As should be clear, each leader practiced the four basic roles in a somewhat different, but highly effective, fashion.

However, in the course of these interviews, a profile of leadership emerged which places in context why these three servant leaders are able to grow other leaders. At the heart of this lie not only certain practices and examples, but also a wider foundation of leadership character and capability. The expanded profiles contained in Appendix III give a more complete picture of the synergy of skills, character, results, and experience that distinguish these leaders.

Appendix III:
Exemplary Leader Profiles

Leo Wurschmidt—Leadership Character and Capability

Leo Wurschmidt's leadership character and capability attributes coalesced around six prominent features that were consistently identified by those interviewed:

- Unquestioned integrity of commitment to live out values
- An abiding focus on the core purpose of public service
- A deep belief in the worth and capabilities of people
- Courage—a willingness to take personal and organizational risks
- Personal caring about people
- A builder of partnerships among all stakeholders—a service family team

Unquestioned integrity of commitment to live out values

Often this is seen as an important trait, but difficult to pin down. In Wurschmidt's case, this attribute was described in vivid terms. For example, one person said that if Wurschmidt ever said something was going to be done for an employee or a stakeholder, he meant it, whether it took long hours to get it done or extraordinary initiative. He lived this way and expected others to carry out their word as well. The central theme of many was that "Leo was a man of his word, and every employee knew it."

Another facet was that he would speak up with great courage about issues and initiatives in the face of opposition, unpopularity, or the views of senior officials. Others mentioned that he would not bow to political pressure in making decisions. He was known to make the right decisions based on the facts and would back up employees who did so even when pressured to reverse a ruling.

An abiding focus on the core purpose of public service

For many people, what seemingly fueled Wurschmidt's life was a deep commitment to serving VA's "customers"—the nation's veterans. Perhaps it was his own service during the Vietnam War, but his motivation was public service to those that served when called.

One person said, "Leo's legacy is to the veterans, which comes from his dedication to the mission and to his personal relations with veterans and those that serve them daily. For those that worked with Leo, it is difficult not to focus on getting the job done and done well."

A deep belief in the worth and capabilities of people

It appears that out of a core value of caring about each person, Wurschmidt also had a bone-deep belief that the best way to bring about change and to accomplish the mission is to leverage the capabilities of all people. A consistent comment was that he trusted people to do the job and valued both their effort and even their disagreements.

Listening and, perhaps more importantly, taking the time to listen were also mentioned as characteristic of how he led in a way that made employees feel they had a real voice in the things that affected their work lives. Appreciative employees said particularly that he was not a micromanager—an attribute greatly appreciated by those on the front lines.

One top manager also observed that one of the major leadership qualities was how Wurschmidt drove out longstanding fear that had existed before his arrival as the top director. This led to a different spirit among the people and laid the groundwork for innovation and real change. Mistakes were not punished but used as points of learning—as long as learning occurred. The other side of it was a high standard of service excellence that he practiced and expected others to follow. In other words, he created the culture and conditions where people could thrive.

One "result" consistently mentioned was that wherever Wurschmidt came in as a leader, it became a better place to work. He created a culture that facilitated change and personal growth. He drove out fear. He promoted openness. He exuded encouragement in person and in countless notes. He set an example of extraordinarily hard work and very high standards. People were expected to keep their word—Wurschmidt, first of all. The veterans who were served were placed at the top of the list of priorities—not the needs of the organization. A wide range of supportive partners was created. Fun and a family sense were injected. Mistakes were allowed in the pursuit of better service and innovation.

Courage—a willingness to take personal and organizational risks

Another quality that stands out is Wurschmidt's willingness to undertake tests or pilot projects as the seedbed for change within the national change efforts. He was instrumental in testing and developing the notion of satellite benefits offices—an effort to bring services closer to people. The satellite initiative is now a base part of the national change initiatives.

He also pioneered the development of VA benefits services being provided right at the Military Separation Center, again a standard approach now used throughout the country. This initiative has chopped the waiting time for disability claims for separating service members to one quarter of what it was previously.

Personal caring about people

Many of the people interviewed mentioned how Wurschmidt knew everyone's name. A photographic memory, perhaps, but indications are it was clearly something he worked at because he felt it was important. This was not a gimmick, but the first step in being able to relate to each person that worked with him and for him on a personal basis.

One indication of this was that he was known to hand-write thank you notes—literally hundreds of them—to people for a job well done, often putting in long hours to recognize what people had done, even the small things.

While MBWA (management by walking around) has been part of the vernacular for some time now, Wurschmidt was apparently one who religiously practiced it. As one employee said, he spent time "in the trenches with the troops," talking about what was really happening and constantly encouraging and thanking people verbally. The result was obvious—the deep loyalty among people that have worked with him was unfeigned and the admiration genuine.

In addition, he always took time to stop what he was doing to talk to people, to encourage them to grow, to challenge them. No matter how busy he was, people came first, and he was not annoyed by the tremendous amount of time it took. A case in point: One person who came to work for Wurschmidt did so because even he was impressed by the way this director of a large office took the time to meet with him—then just a young analyst visiting the organization on business. This person is now a senior leader in VA and attributes part of the reason to Leo's example that day.

Wurschmidt was always quick to turn a compliment or an achievement from himself to others in his organization. His self-effacing manner and modesty were seen as rare among senior executives in the experience of the interviewees, but a clear demonstration of his belief that it was the people on the front line that matter most.

A story is told that illustrates his ability to relax and be natural with people while maintaining their respect. This occurred at an employee picnic where the director—the leader of 300 employees—was suddenly the object of attention as he mounted a children's hobbyhorse in the local park and proceeded to ride for all he was worth. That resulted in several memorable photos of employees who wanted to be photographed with the "boss."

A builder of coalitions and partnerships as members of a service-family team

Senior leaders must form partnerships and think strategically about collaborating with a wide array of stakeholders. In several comments, it was clear that Wurschmidt excelled at this but with a twist. The consistency of his character and values mandated that all stakeholders be made a part of what one person termed "a community of service." He built this sense of community in each leadership position he held, reaching out to organizations that are often known for fractious relations. These included veterans' service organizations, whose advocacy for veteran's benefits in their lobbying role is often seen by some as at odds with the VA mission. Wurschmidt made them part of the team and part of the solution, and gave their representatives respect, personal time, and a listening ear—much the way he treated anyone who worked with him.

Congressional staffs, who are also known by some as partisan advocates, were also accorded the same courtesy and sense of inclusion in the community of service. Wurschmidt built a strong sense of partnership that did two things. First, it set an example to all of the employees that these external stakeholders were not "the enemy" but people to be regarded with a sense of worth. Second, it allowed both the support for change that would be needed and the capacity to say "no" and to be trusted and respected through it all. This is an often-overlooked leadership quality when opposition to change occurs among external stakeholders.

Within the organization, Wurschmidt was similarly consistent, as new approaches to partnering with the labor unions came into being. He was known as a fair and trusted manager and leader and worked very hard, personally, to make it a success—not turning it over to the HR staff to do themselves. As a result, he was a natural choice for the first VA National Partnership Council formed in 1994, where he was instrumental in developing the "Rules of Interaction." These became the policies and procedures that formed the basis for how partnerships were to operate fairly among the almost quarter million VA employees and their representatives at the local level.

Paul Barnes—Leadership Character and Capability

In several interviews with colleagues and former employees, a picture of Paul Barnes as a leader emerges that is both compelling and worthy of emulation. He has made an impact on people wherever he has been a leader and continues to do so as he help's lead SSA through significant periods of change and establish it as a benchmark public service organization. The key attributes of Barnes that emerge from the impressions of those interviewed are:

- Unquestioned integrity of commitment to live out values
- An abiding focus on the core purpose of public service
- A deep belief in the worth and capabilities of people
- Courage—a willingness to take personal and organizational risks
- Personal caring about people
- A sense of balance in life expressed in optimism and enjoyment

Barnes attributes much of his own bent toward developing younger leaders to others who mentored and helped him along the way. As a young

intern, he had a boss who encouraged him in self-development and reading, and who started a local leader development program that Barnes was
part of. He was also encouraged to work outside of his own job familiarity
and to be as mobile as possible in order to learn and to grow. Another key
person was someone whom Barnes worked for and whom he sought to
emulate in his approach to leadership and management. It is clear that
Barnes has continued to pass on the lessons others taught him, instilling the
same in those he mentors.

Unquestioned integrity of commitment to live out values

One senior official perhaps put it best: "He has a strong sense of personal values and he lives them out every day." A common observation was
that Barnes "walks the talk." As mentioned earlier, genuineness and con-
gruity, of behavior and words is key to a leader's capacity to take an organization through change and to fostering others to become leaders in the
same mold.

Barnes's public service values were summed up by one person who
observed that Paul stressed "three Cs:" caring, courtesy, and commitment.
Those themes would be played out in his own behavior.

He also was someone who was not after leadership as an end for his
own ego. One interviewee said this is not someone who was "power
happy." He blended humility with a strong sense of earned authority.

That apparently came across as genuine to a wide range of people,
whether it was in personal encounters or hearing him speak before groups.
One person said that it was quite common for Paul to receive standing ova-
tions from employees after speaking to a group of them. This person had
never seen a senior executive get such a reception and believed that the
heartfelt reaction was yet another indication of his connection to people
and his genuineness.

Barnes himself attributes his values to his parents who were share-
croppers while he was growing up. What he learned from them, he recalls,
was a daily example of what is important in life, hard work and high expectations for yourself and for others.

An abiding focus on the core purpose of public service

In the interviews conducted, the story that was mentioned by almost
every person was how Barnes would often say, "Treat people the way you
would want your mother or father to be treated." He would observe that
most of the people served by the Social Security Administration were someone's mother or father. This image seemed to stick with people long after
Barnes had moved on.

One interviewee noted particularly that Barnes had "a vision for SSA
and what it could become." This strategic perspective included a deep

understanding of the importance of Social Security to the public, which for him was embodied in the term "security." He saw their role as providing not only support, but support with dignity, giving individuals a sense of ease about the future and removing anxiety. It was this bigger picture and the public service potential that he called people to think about and act on.

Another said that what stayed with him was that Barnes's true devotion to public service and to the mission of SSA was unfeigned. His focus on the core purpose was what he felt helped Barnes ride out many of the ups and downs and the tensions inherent in the transformation of SSA during the last 10 to 15 years.

A deep belief in the worth and capabilities of people

His respect for each person as a unique individual often came across in his ability to work easily with people of differing personalities and diverse racial and ethnic backgrounds. One person said that his "belief in the goodness of people is bedrock."

As a day-to-day manager, Barnes focuses on the "what," not the "how." A frequent comment was that he was not a micromanager. He conveyed a great sense of confidence in people and while he set high standards of excellence, he did not punish mistakes made in taking a risk or learning something new. He trusted people to get the job done with excellence. While he left people with the impression that they could call on him at any time, he also was clear that he was not there to manage the day-to-day details of their work. It was a trust that apparently bred trust.

Courage—a willingness to take personal and organizational risks

One of the risks that Paul Barnes was known to take was on people. Two interviewees stressed that Barnes had taken a risk on them by placing them in positions of wide responsibility and setting high expectations for their performance. In part, this was a strategy for their development, but a failure could have backfired on him. This willingness to take a risk on people set a tone that resonated with others. He also challenged others to take risks on their own to try new things and to work outside their comfort zone.

Personal caring about people

One aspect of Paul's demeanor in the workplace was that he was approachable. He apparently could convey a sense of openness to listening to people that they felt comfortable sitting down to raise problems or issues or to get career advice. One person talked about his ability to listen and summed it up by saying, "He *actually* hears." Whereas some leaders would seem to listen because it was expected, Barnes was known to take the time and to respond with action, indicating he was paying attention to the individual.

Another theme was that Paul was both straightforward with people and honest. This built a foundation of trust by the people of the organization, not just in one place, but in each organization he headed. Trust is an essential component of the ability to lead others in change and of personal leadership development.

A sense of balance in life expressed in optimism and enjoyment

While a balanced life is often mentioned as crucial in the best leaders, it is not typical for humor and enjoyment to surface. Yet, the people interviewed for this report, time and again, cited Barnes's sense of humor, hearty laugh, and ability to keep a balanced perspective in the midst of tension. One person said, "you could always tell when Paul was visiting the building because his laughter could be heard up and down the halls." Others noted that while he had very high standards, he also made work fun, even in difficult times.

Another example of Barnes's sense of balance: No one could ever recall seeing him angry. A story is told of how Paul was in a meeting involving an EEO complaint lodged against a manager with some questionable management practices. This manager was creating great difficulties among people in the organization, yet had recently received high performance marks. Barnes was confounded that such a manager would be rated highly, making correction very difficult. But while he was obviously upset, he simply left the room, walked around the building and smoked a cigar, leaving the staff to talk over some alternatives. When he returned, he calmly dealt with the situation, never showing his obvious anger.

Barnes placed a great, importance on family, often observing that his job was easy compared to the rigors of raising a family. A couple of interviewees also noted that at the time of the death of his first wife, he talked about true priorities in life and how important they should be for everyone.

Dr. Janet Woodcock—Leadership Character and Capability

Dr. Janet Woodcock is somewhat of a different type of leader than the previous two profiled in her own developmental experiences and her level (not necessarily scope) of impact. First, she has occupied for some time now the most senior position in the most visible part of the Food and Drug Administration—the Center for Drug Evaluation and Research (CDER), with all of the external responsibilities as well as access to resources that such a position implies. Second, she is a scientist and an M.D. and has thus traveled a somewhat different road in her own development as a leader. And, third, her public service career is not one of an entire career lifetime but of the last 14 years.

Despite these apparent differences, there are more similarities in the leadership attributes she has displayed in helping followers navigate change and produce results and in providing for the growth of the next generation of leaders at CDER. Dr. Woodcock heads an organization that has been widely recognized for producing significant change under difficult circumstances. Nevertheless, part of her agenda for change has been to develop the kind of leaders that CDER will need to sustain change, many of whom have been through an innovative partnership with the Council for Excellence in Government Fellows Program. In interviews with many people who have worked with her, the following attributes emerge as the most prominent:

- Unquestioned integrity of commitment to live out values
- An abiding focus on the core purpose of public service
- A deep belief in the worth and capabilities of people
- Courage—a willingness to take personal and organizational risks
- Perseverance toward a vision

Unquestioned integrity of commitment to live out values
Those interviewed about Dr. Woodcock consistently mentioned her commitment to identify and draw out leaders, often new leaders, at all levels. Here she was not only looking to the future of CDER, but also using this approach as a means to reshape the culture. It is a strategy that recognizes that some individuals in key positions will not be able to change, and that by raising up new leaders who share the new vision, a more gradual process of transformation will occur over the long term. This, of course, has its risks as well as its potential rewards. Despite a crushing workload and uncompromising external pressures, Dr. Woodcock has been able to maintain her commitment to and demonstrate her faith in growing new leaders by giving her time and energy.

An abiding focus on the core purpose of public service
The driving need for change seems to be a bone-deep belief in Dr. Woodcock. Many of the interviewees said that she strongly believed that the nation's citizens demanded and deserved the best in terms of early access to new medications and that the safety of such medications should not be compromised in the process. One expression of this belief was that people were dying because new drugs were not getting to the market. This was a message that stirred hearts as well as minds.

A deep belief in the worth and capabilities of people
One of Dr. Woodcock's first official acts that has remained in the minds of the people in CDER is she personally visited every single office and attempted to talk to every single person as a way to introduce herself. As visible evidence of her caring about people, this could not be surpassed,

but the fact that it also was completely counter to the reigning hierarchical culture was perhaps just as important. And she continues to impress others with her phenomenal memory for names.

Her introductory visits were not a one-time symbolic act. She continues to solicit the input of people at all levels of the organization and takes a personal interest in them, despite her demanding and highly visible position. She also has widened the participation of people in key meetings, drawing individuals not necessarily from the senior levels and soliciting their input at meetings. This was unheard of prior to her arrival.

One mid-level manager commented that what makes Dr. Woodcock stand out is how she makes people feel valuable and good about themselves. She asks about the issues they are passionate about and is able to identify valuable skills and abilities that the individuals themselves often don't see. Simply by asking questions and listening she is able to draw out people.

There is also a clear sense that although she is highly intelligent and quickly grasps the essence of a complex issue, she is not lofty or inaccessible. There is an openness that she conveys beyond her "open door" to people—even when she disagrees, there is respect for the person.

A key aspect that several mentioned was that Dr. Woodcock has created the conditions that allow greater input, innovation, and change—a more permissive and open atmosphere that draws out people at all levels. Her leadership influence on the culture is one that will continue to take a time and energy to realize. Like other aspects, it is still apparently a work in progress.

She also believes strongly that successful change is a team outcome and is extremely self-effacing, deflecting recognition and praise to others.

Courage—a willingness to take personal and organizational risks

One of the capabilities of leading change is the courage of conviction and the ability to instill courage in others. Many of the early Fellows and other leaders were placed into situations—thinking outside of the box and being engaged in a new leadership program that focused on changing CDER—which were not seen as career enhancing. Even the early classes of Fellows experienced a lack of volunteers because of the perceived "danger" of being associated with such efforts.

Some mentioned that her visible role also included a willingness to tackle some of the political opposition to the changes, which demonstrated her own courage and gave heart to others who were experiencing opposition internally.

Perseverance toward a vision

The primary challenge that CDER was faced with was turning around a slow-paced drug review process that increasingly left none of the stakeholders satisfied with the results: consumers, politicians, drug companies, or patients. Dr. Woodcock's vision was that there needed to be a serious change in the way CDER did business, or it would become irrelevant in a world that demands better, faster, cheaper. But, initially, and even now in the eyes of some, the resistance to change was fierce.

Some interviewees mentioned that Dr. Woodcock is not charismatic in the traditional sense and that it is even possible to underestimate her. What was noted was how her personal character of deeply held beliefs, passion around those beliefs, and consistent enthusiasm and energy toward innovation came through loud and clear when she began to speak to groups or in one-on-one conversations.

This attribute of personal character is one seen in many of the so-called "built to last" leaders of organizations—a sense that "good enough" never is and that making things better must be a daily part of organization life. Dr. Woodcock seemed to be constantly questioning why innovation could not apply to drug review and why new ways of doing things could not be found. She apparently preached that the status quo simply was not acceptable and that she would not defend it. For those who had become comfortable with established procedures, even justifying them against public criticism, this was a hard path to take. But what stands out is how she persevered and continues to do so, challenging the established approach and encouraging others to do so, but without a "take no prisoners" attitude. That likely has allowed change to occur slower than some would like, but without the human turmoil that sometimes accompanies driving change from the top and the bottom of the organization as she has.

Appendix IV:
Annotated Bibliography

The references in the endnotes contain the primary written sources for the published research behind this report. However, for senior leaders or others wishing to explore this topic in more depth, the following references provide a wealth of information about how to grow public service leaders at all levels. These individuals will become the leaders with the character and capability needed to transform the service of government to its citizens for the 21st century.

Leadership—The Overall Perspective

Burns, James McGregor. *Leadership.* New York: Harper, 1978.

The "classic" treatment of transformational leadership, done in a scholarly but readable way. Looks at leadership in every sector and from many angles, contrasting transactional and transformational leadership. Develops a general theory of leadership, which set the stage for later developments. Not nearly as practical, but good on the early theory behind most of what is discussed in this report.

Kotter, John. *Leading Change.* Boston: Harvard Business School Press, 1996.

The single best book to date on the link between leadership and change—the biggest challenge for today's leaders—written by the preeminent thinker and researcher on the subject. It is readable, cogent, and eminently practical. His model, based on eight principles, comes out of extensive work with organizations that have failed to produce significant change. His concluding ideas on organizations of the future and how future leaders can grow to enable them to navigate through times of great change are highly insightful.

Kotter, John. *A Force for Change: How Leadership Differs from Management.* New York: The Free Press, 1990.

John Kotter has examined leadership and management in more practical detail than perhaps any thought leader. His understanding of how they differ in execution and in their results is well worth reading. It elucidates better than any source I have found the way in which public service leaders have gone down a management path that is no longer useful in an era of transformation of government.

Kouzes, James M., and Barry Z. Posner. *The Leadership Challenge*. San Francisco: Jossey-Bass, 1996.

Another excellent framework for identifying the capabilities needed in exemplary leaders. The authors use a framework of challenging the process, inspiring a shared vision, enabling others to act, modeling the way, and encouraging the heart. Their view is that leaders can and do make a difference in producing results through people and can learn to do so. They also include the highly regarded Leadership Practices Inventory for a self-assessment or outside assessment of capabilities.

Rosen, Robert. *Leading People*. New York: Penguin Books, 1996.

Pioneer of the "healthy company" initiative Rosen sets forth a model for leadership based upon eight capabilities or principles: vision, trust, participation, learning, diversity, creativity, integrity, and community. An excellent source that is readable and practical, with great illustrations.

Ulrich, Dave, Jack Zenger, and Norm Smallwood. *Results-based Leadership: How Leaders Build the Business and Improve the Bottom Line*. Boston: Harvard Business School Press, 1999.

Written somewhat as a corrective to the notion that leadership is only about attributes or competencies of leaders. The authors focus on a balanced scorecard of results—people, organization, customers, investors— and how to become more results-focused as a leader. They ultimately conclude that to sustain results, leaders must build leaders.

Leadership—The Leader's Perspective

DePree, Max. *Leadership is an Art*. New York: Doubleday, 1989.
DePree, Max. *Leadership Jazz*. New York: Doubleday, 1992.

Max DePree, former CEO of the highly successful Herman Miller Furniture design company in Zeeland, Michigan, reflects on his views of leadership and on the legacy of leadership he observed and implemented from his father and brother. Perhaps two of the more cogent treatments of leadership from the perspective of an individual who has thought long and hard about the subject and has been there.

Hesselbein, Frances, Marshall Goldsmith, and Richard Beckhard, eds. *The Leader of the Future*. San Francisco: Jossey-Bass, 1996.

These essays frame almost every aspect of leadership with an eye toward the qualities leaders of the future will need in all types of organizations—private sector, public sector, and social sector. Experienced academicians, consultants, and practitioners write on every aspect of leadership.

A rich resource with a variety of useful perspectives from the Drucker Foundation for Nonprofit Management.

Pollard, William. *The Soul of the Firm.* Grand Rapids: Harper Collins Publishers, 1996.
  Pollard, CEO of the top service company in the world, explains his approach to leadership, which centers on a value system that is rooted in the dignity of the individual and a focus on the core purpose of work and the business.

Sullivan, Gordon R., and Michael V. Harper. *Hope is Not a Method: What Business Leaders Can Learn from America's Army.* New York: Random House, 1996.
  Sullivan, former chief of staff of the Army, explains how he helped lead the U.S. Army through a time of great change after the Vietnam War and the Gulf War and prepare it for its role in a changing world. A highly useful perspective from a public service leader.

Leadership—Character

Greenleaf, Robert. *Servant Leadership: A Journey into the Nature of Legitimate Power and Greatness.* New York: Paulist Press, 1977.
  Greenleaf is the godfather of the recent move toward an understanding of the importance of character and values in times of change. It is a study in the paradox of how power is best exercised and received. From the story of Hesse's Journey to the East, Greenleaf draws upon the metaphor of the self-effacing Leo. A servant on the journey, Leo proved to be central to its success, yet was himself a great leader of a monastic movement. A somewhat mystical treatment of leadership, but a philosophy that has endured as a way of leading and serving. An exemplary metaphor for public service leadership.

Guinness, Os, ed. *Character Counts: Leadership Qualities in Washington, Wilberforce, Lincoln and Solzhenitsyn.* Grand Rapids. Baker Books, 1999.
  Character in leaders is often caught as much as taught. It is learned through observation and interaction. Guinness profiles four leaders—three from public service—and highlights how they developed character as leaders and how they lived it under the most trying of circumstances. This is not a "how to" but rather a call source of inspiration for those in public service.

O'Toole, James. *Leading Change: Overcoming the Ideology of Comfort and the Tyranny of Custom*. San Francisco: Jossey-Bass, 1995.

This is a somewhat unorthodox treatment of the subject of leadership and change that draws upon history, moral and political philosophy, and practical experience. O'Toole served as the head of the Aspen Institute Executive Seminar and used his work with senior leaders over the years to diagnose the reasons for failure to produce significant change. He identifies the aspect of character, the moral foundation, as being where trust is built or erodes by profiling five "Rushmorean" leaders who have demonstrated the critical role of values-centered leadership. An excellent companion to Kotter's eight change principles.

Thrall, Bill, Bruce McNicol, and Ken McElrath. *The Ascent of a Leader: How Ordinary Relationships Develop Extraordinary Character and Influence*, San Francisco: Jossey-Bass, 1999.

One of the few books that tackles the notion that character in leaders can be developed within organizations that foster a culture of principles and values within senior leaders. The authors use the metaphor of "ladders"—leaders growing as they face ascending challenges related to both character and capability. They show how the two "ladders" must be combined to produce leaders for the future whom others can trust and follow. Through mentoring and coaching relationships, they contend, character is grown in the right culture.

Growing Leaders—The Practical Research Behind "Best Practices"

McCall, Morgan. *High Flyers: Developing the Next Generation of Leaders*. Boston: Harvard Business School Press, 1998.

Morgan McCall, now head of the Executive Leadership Program at the University of Southern California, distills the best knowledge of how leaders grow from his days as head of research for the Center for Creative Leadership and from his experience in developing senior executives. A highly readable and practical primer on how to grow leaders.

McCauley, Cynthia D., Russ S. Moxley, and Ellen Van Velsor, eds.. *The Center for Creative Leadership Handbook*. San Francisco: Jossey-Bass, 1998.

Perhaps the best single reference source for organizations seeking to grow leaders. Contains excellent, research-based sections on the experiences that grow leaders (360-degree feedback, skill-based training, challenging job assignments, developmental relationships, and hardships). Also included is an excellent review of a systematic process to grow leaders and some of the key issues organizations are likely to face—race, gender, and cross-cultural concerns.

Growing Leaders—"Best Practices" in Organizations

Collins, James C., and Jerry I. Porras. *Built to Last: Successful Habits of Visionary Companies.* New York: Harper Collins, 1994.

This contains perhaps the best work done to date on benchmark companies, which are also excellent for comparison to the public sector. These are all companies that have endured over time, experiencing both short-term failure and long-term success. Rooted in core purpose and core values, they build organizations that home-grow leaders with the values and cultural orientation that will ensure long-term stability and continuous, even dramatic, change. For those who think that the private sector has nothing of value for public sector situations—particularly the cultural foundations for growing leaders of character and capability and for a clear-eyed focus on *results.*

Conger, Jay A., and Beth Benjamin. *Building Leaders: How Successful Companies Develop the Next Generation.* San Francisco: Jossey Bass, 1999.

An excellent and up-to-date benchmarking of how the best develop leaders. Contains excellent cases of current best practices and an examination of how leaders are developed on the job including the use of action learning. A good discussion of the capabilities needed by future leaders is also included.

Managing Succession and Developing Leadership: Growing the Next Generation of Public Service Leaders. Washington, D.C: National Academy of Public Administration, 1997.

This is a benchmarking study of the best practices of both excellent public sector and private sector organizations and the systems that are most appropriate for public sector use. It also contains a practical guide to organizations wanting to take a strategic approach to leader development and succession management and has many excellent references including an annotated bibliography and a list of leader programs aimed at the public sector.

Tichy, Noel. *The Leadership Engine: How Winning Companies Build Leaders at Every Level.* New York: Harper Collins, 1997.

This is perhaps the best inside look at how companies that have a reputation for growing leaders do it. The insights of Tichy, a long-time consultant to Jack Welch at GE, offer practical applications to the theories of leader development and root it not in systems, but in the leaders themselves. An added bonus is an excellent practical application for senior leaders who want to identify their teachable points of view and shape them into stories to grow other leaders in their organization.

Vicere, Albert A., and Robert M. Fulmer. *Leadership by Design: How Benchmark Companies Sustain Success Through Investment in Continuous Learning*. Boston: Harvard Business School Press, 1996.

Very good on the strategic use of leader development as a means to drive the organization forward. Not as useful from the individual leader development perspective.

Growing Leaders—Mentoring

Bell, Chip R. *Managers as Mentors: Building Partnerships for Learning*. San Francisco: Berrett-Koehler, 1996.

Oriented almost exclusively toward techniques that a leader or manager who wants to become an effective mentor can use. It is cogent and practical.

Biehl, Bobb. *Mentoring: Confidence in Finding a Mentor and Becoming One*. Nashville: Broadman and Holman, 1996.

Written for both potential and current mentors and for mentees as well. An excellent basic guide to finding mentors and mentees and what to do once the relationship begins.

Hendricks, Howard, and William Hendricks. *As Iron Sharpens Iron: Building Character in a Mentoring Relationship*. Chicago: Moody Press, 1995.

As the title implies, this looks at mentoring as a lifelong relationship that helps shape character in another. Written from a spiritual perspective, it is still down to earth, practical, and aimed at both mentors and mentees, with a good discussion of the notion of legacy.

Stanley, Paul D., and Robert J. Clinton. *Connecting: The Mentoring Relationships You Need to Succeed in Life*. Colorado Springs: NavPress, 1992.

Built solidly on the importance of shaping relationships, the authors do a better job of making distinctions among the various mentoring roles—the intensive, occasional, and even passive role. They dig deeply into the nature of these different relationships and draw upon historical situations and cases to illustrate their findings. A thorough and unique treatment of the nature of developmental relationships over a lifetime rather than a specific career.

Growing Leaders—Coaching

Cotlich, David, and Peter Cairo. *Action Coaching: How to Leverage Individual Performance for Company Success.* San Francisco: Jossey-Bass, 1999.

An application of the action learning approach to growing leaders, this focuses on the coaching practices that leaders can use to help grow leaders within their organizations. It is based on using real life experiences in organizations and on the development of a few tools and skills that will help develop others and move the organization forward at the same time.

Hendricks, William, ed. *Coaching Mentoring and Managing.* Franklin Lakes, NJ: National Press Publications, 1996.

Covering the gamut of leader roles in relation to growing leaders, this book includes several case studies, analyses of specific situations, and tools to be used. Can be used as a text for a course for leaders or as a reference for particular issues or skill development.

Peterson, David B., and Mary Dee Hicks. *Leader as Coach: Strategies for Coaching and Developing Others.* Minneapolis: Personnel Decisions International, 1996.

Practical and highly readable approaches for leaders with coaching aspirations but who need a place to start. The authors identify ways in which good leaders can build trust and understanding partnerships with people, inspire commitment and motivation, grow the skills of others, and promote persistence undergirded by a supportive culture.

Endnotes

1. I would particularly acknowledge all those who were interviewed for this effort from the Department of Veterans Affairs, the Social Security Administration, and the Center for Drug Evaluation and Research, as well as others who were interviewed for this project. Their candid observations regarding their leaders, colleagues, and former colleagues offered keen insight into the nature of servant leadership in the public service.

2. Frances Hesselbein, "The One Big Question," *Leader to Leader*, Fall 1998, pp. 7-9.

3. Warren Bennis, *Managing People is Like Herding Cats* (Provo: Executive Excellence Publishing, 1997), p. 21.

4. John Kotter, *A Force for Change: How Leadership Differs from Management* (New York: The Free Press, 1990), p. 139.

5. Mark W. Huddleston, *Profiles in Excellence: Conversations with the Best of America's Career Executive Service* (Arlington, Va.: The PricewaterhouseCoopers Endowment for The Business of Government, November 1999), pp. 14-16.

6. *The National Survey on Public Leadership: Abridged Results* (Boulder: The Leadership Development and Education Institute, 1999).

7. Kotter, p. 138.

8. Huddleston, p. 9.

9. For a more detailed discussion of these findings see Morgan W. McCall, Jr., Michael M. Lombardo, and Ann M. Morrison, *The Lessons of Experience: How Successful Executives Develop on the Job* (New York: Simon and Schuster, 1988).

10. Noel Tichy, *The Leadership Engine: How Winning Companies Build Leaders at Every Level* (New York: Harper Collins, 1997), p. 3.

11. Tichy, p. 3.

12. John P. Kotter and James L. Heskett, *Corporate Culture and Performance* (New York: The Free Press, 1992), p. 150.

13. Bobb Biehl, *Mentoring: Confidence in Finding a Mentor and Becoming One* (Nashville: Broadman and Holman, 1996), p. 46.

14. In a 1999 study of best practices in developing leadership, the major findings were that action learning followed by cross-functional rotations, 360-degree feedback, and exposure to senior executives through mentoring were the top methods used. More importantly, the top organizations took a systemic approach and formed what might be called leadership learning communities where "graduates" and senior leaders were the coaches and instructors. See *Best Practices in Leadership Development Handbook*, Linkage, Inc, 1999.

15. For a more detailed discussion of the SSA Leadership Development Strategy, see chapter four.

CHAPTER SIX

Reflections on Mobility:
Case Studies of Six Federal Executives

Michael D. Serlin
International Institute of Business Technologies
Washington, D.C.

This report was originally published in May 2000, revised February 2002.

Introduction

In an era of changing public expectations of government and rapid technological innovations, interagency cooperation and broadly experienced
career public servants are a necessity. Yet federal careers within a single
agency have been the norm, often leading to parochialism and bureaucratic
turf disputes, rather than promoting the joint efforts and changes needed to
enhance the level of service and keep costs down. True mobility by senior
executives among agencies has been an oft-preached but seldom practiced
phenomenon in the executive branch of the U.S. government.

The Civil Service Reform Act of 1978 (PL 95-454), which established
the Senior Executive Service (SES), envisioned a corps of top administrators
who could be transferred to senior positions in various agencies based on
government need. Discussing development for and within the SES, the final
legislation included the following provision:

"The Office of Personnel Management shall encourage and assist individuals to improve their skills and increase their contribution by service in
a variety of agencies as well as by accepting temporary placements in state
or local governments or in the private sector."

In the ensuing years, transfers among agencies by career senior executives have not been widespread, but the common wisdom that it almost
never happens is a myth. There are many federal career managers who could
have been included in this study, but this limited sample of six senior executives includes people who have worked in 11 of the 14 cabinet departments and 12 independent agencies. Within the cabinet departments,
several have worked both at the department level and within major bureaus
or other component organizations of the departments. Although the majority of the positions have been in the Washington, D.C. area, three have held
positions in federal field organizations at some point in their careers.

The six career senior executives in this study are June Gibbs Brown, for-
mer inspector general of the Department of Health and Human Services
(HHS); Carson K. Eoyang, professor of management, Naval Postgraduate
School, Monterey, California; Dennis J. Fischer, former commissioner of the
Federal Technology Service (FTS) at the General Services Administration
(GSA); Robert A. Knisely, former director, Analysis Service, Office of Student
Financial Assistance, Department of Education; Eileen T. Powell, director,
Administrative Accounting, and deputy chief financial officer, Internal
Revenue Service, Department of the Treasury; and Chris Sale, deputy to the
chair and chief financial officer, Federal Deposit Insurance Corporation
(FDIC). Chris Sale sometimes refers to herself as the "Poster Child for Exec-
utive Mobility," but Bob Knisely, who has worked in seven federal depart-
ments and seven independent agencies, could give her stiff competition.

The profiled executives were interviewed for this chapter to identify the characteristics and experiences they have in common that have enhanced their ability to favorably impact a broad range of federal agencies with differing missions and cultures. The success of all six individuals is well documented in the numerous Presidential Rank Awards and other recognition they have received from different agencies. The new perspectives they brought and changes they introduced are outlined on the following pages.

Case Studies

June Gibbs Brown

June Gibbs Brown, former inspector general (IG) for the Department of Health and Human Services (HHS), arguably was one of the most widely known and respected IGs in the federal government. With a department that spends more than $376 billion annually on such high-profile programs as medicare, Brown's prominence was inevitable, but respect is something she earned. Serving as IG at HHS from 1993 to 2000, she brought to the position the knowledge and experiences she gained while serving as IG at three other federal departments, a major independent agency, and a Navy component. She consistently demonstrated a strong ability to lead people with differing areas of expertise to work together to achieve a common goal, a vital skill for responsive leaders.

Navy Department

Brown did not initially plan a federal career; she raised a family while working during the day in real estate and later for a CPA firm, and went to college at night. The General Accounting Office (GAO) was recruiting accounting majors at her college, Cleveland State, and she was ready to accept a position with GAO when it had a hiring freeze. A GAO recruiter advised her that he had recommended her to the Navy Finance Center in Cleveland, which was hiring. As Brown recognized that she could make a difference by working in the federal government, and that the standard pay structure and benefits across all agencies meant multiple work opportunities, she signed on as a grade GS-9 accountant with the Navy. She was promoted to GS-11 the following year and subsequently became director of internal audit and quality control at the Navy Finance Center. Continuing her education at night, she received a master's in business administration from Cleveland State University in 1972 and ultimately a juris doctor from the Denver School of Law in 1978.

June Gibbs Brown

1963 – 1968	Real Estate Broker, Northeast Realty, Cleveland
1970 – 1971	Staff Accountant, Frank T. Cicirelli, CPA, Cleveland
1971 – 1971	Assistant to Comptroller, S.M. Hexter Co., Cleveland
1971 – 1972	Graduate Teaching Fellow, Cleveland State University
1972 – 1975	Director of Internal Audit, Navy Finance Center, Cleveland
1975 – 1976	Director, Finance Systems Design, Bureau of Land Management, Denver
1976 – 1979	Project Manager, Bureau of Reclamation, Denver
1979 – 1981	Inspector General, Department of Interior, Washington, D.C.
1981 – 1985	Inspector General, National Aeronautics and Space Administration (NASA), Washington, D.C.
1985 – 1986	VP and CFO of Systems Development Corporation, Washington, D.C.
1986 – 1987	Associate Administrator, NASA, Washington, D.C.
1987 – 1989	Inspector General, Department of Defense, Washington, D.C.
1990 – 1993	Deputy IG, then IG, U.S. Navy Pacific Fleet, Pearl Harbor, Hawaii
1993 – 2000	Inspector General, Department of Health and Human Services

When she began working at the Navy Finance Center, the congressionally established savings program for all overseas Navy members had never been in balance, and teams of Navy and contractor accountants from Washington, D.C., had not been able to identify the problems. Working with the Cleveland staff, which had maintained meticulous records, she was able to identify several computer programming problems, reverse their effect, and reconcile the multimillion-dollar accounts to the penny within her first five months.

Interior Department/Initial Inspector General Position

When her husband was transferred to Denver in 1976, Brown obtained a position as a GS-13 at the Interior Department's Bureau of Land Management in charge of financial systems design.

As her career progressed, she discovered that most federal agencies have large chronic problems, and she developed a pattern of seeking them out and volunteering to tackle them. Although this involved risk, helping to solve long-standing problems increased her visibility and opened up new opportunities. In that regard, she applied for and was selected in 1979 as project manager at the Bureau of Reclamation, which led the effort to consolidate the Department of Interior's seven separate pay and seven separate personnel systems into one consolidated pay and personnel system for the entire department. She was promoted to GS-14, then to 15 and 16 in the process. In fact, the effort was so successful that 18 years later the updated version of Interior's system, based on her original model, is being used by all of Interior's bureaus, the Social Security Administration, the Federal Trade Commission, and several other federal agencies and non-federal foundations.

When a 1978 law established IGs in 12 federal departments, Brown requested consideration for a presidential appointment, seeking and receiving support from the Denver area's congressional representative and both Colorado senators. She was already well known and highly regarded in the Department of Interior based on her leadership of the consolidated payroll/personnel effort. These factors led directly to her being selected as Interior's first IG, following 177 interviews (she kept count)!

The skills she had developed at Navy and in her prior positions at Interior, particularly in getting large numbers of people from different staffs to work together, were fully tested. As the first person in this new position, she comments, "I had to consolidate a number of independent auditing and investigative staffs and get them to stop debating who should be handling which jobs. I had to get them to concentrate their energy on developing appropriate and accurate work products that would be accepted and used within the department."

A criticism of many federal IGs has been that they spend their efforts on the less controversial nickel-and-dime issues, rather than on the more complex ones that could have bigger payoffs. A second criticism has been that their reports are disputed or even ignored by agency management. Brown concentrated on the major issues and worked with Interior's management to assure action, as exemplified by her development of the investigative audit, the "audigator" concept.

At the time she began service as Interior's first IG, Secretary Cecil Andrus was negotiating with a highly skeptical congressional appropriations committee regarding funding for a visitor center as part of a larger rehabilitation project of Washington, D.C.'s Union Station. Secretary Andrus told the committee he would seek a review by the independent IG, and based on that review the committee could decide if the project was sound and deserved further funding. Brown met with the heads of the audit and the investigation staffs, determined that they could consolidate the results of numerous visitor center work products already completed, and monitored development of this highly visible report as it progressed. When the audit chief presented the final report on schedule, she personally delivered a copy to Secretary Andrus and to all committee members. The next day, to her astonishment, the head of investigations came to her with his separate report.

When Brown brought the head auditor and the head investigator together, they were surprised to learn that she had expected one joint report. Each had reasons why he couldn't accept the other's report as definitive. Auditors contended that investigative reports were filled with hearsay and did not follow rigorous standards, while investigators felt that audit reports were too generalized and lacked clear evidence necessary in cases where wrongdoing may have been involved. Brown says, "That was a defining moment in my career. It was clear to me that auditors and investigators needed to communicate. Because they hadn't in the past, Billie Sol Estes had been better able to conceal his fraudulent activities, and wasn't that part of the history of why inspectors general were established?" It was clear to her that a new type of work product, an investigative audit, needed to be created for special situations.

She began to develop "audigators," auditors who would recognize and prove that some apparently innocent errors are made on purpose, or "with intent," and investigators who would recognize that problems detected in a specific case could exist elsewhere, leading to follow-up work and potential recommendations for system, policy, or legislative changes. This concept established an excellent precedent for those who followed in her footsteps at Interior, and Brown introduced the same approach at her subsequent agencies. In fiscal year 1997, audigator teams at HHS were instrumental in recovering $750 million in fines, restitutions, and other settlements.

NASA/Private Industry/Return to NASA

Upon taking office in 1981, President Reagan fired all federal IGs. Brown began to explore a law school teaching position, but she also reapplied for an IG appointment. Her reputation as the Interior Department's successful first IG helped her to land the IG position at the National Aeronautics and Space Administration (NASA), where she served for four years. NASA accepted the IG role more readily than Interior. "There had been resentment at virtually all departments of the new congressionally mandated Offices of Inspector General. The culture at NASA was more accepting. Its scientific methodology (testing theories) encouraged these scientists to be open to criticism, and they appreciated professional work products," notes Brown. At NASA she earned the NASA Exceptional Service Medal following a major case which disclosed that a contractor had falsified X-ray documentation verifying the integrity of weld points. The space shuttle had to be "torn down" to assure the safety of the work performed by that contractor. Brown also was recognized for her "innovative leadership in introducing microcomputer technology within the audit and investigative disciplines of government."

In 1985, she left the federal government, accepting the position of vice president and chief financial officer at Systems Development Corporation (now part of UNISYS). She found the work more lucrative but less meaningful than her government service. It was during her time at Systems Development Corporation, with no relationship to NASA, that the Challenger disaster occurred. She wondered, like almost all who had ever been associated with NASA, whether she could have helped to prevent the tragedy if she had been there. When Dr. James Fletcher was asked to become the NASA administrator in 1986, he asked Brown to return as associate administrator for management. She jumped at the chance to return to the challenges of public service, notwithstanding a substantial pay cut.

Department of Defense (DoD) and Navy

In 1987, to her surprise, she was informed that Secretary of Defense Caspar Weinberger wanted to speak with her about DoD's IG position. She ultimately accepted it and served as the DoD inspector general for two years.

DoD provided a tremendous challenge, but also is illustrative of her approach to joining a new agency. As she points out, "Every agency has a different culture. You need to be sensitive to it. There's no sense in going in to change it—you need to adapt and work within the culture, learning the language, including the acronyms."

With large-scale, long-term procurements involving hundreds of contractors and subcontractors, DoD has historically had thousands of on-site auditors. Brown reviewed the levels of risk associated with various contractors and initiated a program in which her office produced "Contractor Risk Assessment Guides." Contractors could follow the guide, an Internal Control Program, and the number of on-site auditors would be reduced. This self-monitoring objective was adopted by the largest and most progressive contractors, who developed their own forums on best practices.

When physical health problems dictated the need for a less stressful job, she applied for and was selected as deputy IG for the Navy Department's Pearl Harbor based Pacific Fleet, where she was soon promoted to IG and served from late 1989 until 1993, when she returned to Washington for her position at HHS.

Department of Health and Human Services

Content as IG of the Pacific Fleet operating out of Pearl Harbor, Brown had not sought a job change when she was contacted by newly appointed Secretary of Health and Human Services Donna Shalala, whom she had never met. Secretary Shalala, searching for an experienced person for the sensitive IG position, had received recommendations from several sources that she consider Brown, and the two quickly found that they had similar views on how an IG can be most effective. Their discussions went well and Brown returned to Washington, where she was confirmed by the Senate for another IG position, HHS, whose responsibilities then also included the Social Security Administration.

Brown's non-IG management experiences at the Navy Finance Center, Interior's Bureaus of Reclamation and of Land Management, her tenure as NASA's associate administrator for management, and her work in private industry—coupled with successful techniques learned or introduced at Interior, NASA, and Defense—contributed to impressive results in the HHS position.

The massive $200-billion-a-year Medicare program illustrates this point. When the Health Care Financing Administration staff were developing new regulations to reflect legislative changes in 1997, Brown and her staff were involved, at Secretary Shalala's request, to help avoid creating loopholes in the regulations. The fiscal year 1998 growth of the Medicare program was $3 billion instead of the previous year's $16.5 billion, and the error rate (improper payments) was halved between 1996 and 1998. The Medicare trustees' recent announcement extending the likely solvency of the fund under current law by seven additional years, to 2015, was partly credited to the department's anti-fraud and anti-abuse efforts, led by the IG's office.

Brown introduced at HHS a voluntary self-disclosure protocol, a program modeled after the one she introduced at DoD, publishing model compliance guidance programs for health-care providers. In return for self-monitoring and adopting a viable compliance program, entities are assured that if HHS auditors or investigators find problems, the sanctions will be less severe when a good faith effort to comply with laws and regulations has been demonstrated. This approach both saves taxpayer money and creates a more positive customer-oriented relationship.

As HHS Secretary Donna Shalala stated in a 1998 interview with *Government Executive* magazine, "I promised June she would be part of the senior management team, while I would protect and enhance her independence." Brown, in turn, developed a staff well drilled in the importance of gathering all the facts and presenting them in a balanced fashion. Recognizing the value of broadening experiences through interagency work, she encouraged her staff to be active in professional organizations and to participate in interagency efforts. While she lost some talented staff this way, many others received offers and stayed; her office gained a reputation as a place where many from outside HHS would like to work.

Interagency Leadership and Training

Throughout her federal career Brown has been active in professional organizations and interagency groups. She served as national president of the Association of Government Accountants in 1985-86, then a 11,800-member professional organization which has since continued to grow and, while in Hawaii, served on the board of directors of the Hawaii Society of CPAs. She also is a fellow of the National Academy of Public Administration.

Brown twice served as vice-chair of the President's Council on Integrity and Efficiency (the PCIE—the Federal Interdepartmental Inspector General Council). Charles Dempsey, former vice-chair of the Council and former IG of the Department of Housing and Urban Development, credits her for being instrumental in setting up computer training for the IG community at the Federal Law Enforcement Training Center and the U.S. Department of Agriculture Graduate School. She also has chaired an interagency committee on information resources management and has served on several other interagency boards.

Brown's management and leadership training has been a combination of her work in obtaining her academic degrees, attending the 13-week Harvard Advanced Management Program in 1983[1], and on-the-job observation of effective leaders. "The experiences of working with Administrators James Beggs and Dr. James Fletcher at NASA, Secretaries Caspar Weinberger and Frank Carlucci at Defense, and Secretary Donna Shalala at HHS have been invaluable in learning models of effective leadership," she notes.

Brown's broad experience and seasoning across a variety of agencies, coupled with a departmental secretary who understood and valued the inspector general role, produced major dividends for taxpayers and for the professionalism of federal service.

Carson K. Eoyang

Carson K. Eoyang, professor of management at the Naval Postgraduate School, Monterey, California, recently completed a special assignment to the Office of Science and Technology Policy in the White House. Eoyang has more than 25 years of federal experience, which includes teaching, research, consulting, and executive positions with the Departments of Defense, Navy, and Transportation, and with the National Aeronautics and Space Administration. His extensive experience in both field and headquarters organizations, and continuous research in cutting-edge approaches to individual and organizational effectiveness, has earned him

Carson K. Eoyang

1968 – 1970	Staff member, Office of Technical Manpower Planning, McDonnell Douglas Astronautics Co., Huntington Beach, California
1970 – 1974	Research Assistant, Graduate School of Business, Stanford University
1974 – (1989)	Associate Professor, Naval Postgraduate School, Monterey, California
1984 – 1985	Technical Assistant, Office of Chief of Naval Operations, Washington, D.C.
1986 – 1989	Director, Defense Personnel Security Research Center, Monterey
1989 – 1996	Director, Training and Development, NASA, Washington, D.C.
1996 – 1999	Program Director for Training, Federal Aviation Administration (FAA), Washington, D.C.
Since 1999	Professor, Naval Postgraduate School, Monterey

wide respect. He has been able to lead change in the agencies where he has worked, while also influencing changes government-wide.

Navy Department

After receiving his bachelor's degree in physics from the Massachusetts Institute of Technology and his M.B.A. from the Harvard Business School, Eoyang worked for three years at the McDonnell Douglas Astronautics Company in Huntington Beach, California. He subsequently returned to graduate school, obtaining a Ph.D. from the Stanford Business School, focusing on organizational development and design. His first federal position, in 1974, was as an assistant professor of management at the Naval Postgraduate School at a level equivalent to GS-13. He remained on the faculty for 15 years. During that time, he also had two tours in Washington, D.C., on the staff of the Chief of Naval Operations (CNO), initially in 1977. He returned in 1983-1984, serving as a principal consultant in the Office of the CNO focusing on programs regarding organizational effectiveness, human resource management, equal opportunity, and leadership and management training.

From 1986 to 1989 he served in his first federal supervisory position as the second director of the Defense Personnel Security Research and Education Center in Monterey, at grade GM-15. He supervised a mix of civil service and contractor personnel. The center's numerous research efforts included a report indicating that gays in the military did not pose special security risks, a finding that differed from past Defense policies and practices. The report stirred intense controversy in the Pentagon and resulted in various tensions, which complicated the research mission of the center.

NASA

When a former student who had joined NASA encouraged Eoyang to apply for the position of director of human resources and organization development in Washington, he did so and was selected for his first SES position in 1989. He comments, "The vast majority of career SES appointments come from within the ranks of the appointing agency, and NASA was no exception. My immediate supervisor at NASA advised me that I needed to learn the NASA culture and traditions quickly and not rely excessively on my experience and connections in Defense. I followed this sage counsel." He found that is technical education and previous aerospace work experience helped in his assimilation into the NASA family.

During his tenure at NASA, Eoyang published a book with two of his earlier colleagues, *Citizen Espionage: Studies in Trust and Betrayal*, which was based upon their research on personnel security and reliability at the Monterey Center. As chief training officer, he led improvements in the quality of various training programs for NASA's 24,000-person workforce, leading to recognition by the Training Officers Conference and by OPM, which conducted a survey of customer satisfaction throughout government that showed NASA to have the highest employee satisfaction with training.

While at NASA, Eoyang was active in many interagency organizations. He served as founding co-chair of the OPM-sponsored Federal Human Resource Development Council; on the board of directors of the Training Officers Conference, an advisory group on federal training; on the board of directors of the American Society of Training and Development; and as the founding chair of the Asian American Government Executive Network. Also he received a Presidential Rank Award for his contributions to NASA and DoD.

Eoyang was recruited by Vice President Gore's National Performance Review to lead the team on "Rethinking Program Design" in developing the initial government reinvention report in 1993. The work of his team subsequently became a chapter in the second edition of the *Handbook of Public Administration*, published in 1995. In addition to the report, Eoyang found the six months to be a valuable learning experience. "This short but intensive experience proved highly beneficial in terms of providing illuminating insights into the political dynamics at the highest levels of government. There was a great urgency for high-profile early results balanced against the need for fundamental changes, and managing expectations both within and outside government was important," he observes.

FAA

In 1996 Eoyang was offered the opportunity to become the chief training officer of the Federal Aviation Administration (FAA), an organization with more than double the number of employees at NASA and five times the training budget. He helped transform the training function from a demoralized, shrinking bureaucratic function into a rejuvenated, entrepreneurial, customer-focused element of the agency's strategic reinvention. He chaired FAA's Subcommittee on Educational Technology, accelerating its investments and future direction to distance learning and computer-based instruction. Drawing on his previous experience in race relations and equal opportunity at Navy, Eoyang led the redesign of FAA's diversity training programs, working closely with the Office of Civil Rights to support the agency's commitment to developing a model work environment for the entire federal government.

A lesson he had learned in making the transition from Navy to NASA was also relevant to his transfer to FAA. Trust and acceptance were vital not only between newcomers and longtime employees in the agency, but also between headquarters executives and management in the field. At NASA he made special efforts to visit all 10 major field centers as an instructor, consultant, and program manager. He also held agency-wide conferences in the field, as well as at headquarters, to help reduce parochialism.

Similarly, following his start at FAA, he served as the acting superintendent of the FAA Academy in Oklahoma City for six months, commuting regularly from Washington, D.C., while the search process for a new superintendent was conducted. He directed the transition of the FAA Academy from a centrally funded training center to a customer-oriented fee-for-service learning institution, with a congressionally authorized international training franchise and revolving fund.

Eoyang's experience as acting superintendent gave him direct knowledge of the core technical training essential to the FAA mission as well as exposure to key management and union personnel outside of headquarters. The close working relationship with the field was confirmed by Robert Igo, the deputy superintendent, who observed, "During Carson's time as the interim superintendent of the FAA Academy, he was able to deal firsthand with some of the unique projects and challenges at the 'worker level.' He was able to share the perceptions of headquarters organizations to which we provide training services. In turn, he was able to take back to Washington a better understanding and appreciation for the work, daily problems, accomplishments, and capabilities of the people conducting the FAA's training programs."

Return to Navy

In 1999, Provost Dick Elster of the Naval Post-graduate School persuaded Eoyang to return as a full professor to help transform the school into a graduate institution that would make full use of modern education technology and expand its distance learning programs. Eoyang believes that the impending revolution in education and training, stimulated by the explosive growth of the Internet, is creating enormous opportunities and challenges critical not only for the Navy, but also for the entire federal workforce.

Interagency Leadership and Training

To strengthen his understanding of the current state of the art and future trends in advanced distributed learning technologies, Eoyang arranged for a short-term detail to the White House Office of Science and Technology Policy prior to reporting to the Naval Postgraduate School. In that capacity, he chaired an interagency working group responsible for implementing the requirements of a Presidential Executive Order on training technology.

Eoyang's experiences at a variety of agencies, coupled with several temporary assignments including two at the White House level, have been invaluable in forging collaboration and partnerships among federal agencies in promoting greater use of educational technology and resources. His experiences have included teacher, policy analyst, researcher, and consultant. His varied contributions resulted in his being elected to the Cosmos Club of Washington, D.C., in 1999. The impact of his efforts will significantly affect all federal agencies over the next decades.

Dennis J. Fischer

Dennis J. Fischer, former commissioner of the Federal Technology Service at the General Services Administration (GSA), was the chief executive officer for information technology and telecommunications provided by GSA to federal government agencies, a $4.2-billion business. His experiences in both financial management and information technology for three federal departments were instrumental in his successfully initiating major changes at GSA, first as its chief financial officer and, from 1997 to 2000,

Dennis J. Fischer

1961 – 1962	Jr. Accountant, Southern Bell Telephone Company, Atlanta
1962 – 1964	Systems Analyst (Commissioned Officer), U.S. Army, Washington, D.C.
1964 – 1964	Accountant, Southern Bell Telephone Company, Atlanta
1965 – 1966	Systems Analyst (Commissioned Officer), U.S. Army, Washington, D.C.
1966 – 1970	Systems Analyst; Project Manager; Assistant Department Manager, Aries Corporation, McLean, Virginia
1970 – 1973	Systems Manager, Office of Education, Washington, D.C.
1973 – 1978	Project Leader; Chief Department Systems Branch, Department of Health, Education and Welfare
1978 – 1981	Director, Office of Financial Management Services, Health Care Financing Administration (HCFA), Washington, D.C.
1981 – 1982	Director, Bureau of Data Management and Strategy, HCFA, Washington, D.C.
1982 – 1984	Director, Office of Management and Budget, HCFA, Washington, D.C.
1984 – 1986	Associate Director for Policy and Management, U.S. Mint, Washington, D.C.
1986 – 1992	Deputy Assistant Secretary, Finance, Department of Health and Human Services, Washington, D.C.
1992 – 1997	Chief Financial Officer, General Services Administration, Washington, D.C. (Acting Administrator in 1993)
1997 – 2000	Commissioner, Federal Technology Service, General Services Administration, Washington, D.C.
Since 2000	Vice President, Sales and Integrated Solutions, Visa U.S.A.

leading the Federal Technology Service. Throughout his career he reduced the overhead cost of government through using new technology and leveraging industry competitiveness. Serving in a central management support agency for eight years, he introduced major service improvements and cost reductions affecting all agencies.

Office of Education

Fischer, with more than 35 years of federal service, worked in computer software and operational support for two commercial organizations prior to beginning his full-time federal civilian career with the then U.S. Office of Education in 1970 as a GS-14 systems manager. The financial condition of the private contractor for whom he had worked on a contract with Education was uncertain, so he decided to accept a position with the client.

Department of Health, Education and Welfare/Health Care Financing Administration

After almost three years at Education, Fischer was selected (and promoted to GS-15) as the project leader to develop an umbrella accounting system for the parent Department of Health, Education and Welfare (HEW), designed to support all its regional offices. He later became chief of the Departmental Systems Branch in the same office, and he successfully implemented the regional accounting system and began development of a grants payment system for most HEW grants. In 1977 he tried but failed in an attempt to develop a new generation automated data processing accounting system on an interactive basis using a minicomputer. He served in department-level jobs for four and a half years.

Fischer transferred laterally in early 1978 to the Health Care Financing Administration (HCFA) as director of its Office of Financial Management Services. Using lessons learned from his previous failure, he tried once again to develop an online minicomputer automated accounting system. This time he succeeded, developing the first ever implemented in the federal government in 1982. It resulted in better and more timely information and a 60 percent reduction in annual costs. The system was subsequently adapted for use by several other federal agencies and was the forerunner for a system now marketed by a commercial vendor.

Fischer was promoted to his first Senior Executive Service position (ES-2 level) 16 months after he joined HCFA. When HCFA created the Bureau of Data Management and Strategy to establish a focus for its information activities, he was promoted to ES-3 in December 1981, an opportunity that broadened his experience beyond financial systems. In May 1982 he was chosen as HCFA's director of the Office of Management and Budget, at the ES-4 level, encompassing the full range of administrative services. He held this position for two years until moving to the Treasury Department. It was during this time that he helped HCFA to reach a final agreement with industry on a uniform hospital bill that could be used for both Medicare and Medicaid, saving the Medicare program $22 million and the hospital industry $65 million in 1982, the first year of its implementation. He also gained experience in standing up as a careerist to internal political pressure. The general budget strategy at the time was to seek a balance in HCFA's various programs, yet the political appointee in charge of Medicare, which was diminishing at the time, was pushing for a larger share of the total HCFA budget. Fischer opposed him and was subsequently backed by the administrator. The lesson he came away with was, "You need to learn to tell your boss what you believe; don't be intimidated."

Fischer had worked for the Health Care Financing Administration for six years. He explains, "My general philosophy is that I owe any job about two years, but probably not more than about five. I've never left a job I didn't love, but I like to move on to bigger challenges." When HCFA was about to move its central office to Baltimore, Fischer contemplated his potential commute from his home in Reston, Virginia, and considered other options.

Treasury Department: U.S. Mint

Fischer learned from his executive assistant, who was married to the personnel director of Treasury's Financial Management Service, that another Treasury bureau, the U.S. Mint, was looking for an associate director for policy and management. Unlike his previous transfers, in which Fischer had been asked to apply based on previous joint work with the organization, he applied and was selected (at the same SES level) without having previously worked with any of the Mint's management team. He served at the U.S. Mint for two and a half years, using his HEW experience working with industry and contractors to convert the U.S. Mint's operation from processing customer orders for products to a contract with a commercial bank. This cut processing time in half and saved the U.S. Mint more than $1 million annually. He also instituted the use of credit cards in Mint sales programs, and directed start-up marketing for the sale of American Eagle gold and silver bullion coins, which raised more than $1 billion for the Treasury in its first year of operation.

Fischer's previous unfamiliarity with the Mint management team and his acceptance as a transferee highlights his technique in joining a new agency. "My approach is to tiptoe in, talking in depth with my predecessor in the job, if possible, and to begin getting a sense of the people and where the points of power are in the organization. I try to assess the staff and make the most of the current people and organization, rather than coming in with a group of my own staff from a prior agency. If there has been an inside candidate who didn't get the job, I make an effort to work supportively with the individual."

Department of Health and Human Services

Fischer's prior reputation at HEW, now renamed the Department of Health and Human Services, led to a new position in 1986. The staff of Assistant Secretary Anthony McCann suggested that Fischer be asked to serve as the deputy assistant secretary for finance. He accepted the position, receiving a promotion to the ES-5 level. With implementation of the Chief Financial Officers (CFO) Act of 1990, he also was designated as the department's deputy CFO in 1991. While in this position he built upon the efforts initially begun at HCFA as he completed development of the Department of Health and Human Services Payment Management System. This automated system pays all HHS grants and those of approximately 30 other federal agencies on a cross-servicing basis, accounting for $100 billion annually in faster service to states, local governments, and universities while simultaneously providing significant cash management savings for the federal government.

During his time as deputy CFO at HHS, Fischer became increasingly active in several government-wide organizations, most notably as the civilian agencies' representative on the Steering Committee of the Joint Financial Improvement Program (JFMIP), a cooperative executive and legislative branch endeavor whose principals are the director of OMB, the secretary of the treasury, the director of OPM, and the comptroller general.

General Services Administration

After learning from an ad in the *Washington Post* that the General Services Administration was seeking its first chief financial officer, Fischer applied for the position. He joined GSA as that agency's first CFO in 1992, achieving the highest senior executive level grade of ES-6. In addition to financial and budgetary responsibilities, he oversaw the agency's executive information systems and its strategic and performance planning process.

Upon arrival Fischer realized that the available funds for GSA to implement the CFO Act were insufficient. Familiar through his interagency work that the Department of Justice had legislative authority to carry over unexpended funds into the next fiscal year for financial and management improvement, he successfully sought the same authority for GSA. A major restructuring of GSA's financial management systems organization ensued. Results such as the exponential growth of credit cards for federal procurement and travel (making effective use of the federal government's buying power as well as competition among financial institutions for lowest prices and rebates) have revolutionized the way the federal government does business.

During a five-month period in 1993, Fischer was asked to be the acting administrator of GSA. A careerist serving in any political position might find it to be a challenge, but serving as an agency head during a transition between political appointees can be especially daunting. Fischer comments,

"I had no one to go to for answers, but I resolved not simply to tread water. I used the opportunity to get to know better all of GSA's functions and the people, and to position the agency for its transformation." In addition to the normal day-to-day operations of GSA during that time, the agency was called upon to provide logistics and administrative support to the highly visible National Performance Review led by Vice President Gore, which it accomplished smoothly and in record time.

Former GSA Administrator David Barram appreciated Fischer's work in helping GSA move more into the mode of a competitive provider of choice, and he found that they worked well together. When Bob Woods, commissioner of the Federal Technology Service, retired in 1997, Fischer was one of three possible successors Woods suggested to Barram; Fischer was appointed.

Fischer did not rest on his laurels. He spearheaded GSA's "seat management" program, where agencies can pay a fixed amount to assure that they have the most advanced hardware and software fully maintained for an annual fee per desk-top computer. This contrasts with traditional prior approaches, which were costlier and often left agencies with outdated equipment and periodic lengthy procurement efforts. He continually found ways to lower federal overhead costs by consolidating the federal government's buying power, maximizing industry competition, and identifying technological trends. One example was telecommunications. While various companies advertise 10 cents a minute or five cents a minute for long distance business or personal calls, the U.S. government now pays one cent a minute under its latest contract.

Interagency Leadership and Training

Fischer was active in a variety of interagency groups and professional groups during his career. He is particularly proud of the role he played during 1994 in re-energizing the federal Chief Financial Officers Council, establishing an elective structure of officers under the single legislatively mandated OMB deputy director chair. Fischer served as the first elected secretary-treasurer, and the Council has become a model for interagency cooperation. He served on the government-wide Information Technology Services Board.

A tangible result of Fischer's interagency leadership was exemplified by his efforts to address travel reengineering in 1994, which resulted in a December 1995 JFMIP report "Improving Travel Management Government-wide." The report was developed by an interagency task force effort and resulted not only in agencies streamlining their own procedures, but also in the passage of laws implementing its legislative recommendations. The results are not only beginning to reduce government travel overhead costs, but also to reduce frustration levels among federal travelers.

Fischer's management and leadership training included a three-week course in 1983 for senior managers at the John F. Kennedy School at Harvard. He feels that he learned a great deal from the various managers for whom he has worked, singling out former GSA Administrator David Barram as the political appointee who had been the most willing to look at the long-term good of the agency over the short term, by moving managers into roles where they are not immediately expert but can offer fresh perspectives.

By working for agencies with large operational programs or central management support agencies, Fischer was in a position to impact the overhead cost of the federal government significantly. He stayed aware of technological changes, and constantly updated his knowledge by meeting regularly with many people across the federal and industry spectrum. He encouraged them to offer their ideas, shared his own insights, found common ground, and then got everyone working together in implementing improvements.

When he joined a new agency, Fischer was quickly accepted. When he left an agency, he left behind not only improved operations, but well-trained people to continue that agency's progress.

Robert A. Knisely

Robert A. Knisely was the director of Analysis Service in the Office of Student Financial Assistance at the Department of Education. It was the federal government's first Performance Based Organization (PBO), patterned after Great Britain's "Next Steps" program, which gives executives greater flexibility to achieve contractual goals in return for less job security but potentially greater rewards. Education was the seventh federal department for which Knisely worked since beginning a federal civilian career as an operations research analyst at the Navy Department in 1964. He also worked for seven non-departmental agencies and spent five years in the commercial sector during the last 35 years. He was consistently called upon for high-pressure, short-deadline special efforts in a wide variety of federal programs.

Department of Health, Education and Welfare

Knisely was a 1962 graduate of Harvard University and subsequently earned a law degree from Georgetown University while working full-time. Knisely began his federal civilian career with the Navy Department as a grade GS-5 operations research analyst, subsequently participating in Navy's management intern program. He spent three years with the Navy, then joined the Office of Economic Opportunity's community action pro-

Robert A. Knisely

1964 – 1967	Operations Research Analyst; Systems Analyst, Navy Department, Washington, D.C.
1967 – 1969	Community action program monitoring staff, Office of Economic Opportunity, Washington, D.C.
1969 – 1972	Chief, Evaluation and Urban Systems Branch, Center for Community Planning, Department of Health, Education and Welfare, Washington, D.C.
1972 – 1973	Program Chair and Director, Community Management Systems Division, USAC Program, Department of Housing and Urban Development, Washington, D.C.
1973 – 1974	Sr. Attorney–Advisor, Federal Energy Administration, Washington, D.C.
1974 – 1975	Deputy General Counsel and Staff Director, Presidential Clemency Board, Washington, D.C.
1975 – 1977	Director, Office of Program Evaluation, Commerce Department, Washington, D.C.
1977 – 1978	Director, Office of Planning and Budget Systems, Department of Energy, Washington, D.C.
1979 – 1981	Executive Director, Consumer Product Safety Commission, Washington, D.C.
1981 – 1982	Executive Assistant to the Director, ACTION, Washington, D.C.
1982 – 1984	Deputy Chairman for Management, National Endowment for the Arts, Washington, D.C.
1984 – 1989	Senior Member, Systems Research and Applications Corporation (SRA), Washington, D.C.
1989 – 1991	Deputy Assistant Secretary for Budget and Programs, Department of Transportation, Washington, D.C.
1991 – 1992	Special Assistant to the Secretary and Director, Office for Drug Enforcement and Program Compliance, Department of Transportation, Washington, D.C.
1992 – 1999	Deputy Director, Bureau of Transportation Statistics, Department of Transportation, Washington, D.C. (Acting Director in 1992 and in 1998)
1999 – 2000	Director, Analysis Service, Office of Student Financial Assistance, Department of Education, Washington, D.C.

gram monitoring staff in 1967. He had learned about the position from a fellow Marine Corps reservist. This subsequently led to his first promotion to a supervisory position, at grade 14 and later 15, as a branch chief at the Center for Community Planning under the Department of Health, Education and Welfare. He served as HEW's representative on the Urban Information Systems Interagency Committee—the USAC project—involving close coordination with the Department of Housing and Urban Development's (HUD) Model Cities Program and with other agencies. This led to his becoming chairman of the USAC program, working for HUD as director of the Community Management Systems Division in 1972 and 1973. The project, sponsored by components of seven cabinet departments, the National Science Foundation, the Office of Economic Opportunity, and the Office of Management and Budget, used advanced information technology to build integrated municipal information systems.

Federal Energy Administration

An acquaintance at OMB requested that Knisely be detailed in 1973 to an OMB energy task force, which led to his joining the Federal Energy Administration as a senior attorney/advisor, implementing the Mandatory Petroleum Allocation Act of 1973, contingency plans for gasoline rationing, and related issues. In 1974, a fellow attorney, Rick Tropp, who had worked with him on the energy crisis, asked Knisely to be detailed to the Presidential Clemency Board, where he served through 1975 as deputy general counsel and staff director. The staff of more than 600 detailees (including 450 attorneys) to this White House board processed approximately 16,000 applications in less than a year. Knisely then organized the phase-out of this temporary board. "Virtually all my changes in jobs were initially by detail at the request of someone I had worked for or had worked with me, with an actual transfer to an agency following," Knisely explains.

Department of Commerce

Knisely's first position at the senior executive level (GS-16, prior to establishment of the SES) was with the Department of Commerce in 1975, where he created and staffed a new departmental program evaluation office. He had been recommended for the position by Joseph Kasputys, for whom he had developed the federal energy regulations. He also operated the department's management by objectives (MBO) system for Secretary Elliott Richardson.

Return to Department of Energy

With the change in presidential administrations, Knisely searched for a new position. Fellow careerist Bill Strauss, who had worked with him on President Ford's clemency board, told him of opportunities in the new

Department of Energy. In 1977 he joined the department as its director of the Office of Planning and Budgeting Systems, where he designed, built, and operated a multi-year planning and budgeting system—all at the same time. As part of this effort, he designed the department's first multi-year planning process.

Consumer Product Safety Commission

Responding to a job announcement at the Consumer Product Safety Commission (CPSC), Knisely served as its deputy executive director from 1979 to 1981. His earlier experiences in program planning and budgeting helped him to redesign the agency's management structure so that project managers could have greater control over staff and dollar resources. While at CPSC he concluded that the federal budget development process was analogous to a ping pong game in its various submissions, reviews, and appeals processes. It was important to provide the maximum number of iterations on a level playing surface so that each side—program people and the various levels of budget reviewers—felt the process had been complete and fair. A fair game clarified expectations and achieved the best results. This perception of fair play included assuring publication of a master budget calendar so that all could know each side's time commitments in advance. As Knisely admits, "A published schedule may not be met perfectly, but it can be altered in future years to reflect the actual experience." He brought this technique to future agency budgeting whenever possible.

ACTION/National Endowment for the Arts

Knisely's previous experience closing the Presidential Clemency Board led to his interest in joining the ACTION agency as executive assistant to the director for 10 months, directing a reduction in force of 247 employees and the transfer of 300 joint support staff to the Peace Corps. He accomplished this objective without challenge.

From 1982 to 1984 Knisely served as deputy chairman for management at the National Endowment for the Arts. He had been recommended for the position by Kasputys, his former supervisor at Commerce, who was then in the private sector. Knisely directed an effort to streamline the endowment's grant processing system, which reduced processing time almost by half. He also established cost centers and obligation tracking systems similar to those that helped improve operations at CPSC.

Knisely's graphs on grant processing time revealed in the middle of fiscal year 1982 that only one-third of the budget would be obligated by year's end. The graph revealed that the bottleneck was the chairman, who was interested in studying each grant application at his own pace. Instead of confining himself to talking privately with his boss, Knisely indiscreetly showed his charts to others, which eventually led to his job's abolishment.

Private Industry/Department of Transportation

Knisely left federal service for five years to go with a commercial firm, Systems Research and Applications Corporation, returning to federal service in 1989 as the deputy assistant secretary for budget and programs at the Department of Transportation (DOT). The offer came about because he had joined a former fellow worker from the clemency board, Rob Quartel, on President Bush's transition team and caught the eye of the new transportation secretary, Samuel Skinner. While Knisely came in as a careerist on a civil service reinstatement, two years later Skinner wanted to fill the position with a political appointee; in 1991, at the request of the secretary, Knisely moved to the position of director of the Office of Drug Evaluation and Program Compliance.

That same year Congress approved establishment of the new Bureau of Transportation Statistics (BTS). Knisely had watched momentum for the new agency develop from his previous positions with Transportation and lobbied to become its first deputy director. He held this position (and also served as acting director for much of the time) until 1999. Excerpts from his farewell message to his staff provide a sense of both his accomplishments there and his work philosophy:

> "I am immensely proud of what we have accomplished at BTS since that frantic DOT press release in October of 1992. We have built a new national statistical agency, one of America's top 10 principal statistical agencies, with a seat at OMB's Interagency Council on Statistical Policy. We have created the 10th operating administration within the Department of Transportation. We have produced 30 CD-ROMs (115,000 distributed) and 78 publications (325,000 distributed). We have created a virtual National Transportation Library, an award-winning website.... To everyone's surprise, in only six years we have become a presence in the world of American transportation and TEA-21 [the Transportation Equity Act for the 21st Century] increased our funding for the next six years by 107%....

> "A recent *Post* article on a retired Marine Corps commandant described his father as a 'five and dime setup man.' His job was to go to a city, buy land, get a store built, stocked, and in operation, and move on to the next city. Looking back on my career, I have enjoyed most of the jobs in which I was a five and dime setup man. I've done it six times: first for the energy crisis, President Ford's Clemency Board, the Department of Commerce, the Department of Energy, the National Performance Review, and the Bureau of Transportation Statistics."

National Performance Review

Knisely's reference to the National Performance Review was to the task force work he had done in 1993 and 1995. For six months in 1993 he had been a member of the senior management team (one of three civil servants) that directed Vice President Gore's National Performance Review, and he continued in an advisory capacity during subsequent years while working at the Department of Transportation. Accomplishments during these details included initial staffing of the 250-person six-month task force that wrote the original report; bringing in presidential management interns to serve as members of the 20 separate teams to assist in cross-communication among the teams; and serving as a staff director in 1995 at the request of Vice President Gore to coordinate all the key agencies engaged in regulatory reform review. Savings from the regulatory changes were estimated at $16 billion.

Department of Education

In 1999 Knisely joined the first congressionally mandated federal Performance Based Organization (PBO)—the Office of Student Financial Assistance in the Department of Education. The chief operating officer selected to lead it, Greg Woods, had worked with Knisely at NPR, where Knisely had proposed a customer-service initiative to Woods. Woods had been leading the customer-service effort prior to his selection to lead the Office of Student Financial Assistance. He asked Knisely to join as the director of his Analysis Service.

In that position, Knisely assessed the weekly meeting of managers from all over the agency. This "program management" meeting brought together GS-13–15 managers to update one another, seeking to bridge the inevitable stovepipes in an organization of 1,200 employees who oversee $50 billion annually in student grants, loans, and loan guarantees. This type of meeting has taken place for 20 years, sometimes monthly instead of weekly, with varying participants. Have they succeeded, in the face of constant changes in congressional direction and senior leadership? Not entirely, Knisely noted, but they held the agency together through persistent, conscientious, wonderful leadership. He wonders where else in Washington such ongoing meetings can be found.

Interagency Leadership and Training

Bob Knisely consistently volunteered for difficult "startup" work, which is what he did at the first PBO. In his prior position, the new national statistical agency that he helped build in record time earned awards, recognition, and respect from a large and diverse clientele. As part of his professional training, he regularly attended an annual conference on the strategic use of computers and telecommunications in the public sector at Harvard's Kennedy School. Earlier work on the energy crisis, President Ford's

Clemency Board, made significant contributions in a leadership role with the Vice President's National Performance Review, and a variety of other activities represent only a partial summary of his ubiquitous presence when a new issue is being faced and a volunteer executive to manage it is needed.

Eileen T. Powell

Eileen Powell is the director, Administrative Accounting, and deputy chief financial officer, Internal Revenue Service, Department of the Treasury. She joined the IRS in 2001, after three years at the Department of Veterans Affairs (VA), where she was the associate deputy assistant secretary for financial operations. The VA title provided only the vaguest hint of her actual responsibilities, which included directing VA's pioneering electronic commerce and entrepreneurial agency cross-servicing programs. Prior to joining the VA in 1998, she spent 10 years at the Department of Transportation and 16 years with the Treasury Department. Her ability to bridge organizational suspicions and earn the trust of all sides in achieving common goals has been a consistent theme throughout her career.

Treasury Department

Powell, a 1971 honors graduate of Virginia Tech in accounting, began working that year with the Treasury bureau—now named Financial Management Service (FMS)—as a GS-7 auditor. The bureau had a five-year internal rotation program in the accounting and budget fields, which she found provided an excellent grounding for her career. She was promoted to her first supervisory position in 1980 as the bureau's budget officer, then in 1983 broadened her experience when selected for the GS-15 position of deputy chief disbursing officer. This line management position involved supervising a headquarters and field organization of over 800 people responsible for issuing 700 million U.S. Treasury checks, direct deposit, and wire transfer payments annually for Social Security, veterans benefits, tax refunds, and other payment obligations of the federal government. After three years in this position, she then served for two years as the bureau's planning officer.

Among her experiences at FMS that would prove invaluable as she joined other departments was the development of closer collaboration between Washington headquarters and field installations. At the time she became deputy chief disbursing officer, a decision had just been made at headquarters to replace the computers at the disbursing centers with those of a different manufacturer, and the field organization was strongly opposed.

With about half of the bureau's workforce located in the disbursing field offices, and no margin for error without media headlines (e.g., if Social Security payments were ever misdelivered or delayed), good communication

Eileen T. Powell

1971 – 1973	Auditor, Bureau of Accounts, Treasury Department, Washington, D.C.
1973 – 1976	Accountant, Bureau of Government Financial Operations (after merger of two Treasury Bureaus), Washington, D.C.
1976 – 1980	Budget Analyst, Bureau of Government Financial Operations, Treasury Department, Washington, D.C.
1980 – 1983	Budget Officer, Financial Management Service (Bureau renamed), Treasury Department, Washington, D.C.
1983 – 1986	Deputy Chief Disbursing Officer, Financial Management Service, Treasury Department, Washington, D.C.
1986 – 1988	Planning Officer, Financial Management Service, Treasury Department, Washington, D.C.
1988 – 1991	Chief, Working Capital Fund, Department of Transportation, Washington, D.C.
1991 – 1995	Deputy Director of Financial Management, Department of Transportation, Washington, D.C.
1995 – 1998	Director of Financial Management, Department of Transportation, Washington, D.C.
1998 – 2001	Associate Deputy Assistant Secretary for Financial Operations, Department of Veterans Affairs, Washington, D.C.
Since 2001	Director, Administrative Accounting, and Deputy Chief Financial Officer, Internal Revenue Service, Department of the Treasury

and mutual trust between headquarters and field was essential. The environment encouraged considerable initiative in decision making while requiring thorough, timely, and accurate information at headquarters.

Powell stepped into the fray to help both sides find a middle ground of mutual trust and ameliorated the field concerns. The new machines were installed without serious problems or any disruption of payments during the five years they were in operation. She also implemented electronic certification as the first major payment vehicle in government to employ electronic signatures—a system that is still in use today.

Department of Transportation

In 1988, on the recommendation of a former FMS colleague then at the Department of Transportation, she was asked to join Transportation on a lateral transfer as chief of the Working Capital Fund. After three years in this position, she was selected for her first Senior Executive Service position: deputy director of financial management for the department. She served in that position almost four years, and then in 1995 was promoted to director of financial management.

While at Transportation, her skills in ameliorating resistance to headquarters decisions, initially developed while she was deputy chief disbursing officer at FMS, were tested. The department sought to have a single Oracle Enterprise department-wide solution for financial processing and reporting. Normally each administration would fight the department to retain the system with which it was familiar, but her ability to listen, reach reasonable accommodations, and develop an attitude of mutual respect prevailed. Her experience and familiarity with the budget and planning processes in her FMS positions enabled her to develop and institutionalize structured management of the Department of Transportation's $150 million Working Capital Fund—improving billing practices from six months' delinquent to timely, establishing a planning and evaluation function, and keeping both fund customers and the board of directors fully apprised and involved through training, quarterly meetings, and reliable reports.

While reaching a compromise has been appropriate for many situations she has faced, there are times when Powell has taken a strong position and withstood pressure to change. One of her responsibilities was to ensure that travel policy was consistently implemented. In June 1995 the terrorist Unabomber had not yet been captured and had made threats to place a bomb at Los Angeles International Airport. FAA was publicly telling the nation that the airport and planes were safe when a member of the secretary of transportation's immediate staff decided to change the secretary's flight from Los Angeles to a train trip as a security precaution. Powell said, "No." The secretary flew from Los Angeles without incident, and the only repercussion was an increase in respect for her by others in the department.

Department of Veterans Affairs

When a vacancy through retirement occurred at the Department of Veterans Affairs for the manager of their financial operations, Deputy CFO Frank Sullivan asked colleagues whom they would recommend. Dennis

Fischer, then commissioner of the Federal Technology Service at GSA, whom Sullivan knew from work they had previously done together on the CFO Council and in professional organizations, recommended Eileen Powell. Bob Woods, director of the information technology program at VA, who had held a similar position at the Department of Transportation, also recommended Powell. She was interviewed and ultimately offered the job, starting in the spring of 1998. "I was surprised Dennis had recommended me, since I had only worked with him a few times on travel issues," she observes. When Fischer was interviewed for this chapter, he explained that he had been impressed by her leadership abilities and responsiveness in addressing the issues. She was the top person he thought of when contacted for a recommendation.

Once again her communication skills (including those between field and headquarters organizations) were tested. She explains, "I was responsible for giving advice and counsel regarding the department's Franchise Fund finances and for marketing the overall fund. The Franchise Fund cross-services other federal agencies in a competitive environment. I discovered that the six franchise business units, four of which are in the field, considered my Washington-based business office to be an unwanted burden. They neither needed nor wanted help from my office. I met and worked closely with each and am convinced they now realize the value added by the office." The Department of Veterans Affairs is one of the best managed of the six agency Franchise Fund pilots under the Government Management Reform Act, having received an unqualified opinion by a private sector accounting firm in its most recent audit.

Frank Sullivan, the deputy CFO for the department who hired her, commented, "The department's culture is very conservative and it takes a lot for someone to earn people's trust. I have been pleased and floored by how quickly, within just a year, she has become trusted."

Interagency Leadership and Training

Throughout her federal career, Powell has taken the initiative to broaden her experiences both through training and interagency work. While at FMS, when she was selected for senior executive development training in 1988, she arranged for a training assignment outside federal service with Marriott Corporation. She did well in it (they offered her a job), but she was committed to a federal service career. Also, while at the Department of Transportation, she attended the Federal Executive Institute in 1991. She comments, "I learned a great deal about management and leadership from my various training courses and assignments, but I also learned a lot about what *not* to do as a manager simply by watching others."

While at DOT she was active in the interagency committee developing new travel policies. In addition to impacting all federal agencies through this work, one direct benefit to the department was implementing a fully electronic travel management system that eliminated paper and reimbursed travelers' bank accounts within four business days of approval. Supporting a broad, government-wide view of agency accounting interactions, she currently chairs the Interagency Advisory Board on Intergovernmental Transfers.

Powell's 28 years of federal service have included a variety of staff and line management positions in the financial field for three agencies. She has brought to each position, knowledge and techniques learned from previous ones, gained additional knowledge, and brought that to bear on solving subsequent problems. Although the current department for which she works has a national image of old-line conservatism, it has been one of the leaders in the federal government in the use of electronic technology during the past decade. Powell's prior experiences in innovations wherever she has worked, coupled with a fast learning curve in new positions, offer the likelihood that the Department of Veterans Affairs will continue as a program agency leader in accelerating the electronic revolution in federal services.

Myrta (Chris) Sale

Chris Sale is deputy to the chair and chief financial officer for the Federal Deposit Insurance Corporation (FDIC). Her duties there include managing the FDIC's financial activities, its receivership and resolution functions, and its personnel and administrative programs. A unique requirement of the job is managing the investment of FDIC's $40-billion insurance funds. Her career in public service includes management positions with a nonprofit organization and a state government as well as federal service. She exemplifies the career senior executive who earns the trust of political appointees by helping them accomplish key objectives in an innovative manner that brings forth an organization's best efforts.

Civil Service Commission

After receiving her bachelor's degree in psychology from Boston University, she began her federal career in 1972 as a GS-7 budget/program analyst with the former Civil Service Commission, now the Office of Personnel Management. She spent eight years there, receiving frequent promotions. She was a grade 13, serving as the agency's acting budget officer (a grade 14 position) when she left to become director of financial management for the Peace Corps.

Peace Corps/State of Ohio/National Public Radio

A former OPM colleague, Nancy Kingsbury, had invited Sale to help the Peace Corps set up its new budget office as it was separating from the

Myrta (Chris) Sale

1972 - 1980	Budget analyst, Civil Service Commission, Washington, D.C.
1980 - 1982	Director, Financial Management, Peace Corps, Washington, D.C.
1982 - 1984	Director, Office of Budget and Management, State of Ohio, Columbus, Ohio
1984 - 1985	Vice-President, Finance and Administration, and Treasurer, National Public Radio, Washington, D.C.
1985 - 1989	Director, Finance Service, Veterans Administration, Washington, D.C.
1989 - 1991	Chief of Staff to Assistant Secretary for Finance and Planning, Department of Veterans Affairs, Washington, D.C.
1991 - 1993	Executive Associate Commissioner, Immigration and Naturalization Service (INS), Department of Justice, Washington, D.C.
1993 - 1997	Deputy Commissioner, INS, Department of Justice, Washington, D.C. (Acting Commissioner in 1993)
1997 - 1998	Chief Operating Officer, Small Business Administration, Washington, D.C.
1998 - 1999	Director of Management Initiatives, Office of Management and Budget (OMB), Washington, D.C.
Since 1999	Deputy to the Chair and Chief Financial Officer, Federal Deposit Insurance Corporation (FDIC), Washington, D.C.

ACTION agency. The position was in the Foreign Service, effectively a promotion to grade 15. Over her two years there Sale assumed broader duties in finance and contracting and participated in the negotiations to administratively separate the two organizations.

In 1982 former Peace Corps Director Richard Celeste was elected governor of Ohio. Sale explains, "He was looking for someone with technical skills whom he could trust. He invited me to become his director, Office of Budget and Management. When I assumed the office, the state was projecting a $500 million deficit; six months later when we closed the books, the state had a surplus of $80 million." This remarkable turnaround occurred because the state legislature approved a plan she presented that defined the size of the problem, and—in a "burden sharing mode"—effectively reduced half the gap by increasing state taxes and fees and the other half by reducing appropriations. The state also took aggressive steps to increase federal matching funds.

When Sale took the job in Ohio, her husband, a Washington-based federal careerist, took a year's sabbatical, but not having found suitable work in Columbus, he needed to return to his job at the United States Information Agency. With two children to raise, they didn't consider commuting an option, so in 1984 she began inquiring about opportunities in Washington. Douglas Bennett, then president of the private, nonprofit National Public Radio (NPR), was a colleague of Governor Celeste and had become familiar with Sale's work at the time Celeste considered her for the Ohio position. Bennett offered her the position of vice president for finance and administration and treasurer of NPR.

Veterans Administration: Department of Veterans Affairs

"After I had been with NPR a little over a year, I received a call out of the blue from Conrad Hoffman, controller at Veterans Administration, to become director of VA's Finance Service, my first SES position. He had been one of the people with whom I had interviewed two years earlier when I was looking to return to Washington," Sale explains. She served in the position for four years. During her tenure from 1985 to 1989 she helped lead VA into its initial pioneering efforts in electronic data interchange for business transactions, providing major cash management savings as well as operational benefits. Drawing on knowledge gained working for the state of Ohio and NPR, she also directed the first issuance of certified commercial-type financial statements by VA. This occurred almost a decade before federal agencies were required to do so.

The law that established the Veterans Administration as the Department of Veterans Affairs had the unintended effect of leaving her ineligible for what had become the deputy assistant secretary position, which she had been performing and helped to establish. In an effort to assure that the position would be filled by a career professional, the law required that the occupant must have five years of continuous federal employment immediately preceding the appointment to deputy assistant secretary. Sale was short by less than a year. She then spent several months as chief of staff to Anthony

McCann, the first statutory CFO in the federal government, helping to establish the CFO office at VA and receiving the Secretary's Exceptional Service Award for her efforts.

Department of Justice: Immigration and Naturalization Service

The Justice Department was looking for a budget director for the Immigration and Naturalization Service (INS). After calling various agency finance offices, Kris Marcy, assistant to the deputy attorney general, received a recommendation that she call Chris Sale at the Department of Veterans Affairs. "I gave her four alternative people to contact, and mentioned to her that if the budget director's *supervisor's* job ever opened up, I'd be interested," notes Sale. Three months later it did, so in the spring of 1991 she left Veterans Affairs and became the executive associate commissioner for management at INS.

At INS, Sale experienced some of the highlights of her career and some of the greatest frustrations. She served there over six years, first in her initial job, then as acting commissioner, and finally as the deputy commissioner when a commissioner had been confirmed.

As executive associate commissioner, she built the newly established office and a unified administrative support system, redesigned and validated the training curricula for law enforcement employees, and revitalized the information resources program. In January 1993 she began serving as the acting commissioner of INS, awaiting appointment and Senate confirmation of a new commissioner during the presidential transition. It took nine months before Doris Meissner was appointed commissioner.

As a career senior executive in a political position leading an agency that was regularly in the news, Sale dealt with accelerated boat migration from Haiti, the initial large-scale smuggling of Chinese on boats into the U.S., the World Trade Center bombing, and the shooting at the Central Intelligence Agency by a citizen of Pakistan. She testified frequently before Congress and represented INS positions at the National Security Council. In the fall of 1993 when Meissner was confirmed as commissioner, Sale became deputy commissioner and continued in that role for four years.

Both her proudest accomplishment and her most frustrating experiences happened at INS during her acting commissioner and deputy commissioner tenures. Each involved rapid increases in workload. The INS citizenship program, under heavy pressure due to growing backlogs, expanded sharply. Processing errors during that period improperly added many people to the ranks of U.S. citizens. Later, when the flaws in the program were highlighted in Congress and by the media, Sale paid the price, although she was a careerist. Her assessment of the situation was that a flawed existing system expanded with additional people and locations without providing adequate time to establish quality control and to absorb growth.

Sale's proudest accomplishment at INS has never received equivalent media coverage, but is likely to produce the longest-term beneficial impact. With a political mandate, the INS budget was doubled in just four years, from $1.6 billion to $3.2 billion (with staff increases from 19,000 to 27,000 people), to bring order to the most volatile areas on the southwest border and other extraordinary migrant flows. The border patrol actually tripled in size. She redesigned assessment tools for screening candidates for initial hiring and for promotions, improved the system for training, and required individual development plans. The results were a drop in the attrition rate from 25 percent to 5 percent, increased respect for the professionalism of INS law enforcement personnel, and no major scandals. INS's career development, assessment, and promotion programs are now being emulated by other federal law enforcement agencies. To understand the dangers avoided in this program of rapidly increasing the law enforcement staff, one need only look at the District of Columbia's experience in a similar rapid expansion of its police force 10 years ago in which hundreds of new officers were hired and significant numbers were subsequently convicted of felonies.

Small Business Administration

As the focal point for criticism of the INS citizenship program, Sale felt it would be best to leave the agency, although Commissioner Meissner was reluctant to lose her.

Linda Gwinn, a former colleague at INS now with the Office of Federal Housing Enterprise Oversight, knew Sale was looking and also knew that Director Aida Alvarez of the Small Business Administration (SBA) needed an experienced chief operating officer. Sale joined SBA in the autumn of 1997.

Her INS management experience became immediately useful to SBA. At INS, Sale had each unit of the organization identify clearly the outputs it expected to achieve from a finite level of resources, then held quarterly meetings with managers in the field and made necessary adjustments. The process highlighted not only individual programs, but clarified the nexus among programs drawing on the same resources. When she joined SBA, Sale introduced a similar system to help meet Chairman Alvarez's aggressive set of objectives. The lessons of program integration learned at INS helped SBA in developing its first plans under the Government Performance and Results Act.

Office of Management and Budget/Federal Deposit Insurance Corporation

While at SBA, Sale was approached for a position at the Navy Department. When she began making inquiries at the Office of Management and Budget about the Navy position, G. Edward DeSeve, the former controller and deputy director for management at OMB, asked her to consider taking his former job, a political appointment requiring Senate confirmation. Prior to her receiving Senate confirmation, she was asked to speak to Chairman Donna Tanoue about becoming the CFO for FDIC. She did so and began serving in her current position in 1999. As with several of Sale's previous transfers among agencies, she had first met and impressed her new supervisor when asked to recommend people for several other positions for which the agency had been recruiting at the time.

Interagency Leadership and Training

Throughout her career, Sale initiated or has been active in various interagency task forces. "While at VA I felt that there needed to be better coordination among agencies involved in large payment systems. I was active in a finance officers consortium which was a precursor to today's CFO Council." While at INS she sponsored and supported efforts to improve customer service at the nation's borders, bringing together the deputies for Treasury's U.S. Customs Service, Agriculture's Plant Inspection Service, and the State Department's Consular Affairs.

She obtained her master's in business administration in 1979 from American University while continuing to work full-time. Additional management and leadership training has been primarily on the job, observing others.

A native of Puerto Rico and fluent in Spanish, her experiences in quickly understanding the varying work cultures in a wide range of agencies, her willingness to listen carefully in considering alternative actions, and her wide range of friends and colleagues who have worked with her and have great respect for her professionalism have benefited both Sale and the agencies where she has been employed.

Conclusions

Adding Value Through Prior Agency Experience

All of the individuals featured in this chapter introduced approaches in the agencies they joined by building on past managerial experiences and knowledge. A summary of the techniques they used, or the results they achieved in one agency and successfully introduced in others, underscores this point.

June Gibbs Brown's experiences working with many different staffs in leading consolidation of the Department of Interior's pay and personnel systems were invaluable when she became Interior's first IG. She combined many independent audit and investigating staffs and got them to work together. Her development of the investigative audit ("audigator") concept at Interior was introduced in those agencies where she later served as IG, and has paid very large dividends to this day in Medicare and other HHS programs. Jack Mills, the former head of ABC Home Health Agency who is currently serving a seven-year prison sentence for Medicare fraud, stated after his sentencing, "I would rather face a punk with a gun than an auditor with a sharp pencil." Similarly, the voluntary self-disclosure protocol she initiated for health care providers, which has saved auditing costs and created a more positive relationship is patterned after her experiences with the Department of Defense program.

Carson Eoyang's experiences as director of the Defense Personnel Security Research and Education Center and as a principal consultant to the Chief of Naval Operations on equal opportunity and management training were instrumental in helping FAA develop and implement much needed diversity training in order to establish a model working environment. Having worked with a high-technology and geographically dispersed agency (NASA), he built upon his skills to forge a closer relationship between FAA headquarters and field offices and accelerated the agency's investment in computer-based instruction and distance learning. He chaired an interagency working group on implementing a Presidential Executive Order on training technology and is now planning to further these efforts at the Naval Postgraduate School in Monterey, California.

After learning from his mistakes attempting to develop a new generation minicomputer-based online automated accounting system for the then Department of Health, Education and Welfare, Dennis Fischer successfully developed the first one for the federal government after joining the Health Care Financing Administration. Fischer used his HEW and HCFA experiences dealing with contractors to convert U.S. Mint customer orders for products to a contract with a commercial bank, thereby saving money and reducing order processing time in half. He also introduced the use of credit cards for these programs. At GSA, his leadership in expanding the use of credit cards for all agencies had a profound effect on the manner in which the federal government now operates.

Robert Knisely's many experiences with starting new organizations, whether as permanent entities (the Department of Transportation's Bureau of Transportation Statistics) or temporary ones (the Energy Task Force, the Presidential Clemency Board, and the National Performance Review), have led to his being called upon frequently by careerists and political appointees from both parties. In addition to bringing past experiences to bear, he has been instrumental in helping organizations refine their budgeting and performance systems, starting in 1975 when he operated the Commerce Department's management by objectives system.

Eileen Powell's experiences as deputy chief disbursing officer and bureau planning officer at the Treasury Department's Financial Management Service (FMS) helped her to develop skills in inspiring mutually reluctant headquarters and field organizations to appreciate the other's value and to work together. The Department of Transportation's single Oracle Enterprise system for financial processing and reporting and the Department of Veterans Affairs' field acceptance of the useful role of its Franchise Fund business office are direct results of her prior experiences. Improving billing practices from six months' delinquent to timely for the Department of Transportation's Working Capital Fund was an immediately transferable experience when she assumed responsibility for the VA Franchise Fund, a working capital fund for business-like cross-servicing operations completely dependent on earned income to survive. Her prior experience at FMS in pioneering the federal electronic certification system is also directly applicable to her responsibilities in furthering VA's electronic commerce initiatives.

Chris Sale's budget and financial management experiences with the Peace Corps, the state of Ohio, and National Public Radio helped her to develop the first certified commercial-type financial statements for VA, a decade before federal agencies were required to do so. Her development at INS of a system by which each unit identified its expected outputs for a given level of resources, thus clarifying the relationships between programs, was of immediate use when she developed a similar system at SBA. That system helped the agency to meet the chairman's aggressive set of objectives and produce its first plans under the Government Performance and Results Act.

Additionally, many of these executives' innovations have been emulated by others, producing an impact far beyond the agencies in which they worked. An updated version of the consolidated Department of Interior pay and personnel system, developed 19 years ago under the direction of June Gibbs Brown, still is used not only by all the bureaus in Interior, but also by the Social Security Administration, Federal Trade Commission, and several other federal agencies and private foundations.

Carson Eoyang's experiences in advanced distributed learning technologies and identification of the opportunities presented by the explosive growth of the Internet are likely to benefit not only the Naval Postgraduate School but the rest of the federal workforce as well.

Dennis Fischer's online automated accounting system, developed for a mini-computer in 1982, was adapted for use by several other federal agencies and was the foundation for a system marketed today by a commercial vendor. The automated payments management system he developed as deputy assistant secretary for finance at HHS continues to pay grants to cities, universities, and others from HHS, and to about 30 other federal agencies on a cross-servicing arrangement. His leadership in various positions at GSA has led to maximizing industry competition for federal business; lowered net cost for credit cards, computer, and other automation services; and dramatically reduced costs for telecommunications services.

The hiring and training practices Chris Sale introduced at INS during its rapid staff expansion have been emulated by other federal law enforcement agencies.

Common Characteristics of Uncommonly Mobile Executives

The six senior executives interviewed for this chapter have demonstrated success in a variety of agencies. Four have received SES Presidential Rank awards and all have received other awards that attest to the results they have accomplished. Reviewing their careers reveals that they have the following characteristics in common:

- All are self-confident risk takers, with a strong sense of integrity and the courage of their convictions; they are resilient when things go wrong.
- All have been active in professional and/or interagency groups and task forces, often initiating such organizations or assuming leadership positions in them.
- All are energetic, focused lifetime learners who stay current with technological and management trends and readily adapt them to achieve organizational objectives; they are willing to spend the extra time required for advanced degrees or leadership training.
- When joining an agency, all adapt to the culture, demonstrate confidence in people, and inspire the staff to work together toward common goals.

Risk Takers

June Gibbs Brown discovered early in her career that most agencies have large chronic problems, and she made a point of seeking them out and dealing with them, such as consolidating the Department of Interior's many payroll and personnel systems. As an IG, she created a team that brought together the separate disciplines of auditing and investigations when problems demanded a new approach. When President Reagan fired all the IGs in 1981, she could have simply left the federal government and taught in a law school, but she reapplied for an IG position and was selected as the IG at NASA.

Carson Eoyang knew that his center's research (indicating that gays in the military did not pose special security threats) would not be a popular conclusion, but nonetheless he issued the straightforward report. When the reaction began impacting other work at the Defense Personnel Security Research and Education Center, with him as the lightning rod, he joined NASA for his first Senior Executive Service position.

Dennis Fischer turned the lessons he learned from an unsuccessful attempt to develop a new online accounting system for the Department of Health, Education and Welfare into another try, which did work. He developed a pioneering system for the Health Care Financing Administration, which is the foundation for a system used by many agencies today. It also was at HCFA that he stood up to pressure by a political appointee who sought a higher allocation for his program in the HCFA budget, and received backing from the administrator. At GSA, he accepted the opportunity to become its acting administrator during the transition between Senate-confirmed appointees. Instead of assuming a caretaker role, he actively pursued a course of transforming GSA to a provider of choice, while preparing for the new administrator. Once David Barram had been confirmed as administrator, Fischer could have simply continued as one of the best known and highly respected chief financial officers in the federal government, but instead accepted the challenge of changing professional fields to become commissioner of the Federal Technology Service.

Robert Knisely's involvement in startup efforts in uncharted territory, from various presidential boards and task forces to establishing the Bureau of Transportation Statistics and joining the federal government's first Performance Based Organization, is the hallmark of his career. Most of the jobs he has taken have involved constant risk and resilience in high-pressure situations. His enthusiasm and candor sometimes caused setbacks (such as his experience at the National Endowment for the Arts), but he consistently emerged as an energetic, experienced executive in demand who has led successful change.

An example of Eileen Powell's standing up to pressure was when she overruled a member of the Secretary of Transportation's staff who wanted the secretary not to take a flight from Los Angeles due to a publicized bomb threat when the FAA was assuring the public that it was safe to do so.

Chris Sale's willingness to take risks, like Dennis Fischer's, can best be exemplified by her nine months as the acting commissioner of INS, awaiting the confirmation of former Commissioner Doris Meissner. She could have declined the role in this high-profile agency or, once there, could have served as a caretaker. Instead, she used the opportunity to raise recruitment standards and training during an unprecedented staff expansion; initiate closer cooperation among the various agencies with responsibilities at our nation's borders; and begin dealing with the many challenges that happened during her tenure, including the initial large-scale smuggling of Chinese immigrants.

Interagency Leadership

Probably the most striking common factor among the six executives is their involvement in interagency task forces or groups and in professional associations.

Brown served twice as vice-chair of the President's Council on Integrity and Efficiency (the departmental and large agency IGs), chaired the Interagency Committee on Information Resources Management, and served on the boards of directors of the Federal Law Enforcement Training Center and the Interagency Auditor Training Program at the USDA Graduate School. She also was a member of GAO's Advisory Committee on Government Auditing Standards. The now retired former IG at HUD and vice-chair of the PCIE, Charles Dempsey, credits her for being instrumental in setting up computer training for the IG community. Her professional association work has included serving as national president of the Association of Government Accountants and on the board of directors of the Hawaii Society of CPAs. She is a fellow of the National Academy of Public Administration.

Eoyang was the founding co-chair of the OPM-sponsored Federal Human Resource Development Council and the team leader on "Rethinking Program Design" for Vice President Gore's National Performance Review, and is a board member of the Training Officers Conference. He was founding chair of the Asian American Government Executive Network and recently was elected to the Cosmos Club in Washington, D.C.

Fischer served on the Government Information Services Technology Board; was a member of the Steering Committee of the Joint Financial Management Improvement Program; and was the first elected Secretary/Treasurer of the Federal CFO Council. He has represented all federal civilian agencies on the Cost Accounting Standards Board and served on GAO's Governmental Auditing Standards Advisory Council. His interagency leadership style benefiting all agencies is exemplified in his efforts to address travel reengineering in 1994, which resulted in the JFMIP report "Improving Travel Management Government-wide." The report was the product of a multi-agency task force cooperative effort and resulted not only in agencies streamlining their own procedures, but also in the laws implementing the report's legislative recommendations.

Knisely's many interagency task force experiences have been outlined earlier in this report, with the most recent ones being service as a deputy director of Vice President Gore's National Performance Review and coordinating key agencies engaged in regulatory reform review. One of his initiatives in 1993 was to arrange for presidential management interns to be brought in to work with each of the two dozen NPR teams, thus providing an early interagency experience and opportunity for these future federal executives at the start of their careers to work with senior careerists from across the federal spectrum.

Powell worked on the interagency committee developing travel policy, and she chaired the Interagency Advisory Board on Intergovernmental Transfers.

Sale has initiated interagency groups or task forces to deal with a variety of cross-agency programs. At VA she organized a finance officer's consortium to improve coordination in the Pell Grants student loan program; while at

INS she sponsored and supported efforts to improve customer service at the nation's borders, bringing together the deputies for the Treasury Department's U.S. Customs Service, the Agriculture Department's Plant Inspection Service, the State Department's Consular Affairs, and INS. She also served as INS representative on the Department of Justice's Executive Officers Group.

Lifetime Learners

Whether they sought advanced degrees while working, stayed current with technology, attended leadership training, or closely observed effective political leaders and careerists in their agencies or on interagency projects, all six principals have consistently exhibited a high level of energy, curiosity, and dedication to learning.

All of Brown's post-secondary education, from her bachelor's and master's degrees from Cleveland State University to her J.D. from the Denver School of Law, were earned while she worked. Additionally, she attended the 13-week Harvard Advanced Management program. She also comments that working with two administrators at NASA, two secretaries of defense, and the secretary at HHS has provided invaluable learning models for effective leadership.

Powell, a magna cum laude graduate of Virginia Tech, participated in an extensive rotational training program for newly hired accountants at the predecessor Treasury bureau to the Financial Management Service. Some years later she was selected for senior executive development training and took the initiative to obtain an assignment with a major commercial company to broaden her experience. She feels she has learned a great deal about management and leadership from her training, but comments that she also has learned much by observing various federal managers, including what *not* to do. She has attended the Federal Executive Institute and other management training for positive models as well. Her pioneering leadership in implementing the federal government's first electronic signature system for payments and her efforts in VA's electronic commerce initiatives reflect how she continually updates her applied-technology expertise.

Knisely, a Harvard University graduate, earned his law degree from Georgetown University while working full-time. His primary executive-level training had been to attend an annual national conference on the strategic use of computers at Harvard University's Kennedy School of Government. Practical use of his continually updated technology learning includes establishing the award-winning Internet website of the Bureau of Transportation Statistics and other efforts to make data readily available to the public.

Fischer holds a bachelor's from Vanderbilt University and earned his master's from George Washington University at the time he began his federal career. He attended the three-week course for senior managers at Harvard's

Kennedy School. He also cites the value of on-the-job learning from working with effective leaders. His leadership in establishing fundamental changes in the federal government's ordering and payment systems through credit cards and online information attests to his zeal in maximizing service and lowering costs through planned implementation of current technology.

Eoyang received a bachelor's degree in physics from the Massachusetts Institute of Technology, a master's in business administration from Harvard, and a Ph.D. from the Stanford Business School prior to his work with the federal government. His extensive experience managing training at the Naval Postgraduate School, NASA, and FAA, coupled with his White House and Chief of Naval Operations details, have exposed him to key leaders. His primary formal training has been with the National Training Laboratories. The distance learning technologies he introduced and expanded at NASA and FAA will be further enhanced as he explores ways to maximize use of the Internet.

Sale earned a master's from American University while working for the federal government and has gained leadership skills through working with other leaders in her varied career. Her state of Ohio and nonprofit work experiences have been valuable as she has adapted standard business financial reporting practices to federal agencies, an approach which will be particularly useful to FDIC in the coming years.

Joining Agencies and Inspiring People to Work Toward Common Goals

The wide variety of agency missions in the federal government has led to widely differing work cultures. When someone new comes into an agency at a management level, there always is some level of uncertainty regarding his or her acceptance. Trust must be earned—it is not automatically conferred by virtue of position. The individuals interviewed for this chapter have been able to make an impact rapidly. Their comments on how they approach each new position provide great understanding.

Brown points out that she recognized every agency has a different culture to which you need to be sensitive. It is important to understand that you need to adapt and work within the culture rather than trying to change it. She sought to learn the language and the acronyms quickly.

Eoyang was advised by the person who hired him for NASA that it was important to learn NASA's culture and traditions swiftly, and minimize references to his Defense Department experiences. He did so and found that, combined with his technical training and previous aerospace industry experience, he was soon accepted. When he transferred to FAA some years later, he not only followed the same approach, he jumped at the chance to serve in an acting capacity in a critical field position and thus gained a more thorough understanding of the entire agency.

Fischer described his approach as "tiptoeing in," talking in-depth with his predecessor in the job, if possible, and starting to get an understanding of the people and points of power within the organization. He also tried to work supportively with any inside candidate for the job who was not selected.

Knisely's transfers among agencies normally have come about after he had been serving on a detail at the request of someone in the agency. He points out that at any agency there is always someone who has been there for many years and knows the agency backwards and forwards—the people, the process, the products, the budget, and the agency's idiosyncrasies. He finds them quickly, then listens and learns.

When joining a new agency, Powell talks to many people to gain their insights and ascertains who the key people are who get things done. She learns the culture and talks with agency customers to gain their views, then seeks to produce some tangible quick results.

Sale seeks to learn the agency's business as quickly as possible and establish credibility with the careerists who have worked there. She gets around and talks with many people who are doing the agency's daily work, and tries to respond and act in a timely manner and always keeps her word.

The common elements among all six executives are an emphasis on listening, adapting to the culture, and developing a bond of trust—with employees, other executives, and agency customers. They are then in a position to introduce new ideas to solve long-standing problems, such as Brown's introduction of the "audigator" concept at Interior and subsequent agencies, and Powell's convincing the independent VA field offices of the value of the Franchise Fund management office. Producing results based on previous management experience—such as Fischer's obtaining legislative authority for carryover of unexpended funds to improve CFO operations at GSA, and Eoyang's helping FAA develop a credible diversity training program—can quickly deepen the level of trust and set the stage for major improvements in products, services, or cost reductions in the years to come.

A further overarching characteristic of the principals is *flexibility*. Opportunities for training, task forces, or positions do not always occur in a predictable and orderly linear fashion. A general sense of career planning is useful, but a broad set of experiences and work colleagues can lead to some unexpected opportunities. Several of the executives profiled ascribed some of their invitations to apply for positions in other agencies to luck. It was not pure luck—they were known, respected, and ready to risk a new challenge.

Factors That Enhance Mobility

All of the executives were asked about the factors that contributed to their success in being selected to work in a variety of agencies and were invited to offer their thoughts about greater mobility for others in the future. All felt that their wide range of personal connections was a significant contributing factor. Fischer described how he sought in all his positions to identify people with a community of interest, to establish groups and hold off-site meetings to discuss common problems, and to turn to these people for help in resolving issues. While the primary objective has been to help people from all the involved agencies to work better together, the secondary result has been to enhance mobility among agencies when positions need to be filled.

Brown pointed out that she has always enjoyed a wide interest in the different aspects of government, and she encouraged her staff to embrace this viewpoint. Most jobs have some overlap among agencies; she encouraged her subordinates to become involved in interagency work. Although she sometimes "lost" good staff members to other agencies this way, the federal government gained and interagency cooperation was enhanced.

Eoyang suggests that interagency mobility could be enhanced by developing senior executive positions selection criteria that give explicit and substantial credit to experience across a variety of agencies. Encouraging significant interagency rotational assignments could be another means of broadening this experience.

Fischer urged his staff to do what he did—be willing to move laterally between agencies instead of only doing so for a promotion. People at the receiving agency feel they are taking less of a risk, and the mobile executive can then earn trust and a promotion by performance. He adds that senior executives should not lose a year's deserved bonus simply because of the timing of their move.

Knisely stressed the value of providing assignments for senior executives in other agencies either through the requirement of a 90-day assignment to "vest" permanently in the SES, or through developing a tradition of using senior executives from various agencies for significant temporary leadership assignments, such as starting up (or closing down) a function. He also felt that more emphasis should be placed on helping presidential management interns stay in touch with one another and continue their leadership growth in government.

Sale attributes her positive career experiences to making it known that she was available to take on difficult assignments, and she believes others should do the same. When filling top jobs, it is always important to learn more about an individual's capabilities and capacities than paperwork and an interview may reveal. She suggests the assessment center process. INS arranged for people to have both a "self-assessment," which was kept private, and a public assessment. Only those who had participated in the assessment center process could be considered for senior management positions.

Powell stated that it may be a bit scary to leave the comfort zone of work and an agency with which you're familiar, but that it can be very satisfying when you do. Significant temporary assignments in another agency can help to overcome reluctance. One discovery she made, shared by Eoyang, is that there is a larger gulf to overcome between headquarters and the field within many agencies than there is among agencies. Problems in different agencies are not so totally different.

Factors That Inhibit Mobility

Although the majority of factors inhibiting interagency mobility identified by the individuals profiled reflect reluctance of senior managers to hire outside their home agency, some interesting individual and systemic problems were also mentioned.

Knisely commented that federal careerists tend to communicate vertically—within their agency structures—rather than horizontally, as most political appointees do. This limits both their awareness of opportunities elsewhere that could fit their skills, as well as other agencies' knowledge of their abilities and potential availability. Brown attests to this comment by pointing out that many of her best people were not well known outside HHS.

The four other executives make a point that sometimes is overlooked in mobility discussions, which often focus on the reluctance of agencies to hire someone from the outside: Many senior executives are very comfortable remaining in their agencies and have no desire to work elsewhere. They are familiar with the culture and the people, are considered expert in their area, and do not wish to risk working in an unfamiliar environment for people who might not be as appreciative. Others might be interested in changing agencies, but only within their normal commuting area; thus they equate the term "mobility" with geographic mobility. Fischer also raised the point that some senior managers do not want to lose the opportunity to earn an annual bonus; this usually is missed in the first year at a new agency when they are proving themselves. Powell highlights the fact that the increased flexibility among agencies in such areas as flextime and commuting subsidies may also reduce the interest of some executives in considering a position with an agency that has more restrictive rules. This issue of benefits may eventually pale by comparison when the increasing number of unique pay scales among agencies grows.

There are additional inhibiting factors, including the fact that not all senior management jobs are fungible. The "generalist" vs. "specialist" debate has raged since the inception of the Senior Executive Service. Clearly there are many program management positions requiring a high degree of subject matter expertise. On the other hand, there are many others where general management skills, including the ability to recognize and reward top technical performers, would produce meaningful results.

More commonly, people who discuss factors that inhibit mobility mention the reluctance among political and career senior executives to lose good managers from their agency or to hire someone who has not worked their way up within the agency. In the 1980s, at an OPM-sponsored interagency review of the Senior Executive Service, the chief of the U.S. Forest Service joked that his agency traditionally promoted only people who wore green underwear.

Fischer pointed out that political appointees and senior careerists in most agencies discourage interagency mobility, focusing on current work demands rather than risking the learning time for someone new who might later benefit the agency. He was impressed that the former GSA administrator, David Barram, selected executives for positions based on the long-term good of his agency, counter to the conservative trend. Powell believes that senior managers are reluctant to hire outside the agency because they fear the learning curve for the new manager will be too steep. Sale adds that there sometimes is a stigma attached to interagency applicants. Some managers wonder why the applicant has not been promoted at the home agency. She also makes two additional points: Many managers tend to hire whom they know best, and some feel bad if they do not "give" the job to an inside candidate. Eoyang contends that the criteria for job selection frequently reflect the biases of the selecting official toward people who have grown up within the organizational stovepipes.

Recommendations

Recommended Actions: Office of Personnel Management

In recent years, the Office of Personnel Management has been moving away from a policing and broad range technical-training organization to assuming more of a research and consulting role, directions generally appreciated by the program agencies. At the same time, OPM's drastic staff downsizing, elimination of some functions, and related changes have resulted in the loss of much of the agency's central corporate memory and effectiveness in communicating with the federal workforce. It needs to strengthen its database and ability to make pertinent and timely information readily available to all in order to become a more useful research, consulting, and training institution. Specific actions OPM should take to enhance inter-agency executive mobility are:

1. Establish and maintain a complete and current database on the careers of all federal employees at the grade of GM-15 and SES (or their equivalent), readily Internet accessible to all agency managers, with appropriate search capabilities.
2. Recognize that with an increasing number of executives under the Federal Employees Retirement System (with pension portability), public service careers are more likely going to include public, nonprofit, and private sector work experience. Explore ways to maximize the cross-training value, developing incentives to encourage executives who leave federal service to return later in their careers. Work with the Office of Government Ethics to minimize potential conflicts of interest.
3. Conduct research on ways of ameliorating the increasing differences in pay and benefit systems among agencies in order to ease transfers.
4. Establish a well-staffed and knowledgeable executive search office to assist agencies in filling key positions.
5. Invite current executives who have worked in several agencies to serve as guest speakers or adjunct faculty at each training class at the OPM Executive Seminar Centers and the Federal Executive Institute. Their credibility in answering questions will have far greater motivational impact than even the most committed regular instructors.
6. Strengthen the follow-up interagency program for presidential management interns. Although this chapter has focused on mobility of federal executives already at high career levels, OPM could set the stage for executive mobility in future years by greatly strengthening the follow-up programs for these interns. Including them in regular government-wide seminars and calling upon them to serve on interagency task forces, as occurred with the National Performance Review, is likely to increase their enthusiasm for federal service and consideration of broader experiences than limiting their careers to a single agency.

Recommended Actions: Individual Agencies

Agency program managers, working with human resource and training managers, can take several actions to increase the likelihood of finding talented executives they have not previously known who can benefit their programs:

1. Make changes in their normal search and selection process:
    *   Review potential selection criteria for all GM-15 and SES (or equivalent) positions with the intent of maximizing the ability to attract applicants from outside the agency. This could include specific credit for experience across a variety of agencies or on interagency groups.

- Have at least one individual from outside the agency included as a selection panel member for any executive position. The individual could be someone from an agency with related functions or a "customer" agency.
2. Become involved and encourage other agency managers to become involved in working with other agencies:
   - Serve on interagency task forces.
   - Participate actively at conferences involving more than the home agency; serve on planning committees or panels.
   - Seek to arrange extensive details into positions with partner agencies, possibly trading positions for a period of time with a counterpart.
3. Insure that anyone promoted to an executive position has attended residential leadership training, not limited to home agency personnel, either before or within two years of appointment.

Final Comments

This chapter profiles the careers of six highly successful federal career executives who have worked for a variety of agencies. It describes how their experiences at one agency benefited another and gives several examples of how their government-wide impact has benefited the nation. It demonstrates that mobility among agencies can and does happen. It describes the common characteristics that enabled the profiled executives to transfer and swiftly make valuable contributions at their new agencies.

The executives profiled and almost all the members of the Senior Executive Service today represent the last cohort of federal executives working under the old Civil Service Retirement System, which has tended to keep people in the federal government for entire careers. The Federal Employees Retirement System (FERS) does not create the same incentives. Just as free agency and spending caps have altered the human resources decision-making landscape in professional sports, FERS and the increasingly broad definitions of public service are likely to result in a more mobile workforce that enters and leaves federal service. Worker mobility in our society is becoming more widespread, and the federal workforce is not exempt. A quarter of a century ago, when most federal managers entered the workforce, people who changed jobs more than once or twice in a decade were derisively referred to as "job hoppers." Today, anyone who stays in the same job for 10 years is likely to be suspect.

Mobility can be beneficial both to the individual and to the organizations they join. Planned mobility can leverage the phenomenon to increase the organizational benefits.

Based on the experiences and views of the profiled executives, several specific recommendations for actions OPM and individual agencies can take to facilitate more and more effective interagency mobility in the future are offered. Many of the recommendations will provide benefits to federal agencies even if some individual executives do not join another agency. The exposure to new ideas and different ways of approaching problems through working with people other than familiar home-agency personnel can be useful. To the extent experience is gained in another agency with which executives normally do business, it can lead to closer cooperation in the future.

Many federal human resource issues today require legislation, a solution which is always uncertain and may take years to accomplish. The foregoing recommendations for increasing federal executive mobility do not require legislation—they can be implemented within the executive branch by actions today.

Appendix I:
Career Advice

The foregoing case studies identify useful approaches for individuals who view their careers as encompassing the range of public service:

1. Depend upon yourself, not some wise parent figure, to guide your career. Be flexible, and seek opportunities to work for good leaders and to learn from them.
2. Volunteer for interagency committees and task forces.
3. Seek opportunities for training that include people from different agencies or the private sector (such as the Federal Executive Institute, Harvard's Advanced Management course, advanced degrees).
4. Join professional organizations whose membership involves people from many agencies and, when appropriate, the private sector.
5. Be willing to accept positions or temporary assignments outside your immediate commuting area. The disruption need not last forever, and the longer-term rewards can be great.
6. Be willing to transfer laterally into a new agency. After you've made a contribution, recognition and promotion are likely to follow.
7. Gain some experience in the private sector. All commercial companies are not necessarily more effective or efficient, but their approaches and motivations are different. With a major increase in public/private part-nering and more instances of blended workforces, it is important to have a clear understanding of the similarities and differences.
8. As a manager, be willing to hire people from outside your organization, and listen to them when they challenge the organizational conven-tional wisdom.
9. Encourage your subordinates to do all of the above. It will help the entire federal government to work more flexibly, efficiently, and effec-tively, and help you in recruiting talented and motivated people who can sustain efforts you have started at an agency if you move on.

Appendix II:
Interview Questions

1. Why did you choose to begin a public service career and what other alternatives did you consider?
2. At what level and type of job did you begin, and were you in any sort of intern or management training program?
3. Did you intend to have a general public service or specifically federal career, and had you planned to be transferring among organizations?
4. What were the biggest challenges you faced when joining a new agency and how did you overcome them?
5. What are some examples of experiences and problem solutions at one agency that you were able to introduce successfully at a subsequent agency?
6. What was the most serious problem you faced in your career, how did you deal with it, and what did you learn from it? Did the political/career interface help or hurt?
7. Which particular job or accomplishment have you found the most satisfying? Did the political/career interface help or hurt?
8. What professional, service, or social groups have you joined over the years and what leadership positions have you held in these organizations?
9. On what interagency task forces have you served?
10. Which mentor(s) were most influential in your career?
11. Did people you know seek you for positions in other agencies, or did you actively search outside your agency?
12. To what extent did your contacts through (a) mentors, (b) professional and other groups, (c) task forces, or (d) training lead to positions in other agencies?
13. What government-sponsored training or additional education outside work have you found most useful?
14. Do you still get together with people from former agencies, task forces, or training experiences?
15. What factors do you believe were most significant in your job mobility?
16. What do you consider the biggest obstacles to SES mobility; how might they be overcome?
17. What other thoughts do you have regarding the factors which facilitated your mobility that might be useful for others?

Endnotes

1. At the time she took the Harvard Advanced Management program, women represented about 3 percent of attendees in this highly competitive program. That was double the number in any of the previous 91 classes. Many, particularly those from countries where women were not considered for executive positions, resented the women's presence. She applied herself, worked on teams in the case study system, and by the end of the course was elected by the class to give the graduation speech. She received a standing ovation prior to and then again immediately after her talk. Professional pioneering has its perils, but also impact and rewards.

PART III

The Workplace Challenge

CHAPTER SEVEN

A Learning-Based Approach to Leading Change

Barry Sugarman
Research Coordinator
Society for Organizational Learning
and
Health Research Scientist
Health Services Research and Development
VERDICT, Department of Veterans Affairs

This report was originally published in December 2000.

Introduction

The concepts and management tools of "the learning organization" and "the learning-based approach to change leadership" have been found to be very useful for better understanding and improving the ways that organizations change themselves. Today all organizations face unprecedented levels of demand for better results—in the government, as much as anywhere else—for new levels of service and response, for greater efficiency to produce more with less resources, and to take advantage of new opportunities, such as the Internet. While most of our experience so far with the learning-based approach to change management comes mainly from the business sector, it is important that we also evaluate this approach in the public sector. That is what this chapter begins to do through several case studies in the U.S. federal government.

Leaders within several federal agencies began a partnership with the Society for Organizational Learning (SoL) to try this approach. That came about as the result of an earlier four-year partnership between SoL and the New England Regional Office of the Environmental Protection Agency (EPA). Interviews and observations were conducted in order to understand the process of change in these agencies. These data are analyzed in the light of our experience with earlier change initiatives in the business world, sponsored by SoL and its predecessor, the MIT Center for Organizational Learning.

The information presented here represents early results from organizational change initiatives that are expected to take much longer to reach full fruition. Unlike many other reports of change projects, these cases were not selected as the pick of the crop of proven successes. This is an interim examination and think piece based on an experiment still in process.

Demands for Change in the Government

There have been significant changes (improvements) in the management of government agencies over the past decade, and there continue to be enormous pressures for these agencies to change more for a variety of reasons:

- The gap between ever-increasing demands and restricted resources constantly expands as the consumer revolution creates demands for higher standards of service to citizens.
- Changes in technology and other external factors create new threats and opportunities.
- Industry groups and others who are subject to government regulation have become more demanding, and elected officials have become more receptive to their demands.

- Meanwhile, there is new thinking about the respective roles of federal, state, and local governments; corporations and industry groups; and private, nonprofit service and advocacy groups. For example, there are notions of *partnership* between government and private groups, as well as between levels of government, in many areas (such as environmental protection; regulating the safety of food, drugs, and medical devices; and ensuring that services are provided to disabled children and their families) which require great change in how government managers define and conduct their work.

- Lastly, the vast changes in our world (many based on new technology) present never-ending new challenges to government—genetic research and new questions of ethics and regulation, the AIDS epidemic, the economic stress on all health-care systems, protection of the infrastructure of the Internet now that both economic and national security systems depend on it. In short, the demand for more change in government will only get greater.

Basic Ideas About Change Leadership

In spite of the huge and relatively recent demand for more change in government, the role of change leader is unfamiliar to many public managers and many have serious misconceptions about it. People's *ideas and assumptions* about change and leadership are very important because they greatly affect how people act (or refuse to act) as leaders and as followers who shape what leaders can accomplish. One deeply rooted assumption is the belief that change depends on some rare, extraordinary kind of individual who calls to us from a high position in the organization ("the hero on the white horse") and that we must wait for the arrival of this charismatic senior change leader before we can make any contribution to change. This idea is highly questionable and may be very harmful. A different view is the idea of the learning organization and the learning-based approach to change management, which suggest a different view of the change process in organizations. This chapter is offered as a brief introduction to that view.

This introduction is intended to be relevant and useful to several groups of readers, not just to senior executives but also to middle managers, supervisors, work group leaders (including official leaders), human resource development staff, individual contributors who are frustrated by the limits the organization places on their talents, and to "live wires" of all kinds. Hidden (or perhaps not hidden) within government agencies are plenty of people with good ideas and the ability to develop significant improvements, but there are serious barriers to these potential change agents being heard and working together. Therefore, the role of the change leader is basically to encourage them and to remove those barriers.

Lucky senior executives may find members of their agencies coming forward with proposals for change that they want to implement, just asking for a little support; but more often the senior executive who wants to promote meaningful change will need to signal to staff that such efforts will be appropriately supported. What is "appropriate"? What does it take to create a change initiative? That is the focus of this chapter. At a very introductory level we shall present some of the necessary elements needed in a learning-based organizational change initiative.

Important ideas are often truly simple at their core, but they get overlaid by related but non-essential elements. In this case the central idea is the following: *There is sufficient talent and energy at the grassroots level of most organizations to make significant improvements, but long experience with organizational barriers has led those people to be frustrated and discouraged, which then leads them to develop beliefs that change is impossible in this agency.*

It is impossible, they believe, because "the others" (their colleagues and bosses) would not support or allow it. "They" appear to be major barriers. But originally, they were just like the would-be innovators, full of ideas and energy to make things better. Over time, many have become trapped in a vicious cycle of disappointment, in which we refuse to get hurt anymore, so we protect ourselves behind defensive beliefs that cloak the fact that we care about making things better. This creates a cycle in which we each confirm the fears of our colleagues ("they would not stick their necks out to support a new idea"), while we all retreat into defensive cynicism. In the business world the competitive marketplace tends to blast employees out of that situation, with big rewards for those who succeed and job loss for those who fail.

The Public Sector's Advantage

The public sector faces a big challenge to meet vastly increased expectations with tighter resources and with some significant structural barriers not faced in the private sector. Yet the public sector also has one special asset—its public, common, patriotic purpose. It exists to create public value—for example, safe food and drugs, security against crime and external enemies, clean water, safe air travel, a banking system and financial institutions with integrity. This work is essential to the foundations of our civic society and to the survival of the nation. It is work to be proud of, and many government workers choose it for that reason. This commitment to the ideals of the public good, held by many government workers, should be a big asset to those who wish to light more fires of change in government agencies. For the learning-based approach believes that one crucial element in leading change is to rediscover how much we really care about making things better and to help others to rediscover that they do, too.

We shall now introduce the learning-based approach to leading change in two parts. First, we present the idea of the "learning organization" as the ideal state towards which we are aiming to move. Then we present a very simplified version of the change process involved, the process that leaders at all levels can understand and use, which we call "the learning-based approach to leading change."

What Is a "Learning Organization"?

Organizations that understand how fast the world is changing and what that means for their survivability aspire to be "learning organizations." For Peter Senge [Senge, 1990, 1999], a "learning organization" is an organization that is continually improving its ability to be more effective in meeting goals that are really important to its members. A one-time improvement, however impressive, does not make a learning organization; it requires a state of continuous improvement and improving the way that improvements are made. A learning organization is capable of reinventing itself when necessary.

The learning organization can also be called a "new model" organization. Either way, the difference between "old model" and "new model" organizations is profound. The "old model" organization operates by a *basic formula* that defines how to run the organization: how to obtain the necessary inputs (including resources, licenses, and charters), how to transform them into the appropriate products and services, and how to get them into the hands of those who need them, earning appreciation or at least support for the organization's continued existence. That broad definition should cover both government agencies and businesses in the free market.

The "old model" formula-driven organization spends little time or effort on innovation or improvement. The "new model" or "learning organization" is the opposite. It devotes a major part of its efforts to discovering new ways, not presently known to it. It seeks new formulas, knowing that they can last only a limited time before needing replacement. The way that the old model organization depends on its embedded formula, without giving it any thought, does not exist in the new model, learning organization. Here there is much thought given to how and why things are done a certain way, because they must be improved on continuously, and because they may need to be replaced in the event that sudden changes in the environment should make the old way unviable. The new model, or learning organization, lives in a state of permanent change. Naturally, it requires a very different kind of organization and very different behavior and thinking from all its members.

This contrast between old model and new model is deliberately over-simplified in order to make an important point. We are not describing actual cases right now. In fact, these two models or types do not exist in the real world; they are mental constructs which we may use to help us understand the real world—or we may reject them. Most real organizations have some features of both types; there are very few, if any real examples that are as simple or as extreme as the models. Yet they can be useful in helping us to understand how organizations differ in the way they function. The old and new models may be considered as end points on a continuum where few examples lie at the ends, but many are close enough to be classified as nearer to one model than the other.

The "New Model" or "Learning" Organization

Organization researchers, looking at both government and business sectors, have contrasted the "old model" of modern administration, known proudly as "bureaucracy," with newer models of organization that have been emerging in the latter part of the 20th century. By contrast with the old bureaucratic model that laid the foundations of the modern state and the industrial revolution in the late 19th and early 20th century, these newer models of organization aimed to add new kinds of flexibility onto the base of dependability which was a large part of the legacy of the old model.

The business sector discovered its need for a "new model" of organization and management as it entered an era of intense global competition, the info-telecom revolution, and the knowledge-based economy. (Burns and Stalker, Lawrence and Lorsch, Mintzberg, Ouchi, Pascale and Athos, Quinn.) Whereas the old model of production and distribution had enabled the Allies to win the Second World War and to rebuild during the post-war era of shortage, the new economy of abundant supply, fierce global competition, empowered consumers, and more talented workers demanded a different model. That new model was, in effect, the learning organization.

The government sector experienced its own shake-up in terms of significantly changed demands from its "customers." The traditional model would no longer suffice here either, in the face of new levels of demand for improved service and efficiency in large-scale programs, and for new effectiveness in specially challenging areas, such as preparing for Y2K, mapping the human genome, defeating global terrorism, exploring Mars, and reducing welfare dependency. Max Weber's classic model of stable, honest, rule-governed bureaucracy is no longer a suitable standard for an excellent government agency in the new millennium. In the words of a recent commentator, "Reinventing government means more than creating a government that works better and costs less. It means going beyond the industrial-age model of governance." It requires new thinking and a new model.

We may contrast the new and old models on seven key points. The same differences in organizational design between new and old models will be found to be important, I maintain, in both government and business sectors.

The basic **strategy** of the old model organization is replication or mass production, always following the basic formula, pattern, or rule book, while the new model is innovation as needed to meet (or anticipate) the requirements of the customer, current or anticipated.

The basic **structure** of the old model organization is hierarchy, with emphasis on respect for the chain of command. At the top of the hierarchy are the few who alone have the whole picture of the organization's strategy, so staff must depend on them for approval of any initiative. The new model approach of structure is heterogeneous, with many project teams. Many people (possibly all of them) have the big picture.

The basic **system** of the old model organization is formalized, with explicit rules, policies, and procedures being used. It runs by its standard operating procedures, which are documented and available to all, unlike the new model where systems are more informal, because they are frequently evolving and changing. Staff mutually adjust and coordinate informally (without waiting for supervisors to tell them how) in the new model.

The basic **style** of the old model organization is one of conformity and "please the boss," whereas the new organization emphasizes learning and creativity to please the customer above all. This is sometimes described as a shift from a vertical (hierarchical) emphasis to a horizontal (customer-focused) emphasis, with the value-chain flowing horizontally across all the components of the organization as they contribute to the final result, which is delivered to the all-important customer.

The **staffing** of the old model organization is based on clarity about roles and duties (i.e., job descriptions are taken very seriously), whereas the new organization is flexible about job boundaries, allowing staff to adapt their jobs as they innovate. The new organization encourages staff to be passionate about their work, unlike the old model bureaucracy which expected staff to be impersonal and dispassionate, leaving their personal "baggage" at home.

The **skills** model of the old type organization was to have narrowly specialized roles, but the new model organization prefers skill clusters and cross-training of staff so they can be more versatile and support a flexible system, with workers switching their duties as the need arises. Therefore, the number of different job categories tends to be reduced in the new model.

Finally we compare the old and new models in terms of their purpose or **superordinate goals**. In the old model these ultimate goals are different for the public and private sectors. In the private (business) sector the old model goals are to create profits and rising share values for investors, while in government the old model goals are to administer programs and policies authorized by the legislature and created by senior officials of the executive branch. Because the thinking of the new model about organizational purpose is quite different, it is possible to combine both public and private under one set of superordinate goals: to fulfill a shared vision of the organization's mission through creative work in a community of employees, partners, and stakeholders (see Figure 7.1).

This view of the purpose (superordinate goal) of a public (government) agency is idealistic. It presents the ideal of an organization staffed by workers, managers, and leaders who strive to develop a shared understanding of its mission, together with the various customers and other stakeholders. Their creativity is required both for negotiating this shared vision and for the continuous improvement of performance, with ever tighter resources. A degree of success in this context offers considerable intrinsic rewards, more so than did the old model. Instead of being just a program administrator, as in the old model, the new model public manager tries to act as a significant player in a process of negotiating among diverse stakeholders. "Instead of simply devising the means for achieving mandated purposes, they become explorers who seek to discover, define, and produce public value." [Moore, 1995, p. 20.]

A Learning-Based Change Model

In the previous section, we summarized the main differences between the old model with which today's generation of managers grew up, and which they took for granted, and the new model, which increasingly seems to have answers to the shortcomings we find in our organizations. Making changes in the direction of the learning organization is a huge challenge, but it has begun.

On a much smaller scale, the partnership between the Society for Organizational Learning and five federal agencies has directly taken up this challenge of moving to the new model. Senior managers who are also natural leaders for such change initiatives were sought out and supported in preparing themselves for their new role. Outside experts were brought in who had prior experience in leading similar change initiatives and in training and coaching change leaders. For the most part, though, the leaders of these government change initiatives would have to learn their new roles in the same way that their predecessors had learned—not in the classroom but in the learning lab and on the job, experimenting in how to apply the new

Figure 7.1

	Old Model Bureaucracy	New Model Learning Organization
Strategy	Replicate. Follow the formula. Mass produce.	Innovate to please the customer.
Structure	Hierarchy. Vertical. Chain of command. Big picture held at the top.	Networks. Horizontal. Many project teams. Maybe matrix. Everyone has the big picture.
Systems	Formalized. Coordination by rule book. Standard operating procedures very important.	Informal. Coordination by mutual adjustment.
Style	Conformity. Please the boss. Politics. "Everything in its place."	Creativity. Learning. Participation. Dialogue. Politics (rivalry) over priorities and strategies.
Staffing	Role clarity. Dispassionate.	Flexible job boundaries. Passion about their work.
Skills	Narrowly specialized.	Versatile. Cross-trained.
Purpose (Superordinate Goals)	Create profits and rising share values for investors. (BUSINESS) Administer programs and policies authorized by the legislature. (GOVERNMENT)	Fulfill a shared vision of organization mission through creative work in a community of employees, partners, and stake-holders. (BOTH GOVERNMENT AND BUSINESS.)

principles and tools, and making mistakes along with their colleagues. Leadership and learning are intimately related in the new model of organizational management and change—"the learning organization."

Having defined the learning organization, the new model or ideal, we must now define the change process that is required to move in that direction. This will be called the "Learning-Based Change Model," which differs in some important ways from the traditional or mainstream model of organizational change. We shall highlight some of these differences before we present a checklist of the major steps involved in applying the Learning-Based Change Model, based on the principles of the learning organization.

In its simplest terms, the Learning-Based Change Model relies on the approach of introducing the germs of new ideas, then nurturing and protecting them while they grow stronger, propelled largely by their intrinsic appeal. It is a model of change that relies as much as possible on the power of the grass roots. The traditional model, by contrast, relies on the "leader on the white horse" setting direction and impetus from the top. A more systematic breakdown into two columns can be seen in Figure 7.2.

Figure 7.2

Traditional Change Model	Learning-Based Change Model
Change is *pushed* from the top level.	Change bubbles up from mid-levels and grass roots.
Change program presents a full set of *answers* (formula).	Change approach offers some key answers plus opportunity to *learn together* the rest of what is needed.
"Here's my (top level) vision ... This is how we shall do it."	"Here's my (top level) vision ... How does this connect to what is important to you? How will you contribute to this vision?"
Change behavior through changing policies and reward systems.	Develop new *thinking*, which will shape new behavior.
Exhort, encourage, push, threaten.	Put down roots, feed them, let them spread.
Urgency to show clear, tangible results.	Emphasis on building a foundation for *sustained* change and improvement.
Setting a tough mandate and deadline (from the top).	Work on *several local* level areas of improvement and what arises.

Key Success Factors for the Learning-Based Change Model

What is actually involved in cultivating a learning organization, following the learning-based change model? The following checklist highlights some of the key building blocks needed in order to be successful in that challenging undertaking. If the first section aroused or rekindled the reader's interest to the point of asking, "What specifically is involved in this?" here is a brief answer. It is based on the experience of a dozen change projects guided by the ideas of the learning organization, plus the experience of other change experts, two approaches which agree in some areas and not in others.

Since this chapter is designed for public managers and others with a practical interest in the subject, not for scholars, we shall not attend to these differences, but go straight to a combined checklist of key factors related to success. We do not promise success if they are followed but we confidently predict problems if careful attention is not paid to all of them.

The Change Model Checklist

Each of the items on the checklist will be described briefly. This explanation offers a very "applied" version of the learning-based theory of change, but you will note at one point where I borrow carefully from the traditional (mainstream) theory in order to fill in a weakness in the learning-based theory as we have known it. The goal of both change theories might seem similar—to move closer to the ideal of the learning organization—but only the learning-based theory makes the change in a way that really leads to a strong learning organization.

PHASE ONE: Getting Ready
First requirement: Leaders who want to do this
No factor is more important than the sincere commitment of the leaders to this change effort. They must be volunteers; it is not enough to be a "good soldier" leading this because you were assigned by the boss. The ideal leader for a learning-based change project does not wait to be assigned but creates the assignment for him/herself and then seeks a senior sponsor or champion. In terms of position in the organization, the "ideal leader" is not one person but a coalition of three individuals: (1) one is in a line (rather than staff) management position, (2) one is an internal consultant or networker (e.g., someone in human resource development (HRD), and (3) one is a senior level sponsor. If you, the reader, fit one of these standards, you may nominate yourself for the leadership role. Just be sure that you also find the other two partners you need.

Example: In the partnership between SoL and the Committee for High-Performing Federal Agencies, the Committee played the role of seeking out potential leadership candidates in several agencies, line leaders (mostly from an office of around 100 staff) who would welcome this opportunity and challenge.

Help leaders build skills, understanding, and commitment: find advisors, coaches, or consultants

This is the special responsibility of the internal consultant (HRD, staff position), the second member of the leadership group—in the sense that this person has some knowledge of change management and good access to other resources for training, coaching, and consulting. Leading change and

---

An Implementation Checklist

PHASE ONE: Getting Ready

- Find leaders who want to do this (first requirement)
- Help leaders build skills, understanding, and commitment: find advisors, coaches, or consultants
- Establish senior level support
- Engage others who want to do this ("partners")
- Have partners get to know each other
- Form a core learning/leadership group

PHASE TWO: The Pilot Project

- Select pilot project, ensuring alignment with the strategic direction of the parent organization
- Implement pilot project and initial goals
  - Check out assumptions and "mental models"
  - Identify systemic issues
- Assess your progress frequently, both results and process
- Help all members build their skills, understanding, and commitment

PHASE THREE: Building on Initial Learning

- Make the necessary changes to structures, policies
- Build more capacity
- Keep the neighbors (and boss) informed
- Renew the vision and feed the passion behind the effort for change
- Make and keep contact with other groups making similar change efforts, create a mutual learning support system

creating change together with other people is extremely demanding in terms of skills and in terms of character. Some people start out with more natural aptitude than others and some pick up related "management development" gains in this area during their careers. But few (even the most fortunate) would choose to jump unprepared into this role if there were a chance to prepare. SoL's experience has been that several days spent preparing themselves off-site with other leaders who are approaching such a change venture can be very valuable. This was in fact provided to the volunteer leaders through the Society for Organization Learning's core competencies course.

Establish senior level support

The senior sponsor (or "champion") is the third essential member of the leadership team. This person's main function is to give legitimacy to the initiative, in case it should be challenged by others, even at senior levels. So it is important that the sponsor understands and accepts the rationale for the initiative and the theory of change. The sponsor's contact with the change leaders can be quite infrequent, unless this is the leader's direct boss. Sometimes the sponsor is the first to get the idea of the change initiative and encourages the others; sometimes the line manager is the first one; sometimes it is the HRD internal consultant.

Example: In our case at an EPA Regional Office the initiative suffered greatly because the senior sponsor (who was the regional administrator) and the change leader did not have a good shared understanding of what would be required to make the change work. They agreed on the grand vision of the change but not on how it would be managed and how the active resistance of some other managers would be handled. As a result, the initiative was more limited in its success until the regional administrator left; and the burden of personal stress was much greater than necessary.

Engage others who want to do this ("partners")

All change management models emphasize the need for the leader to present a clear and compelling vision for the change needed—why it is necessary, what the future state will be like, and how they can get there. *Traditional* change models expect the leader to push hard for all employees to follow, to adopt the same vision, and to act accordingly, offering rewards for those who do. However, the *learning-based* change model seeks to get as much mileage as possible out of the voluntary support of those who find this new vision genuinely attractive (even though it may be a small proportion).

These small groups of enthusiasts will encourage each other; their commitment will lead to some early creative efforts and successes. These start a reinforcing cycle or positive growth loop, which may attract other volunteers. The leaders allow others to *participate* in developing and shaping the initiative. It is *not* a top-down, pre-ordained program. Although this way may take longer to get up steam, it seems to have more lasting power to keep on trucking over the long haul, whereas top-down initiatives are more vulnerable to collapse as soon as the leader's full attention waivers.

Early adopters of the learning organization concept are low-key evangelists, always willing to talk about their ideas and ready to invite colleagues who are interested to attend learning labs or other meetings where they can see more of what it is about.

Have partners get to know each other

Not only do the initial group of change leaders and supporters work together in a collaborative, participative way, but they get to know each other as individuals. Our experience indicates that people learn more and work more creatively when they give up trying to leave "personal stuff" at home and are able to "be fully present" in the work group. Whereas the old model of organization would strive for a complete separation between the official role and the private life of the office-holder, the learning organization prefers that workers and managers acknowledge their private lives, interests, and values, while still being held to the usual standards of performance and fairness. Research shows that organizations in fact get better results when they give consideration to the personal lives of employees [Bailyn, 1997].

Form a core learning/leadership group

This is a very important part of the entire learning-based change leadership process. It is where the founders get together and develop their shared vision, which guides the change initiative. Since they are working with a new model involving new concepts, they need to experiment with them. They are learning about each other as individuals and how they each think, building trust and shared commitment. All these activities depend on unusually strong skills at conversation, which participants and change leaders must continue to develop.

At the beginning (before the pilot project), the core group of change leaders and fellow enthusiasts will probably be small enough (say 4 to 10) to function with everyone participating in all discussions. Later, during and after the pilot, the numbers of people and groups involved grow larger and a steering group may become useful.

- Leaders need support and feedback from trusted colleagues and reflective partners.
- They need to model how to be good learners, acknowledging what they do not know, being willing to risk making mistakes, and learning from those mistakes.
- The learning process within this group sets a pattern that can spread through their followers to "infect" wider areas of the organization.

Example: In the case of the Office of Special Education Programs (OSEP) in the Department of Education we see a clear example of such a core group. Formed around Patty Guard (the senior career civil servant) is a group of four (including herself and two of the three next-level managers (her direct reports), plus their in-house HRD consultant). This group is part of the OSEP management team. Core group members went through the SoL orientation and training. They meet frequently to plan the work of the office and the organizational learning activities, and they meet following many of these activities to debrief.

PHASE TWO: The Pilot Project
Select a pilot project, ensuring alignment with the strategic direction of the parent organization

A major outcome or culmination of the core learning group's initial gestation period is to select a pilot project in which it will apply the new approach to change and improvement. The kind of *goal statement* needed for the pilot project involves two things: (1) some improvement in an area that is important to the parent organization, and (2) to be achieved through improvements to the basic business processes involved. This alignment of the process improvement with strategic goals of the parent organization is crucial, though sometimes not receiving sufficient attention. (This is an area where the learning-based approach can learn something important from the mainstream.) Having established that we are pointed in the right direction, the next item looks at the implementation of the project itself.

Implement pilot project and initial goals
Check out assumptions and "mental models"

Pilot projects typically have goals requiring major improvements, more like 40 percent than 10 percent gain, the kind that cannot be achieved just by working harder or by other incremental effort, but by requiring a different approach, a different way of thinking about how the work is done. The assumptions (usually unspoken) that workers (including managers) make in the workplace are brought to the surface and examined by them in reflective conversations. In this way, the mental models that people tacitly use in thinking about the program, its purpose and methods, its customers and how they are approached and treated, its suppliers, etc., are all reviewed and tested for their validity. Alternative assumptions are considered and may become the basis for a new approach, promising major improvements. An example of this can be seen in the Office of Special Education case. (See "The Power of Reassessing One's Mental Models," on page 292.)
Identify systemic issues

The causes of problems are not always obvious, since events can have multiple causes and multiple consequences, and some of the consequences

Reviewing Progress in Process Improvement

A meeting involving seven "learning leaders" and senior executives of the Office of Surveillance and Biometrics (OSB) in the Food and Drug Administration's (FDA) Center for Devices and Radiologic Health (CDRH) took place in March 2000 to review the progress of the organizational learning initiative. The meeting was called by Larry Kessler, director of OSB. Among the examples narrated of areas where the new learning had been applied were the following:

> I have noticed a lot more meetings that I've attended where we tend to behave differently—using the ladder of inference* and trying not to climb up too far, keeping in mind our behavior and how it reflects on others and how people can react to that.
>
> I see the use of the ladder* [of inference] on a day-to-day basis, often in a light- hearted manner.
>
> We seem to be more careful than we were before about climbing the ladder of inference. An example is talking about exploring other people's perspectives—I think that's something we didn't do nearly as well three years ago.
>
> More recently [my division has] begun to think about how we can use SoL ideas to address how our partnership, our relationship is with this other office [which is our major customer...]

According to this discussion, the main changes at OSB since their involvement in the SoL partnership are not so much different products, procedures, or policies (at least not so far) but "how we deal with our colleagues."

> One of our senior staff said to me, "I think SoL is the way we do business every day, and I try to have my division work like this anyway, and we try to keep these kinds of principles living and growing in the way we do business."

As Kessler summarized it: "This [organizational learning] has become part of our culture here."

---

* The "ladder of inference" is a learning tool or metaphor designed to increase our awareness of the degree to which we go beyond the hard facts in everyday perceptions and judgments. At the bottom of the "ladder" we stick close to verifiable facts with minimal interpretations. At the top of the ladder we use major assumptions or biases in order to draw interesting but speculative conclusions. Both can be useful—at times—but it can be valuable to be aware of when we are betting on a major assumption in case it is not correct for this instance.

can be delayed and unnoticed. Some of these unintended and unnoticed consequences can loop around and bite us in unexpected places. The usual method of making a list of causal factors, then tackling them one at a time, sometimes fails to fix the problem. A series of "solutions" that each worked for only a short time may be an indication that this problem needs stronger (more systematic) medicine. As participants in a problem situation, we must listen carefully to each others' "stories" from different roles, as we sort out the specific consequences of things that happened and map them. Then we construct a systemic view from which new insights and solutions can be derived. In a learning organization there is careful communication and analysis using systems thinking.

Often, dedicated work is entirely focused on "our" piece of the organization, but not on the purpose of the whole—sometimes to the detriment of the whole—perhaps without our even realizing what we do. It takes a little systems thinking to gain perspective. The EPA spent many years pursuing polluters to impose penalties. After 20 years, many of the worst offenders were dealt with, and the general public learned from the example of these prosecutions. Then some EPA strategists, taking a systems view, began to ask whether more could be achieved to stop pollution and protect the environment by negotiating broader agreements with certain industries instead of enforcing just what the law provided for. This went against the inclination of the enforcement division, since it had always been judged on how many court actions it won. This shift in perspective is at the heart of the EPA change case.

Assess your progress frequently, both results and process

One of the defining marks of the learning organization is that members frequently check on "how are we doing?" This usually falls into two areas: (1) how do we feel about the way we are working together? (work process), as well as (2) how well are we progressing towards our major goal to improve the standard of what we do for our customers? (performance results).

Progress on performance goals must be measured. The host organization usually has its own measures, but the work group may supplement these with its own. These internal measures, which do not have to be shared outside the work group, may be "fuzzy," broad, and subjective—as applied to both the output goals and work process—provided that the group members are ruthlessly honest with each other. This is possible if a culture of trust has really been developed, along with a fierce commitment to the performance goals. Where this exists, the fuzzy, gut feelings of members about how they are progressing on a tough, complex task may be more valid than the precise but narrow official measurements.

Help all members build up their skills, understanding, and commitment

This is the special responsibility of the second member of the leadership group, the internal human resource development consultant. This person should have some knowledge of change management and ready access to other sources for training, coaching, and consulting. This person needs to know a variety of qualified people who can be trusted and who know and accept your approach as important.

Learning from peers and learning in the actual context of work ("adult learning" or "experiential learning") are to be encouraged. "Learning labs" that present concepts and tools of change management in the context of work issues—and that support learners while they apply the new learning— have been found to be an effective approach. Coaching takes place in the labs and during normal work time. It is done initially by internal consultants and then, increasingly, by their line managers, colleagues, and supervisors. As the pilot project expands, the organization must also expand its investment in learning labs and on-the-job coaching for the new roles that the change initiative is introducing.

Example: In the OSB case, the change leaders decided to create a full-time detail position, with 90-day rotations, for a staff member to support their organizational learning initiative and to help it take root. (So far this approach is unique among the partnership projects). The first appointee was a branch chief within the office, who left those responsibilities for three months while she served on this detail. She estimated that during the detail she spoke to about 80 percent of all staff members. Some approached her, asking for help, but she also asked to be invited into some regular meetings to speak to work groups. (See "Apply Organizational Learning.")

PHASE THREE: Building on Initial Learning
Make the necessary changes to structures, policies

Organizations have many structures that guide the behavior of their members along certain paths and away from others simply by making it easier to get one kind of resource rather than another, under certain conditions rather than others. In addition to all these indirect structures, there are also direct reward systems, especially those based on performance appraisal.

Example: In the case of the EPA Regional Office, where the change initiative was centered on integrating the work of separate environmental programs around common *results* (cleaner air and water) in place of the old *program activity* goals, the change leaders realized that they should incorporate these new expectations directly into the performance goals of senior managers and so on down the management hierarchy. However, it is important to realize (as they did) that this kind of structural change only works when combined with fostering and teaching the new thinking that goes with it. This requires engaging managers in dialogue about how they can

Apply Organizational Learning

In an interview, Mary Brady, the first person detailed to this position, stated: "I felt people needed to bite off a little at a time. People in the government don't handle change well. I've been in government 16 years, and there is a lot of this type of training—one more thing the government is going to talk about and not act on. But I also felt they would be overwhelmed.

"The role I played was to remind people of what they learned in July. I started in November and I asked: What can we succeed in right away that will show something tangible? What can we work on that will be individual and not have to add to their daily activities? So I thought of the mental models. Everyone seemed to enjoy that part the best. And what I did was focus on how we behave, how we react to others, how we're thinking—just being more cognizant of that on a daily basis. It might take six to eight weeks just for this part. I put them through a dog-and-pony show at all meetings and I worked with individuals who requested it. It was all voluntary. You don't need to comply, but you need to be aware of it when talking to others. We looked at the ladder of inference, mental models, [left-hand] columns*. [My aim was to get them] to practice in meetings, in and outside the organization, and see how it feels to be using this. For the most part, everyone thought it was a good idea learning how to deal with difficult people, keeping your left-hand column intact, how can you deal with others? ... I ended up talking to virtually the whole office—80 out of 100..."

---

* The "left-hand column" exercise asks people to write down a conversation they were dissatisfied with. In the right-hand column they write what each person said; in the left-hand column they write what they themselves were thinking or feeling but did not say. This exercise was developed by Chris Argyris. [1985; 1996, first published 1978.]

rethink their work plan, focussing on the new priorities. This cannot simply be imposed from above. Then each manager who has redesigned his/her own performance goals must hold that dialogue with his/her own reports. Only if there is meaningful dialogue and participation at every level can the change work. As a last resort, those managers who refuse or fail to comply may have to be removed or transferred; the success of the change, however, depends on how many can be engaged in the new way of thinking and express it through their performance goals.

Where dysfunctional policies and structures of the organization itself form barriers to improved performance based on a systematic analysis of the root causes of problems, these should be changed. Often this is much harder than it sounds, because organization-wide policies are involved. Now we discover how much investment the highest levels of management have in the goal of becoming a learning organization. In large organizations, top managers have little awareness of the change initiative, off in a corner of one of their divisions. The influence of the senior sponsor (and how close this person is to the top levels) can be significant here. Many change leaders will learn that it is much easier if they confine their ambitions to changes that can be managed within their own area, without seeking collaboration from other parts of the larger body, i.e., without causing that entity to change itself. Initiatives that were sponsored from the top with the intention of instigating wide change (quite rare creatures) will be treated differently.

Build more capacity

This is a continuation and expansion of the item in phase two named "help all members build their skills, understanding, and commitment." It is the special contribution of the internal human resource development consultant, who should have ready access to sources for training, coaching, and consulting. As the pilot project expands, the organization must also expand its investment in learning labs and on-the-job coaching for the new roles that the change initiative is introducing. This is needed both for the early-adopter, the enthusiastic group as it expands, and also for the larger group of employees who are complying like "good soldiers" due to peer pressure, the urging of top managers, and their sense that "this is the way things are going around here"—although they don't (so far) feel the depth of conviction of the enthusiasts' group.

Keep the neighbors (and boss) informed

This is not just common sense and good manners but can be a matter of life and death for a new initiative. The change initiative introduces some very different ideas and role behavior. Outsiders who see or hear about things that are happening due to the initiative, without understanding the context and reason, could get a very wrong impression.

Example: In the Epsilon new car project there was a big effort to get engineers to report right away when they anticipated problems, so that all could get involved in resolving them and so that others would not count on a component staying unchanged when there was a known problem with it. This openness had never happened before, due to lack of trust. Building up trust was a central goal for the Epsilon program managers, and higher numbers of reported problems were an indicator (to them) of increased trust. Seeing more problems in the open than previously (before the start of the initiative) was interpreted within the initiative as a good sign. But to their boss, who had paid little attention to the nature of the change initiative and resisted their efforts to keep him informed, the large number of problems was very distressing, because (to him) it meant that the program was "out of control." That is what such a number traditionally meant in the old culture.

The new behavior in the change project (e.g., workers sharing duties in new ways that they devised and acting more autonomously by not checking every move with a supervisor) can also seem threatening to those still accustomed to the old ways. Just the enthusiasm and esprit de corps of the pioneers can seem like a "cult" to those who do not know their plan and purpose. This "public education" for neighbors and bosses also helps the new knowledge of other ways of management become available to other parts of the organization.

Renew the vision, and feed the passion behind the effort for change

This item is a reminder that basic to the learning-based approach is the notion that a major energy source for the change process is the personal vision and deeply felt aspirations of individuals, the goals and values they really care about. In addition to the importance of skill development to meet these new challenges, there is also a need for periodic reminders to participants about why they are involved in this change effort, invoking symbols that rekindle the passion. Examples include celebrating recent successes, commemorating old ones, retelling the stories of early struggles, and hearing from people who represent personal and poignant examples of the need to which the work of the organization is dedicated. From a shared vision like this, the wells of positive motivation run very deep and strong.

Make and keep contact with other groups making similar change efforts, create a mutual learning support system

Change leadership in this model is all about learning together to do things one has never done before. It involves making mistakes and learning from them. It involves recognizing the assumptions that invisibly guide our behavior and choices, and sometimes revising them. That reflection occurs both individually and jointly, sometimes in groups and sometimes between two individuals. It is a natural extension of learning within each group and change initiative to include learning across several initiatives. It is useful to share learnings and best practices, and to get advice or help with difficult problems. The perspective of the outsider can be valuable in spotting problems that those on the inside couldn't see.

Example: Among the five federal government agencies participating in the partnership with SoL there is a conference call every three months involving the two main leaders, several members of the High-Performing Federal Agencies Committee, SoL staff, and consultants. There have also been two larger, longer, face-to-face meetings in less than two years. These meetings share encouragement and best practices.

The EPA New England Initiative: Changing Thinking and Organizational Structures

*To get the best results from an organizational change it is usually necessary for participants to change their **thinking** (purpose and mental models) at the same time as organizational **structures** are changed.*

In the first year of the EPA New England initiative, the strategy was designed to be vision—driven. After engaging with the vision, staff members were expected to design the modified structures and policies that would be needed to create an integrated, results-oriented environmental system. However, powerful distractors got in the way and not enough managers became sufficiently engaged in this process to the point where they felt joint ownership of the vision. In one major area, however, the initiative went ahead very much according to plan. This was in the newly created "state offices," which manage relations between the EPA and each of the states (to provide the state environmental agencies with "one-window shopping"). These "state offices" embodied fairly well what the new strategy and vision called for. As for the rest of the regional office, however, progress in getting collaboration and integration of efforts across units was quite limited.

In the third year of this change initiative a—group of change leaders/senior executives who were looking to accelerate the change process decided to use the staff performance management system (PMS) as a tool for this purpose. PMS had existed on paper for several years but was ineffective. It was an empty, required ritual. In the first year of the change initiative, managers were, in effect, *invited* to participate in conversations about the new vision and mental models, but they were not pushed to set performance goals for their units and themselves in line with the new thinking. Now, in the third year, managers and their reports were *expected* to talk together about the goals for their units and themselves, and then to set goals appropriate to the new thinking. Training was provided for all levels of staff to help them with this.

In the new (third year) strategy it was considered essential that every manager have good conversations about which unit and personal performance goals would fit with the agency's new vision of integration around environmental results. Each top manager would have this—conversation with his/her direct reports, and therefore every manager and employee would eventually have such a conversation with his/her boss. In the new strategy staff members were told that they and their supervisors would be evaluated both on the way these goals were written (now) and on how well they were met (later). Thus the PMS was intended to provide a structure for shaping and supporting the behavior and thinking of staff (at all levels) who were not opposed to the new direction (vision) but were not going to enact it without more help. For staff who were opposed to moving in this direction, PMS might be experienced as a coercive structure.

Case Studies

The Partnership Between the Society for Organizational Learning and the High-Performing Federal Agencies Committee

The idea of trying a learning-based approach in the federal government arose out of conversations between the Society for Organizational Learning and the High-Performing Federal Agencies Committee of the Inter-agency Human Resource Development Council (HRDC). This idea built on the pioneering efforts begun in 1995 at the Environmental Protection Agency's New England Regional Office in its partnership with SoL and several of its consultant members. Georgie Bishop, one of the leaders of the New England EPA initiative, was a member of the High-Performing Federal Agencies Committee and shared with her colleagues some of their early experiences. This aroused their interest and led in 1998 to the start of a partnership between the committee and SoL.

The committee sought out and selected other government executives interested in becoming involved with the partnership and developing their own initiatives. These volunteers, senior executives from four different agencies, with the consent of their superiors, joined the partnership. They attended a five-day introduction course in the "core competencies" of the learning organization, along with one or two staff from their respective units, all of them carefully selected. At the "core course" they met colleagues from many other organizations—mainly non-governmental—on a similar career journey. Upon their return, this group planned with SoL consultants an in-house workshop ("learning lab") to introduce some of their own staff to the new approach. Each unit then planned, with the help of its consultants, how to take the initiative forward. Four times during the first year several leaders from each of the four projects talked together, three times via conference call and once at an all-day in-person meeting. Other times this networking group might meet when invited to an initiative-related event at one of the participating agencies. For example, the Department of Education invited them when they hosted a presentation by the two EPA leaders to their own staff in June 1999. Members of the networking group also would attend meetings at SoL. In fact, the SoL annual meetings in 1999 and 2000 included presentations by leaders of government projects about the work being done in the federal government.

The role of the Committee for High-Performing Federal Agencies (HPFA) was crucial in three areas: 1) in sponsoring and legitimating the idea of this experimental partnership from the outset, which included the recruitment of participants; 2) in facilitating the contracting process between SoL and the federal Office of Personnel Management; and 3) in finding suitable pilot agencies and appropriate leaders within the agencies to participate.

In their individual HRD roles, several committee members have also taken part in facilitating learning laboratories and providing ongoing on-site consultation with the application of the concepts and tools in the specific agencies. The quarterly conversations among project leaders were planned and sponsored by the HPFA Committee. The leadership role of the Committee on High Performing Federal Agencies was recognized by their peers who selected them to receive the Distinguished Service Award "For Service to the Federal HRDC Community" from the Training Officers Conference in June 1999.

Four pilot projects for the first year of the contract were started within the following agencies:

- National Aeronautics and Space Agency (NASA)
- Department of Veterans Affairs: Vocational Rehabilitation and Employment (VRE)
- Department of Education: Office of Special Education Programs (OSEP)
- Food and Drug Administration: Center for Devices and Radiological Health, Office for Surveillance and Biometrics (OSB)

Historically, the first project was undertaken at the Environmental Protection Agency, New England Regional Office, which began its own partnership with SoL in 1995. The leaders of that project, Georgie Bishop and David Fierra, are considered valued mentors within the group and are regular participants in meetings of the partnership. The last case study in this chapter focuses on the work done at the EPA. The first two case studies highlight initiatives at OSEP and OSB.

The recruitment of government executives to be "learning leaders" for these initiatives (through the HPFA Committee) represents the first of three key elements required for introducing organizational learning initiatives into the federal government. The second key element is the availability of internal human resource development consultants who could coach and support the projects; and the third is the outside expertise and support brought in by SoL supporting staff and SoL-affiliated consultant-trainers (primarily Fred Simon and Nick Zeniuk).

Each of the four agencies taking part in this partnership followed its own timeline, but the sequence of major steps was the same: after attending the introductory course in the Boston area, the learning leaders and internal HRD consultants next scheduled a "learning lab" for a group of their staff members, to be presented by outside consultant-trainers recommended by SoL. This learning lab, presented locally for some 25 to 40 staff members of each pilot agency, introduced them to some basic organizational learning methods in the context of a "practice field" where they could begin working out how to apply these methods to a selected challenge that they faced. Not only the learning leaders (executives) but also the staff and supervisors involved in these pilot initiatives were all volunteers—a basic principle of the SoL approach.

As we shall see in the case studies, participants learned to improve their effectiveness in communicating and working together. At NASA, for example, the human resources development staff (which was the host for one of the initiatives) noted that its widely dispersed membership was able to increase its productivity as a group, as a result of developing together a shared vision and strategy in the learning lab. At the Department of Education, the division responsible for monitoring state programs of special education and early intervention for children with disabilities was able to improve significantly its whole system for working with state agencies, based on rethinking some of its basic assumptions and mental models.

The informal assessment of the first two years' achievements, both by federal participants and SoL partners, is that much important progress has been made and that the beginnings of healthy roots have been put down. The SoL approach is to invest heavily upfront and to continue patiently, building up a healthy orchard to support extensive future harvests and growth. SoL's program manager for this partnership is Jeff Clanon.

Case Study: The Office of Special Education Programs (OSEP) in the U.S. Department of Education

Overview

This change initiative went through the steps outlined earlier. During phase one (getting ready) a core learning team was formed to lead the effort, headed by Patty Guard, deputy director of OSEP and senior career servant in OSEP, and included two of her direct reports and an internal consultant. Their pilot project (phase two) turned out to be redesigning the work of the State Monitoring and Improvement Division. This project was led by Ruth Ryder, director of the division, with the rest of the core learning team staying in the background to act as her support group and reflective partners. The core learning (and leadership) team in OSEP then moved the initiative into phase three, expanding its scope from the pilot project in one division to a more complex project that cut across several divisions of OSEP. The impressive progress made by the pilot project encouraged the three-person leadership team to get more ambitious and take on a larger and more complex project that involved several segments of OSEP that needed to collaborate in new ways. The success of both phases gave credibility to the goal of making OSEP into more of a learning organization.

Phase One: Getting Ready

About one-third of OSEP staff (about 30 people) took part in a two-day learning lab run by two consultant-trainers from the Society for Organizational Learning, presented on-site at the agency, to introduce them to the basics of some tools of organizational learning. For three OSEP executives and their internal HRD consultant, their involvement began at least two months earlier when they attended the five-day "core competencies course" in Boston, along with other change leaders from a number of organizations. These three took the lead in planning the in-house learning lab and in OSEP's whole venture into organizational learning with its outside partners (consultants) from the Society for Organizational Learning. The four who attended the core competencies course became the core learning team for OSEP's learning-based change initiative: Patty Guard, two of her direct reports—Ruth Ryder and Lou Danielson—and their internal consultant, Bette Novak. From the start they had the support of the OSEP office director (a political appointee), and when he left the position, Guard took care to acquaint the new director with what they were doing, so that he too became a firm supporter of this change initiative.

Phase Two: Pilot Project in the State Monitoring and Improvement Planning Division

Immediately following the two-day learning lab in March, staff who had participated began to experiment with applying the tools and concepts to their work. One group in particular found itself in a painful bind: They really wanted to put their new learning to use, but they faced a huge backlog of overdue reports on the state reviews for which they were responsible. They felt that they dare not take the time necessary to plan an organizational learning initiative. Yet they really felt the need to improve the way they managed the situation instead of continuing to push the boulder up the mountain.

They felt this dilemma acutely. But it was not long before they broke through "the wall" with a question about their mental models around the state monitoring process: How might they have caused themselves to be in this bind? And what would be another mental model for what they were trying to do that would somehow reduce this dreadful workload?

That proved to be the essence of the solution they found. It still took a lot of hard work, talking and thinking about the purpose of their program and the assumptions they made about their counterparts in the state agencies. The rhetoric of recent American political philosophy called on federal government to think of their state counterparts (and even the private sector) as "partners." But the long history of more adversarial roles between state and federal agencies (not to mention the government and private sector) carried a legacy of less trusting mental models, which supported a particular approach to monitoring, accountability, and reporting back to the states. What if they could truly adopt a partnership model? How could that change the monitoring and reporting process? And could that be less onerous to both sides, and perhaps more useful to the states and more beneficial to the real customers—the disabled children and their families? The "magic" of mental models work—the surfacing of tacit assumptions that invisibly guide people and reflecting on their implications—makes possible such significant breakthroughs in problem solving. This work is not unilateral, of course, for the partners also need to be involved in the discussions and to agree to the changes that emerge.

Under the leadership of Ruth Ryder, the Division of Monitoring and State Improvement Planning staff met weekly for several months, applying these tools to their "wicked problem" of how to manage the ever-increasing backlog of state reports. An innovative solution was created, and the next steps for implementation are being developed. In this work they have used a variety of tools: mental models, shared vision and team learning, and advocacy, inquiry, and reflection. The staff was very enthusiastic about the process. The comment heard many times was that they felt they had "been given permission to think outside the box." This work has included the entire staff of the division, a significant number of whom did not participate in the learning labs.

Phase Two: Assessment

"We found that the Vision Deployment Matrix (VDM) was a very structured and labor-intensive tool—not one that we would use for our day-to-day work, but one we could effectively use for larger projects such as the ECTA (Early Childhood Technical Assistance) work group," said Bette Novak, internal consultant. "The work group and learning leaders found that the VDM process and other organizational learning tools surfaced many complex and broad-based issues related to OSEP's role in providing technical assistance that may not have been identified without using this process. The major outstanding issues that needed additional attention included work with our sister federal agencies which also have programs

---

The Vision Deployment Matrix (VDM)

The Vision Deployment Matrix (VDM) is a trademarked tool for organizational learning developed by Daniel H. Kim and Diane Cory. It was described by Kim in an article in *The Systems Thinker*, 1995, vol. 6, no. 1. The VDM provides change leaders and work groups with a powerful method of organizing the efforts of a change team, using their understanding of current reality and their aspirations for a different future, focusing on the gaps (and questions) between them, and on the actions they will take to narrow the gap. All that is repeated on five different levels of perspective, from events to patterns to systemic structures to mental models to vision. In total this yields a 5 x 6 matrix, though it is possible to work effectively in a subset of the whole.

The Power of Reassessing One's Mental Models

At the time they attended the first learning lab, the staff of the State Monitoring Division in the Department of Education's Office of Special Education (OSEP) was struggling unsuccessfully with a very sticky issue concerning the state reports, which are at the heart of that division's work. What the division does, in simple terms, is to go out to the various states and monitor their delivery of special education services. They come back from each monitoring visit with "tons of information." The problem has been how to organize that information effectively (and efficiently) into a state report, which can help state officials to move into corrective action or improvement planning. The issue of efficiency was very much weighing on the minds of the staff at the time of the two-day learning lab, because the division was seriously behind schedule in producing these reports and the backlog was getting worse all the time.

With the new energy, skills in organizational learning, and insights that they brought back from that learning lab, staff spent "a relatively short amount of time" looking for (and finding) a new and better approach to the situation. They considered *their vision* for how the state monitoring process and reports to the states should ideally be functioning. They also spent some time examining their *mental models* about the work of the division: the assumptions they made about the state agencies, their motivation, and how they believed the state staff viewed the monitoring process. This produced many pages of chart paper, full of notes on mental models around this issue. From April to August of 1999 small groups of division staff met and came up with a strategy for solving the backlog of reports.

They went "outside the box" for a solution. What led them to the solution was to question the real purpose of the reports. The breakthrough came when they realized that the reports were not an end in themselves, but a means to improve the quality and effectiveness of services to students with disabilities. By focussing on the *results* that mattered, on the true *purpose* of their program, they were able to view the problem in a totally different light. Once the problem was reframed, a solution that was previously inconceivable now became obvious. Stated with a little irony, the solution to having *too many* reports to produce was to produce *fewer* reports—because they saw that the reports per se did not really matter. What mattered was the corrective action that the reports were supposed to lead to—and there were more direct ways to get there. (This is explained more fully in the OSEP case in the Case Studies.)

It takes courage to go forward with such a solution. "It was pretty radical thinking for us," said Ruth Ryder, director of the division. "For 20 years we've been going out, gathering data, doing reports, developing corrective action plans, and going back to states four or five years later and doing the same thing—and a lot of times coming up with the same problems in the states." New thinking always requires hard adjustments—in this case from those who might think that it means that staff have been wasting much of their energy for

(continued)

(continued)

all those years, carrying an unnecessary load. Another thought among some staff was concern that the new approach might appear as if the agency were "backing off" from its responsibility to enforce the law. For some groups, that discomfort would be enough to squash the proposed innovation, if it should ever be suggested. This highlights the fact that innovation requires more than just smart creative thinking. It also requires the strong personal commitment of members to the mission and values of the organization (enhanced by the vision discussion in this case) and to doing the right thing, what is best for the "customers" (the disabled children)—even if it causes some discomfort to the staff. These staffers did care more about a better solution to the problem, regardless of their own discomfort, and they are on their way to creating a learning organization in the Office of Special Education Programs.

for young children, including providing technical assistance, and work with our external customers and partners to develop a 'shared vision'."

Meeting with the supervisors, Guard remarked jokingly that in their current task they would again be using the VDM—"a tool that has become near and dear to our hearts" (laughter). "We seem to use it for everything around here. We are getting better at it all the time and we have learned a lot from using this tool."

Some further assessment of the OSEP experience with the VDM tool was offered at a cross-agency meeting by Lou Danielson, another member of the three-person leadership team for OSEP and director of the Research to Practice Division, who was heavily involved in the ECTA task force, as well as all of the management team meetings. In his assessment, they were "extraordinarily compulsive" the first time they used the VDM; in every cell they pushed the discussion until they ran out of steam. On reflection, that was not necessary, since points that might be missed the first time can easily be added later without loss of effectiveness. Since then, they have learned to work much faster with the VDM: in one case achieving in four hours what they would earlier have taken four days to accomplish. (Researcher's comment: This does not necessarily represent a ten-fold increase in skill because the increased speed probably comes from their increased confidence and the realization that some of their earlier meticulousness was unnecessary.) Ruth Ryder noted (at the same meeting) that they had learned several things about using the VDM: to avoid spending time on discussions of "which box to do next?"; to avoid "wordsmithing" their phrases; to allocate one question per cell; and to use a time-clock to help them keep to a schedule. Although the VDM is a tool designed to foster thinking, not hasty decision-making and just "filling in the boxes," it is possible to be efficient and time-conscious about collective thinking—especially after some practice and with growing skill in the arts of thoughtful listening and dialogue.

Another feature of the VDM, noted by Danielson, is that it can be used effectively without much training—at least in some instances. He cited the example of one staff member who did not attend the learning lab but found herself in a project leadership role where the VDM had been suggested. With only an hour of instruction from a colleague and the benefit of reading the Daniel Kim article on the VDM used in the lab, Bonnie Jones proceeded to experiment with its use in her project group. The group responded positively to the way it helped them to think about their work and the resulting product.

Staff response to the introduction of organizational learning tools has been very positive. Lou Danielson observes that, for once, staff *do not complain* about the extra time that the application of organizational learning tools requires. Another source of data comes from staff feedback collected from OSEP supervisors on how they felt about using the organizational learning tools to do the work of OSEP, including the ECTA task force led by Guard, Ryder, and Danielson. According to staff, the use of new tools changed their experience of the work process because it:

- Increased the feeling of inclusiveness
- Showed evidence of the collaboration and commitment of the three learning leaders to using the tools and concepts
- Engaged everyone in the conversations and decision-making process; it promoted creativity and out-of-the box thinking
- Helped large groups to get a common understanding of the complex area of technical assistance.

Phase Three: Building on the Initial Learning

The success of the State Monitoring and Improvement Planning Division pilot project was an inspiration to their colleagues in the other half of OSEP and encouraged two other formal initiatives, using the organizational learning tools. A third day of the learning lab (held in June 1999) provided the opportunity for staff to review the concepts of mental models and systems thinking and to apply them to work that cuts across all components of OSEP. The work in the learning lab focused on how OSEP currently does and could provide technical assistance and information dissemination in order to get useful research into practice. The Vision Deployment Matrix was introduced and applied more deeply by the management team. Subsequently, OSEP asked for volunteers to serve on a work group to develop a priority to fund a $4 million grant for technical assistance in the early childhood area. This work group used the VDM to consider the future of early childhood technical assistance. In addition, they used other organizational learning tools including dialogue, advocacy, inquiry, reflective thinking, mental models, and systems thinking in their work.

The Vision Deployment Matrix is one tool of organizational learning that has been very useful to OSEP. It looks like a planning tool, but the way it works is different from conventional planning devices whose purpose is to get decisions made. Here the main purpose of the tool is to facilitate *collective thinking* (the formulating of vision, the surfacing of mental models, the analysis of systemic structures, and the alignment across these) that will lead to shared vision across the group, with shared strategies and goals and structures that are in alignment.

Conclusion: Overall Assessment

Results so far would include the following:
1) Reorientation and improvement of the state monitoring program (which represents at least half of the total OSEP workload and mission)
2) Design of a new Early Childhood Technical Assistance System by a task force representing many areas of OSEP
    (Note: Both of these items are considered "results" of the work in applying organizational learning methods, since they go significantly beyond "business as usual" both in their approach and in the extent of the challenge taken on.)
3) A significant increase in collaboration among the top three career executives in OSEP around the core work of the office.

Overall, these three changes represent an increase in the ability of OSEP staff to make improvements in the way they work. Beyond these specific changes, an enhanced capacity is being created for continuous improvement. Obviously, the evidence to support this hypothesis will have to be collected in the next few years. But it is important to state the hypothesis now, so that even the data at this early stage may be examined with this possibility in mind.

In addition to the self-assessment of key participants, which we have depended on mostly here, it can be useful to observe them in action, as I did during a three-hour meeting of the OSEP supervisors' team in May 2000. Thirteen OSEP supervisors were present at the meeting, which was led by Deputy Director Guard. The group worked in a very focused way. It started on time, with no latecomers. They used the Vision Deployment Matrix to address a new issue concerning the changing roles of their support staff. Members were attentive throughout and highly focused on the work plan presented to them that was used to guide the meeting. There was humor and a lot of informal participation after the purpose and procedures had been explained by the leader, but there was an intense focus on the task throughout. Members did a lot of listening. Several times when different members were having trouble getting into the discussion, other members intervened tactfully to help them get a chance to speak. No one went off on tangents. At the cost of negotiating the break time down to barely

10 minutes, the agenda was covered. At the end of the meeting, which went 10 minutes overtime, the group did not protest when the leader asked for extra time for them to assess what they thought of the way they had worked together. That was done quickly and (to this observer) hurriedly, focusing on how the work was organized but not on the interpersonal dynamics.

The bottom line is that this group covered in three hours an amount of work that I estimate would typically take at least a full day. This led me to infer (incorrectly) that this group of 13 supervisors worked together on a regular basis. In fact, I was told it does not normally work together as a single group—though its two divisions and other subsets of the group each do so. In addition, it is very significant that its three senior leaders, the members of the core learning team, have learned a lot in the past two years about working closely together.

After the meeting I asked Patty Guard: "How much difference would I have seen in this group one, two years ago?" She answered that their involvement in the SoL partnership has "made a significant difference" in the way the three senior (career) leaders of OSEP work as a team on issues that cut across the organization. They work much more smoothly together, which has been remarked on by staff. They meet frequently to plan the work of the OSEP and the organizational learning activities, and they meet following these activities to debrief.

In a reflection on her personal experience of this work, Guard concluded: "My involvement in the SoL partnership has been one of the most challenging and rewarding professional growth experiences of my career. It is an outstanding opportunity for senior executive professional development."

Case Study: The Office for Surveillance and Biometrics (OSB) in the Center for Devices and Radiological Health (CDRH) of the Food and Drug Administration (FDA)

Overview

This case followed a fairly typical phase one (getting ready), but its phase two was not focused around one pilot project—not in the way it occurred at OSEP. While there was a pilot project, there was more emphasis on many, small, daily applications of the new organizational learning methods. Another contrast with the prior case is that there is not the same type of cohesive core learning team among the leaders and senior managers, although there are just as many strong supporters of the organizational learning initiative here. In assessing their progress, these leaders are clear that organizational learning has become part of the culture in OSB.

Phase One. Getting Ready

1. All staff (about 100) were invited to learning labs (some 300 person-days of staff development). Plus a review workshop was given, primarily for managers, by Rebecca Pille (an internal consultant from another federal agency).
2. Emphasis is placed on building internal capacity among line staff, as opposed to using external consultants or even internal ones.
3. Creating *the detail position* was a major part of the capacity-building strategy.
4. Encouragement of the use of organizational learning approaches in varied aspects of the work of the Office—especially during the first year at the interpersonal level.
5. "Dialogues" open to the entire OSB have been scheduled regularly, about every three weeks. (Note: This is an unusual locus or format for dialogue—a "town meeting" open to any OSB staff as opposed to a small group with more focus and more consistent attendance. There were some difficulties with guidelines and attendance.)

Phase Two: Pilot Project

After the first year of the initiative at OSB, there are not any specific projects, achievements, or quantified results that would impress the outside world. There was one top-priority project that was selected to be an organizational learning effort. Its tough and important mission was to re-engineer the entire process of postmarket surveillance of regulated medical devices, i.e., most of the work of OSB, which was closely interlocked with other Offices in the Center (the mother organization within FDA). Compared to the state monitoring project at OSEP, this task was entangled with more major external players and faced much tougher constraints. The central reengineering office, which exerted very tight control, was a powerful stakeholder. Integrating the organizational learning approach with the rigid demands of the re-engineering office proved more than this group could manage, especially given the large number of different groups that had to be coordinated. One lesson learned from this experience concerns the wisdom of this choice for a first-year project. Given that the leader wanted to take a risk since the project was so important to the organization, this raises questions about what kind of leadership is needed in such a case—both from the project leader and from the office director.

Assessment and Impressions of Cultural Change

A meeting involving seven "learning leaders" and senior executives of OSB (several occupied both categories) took place in March 2000 to review the progress of the organizational learning initiative. The meeting was called by Larry Kessler, director of OSB, at the suggestion of the researcher,

---

Mission Statement of OSB

"Our mission is to constantly improve patient and provider outcomes related to the use of medical device and radiation-emitting electronic products.
We accomplish this by:

- collecting, analyzing, and generating surveillance information to identify ... product issues;
- ... facilitating development and implementations of postmarket problem solving strategies;
- providing statistical and epidemiological expertise and support in pre- and postmarket product evaluation ... " (from OSB Annual Report, Fiscal Year 1997.)

---

who was present at the meeting. Among the examples narrated of areas where the new learning had been applied were the following:

> I have noticed a lot more meetings that I've attended where we tend to behave differently—using the ladder of inference and trying not to climb up too far, keeping in mind our behavior and how it reflects on others and how people can react to that.
> I see the use of the ladder[2] [of inference] on a day-to-day basis, often in a light- hearted manner.
> We seem to be more careful than we were before about climbing the ladder of inference. An example is talking about exploring other people's perspectives—I think that's something we didn't do nearly as well three years ago.
> More recently [my division has] begun to think about how we can use SoL ideas to address how our partnership, our relationship is with this other office [which is our major customer ...]

What about results? According to this discussion, the main changes at OSB since their involvement in the SoL partnership are not so much different products, procedures, or policies (at least not so far) but "how we deal with our colleagues."

> One of our senior staff said to me, "I think SoL is the way we do business every day," and I try to have my division work like this anyway, and we try to keep these kinds of principles living and growing in the way we do business.

As Larry Kessler, director of OSB, said: "This [organizational learning] has become part of our culture here."

Phase Three: Building Capacity

One important practice used at OSB to help their initiative take root (so far unique among the partnership projects) has been to create a full-time detail position, with 90-day rotations, for a staff member to devote full time to the initiative. So far two appointments have occurred. An interview with the first appointee will be used here. The second appointee has just completed her time, and no decision has been made about continuing the practice.

Mary Brady, the first appointee, is a branch chief within OSB and left those responsibilities for three months to fulfill the detail with much energy. During her detail, she estimates that she spoke to 80 staff members. Some people approached her, asking for help, and she took advantage of some regular meetings to insert something onto the agenda where she could. She also asked to be invited to speak to work groups. We could nickname this the "Jenny Appleseed" approach to promoting organizational learning, as opposed to one that focuses efforts around specific projects or depends on an executive-led, top-down approach.

In an interview Mary Brady stated her approach:

> Larry's [the director's] expectations were different than mine. I felt people needed to bite it off a little at a time. People in the government don't handle change well. I've been in government 16 years, and there is a lot of this type of training—one more thing the government is going to talk about and not act on. But I also felt they would be overwhelmed. Larry wanted me to integrate SoL into our strategic plan. I told him right away to put it on hold now. We need time to figure how to integrate this and get staff buy-in. See what we can do, little by little. People aren't going to understand massive change and where it is in their priorities. He was OK with that.
>
> The role I played was to remind people of what they learned in July. I started in November and I asked: What can we succeed in right away that will show something tangible? What can we work on that will be individual and not have to add to their daily activities? So I thought of the mental models. Everyone seemed to enjoy that part the best. And what I did was focus on how we behave, how we react to others, how we're thinking—just being more cognizant of that on a daily basis. It might take six to eight weeks just for this part. I put them through a dog-and-pony show at all meetings and I worked with individuals who requested it. It was all voluntary. You don't need to comply, but you need to be aware of it when talking to others. We looked at the ladder of inference, mental models, [left-hand] columns. [My aim was to get them] to practice in meetings, in and outside the organization, and see how it feels to be using this. For the most part, everyone thought it was a good idea learning how to deal with difficult people, keeping your left-hand column intact, how can you deal with others? ... I ended up talking to virtually the whole office—80 out of 100...

Mary Brady's approach to change leadership goes beyond being the open-handed teacher and coach (Jenny Appleseed). She also sees the need to recruit, support, and coach other leaders who can extend and multiply the effect. "I looked in each division for someone who could be my goodwill ambassador. I keep reinforcing with them, being a cheerleader and keeping it in the front of their mind, asking them to keep pushing it," Brady says.

Some Lessons Learned and Further Questions

- Using the tools of organizational learning, managers and staff at OSB believe they have improved the quality of workplace relations and the quality of work in several areas, as they learned to question their assumptions more often and to become more aware of how unverified assumptions and feelings may enter into perceptions and judgments, causing misunderstandings.
- An effective way of providing support for OSB staff in the process of incorporating organizational learning (OL) into their daily lives has been to detail an interested volunteer, a middle manager, or a recent learner to play an at-large support role.
- The role of the full-time detail support person, plus the leadership of all those at OSB who believe in the value of organizational learning, in addition to learning labs made available to all staff, have all combined to make some elements of OL "part of our culture."
- Where is the leadership team for the OL initiative? There are a number of dedicated leaders, but they do not function as a team with frequent or regular communication (compared with other initiatives). It could be combined with the OSB director's senior management team, if they want to serve that function, or it could be a separate group.
- They chose reengineering as their pilot project. This was a high visibility, high stakes project that required a high degree of cooperation across boundaries, with powerful outside stakeholders. Was this too tough an assignment for inexperienced change leaders, given the difficult constraints?

Case Study: The Environmental Protection Agency (EPA): New England Regional Office

Overview

This case extended over four years, twice the time of the previous two cases, and it operated on a much larger scale, involving more than five times the number of staff (800). Still, it can be summarized in terms of the same three phases. In phase one, a senior executive conceived a vision for transforming the overall structure of this EPA regional office, aiming to integrate its components around a clear focus on results. He found a major ally in a senior HR colleague. Together they attended a three-day course in learning-based leadership and enlisted outside help in training and consultation, for themselves and later for the pilot project.

In phase two, a major pilot project was launched to inaugurate a newly formed department with major responsibilities for integrating services in entirely new ways. The new department was mandated by the new regional administrator as part of his sweeping reorganization of the entire office, rather than emerging out of the deliberations of a core learning team, as in the classic version of the model. There was much learning from this pilot project (much of it painful), which contributed to the design of phase three, in which the change leaders shifted their focus from the new office (within the regional office) to the whole regional office.

Phase three also featured a strategic partnership with the human resources function to implement a redesigned performance management system that gave more impetus and direction to the drive for change. Finally, there is a phase four, going beyond the basic model, in which a surprise change of top leadership in the organization creates new possibilities for the change initiative.

Phase One: Getting Ready

In 1995, David Fierra, a senior executive in the EPA New England Regional Office, found himself chairing a taskforce to design a new Office of Ecosystem Protection (OEP), intended to integrate the work of the various programs within the regional office. He had sought this assignment, which he felt strongly was essential to this agency regaining a clear focus on its original purpose, but he knew it was bound to be an uphill struggle. Historically this agency (established in 1970) had grown out of a collection of separate federal laws and programs (Clean Air Act, Clean Water Act, etc.) each with its own legislation, funding, structure, sanctions, staffing, and accountability. The EPA had 25 years of accomplishment, but by 1995 it was apparent to a growing number of thoughtful EPA employees and other environmentalists that the environment could not be protected piecemeal and that a more integrated approach would be necessary. This was a formidable challenge since the staffs of each program had mostly spent their whole careers in that program and indeed many of them had been the founders of their program. While they might see some theoretical merit in the integration idea, they were still deeply committed to defending the integrity of their separate programs, as originally conceived, and they felt little resonance with the new vision at first. Making the challenge even more difficult was the fact that EPA headquarters was still organized in program "silos" for accountability purposes.

Fortunately, Fierra found a major ally in this tough leadership challenge in his colleague, senior human resources development specialist Georgie

Bishop, who led him to the second major asset: the approach and methods of organizational learning. "The two of them attended a three-day course, which their thought would be invaluable as an approach to managing the significant organizational changes that they believed to be necessary at the EPA New England Regional Office. And so it proved to be. Georgie Bishop was already acquainted with organizational learning and systems thinking, having heard Peter Senge five times at conferences (ASTD, Linkage, etc.). From the HR training budget she had bought copies of *The Fifth Discipline* and audio tapes. She had organized a study group on *The Fifth Discipline* within the HR department. "It made me think," she said, but exactly how it could be applied was not yet clear to her—until 1995. Fierra sought out her help with his leadership challenge. Had he not done so, she would have offered, since she was impressed by his unusual openness with staff and their trust in him. [Interview 7/8/99]

Phase Two

    The launch of the new office was assisted by a three-day "learning lab" conducted by outside consultants in organizational learning for all 20 of the top staff of the new Office of Ecosystem Protection. As director, Fierra introduced weekly three-hour executive staff meetings (called "EcoLabs") that devoted significant blocks of time to thoughtful conversation aimed at identifying the core issues of the new approach and at examining the "mental models" they were each using to think about problems and solutions, so they could begin new ways of thinking towards better, integrated solutions. Dialogues in the EcoLab also focused on the question of how staffers in different areas of responsibility would interrelate at work. The purpose of these Ecolabs was "not to 'practice the tools [of organizational learning]' but trying to keep in mind what we had learned as we did our work and trying to become a 'learning team.'" These meetings were different from the kind of administrative meetings traditional to this agency, meetings occupied mainly with operational details and tactics. Instead, they kept a focus on defining and realizing the vision. They took themes from the vision statement to work on and they kept a focus on strategy and outcomes, as well as tactics. The meetings were structured but flexible. While they always had a prepared agenda, Fierra was flexible and would change the schedule if a topic with much emotion or energy behind it appeared. [Interview 14/7/99]

    There was some initial resistance to Fierra's insistence that the executive team of the Office of Ecosystem Protection should together generate solutions to major issues. He tried to make them challenge their own thinking, instead of looking to him, as director, to make all the important decisions. He challenged them to understand their interdependencies and how they all contributed (or could contribute) together to achieving better environmental results. He was working from a mental model unfamiliar to them, one that assumed that the leader's proper role is not to make the major decisions but to coach and coordinate the efforts of those who are closer to the situation and who collectively have far more of the relevant knowledge. [Interview 14/7/99]

Results of Phases One and Two

About a year after the establishment of the Office of Ecosystem Protection in the EPA Regional Office in New England, there were indications that various results had been accomplished.

- OEP managers understood that the results the organization should be measuring and emphasizing included cleaner air, cleaner water, and a safe environment (as opposed to numbers of permits issued, or enforcement actions taken, for example).
- The heads of various programs learned about other programs in the regional office.
- OEP managers and staff developed some skills in "the five disciplines" of organizational learning [Senge, 1990].
- A new sense of openness and trust grew among OEP managers.
- Performance Partnership Agreements were developed with each state in the region.
- The states (as "customers") were more pleased with their dealings with the regional office. In fact, there were glowing reports from the states about the new emphasis in the regional office.
- A new strategic alliance formed between executive change leaders and human resource development staff.

Phase Two: Further Developments

In phase one, we told the story of a successful beginning to what was intended to be a process of transformation in a large, complex federal government agency. We told the truth, but not the whole truth. We did not indicate the scale of resistance that Dave Fierra met from certain members of his management team, nor the failure of his boss, the regional administrator, to back him up, nor the consequent level of personal pain and stress suffered by Fierra as he struggled with his leadership challenge in the face of seriously inadequate support. In organizational learning initiatives that are assisted by consultants within the Society for Organizational Learning, this is an uncommon occurrence. One of the basic guidelines is that initiatives should not be undertaken unless they have the commitment of a three-part leadership coalition, including a line manager (Dave Fierra in this case), an internal consultant (Georgie Bishop), and a senior sponsor.

The new regional administrator (head of the regional office), appointed by the first Clinton administration, enjoyed an outstanding public reputation as a dedicated environmentalist and a tough and brilliant public sector leader. He saw clearly the need for integration of EPA's programs and for more partnering outside the agency, and approved the introduction of a new Office of Ecosystem Protection within the regional office, which represented a radical change for that office. However, when Fierra found that two of his senior managers in the new office continued to oppose his efforts, by lobbying senior executives to complain about the changes and by actively disrupting EcoLab meetings on a regular basis, the regional administrator gave him no support in counseling, transferring or disciplining them. In fact, he paid very little attention to this major initiative to realign and integrate the regional office through the new OEP. That is, he did not concern himself with overseeing or supporting the management effort necessary to implement that vision. That was consistent with his management style, which was to provide very strong, directive leadership to his own high-priority projects, with a heavy emphasis on activity *outside* the agency. How the regional office was managed to support his strategies was not a subject that ever got his consistent attention.

The position of deputy administrator might have provided the support that the struggling head of the new OEP needed, but that did not happen. An unusual situation existed where the new regional administrator had divided the functions of the Deputy's office between two different managers, with an "acting" deputy. This significantly diminished the authority of the office and, as far as Dave Fierra was concerned, its ability to back him up effectively.

Earlier the office of deputy had become vacant due to the sudden death of the long-serving, much-loved previous deputy administrator. This loss was a great blow to the people of this agency. It coincided with budget cuts and the threat of major layoffs, as well as the arrival of the brash new regional administrator, who demanded sweeping changes right away, with little time for consultation. It was a deeply disturbing time for all of the employees of the EPA New England Regional Office.

For the main protagonist of this story, Dave Fierra, the result was that he faced debilitating opposition to his efforts to change the organization without the support of a supervisor, either for regular review or for backing up his authority to take drastic action in the last resort (such as transferring managers who refused to cooperate). The fact that he was in this situation was not due to a failure in planning. Rather it was bad luck that the deputy administrator position was not functioning normally at just this time and that the regional administrator directed his leadership to issues outside the agency. That left Fierra in a most difficult situation. Fortunately he had the steady support of his internal consultant, Georgie Bishop. She acted as advisor, planning partner, coach, link to occasional help from outside consultants, and confidante.

Phase Three: Strategic Alignment and Performance Management

In 1997, after two years as founder-director of the Office of Ecosystems Protection, Dave Fierra was reassigned by the regional administrator to a new position as director of strategic planning, charged with building a team of all the office directors aligned around environmental results instead of programs. From his two years of work in establishing the Office of Ecosystem Protection he had come to see a need to focus integration efforts on the other offices within the regional office. From his OEP position he had begun to impact the rest of the regional office, fostering increased collaboration across offices and programs—but mainly at levels below that of office director. In his new position he would work mainly with them, but without having line authority over them. For a year he talked extensively with these managers, both individually and collectively, and began to see some positive changes—at least cognitively.

The office directors agreed to undertake a pilot effort to integrate the work of the regional office across four environmental results areas. These included safe drinking water, restoring water quality in 14 watersheds, eliminating environmental risks in three urban areas, and protecting wetlands in New England. To provide direction and accountability for the pilot stage, workplans were developed for each result area in the spring of 1998. Each work plan was to contain a specific quantifiable environmental objective and a listing of regional work needed to reach it. It was expected that the middle managers from the various offices would provide leadership in integrating the programs to accomplish the objective. Unfortunately, many middle managers (particularly in OEP) resisted collaborating with other programs to integrate their work around environmental results. As a result, the first year of the pilot was largely unsuccessful. The new OEP office director did not take action against the recalcitrant middle managers, stating that these new roles were not clearly defined.

It was now clear to Dave Fierra that many of the managers in the region were not motivated to become leaders and advocates of the newly redefined mission of the organization as he had hoped. "I now believed that it was time to focus the leadership and behavioral changes needed to integrate the work through the performance management and planning system." As it happened, just at this time a mandate from EPA headquarters introduced a change in the format of the performance management system (PMS) to take effect in 1999. This helped to get senior managers in the regional office to pay attention.

Much work went into designing and negotiating a new PMS. Here the HR function enters this story as a strategic partner. A key person was Georgie Bishop, who has been a principal advisor to Dave Fierra since 1995. She now assumed a new role in facilitating a new and more committed approach to performance management in the Regional Office. A key

Some Lessons Learned and Questions for Further Reflection

To change EPA New England from a focus on enforcement *activities* to a focus on environmental results *requires coordinated changes in several areas:*

- changes in the *vision* that members have of the agency's purpose
- changes in many of the members' *mental models*
- changes in the agency's *formal organizational structure,* including setting up the Office of Ecosystem Protection and (within it) State Offices, especially changes in the measurement system or performance appraisal system (changing the individual performance measurement system should have begun earlier)
- changes in *resource allocation* priorities (away from traditional enforcement work)
- changes in the agency's relations with (at least some of) its *major stakeholders,* especially state agencies, congressional representatives, other federal agencies, businesses, national environmental groups, local citizen groups
- new learning opportunities for the new roles and duties, including the nature of *communication* between staff and managers at all levels—change leaders also need opportunities for dialogue and feedback
- support for the learning of new roles in several ways
  - "training" (e.g., how to write the new performance standards and goals)
  - "practice fields" and "learning labs" where coaching and support are provided (by internal or external consultants) while people work on real problems
  - "reflective partners" for the most active change leaders—internal human resource development consultants would be partnered with individual change leaders (as Georgie Bishop was with Dave Fierra) and with a change leadership team (as Bette Novak was with the three OSEP leaders
- reassignment or termination of staff who do not make the necessary changes after a fair interval and proper resources

To make these major changes requires effective *communication via* participation:

- explaining why change is necessary, the direction of the change, and the new thinking behind it
- listening while staff react to this new material, express their concerns, and reflect on what it means to them
- jointly developing ideas for implementing the new direction (even re-inventing the wheel) so that commitment develops to the change goals
- explaining specific implementation plans once they are adopted
- listening to feedback on problems found with the new changes and making use of it

This communication (dialogue) requires the active participation of staff and leaders on all sides of the conversation, in an effort to understand the intent and assumptions of others.

role was also played by the Regional Human Resources Council, set up in the mid-1980's in response to serious morale problems in the Agency. The Council's function was to advise senior managers in the regional office on any matters affecting employees.

Membership of the Council included all levels of employees, including union representatives, and was chaired by the deputy regional administrator. The council could be used, in effect, as a permanent focus group to design and test ideas for new HR policies and programs. So the members were asked how to make the performance management system (PMS) truly relevant to the mission of the agency at the regional New England level.

The old performance management system was widely considered pointless, unproductive, and part of a paperwork ritual that was not taken seriously by staff at any level. So the HR council met in March 1998 to consider two questions: 1) how to get everyone to focus their work plans and goals on environmental results and 2) how to change the culture of the office.

The council created a large training program to launch the new performance management system, recognizing (in the words of Georgie Bishop) that this was an attempt at revolutionary change and culture shift. A total of 750 staff received training in 15 sessions in the fall of 1998. Eighty managers received separate training and then were also involved in the training of their own staffs. Consequently, in January 1999 the entire staff of the Boston Regional EPA Office was engaged in rewriting their individual performance standards, something that had not been done for many years, if ever. Everyone was directed to write their plan so as to answer two key questions: 1) what results do I seek to achieve, and 2) with whom do I need to interact so that this can happen?

Despite the major training effort, leaders of this initiative were not naive enough to think that that would suffice, given the magnitude of the cultural shift involved. Even so, they were surprised at the difficulty experienced in the first year. A Quality Assurance (QA) program was implemented in February and March in which a sample of the 190 plans of individual employees were reviewed, using a general standards guide. This included a review of *all* plans for management and supervisory positions by the Strategic Planning Office. A sample of 70 performance plans were reviewed across the regional office from all levels and areas. QA reviewers were provided by HR, the management team, and the Office of Strategic Planning (Dave Fierra). Written reports were provided to each office with feedback based on the sample plans reviewed. QA reviewers also met with the management team of each office. Fierra offered to meet with each of the office directors individually to discuss changes needed in the individual performance standards submitted by their managers. One office director declined to meet, which resulted in unnecessary confrontation when the QA reviewers met with managers of that Office. At the meetings (about 90 minutes) the reviewers discussed the review of plans sampled from that office and also talked about the need to support this performance initiative with other HR efforts, especially professional development planning and resources.

Later Fierra met with the deputy administrator to review the initial implementation of the performance management system, including the roles played by senior executives in that process. Some had not met their duty to implement the new system to the best of their ability. He was concerned about how this would be handled in the performance reviews of those executives who were reviewed earlier, as Senior Executives, on a different schedule. Would there be accountability for this area, which had been determined by the top management of the regional office to be an essential requirement for their performance plans?

The challenge before the EPA regional office was to shift the vision of its employees to one where they integrated the efforts of all their programs with a focus on environmental results. An important part of their strategy to bring about that change was to implement a performance management system based on the new goals and standards, which would make each manager accountable not only for their own efforts but also for holding their own subordinates accountable for the same goals and standards. From an outsider's viewpoint, this was not so much a matter of redirecting the performance management system but of creating an effective one for the first time and giving it the necessary direction. In Dave Fierra's own words, "The key was to link the regional and national strategies to the individual performance of each individual." In this struggle one could feel the weight of a legacy culture in which these ideas are still quite alien and unwelcome.

Phase Four: Unexpected Change

In November 1999, without any warning, the regional administrator (a political appointee) announced his resignation to take a position at a local university and to enter the private sector. This news came as a complete surprise to the staff. He had recently received some criticism in the press regarding alleged favoritism on a decision (*Boston Globe*, Nov. 16, 1999, p. A37) and on the drop in the number of enforcement actions and permits issued (consistent with the new vision). But he had also won major acclaim for negotiating a hard-fought, major clean-up agreement with General Electric (the toughest of opponents) and for forcing the Army to stop using its firing range on Cape Cod because of ground water contamination. The belief in-house was that he would be around for a while, and there was even speculation that he might be re-appointed by the new administration. He was such a strong factor in terms of policy and leadership style that his departure could hardly fail to be significant. If his replacement were someone who believed in the new vision and also gave it some real support as a top leader, what a difference that could make!

The deputy administrator, who would be promoted to regional administrator, had only been in that office some two years. In that time she had come to understand the need for a more integrated and strategic approach to achieving environmental results, as Dave Fierra had been advocating. Mindy Lubber, the new regional administrator, saw how it made sense in terms of EPA's mission and purpose. And unlike her former boss, she understood how it needed to be implemented—that it involved getting staff to work together in new ways and to think about the work of the agency in new ways. She understood well the need to create management infrastructures for staff development and performance assessment to enable the new direction in how this EPA Regional Office would approach its mission. On January 11, 2000 she held a meeting with the top 80 to 100 managers. Listed first among the half-dozen priority topics she featured was a *focus on environmental results* and the need to integrate programs. Also on that list was the need for an improved *performance management system*. She and five other senior managers recently attended a three-day course in organizational learning, the same "leadership and mastery" course attended by Bishop and Fierra four years ago, when this story was just beginning.

Results

There is progress in this long, hard struggle. "We are now completing our second round of performance plan reviews with each office," says Dave Fierra. "The quality of the dialogue and overall understanding is improving." These are the crucial metrics—not numbers of performance standards completed without errors (for example) but the quality of thought and understanding demonstrated by staff. The new behavior sought from staff needs to be guided by new thinking on their part. So there is progress being made—but considerable resistance continues—and Fierra notes that, too. A change leader needs much patience and forbearance and needs to be capable of living with encouragement and disappointment mixed together.

In more than half a dozen visits to this agency for interviews, I rarely saw the same mood twice in succession: Sometimes there was frustration, but the next time there would be joy; it went back and forth, like a pendulum. We spent many hours talking about these events and sometimes speculating about the dynamics associated with them. Sometimes I heard fatigue and pain, but I also heard passion for working together for a clean, healthy, beautiful environment. I never heard cynicism and I never heard them consider giving up.

Dave Fierra's initial approach to transformation at EPA depended on the power of *vision*. However, his clear personal vision failed to connect with the personal visions of some of his reports. In the first few years, there was no *performance management system* to help carry the burden of alignment that vision alone could not carry. *Assessment* of organizational performance must focus on the quality of the dialogue about goals and standards, and the quality of understanding—not just alignment of standards and goals on paper—and then test for changed results.

Note by comparison that OSEP (working on a smaller scale) had success with the Vision Deployment Matrix as a very structured way to formulate and build upon vision, and also had the advantage of a small, unified top management group. This may have started as a slight advantage but through the organizational learning experience at OSEP, the three-person leadership team became much more cohesive and they then helped the 12-person supervisors' group to become more cohesive also.

Conclusion

Reflecting together on "how are things going?" and "why do we think so?" is an essential part of the process of managing change—both because we need to learn from our mistakes and successes, and because we need to learn from each other. That is, we need to learn how to understand each other better—the people we are supposed to work with. We need to understand better how they think (and how *we* think), how they see things (and how we do), and how they feel about things (compared to how we do). These are the keys to changing the way we behave with each other, especially how we collaborate more effectively across the old barriers that traditionally separate us—barriers of culture, ethnicity, gender, class, occupation, and all the different identities formed within an organization. Improved results for the organization depend on people working together more effectively across these boundaries. We can *learn* to do that if we are determined. It's not like learning computer science, codified knowledge that already exists and just needs to be internalized; it's more like creating new knowledge together—knowledge about us and how we can collaborate better.

The "lessons" listed here may or may not be correct; they may not be the most important lessons to be drawn from these change efforts. They are not so much conclusions as questions for further consideration. The point is that every change initiative must create its own reflections and lessons. That is how learning-based change happens—through people using their thinking and reality-testing abilities to grope forward through the murky, unmapped territory. A learning organization creates new futures, because the old ones do not work well enough anymore. And the only way for this entity we call an "organization" to create anything new is for its members to create it, using their ability to learn. Change leaders, core learning teams, and everyone involved in learning-based change—all have learning to do. This is the point of the learning-based approach. It is not about following some guidelines to "get it right." That's the old model. The new model is about using our capacity to learn in order to move from bad places to better ones, improving our organizations for the benefit of all.

Appendix I:
Creating a Learning Organization in (Part of)
an Auto Company (Case Study)

"AutoCo" is one of the big three Detroit car makers, and "Epsilon" was its program to create a new design and production tools for one of its luxury passenger vehicles (Roth and Kleiner). The program manager and his team were responsible for creating the design and being ready to launch production by a date some three years away, meeting many quality standards, and for staying within a cost budget. This would require the coordinated efforts of never less than 300 and as many as 1,000 employees, mainly engineers.

The program director came in with a personal goal, not only to produce a great car design, but to improve drastically the *process* of program development and the production launch. Having worked on several prior new car programs, he was familiar with the customary period of panic, out-of-control stress, and pandemonium in the last phase, just before launch, where everyone would be working extreme amounts of overtime, trying (always unsuccessfully) to launch on schedule. He was convinced that this was unnecessary and could be avoided by better management. Exactly how, he did not know, but he was fortunate that his deputy had become interested in learning organizations, especially the version being developed at MIT.

A consulting research team from MIT agreed to work with the Epsilon program leaders. While the MIT team had many ideas and tools to offer, they did not have a fully developed "package," and it was agreed that they would work as partners with the Epsilon team in a joint learning experience.

A "core learning team" was formed with 10 Epsilon managers and several staff from MIT, which met every month or two for a period of eight months. They conducted joint assessments on their team working issues and began learning and practicing the basic concepts and tools of organizational learning. Before asking the rest of the program staff to become involved in changes, members of this leadership group first engaged *themselves* in some very serious learning and change. When it was time for the learning labs, some senior Epsilon managers from the core learning team acted as teachers and coaches for the other staff, with the help of internal AutoCo consultants.

The training agenda and content were developed by the core learning team. Several members interviewed other program staff about their "greatest challenges and strengths." The core team used that data to study the central question: "Why are our parts always late?" Working together they created a systems map (causal loops) of many factors, which led to discovering the root cause and point of leverage. It was the fact that engineers who were having a problem with their component would not report this until very late, which would cause other dependent elements to be even further delayed, compounding the problem. Had the problem been revealed earlier, others could have helped to speed up the solution and prevent the escalation effect.

Concealing problems in one's own area, they learned, was a consistent pattern. The core team discussed why this happened, concluding that it was a combination of "engineering culture" (don't report any problem until you know the solution) and a company culture in which reporting problems would be held against someone, downgrading his or her performance appraisals and reputation. The Epsilon core team wanted to change that and realized that it would require establishing greater trust among the program staff, trust that "bearing bad tidings" would be safe. This required change in some other supporting norms and beliefs—the belief that no one has all the answers (even managers) and that cooperation for the good of the whole program was more important than the embarrassment of some individuals because their part of the work was not going well at the time. In other words, the Epsilon team was aiming to create a culture very different from the one that they had experienced over many years at AutoCo. In the new learning organization culture, managers expected engineers to make their own decisions (instead of demanding to control them) and cross-functional collaboration was expected and rewarded. These insights were developed first among the core learning team over eight months of regular meetings.

Several learning labs were held, eventually involving about one quarter of the entire staff, and many briefings and discussions were held with all of them. Much of the focus was on changing the norms of communication. The learning labs included various experiential methods. What made the biggest impact on employees, though, was seeing senior Epsilon managers actually change their own behavior. They became less authoritarian and more open to other viewpoints, and when engineers reported a serious problem delaying their work, senior managers made sure that they got help and did not suffer for their honesty.

The changed work process and culture was successful on the bottom line. Launch of the new model went smoothly and on time (as intended) instead of the usual last-minute panic and pandemonium—an unheard of event in the recent history of this very large company. The project was also well under budget, saving some $60 million in re-tooling costs. Customer reaction and various quality measures on the new vehicle were also well above previous levels. In three years—a short time for serious change in organizational culture—this program achieved impressive strides towards becoming a learning organization.

Note: The two change leaders, who were also the two senior executives of the Epsilon car program, Fred Simon and Nick Zeniuk, left the company shortly after the Epsilon launch to become consultants in this field. Subsequently, they were asked to assist the EPA New England Office with their initiative, which they did over some five years, through learning labs and continuing consultation with the main leaders. When the partnership between SoL and the Committee for High Performing Federal Agencies began, they became the main consultants to each of those projects.

Appendix II:
Environments That Are Unfavorable
to the New Model

"It's different here. You don't understand."

The following factors impact the ability to implement change. Use this list either to select the more promising locales for change initiatives and/or use it to prepare the ground, developing a more favorable environment for learning-based change initiatives.

When an organization has the following factors operating at a high level, it will be harder to improve organizational learning and to build more effective learning organizations—whether it is in the public or private sectors. It is often assumed that these negative factors generally characterize the public sector in contrast to the business sector, but we do not need to make that assumption. (In fact, those who are familiar with the inner workings of *Fortune* 500 corporations will instantly recognize most of the pathologies on this list.) The point is, it will be harder to promote learning-based change and to move towards the learning organization in situations where the following conditions exist:

- The work environment makes use of *blaming* when mistakes happen— especially when the blaming is personal, punitive, and public. All that is bad enough *inside* the organization. It's 10 times worse when your mistakes are considered fair game for the mass media and may be featured in provocative headlines or on the 6 p.m. news.
- Credits for successes are not balanced against a failure—this leads to a risk-averse culture.
- Stakeholders have the power to intervene and micromanage ("Congressman X's office called about … ").
- Change-resistant workers feel that they can wait out (and outwit) the reformist leaders. This is a specific reason for not depending too much on top-level (politically appointed) agency executives as change leaders, because their tenure is short. While they are indispensable for certain kinds of change—e.g., where legislation must be changed—the career service officials can play a broader role as change leaders.
- Dysfunctional structures are locked in by legislation or other hard-to-change means. This is where the political leverage of the political appointee can be valuable in getting the legislative changes. Most effective is an alliance between senior career officials, who may do the

groundwork, both in research and in the preparation of staff for the changes in operational models (changes in thinking) over several years prior to the arrival of the new appointee. (This happened, for example, in the OSEP case.)

- Senior managers *micromanage* or permit stakeholders to interfere in matters of administration through them.
- Poor performers (at any level of the organization) remain long-term without effective evaluation, help, or sanction. This creates a double drag effect on the morale of colleagues and on the performance of the unit.
- *Accountability is weak* and staff members feel they are invulnerable. Change comes as a severe threat to this situation.
- The workforce feels neglected and/or abused. Curiously, this may overlap with the previous two situations.
- Workers consider themselves more expert and/or more dedicated than their bosses.
- The vision of workers is limited to their own job description (*"it's not my job"*), with no regard for the purpose or mission of the whole program, and no concern for those who depend on its outputs (their "customers").
- *Inadequate feedback loops and information* systems leave staff "flying blind."
- A significant part of the workforce has a different vision for the agency from the official one. (This is a serious situation, even more than the others listed here.)
- The *intangibility of the work* leaves workers in disagreement about the nature of their customers, about what they do, and about what is or is not effective, with no ready evidence on which they could agree to settle the matter.
- The customers, those who depend on the outputs of the agency, have no way to reward or penalize the agency based on how well it meets or does not meet their needs. This is a major difference between traditional government services and the world of the marketplace. And this is why there has been so much interest in privatizing public services, making them compete and risking the loss of their franchise if they fail. This approach may work for service programs but would not work the same way for regulatory or security functions.
- The payer (third party) is different from the customer or beneficiary. In effect, there are two customers/stakeholders with possibly different interests, feedback loops, etc.
- Key players remain in position only a short time, often replaced by someone holding quite different assumptions, principles, and policies (*discontinuity of key players and policy*). This occurs in the electoral system of political appointees at the top levels of government agencies,

with a democratic rationale, as the larger political system adjusts to a shift in voter preferences. With increasing volatility in the business world, there may be an element of this discontinuity of key players with or without a shift in policy.

These 17 factors unfavorable to change are hard to avoid—especially (but not exclusively) in the public sector. Perhaps the main value of the list is to enable the prospective change leader to anticipate the nature of the barriers to be faced.

Bibliography

This short list of useful references combines sources that were cited in the text and other related works that are recommended as useful to readers beginning to explore this subject.

Argyris, C., D. A. Schon (1996). *Organizational Learning II*. Reading, Mass., Addison-Wesley.
Bailyn, L., J. K. Fletcher, D. Kolb (Summer 1997). "Unexpected Connections: Considering Employees' Personal Lives Can Revitalize Your Business," *Sloan Management Review*.
Miles, R. H. (1997). *Corporate Comeback*. San Francisco, Jossey-Bass.
Mintzberg, H. (1989). *Mintzberg on Management: Inside Our Strange World of Organizations*. New York, Free Press.
Moore, M. H. (1995). *Creating Public Value: Strategic Management in Government*. Cambridge, MA, Harvard University Press.
Nadler, D. and M. B. Nadler (1998). *Champions of Change: how CEOs and their companies are mastering the skills of radical change*. San Francisco, Jossey-Bass.
Nevis, E. C., J. E. Lancourt, et al. (1996). *Intentional Revolutions: A Seven-Point Strategy for Transforming Organizations*. San Francisco, Jossey-Bass.
Ouchi, W. (1981). *Theory Z: How American Business Can Meet the Japanese Challenge*. Reading, MA, Addison Wesley.
Pascale, R. T. and A. G. Athos (1981). *The Art of Japanese Management: Applications for American executives*. New York, Simon and Schuster.
Quinn, J. B., J. J. Baruch, et al. (1997). *Innovation Explosion: Using Intellect and Software to Revolutionize Growth Strategies*. New York, Free Press.
Senge, P. M. (1990). *The Fifth Discipline: The Art and Practice of the Learning Organization*. New York, Doubleday/Currency.
Senge, P. M. Charlotte Roberts, Rick Ross, Bryan Smith, Art Kleiner (1994). *The Fifth Discipline Fieldbook: Strategies and Tools for Building a Learning Organization*. New York, Currency/Doubleday.
Senge, P. M. Charlotte Roberts, Rick Ross, George Roth, Bryan Smith, and Art Kleiner (1999). *The Dance of Change: The Challenges of Sustaining Momentum in Learning Organizations*. New York, Currency/Doubleday.
Young, G. J. (2000). *Transforming Government: The Revitalization of the Veterans Health Administration*. Arlington, VA, The Pricewaterhouse-Coopers Endowment for The Business of Government.

CHAPTER EIGHT

Labor-Management Partnerships:
A New Approach to
Collaborative Management

Barry Rubin
Professor
School of Public and Environmental Affairs
Indiana University

Richard Rubin
Professor
School of Public and Environmental Affairs
Indiana University

This report was originally published in July 2001.

319

Introduction[1]

The City of Indianapolis has received significant attention for its efforts in reinventing the delivery of many urban services. It developed a system of municipal operations that is the envy of many other cities, both in the United States and abroad. Initially driven by the privatization efforts of former Mayor Stephen Goldsmith, a unique partnership has evolved between labor and management, encouraging cooperation and competition between city departments and their represented employees with private contractors. Because of the city's approach to organizational reform, the massive shift to the private sector for the delivery of city services threatened in the 1992 mayoral campaign never materialized.

While the city's success in improving the delivery of municipal services is known anecdotally throughout the United States and many other countries, little validation of this success exists. Moreover, research that has been conducted has addressed only limited aspects of the city's efforts, has been done by organizations with a vested interest in the outcome of the analysis, or has failed to connect inputs to outcomes. Thus, the reasons behind the city's success are not immediately obvious. Perhaps most importantly, the methods used to achieve successful reinvention of municipal service delivery in Indianapolis have not been fully documented to allow replication by other communities throughout the United States or the world.

Simultaneous with the privatization initiatives and development of the resulting labor-management partnership in Indianapolis, we were refining and testing a conceptual model of collaborative management in the public sector. This model was predicated on an ongoing labor-management relationship and a collective bargaining process that resulted in a jointly negotiated contract addressing all major work issues covered under wages, hours, and working conditions.

Historically, collective bargaining generally has not been adequate to address emerging issues that require cooperation rather than adversarial approaches. Many of the existing responsibilities of local government, and especially those resulting from the recent devolution of federal responsibility to states and municipalities, require cooperation. Quality enhancement, improved cost-effectiveness of service delivery, customer relations, neighborhood development, and welfare reform are just a few examples that require the cooperation of both municipal officials and labor leaders to work collaboratively. This need for cooperation is especially important in the public sector, where, according to the U.S. Bureau of Labor Statistics, unions currently represent 47.9 percent of local government workers in dramatic contrast to the 9.8 percent of union-represented private sector workers.[2]

Implementation of collaborative management—a joint process where both employees and their employer share in managerial decision making—

Definition of Collaborative Management

Reform efforts, in both the public and private sectors, have made use of programs that focus on the increased involvement of employees. In those settings where unions and collective bargaining agreements are present, these programs are dependent on the joint collaboration between labor and management. The Indianapolis labor-management partnership is one example of successful collaboration. Other forms of collaboration—such as site-based management, participative management, and labor-management committees—have been utilized throughout the United States with varying degrees of success.

has become a major topic of discussion among organizational reformers. Organization management theorists have documented that collaborative management improves labor-management relations in the public sector. When designed and implemented effectively, collaborative strategies satisfy both organizational and individual needs, and build lasting relationships between managers and employees.

Despite the currency of such collaborative efforts, little is understood about how such collaboration works. The existing literature on collaborative management is generally descriptive, impressionistic, and piecemeal in focus. Research has failed to reveal those factors that determine successful collaboration or induce the establishment of cooperative arrangements. While some researchers have identified variants of collaborative management with organizational improvement, a conceptual understanding of the dynamics of collaborative management is generally lacking.

The failure to consider the collective bargaining relationship already established between labor and management has been a major deficiency in the research on collaboration, especially since labor unions are likely to have a significant role in determining the initiation and outcomes of organizational improvement programs. Consideration of the pre-existing labor-management relationship must be a fundamental component of research investigating organizational reform and collaboration, especially for local governments.

This chapter utilizes a conceptual model for collaborative management in the public sector that is premised on the traditional labor-management process of collective bargaining and identifies the correlates of successful collaboration.[3] Then, using this model, the City of Indianapolis serves as a case study for the implementation of collaborative management. Initially driven by the privatization efforts of Mayor Stephen Goldsmith, a unique partnership has evolved between labor and management. This partnership encourages cooperation and competition between city departments and

Partnership Ground Rules

The essence of successful partnerships is a parallel structure that changes as a cooperative counterpart to the traditional union-management structure for collective bargaining. Ideally, this parallel structure involves union and management representatives in collaborative decision making at all levels of their respective organizations.

Ground Rule 1: Labor-management partnerships should be limited to those issues of mutual concern outside of the collective bargaining agreement.

Ground Rule 2: All involvement in labor-management partnerships should be voluntary.

Ground Rule 3: Improvements developed through labor-management Partnerships should not result in the loss of an individual's job.

Woodworth, W. P. and C. B. Meek, Creating Labor-Management Partnerships, *1995. Reading, MA: Addison-Wesley (pp. 88-89).*

their represented employees with private contractors. Because of the city's approach to organizational reform, the mass privatization of city services threatened in the 1992 mayoral campaign never materialized.

Application to Other Levels of Government

Our analysis of the Indianapolis experience provides prescriptive recommendations that can help labor and management initiate similar changes in other organizations. Indeed, these recommendations also are applicable to the federal sector as well as state government. In fact, the blueprint we provide can assist all organizations to implement collaborative management, and enable labor and management both to bargain competitively and to deliver services cooperatively. Appendix I provides a brief overview of labor relations in the federal government.

The Indianapolis Partnership: A Case Study

Getting Started

During the 1992 mayoral election, the American Federation of State, County and Municipal Employees (AFSCME) campaigned aggressively against Republican candidate Stephen Goldsmith, who pledged to privatize a wide array of city services. According to the AFSCME state director, Steve Fantauzzo, every job of every AFSCME member was in jeopardy due to Goldsmith's strong privatization position. Fantauzzo also feared that Goldsmith then would have the ability to implement his plan, as the city council was more than two-thirds Republican. During the campaign, Fantauzzo said, "We threw everything we had at them. If we were going to go down, we would go down swinging." Despite the union's efforts, Goldsmith won the election and took over as mayor of the City of Indianapolis in January 1993. Once Goldsmith was elected, grievances within the city departments tripled to between 200 and 300 each year.

City departments also faced myriad internal problems that hindered their ability to fulfill their duties. For example, the procedure for purchasing equipment and materials required numerous signatures, and work crews often were left idle while waiting for necessary supplies. Moreover, workers had little opportunity to participate in requisitioning materials and equipment, which, as a result, often were inadequate. Instead of contributing to management decisions, workers felt as though they were expected to "park their brains at the door" the moment they arrived at work. These expectations —combined with racism, inconsistently applied discipline, and other forms of favoritism—resulted in low morale, high absenteeism, and inefficient work practices.

Faced with deteriorating conditions, Mitch Roob, the mayor's new director of transportation (DoT), approached Fantauzzo with the idea of introducing competition and bidding into the delivery of public services. Presented with an opportunity to try a new approach in worker-management relations, AFSCME negotiated with the city to develop guidelines for the bidding that would allow public employees to compete on a level playing field. AFSCME members also received training, provided by the city, on Activity Based Costing (ABC), which allowed them to understand better the budgetary and bidding processes.

Seventy-five workers attended a two-day workshop in ABC. As a result of this training, Department of Public Works (DPW) employees realized the extent of their overhead costs and, in particular, the costs associated with management. As Fantauzzo said, "ABC allowed us to graphically verify that we had too many bosses and supervisors. There was no way we could compete with one supervisor for every four employees." Further, he challenged

Timeline of the Labor-Management Partnership

January 1993
Stephen Goldsmith takes office as Mayor of Indianapolis.

May 1993
Mitch Roob, Director of Transportation, approaches AFSCME about introducing competition and bidding into the delivery of public services.

June 1993
Workers attend Activity Based Costing (ABC), enabling them to calculate overhead costs associated with the high number of supervisors. Mayor Goldsmith then reduces the number of supervisors, which allows city departments to compete with private contractors.

July 1993
Chuck Snyder is hired as a consultant to improve the relationship between the city and AFSCME.

September 1993
The Re-engineering Task Force (RTF) is formed to address problems between labor and management.

December 1993
RTF potluck Christmas dinner provides a breakthrough in the traditionally adversarial relationship between labor and management.

March 1994
RTF disbands.

Fall 1994
Department of Transportation (DoT) and Department of Public Works (DPW) merge, as do their locals. Steve Quick is elected the AFSCME president.

March 1995
Snyder is appointed Chief Operating Officer of DPW. Snyder and Quick begin to make important changes within DPW, such as cleaning out employees' files and changing the pay scale to attract quality workers. These changes, along with the commitment from both the city and AFSCME, help the joint partnership to take root.

October 1995
The City of Indianapolis is recognized with the Kennedy School Innovations in American Government Award from Harvard University for its introduction of collaborative management. Mayor Goldsmith and Steve Quick jointly accept the award.

May 1998
Since street maintenance workers helped with the fall leaf collection, the Solid Waste Division helps the Streets Division with cleanup after the Indianapolis 500 annual parade. Both tasks are completed in record time.

December 1998
Collective bargaining for the new contract goes smoothly. Negotiations take approximately 40-48 hours compared to the previous negotiations that typically involved five to six hour-long meetings every day for a month.

January 2001
Bart Peterson takes office as Mayor of Indianapolis.

Mayor Goldsmith to cut supervisors to make the city departments more competitive with the private contractors. Though many of the supervisors were strong Republican supporters, Goldsmith responded by cutting 32 supervisors, 18 in the Department of Transportation alone. These cuts dropped the employee-to-supervisor ratio down to 17 employees for every one supervisor. Goldsmith's willingness to reduce the number of management positions, typically held by political appointees, represented a substantial political sacrifice. AFSCME, recognizing this as a signal of Goldsmith's interest in exploring a new approach to labor-management relations, began to encourage and assist its members in preparing bids for DPW services.

To reinforce the administration's commitment to establish a new relationship with AFSCME, Mayor Goldsmith brought in a consultant, Chuck Snyder, to facilitate this relationship. Snyder previously had worked as chief operating officer for a $100 million manufacturing company. During his tenure with that company, management and labor had developed a strong relationship based on open communication and trust. Mayor Goldsmith got a glimpse of what was to come when he indicated to Snyder that he never had asked AFSCME for suggestions to improve working conditions. To this, Snyder simply responded, "You are not going to get anything accomplished until you do."

Chuck Snyder began working within DPW to build trust and confidence with both AFSCME and the city. As Snyder explained, "Persuading workers of my good intentions was a real sales job." To the union, Snyder initially was just a consultant, which was nothing special to the workers. "If we've seen one consultant," said DPW AFSCME President Steve Quick, "we've seen a hundred." For Snyder, selling himself to DPW employees meant meeting personally with every employee and seeking their ideas. He attended midnight meetings and accompanied street repair crews at three o'clock in the morning. Snyder also told Mayor Goldsmith that he would not support any layoffs or job loss. Mayor Goldsmith agreed and kept his promise.

Snyder's dedication to the process became even more apparent in September 1993 when a Reengineering Task Force (RTF) was formed. It was comprised of 12 people from both labor and management, plus Chuck Snyder. The initial task for the RTF was to identify the problems between labor and management. "There were 500 different things wrong with this city that we listed on the walls. The whole room was wallpapered with problems. And 99 percent of it was bad management and poor communication," Snyder explained.

Steve Quick, who at that time was the union steward in the Streets Division, walked into the RTF room, looked at all of the problems listed on the walls, and said, "The biggest problem isn't even listed—it's racism." At the time, the Streets Division was predominantly black while the Department of Transportation was mostly white. To further amplify the racial division, of the seven city garages, some were almost all white while others were almost all

In January 1994, Indianapolis was hit with a particularly nasty blizzard. One of the many benefits of cellular telephones, I discovered, was the increased speed and convenience with which citizens could complain about the city's snowplowing effort. During morning drive-time, my phone and those of the morning news programs rang incessantly as motorists enthusiastically expressed their opinions from their cars. Throughout the day the dissatisfaction grew.

Snow can ruin political careers, so the next morning I visited a city garage where workers were beginning a shift. I asked the snowplow drivers to gather in one room while I first spoke with the managers in another. I told the 15 or so managers that I was puzzled by the unusually high number of complaints, and asked their view. One after another volunteered that the plan had been well executed, that everyone was working diligently, and that without vast new resources, the city was already doing the best it could do.

Moments later, I asked the snowplow drivers the same question. Hands shot up. City mechanics should be out on the streets repairing trucks as soon as they broke, they said. Some of the trucks' blades were operated by a hydraulic system that broke frequently and needed immediate maintenance. Route maps were hard to read and did not reflect current rush-hour traffic patterns, so some busy streets were placed low on the priority list. To save money, the city no longer used salt with blue dye in it, which had helped snowplow drivers see where they had been and allowed them to notice immediately if their equipment malfunctioned. The new salt came in chunks that were often too big to go through the spreaders. On and on it went.

These employees did the work, knew the problems, and had workable solutions. It's funny how few mayors see it that way. Many of us view unions as the very embodiment of government inefficiency, keeping costs high and quality low. Everyone knows, after all, that public employees are lazy and incompetent—why else would they work for the government, right?

Wrong. The unions often have little to do with the problem. Public employees are an easy scapegoat, but when union workers are given the freedom to put their own ideas into action, they can be as innovative, effective, and cost-conscious as their private-sector counterparts—and they can prove it in the marketplace.

— Mayor Stephen Goldsmith
"Can-Do Unions: Competition Brings Out the Best in Government Workers," The Journal of American Citizenship Policy Review, *March/April, 1998, p. 24.*

black. While the city had already formed a committee to address affirmative action and cultural diversity, Snyder preferred to "get down in the trenches, deal with it, and break down walls." This attitude led to the reduction of the seven city garages down to three, which forced integration and compelled people to work together. By easing the racial tensions in its departments, the city could work more efficiently while treating everyone equally.

Through his conversations with DPW employees, Snyder realized that many problems lay within management. In his opinion, there were too many middle managers who emphasized the distinction between managers and labor. "What's the difference," Chuck Snyder asked, "... between the blue collar workers and someone who works in an office?" Snyder also found a wide range of favoritism within middle management, as well as resentment toward the RTF process. To allow the RTF process to move forward, Goldsmith responded to Snyder's concerns by downsizing the number of middle managers within that department.

The RTF continued to consolidate, rearrange, and retrain throughout this process. One key result of the RTF was to reduce the number of job classifications from more than 100 in 1993 down to 12 by 1998. While reducing job classifications, employees were retrained so that they could be assigned to a much wider range of tasks. In addition, the RTF developed a Second Chance Program, through which city commercial driver's license holders who tested positive for drugs could go through rehabilitation and retain their jobs. While Mayor Goldsmith supported this program, other city departments, including Human Resources and Risk Management, strongly opposed it. However, with the insistence of Snyder and the RTF, the program finally was established, and has had much success. Twenty people had gone through the program by the end of 1998, with 17 people successfully completing rehabilitation and retaining their jobs.

"Our goal was not to use privatization as an end, but to use it as a means to an end. We started with a privatization strategy which assumed that the private sector was more efficient than the public employees. We shifted to a competition model which said it is monopolies and bureaucracies that are inefficient.

Public employees are not inherently inferior to private employees—the systems are inherently inferior. So if we compete out public services, we'll be able to save a significant amount of money and at the same time improve the quality of city services."

— Mayor Stephen Goldsmith in an interview with staff
writer Bill Steigerwald *"Saving the City from Itself,"*
Pittsburgh Post-Gazette *March 22, 1998, p. C-4.*

The Second Chance Program was not the only example of opposition from lower-level management. Many departments felt threatened by the power base they saw forming in the RTF. In an unsuccessful effort to diffuse this opposition, Snyder talked with them. He also worked to fight rumors within the workforce by maintaining a continuous dialogue with all DPW employees. As a result, union laborers began to see Snyder as a "straight-shooter" and began to trust both him and the RTF. According to Snyder, "I moved around here pretty much like I owned the place." While this approach potentially could have caused Snyder problems, Mayor Goldsmith and the other members of the RTF did not object to Snyder's activities, because they felt sure that he could make this emerging partnership a success from the city's perspective.

An RTF potluck Christmas dinner proved to be a turning point in solidifying the rapport between labor and management. Snyder, assigned with the responsibility of bringing meat trays to the dinner, appeared with two platters. The first was piled high with an impressive assortment of food, complete

---

When Stephen Goldsmith ran for Mayor of Indianapolis in 1992, he vowed to cut the size of the city government by 25 percent in his first year without touching police or fire. He intended to reach his goals by privatizing a great majority of city services. Mayor Goldsmith invoked the "Yellow Pages" test to determine which operations should be contracted out. As Goldsmith aide John Hatfield explained, "The rule was that if you could thumb through the phone book and find three or more companies that provide a service that government is producing, then government is probably not the best at providing that service." In light of this test, only police, fire, and zoning operations were exempt from the city's bidding wars. Virtually all other municipal functions— such as trash collection, window-washing of city-owned buildings, copying services, and management of the Indianapolis International Airport —were to be awarded to the provider that would deliver the service at the lowest cost to the city. However, Mayor Goldsmith did recognize that there might be times when city workers could provide the best and most cost-effective service. To allow for this, the mayor's focus turned toward competition rather than privatization. City employees would be able to compete and submit bids for jobs, including those jobs which had been slated for privatization before Mayor Goldsmith took office. According to Jerry Richmond, vice president of AFSCME, Mayor Goldsmith basically told the union, "If you can do it, we'll let you do it."

— Jon Jeter
"A Winning Combination in Indianapolis: Competitive Bidding for City Services Creates Public-Private Success Story," Washington Post, Sept. 21, 1997, p. A-3.

with a label entitled "Management." The second, labeled "Union," had a few pieces of bologna, toothpicks, and some carrots. The labels amused both labor and management, and brought an informal, human element to what typically was an impersonal, adversarial relationship.

With an easing of the traditional schism between labor and management, the members of the RTF were able to spend the next three months implementing a number of the solutions they had developed. One such solution was to combine the two AFSCME locals (from DoT and DPW) into one. This move helped unify the employees and made it easier for management to work with AFSCME. However, while these plans were being implemented successfully, people outside of the RTF still were suspicious, believing both management and union leaders had sold out.

These rumors ultimately brought the RTF to an end. Under pressure and allegations that they had sold out, union leaders needed to pull themselves out of the negotiations as a demonstration of commitment to their members. Changes in the upper levels of management also impeded the ability of the RTF to accomplish its goals. In March 1994, the RTF was disbanded. To Chuck Snyder, the close of the negotiations came too early for the relationship between labor and management to truly change. "There was not enough buy-in from people outside that room," Snyder explained. "Either you believe in this partnership and you're in it all the way, or you're out. There's no one foot in, one foot out in this deal."

To allow union workers to compete on a level playing field with private contractors, the city provided training in Activity Based Costing for 75 workers. Understanding job-related costs was a necessary first step in implementing competition. "We have great employees trapped in bad systems," said Skipp Stitt, former deputy mayor of the City of Indianapolis. "Once the system changes and workers know the costs involved with their jobs and are rewarded for holding them down, guys start to see it. They're not bad people." Making workers responsible for obtaining and keeping contracts also sent a message to management that the men and women doing the job know better than anyone what it takes to get it done well. Mayor Goldsmith understands this more than most, as he would join a crew of city employees on the job once a week. "Nobody knows better than the worker how the job can be done more efficiently," he said. "You spend an hour with a guy filling potholes, and he can give you a dozen good ideas about ways to make the service more efficient."

— Dirk Johnson
"In Privatizing City Services, It's Now 'Indy-a-First-Place,'"
New York Times, March 2, 1995, p. A-14.

Before competition was introduced, the Department of Public Works (DPW) did only 30 percent of all trash collection. Since the introduction of competition, DPW won 70 percent of the trash collection contracts. This competition has cut annual trash collection costs per household from $85 to $68, for a total savings over the three-year contract of $15 million. The department also has reorganized from 27 trash collection crews to 17 while increasing the number of homes served per crew by 78 percent over the 1992 level. Absenteeism and worker's compensation claims also have decreased. These gains in productivity allowed DPW to beat their bid price by $2.1 million in 1994, resulting in incentive pay averaging $1,750 per worker.

— Mayor Stephen Goldsmith
"Can-Do Unions: Competition Brings Out the Best
in Government Workers," The Journal of American
Citizenship Policy Review, March/April, 1998, p. 24.

In the months following the end of the RTF, the relationship between labor and management further deteriorated. During this time, the Department of Transportation and the Department of Public Works merged, causing tension within the union. Communication between management and AFSCME was by appointment only. Racism and grievances again were increasing, while the amount of work being accomplished was decreasing.

Snyder Becomes COO

Concerned with the situation, Mayor Goldsmith asked Steve Quick, now AFSCME president of the combined DoT-DPW union, who could take over the position of chief operating officer of DPW and help fix the situation. Quick recommended Snyder for the position. What sold the union on Snyder was trust. According to Quick, "What DPW needed was someone's word that was good." Snyder assumed that position in March 1995.

As the new chief operating officer, Snyder, working together with Quick, made many critical decisions that reversed existing city policies and helped solidify the standing of AFSCME in DPW. To provide everyone with a fresh start within the department, all old files were cleaned out, eliminating prior employee disciplinary records. Given this clean slate, Snyder and Quick also improved the grievance system. Management became more accountable as they now were subject to being "written up," with copies of the write-ups being provided to the union. This increased accountability within DPW and allowed the department to clean out those workers who were not producing their best work, but the old pay scale made it difficult

Jerry Richmond, Chuck Snyder, and Steve Quick.

to attract better candidates. Quick convinced Snyder that to obtain quality workers, they would have to offer competitive market salaries, which Snyder implemented. Many of these changes faced strong opposition from both lower-level management and people outside DPW.

Snyder and Quick had to demonstrate a united front to quell opposition to their new working relationship and to gain the trust and confidence of both labor and management. To do this, the two held meetings in the city garage that provided workers the opportunity to address both their union leadership and management. Snyder and Quick, working as a team, constituted the nucleus of the new partnership. They met with each other daily and talked on the phone several times each day. Many of these conversations involved decisions that easily could have been made without union involvement, but Snyder preferred to involve the union in everything. To Snyder, this was a strategic effort to strengthen the partnership. In his words, "No matter how small or insignificant the decision, bounce it off the people you are trying to partner with." Snyder felt that doing this ensured open communication between the parties and prevented both rumors and ill will from forming within the partnership.

Mayor Goldsmith also played a vital role in advancing the partnership. Because of his aggressive campaign promises for privatization, many union workers distrusted Mayor Goldsmith's support of the partnership. To combat this, monthly meetings were convened that involved just the mayor and workers. Mayor Goldsmith also encouraged all employees to communicate with him via e-mail, and he guaranteed a response. With a means through which they could speak directly with the mayor, and without having to go through middle management, union workers were able to see the mayor as "more human" and as a valuable supporter of the partnership. This open communication worked in both directions, for it proved to Mayor Goldsmith that union workers could make a significant contribution to improving the city.

Maintaining the partnership required great dedication. It was criticized from all sides. Internally, some workers and lower-level management were still trying to undermine Snyder and Quick, while externally the local media were attempting to discredit them. However, Snyder chose to "live or die" by the partnership. "There was never a time I quit believing in what I was doing," said Snyder. "I felt I was improving the workplace and helping city employees. But there were days ..." By working together, Snyder and Quick depended on each other for support. Their teamwork eventually would affect the working atmosphere in DPW as well as the lives of its employees.

For some employees, the partnership resulted in increased responsibility. The managers who remained after Mayor Goldsmith RIFed (Reduction-in-Force) some supervisors were relatively amenable to cooperating with the union. This, combined with the increased job responsibilities of the workers, forced management to depend on union workers as crew supervisors. The crew supervisors assumed some of the management paperwork, while management became more focused on ensuring the availability of proper equipment and material. The new arrangement also allowed DPW managers to widen their perspective on the abilities of union workers. As Todd Durnil, the deputy administrator of street maintenance, observed, "We took the shackles off the guys. We tapped their knowledge and experience instead of telling them what to do."

Partnership Takes Hold

As the partnership took hold, the department as a whole began to come together as a team. "Before [the partnership], you didn't care about your fellow employee. You were your own entity," AFSCME Vice President Jerry Richmond explained. "When people saw how the department came together as a group, they started to care about their fellow employees." This attitude also seemed to permeate the employees' home lives. Prior to the partnership, marital problems and alcohol problems were common among DPW workers. Through training and recognition for their knowledge, the partnership allowed workers to grow as individuals and increase their sense of self-worth. As a result, such personal problems became less troublesome within the department. As Richmond stated, "For many, their life had turned around."

As employees became more involved in the decision-making process, they suggested new work practices to improve quality and efficiency within DPW. For example, trash collection required three people to be on the truck. In the past, all three workers would go with the full truck to the trash dump. Under the partnership, when a truck was full, a different driver would arrive with an empty truck and exchange it for the full one. The new driver then would take the full truck to the dump, while the other three workers were able to continue their route.

This greater efficiency, combined with increased job training, allowed workers to be shifted to whatever task needed immediate attention. For example, starting in 1998, street maintenance workers began helping with leaf pickup, formerly a job solely within the jurisdiction of the Solid Waste Division. By employing this procedure, both leaf collection and trash collection were accomplished in record time with no delays in service. Similarly, the Streets Division always had cleaned up after the Indianapolis 500 parade. In 1998, the Solid Waste Division assisted, resulting in an unprecedented, quick cleanup. This was critical because an NBA playoff basketball game was scheduled later that same evening.

For such special circumstances, DPW and AFSCME implemented an automated callup system which offered overtime work to employees according to their seniority. This eliminated both favoritism and the labor-intensive task of calling and locating off-duty employees. With the automated system, employees were paged and given a number to call for recorded details. After listening to the possible assignment, the employee accepted or declined the offer by pressing a key on the telephone. This process continued until all needed spots were filled.

Improvements like these, however, would not be possible without the proper equipment for the delivery of these city services. Before the partnership, money was spent on equipment simply to spend out the budget. Much

---

Potholes

When Mayor Goldsmith took office, one of the first questions he asked was how much it costs to fill a pothole. At first, no one could tell him, though city officials eventually came up with a price of $425 per ton of asphalt. Mayor Goldsmith and other city officials considered this cost to be too high. They put the job of street maintenance up for possible privatization but invited the Department of Public Works to bid as well. In the end, DPW was able to win the contract for street maintenance by submitting a bid of $307 per ton of asphalt, a 28 percent reduction over those costs before competition was introduced. When the work actually was completed, DPW not only met the overall bid price, but they beat it by $20,000. They also increased the average production of a work crew from 3.1 to 5.2 lane miles per day, a 68 percent increase.

of this equipment was inadequate or inappropriate for the duties of the department, and workers were left to complete their jobs without the proper tools. Under the partnership, workers were given a voice in the type of equipment that was purchased. By understanding the costs of service delivery through their training with Activity Based Costing, workers had the necessary knowledge to select the best equipment. Purchasing rules also were changed to improve the speed with which new equipment could be obtained. While supervisors were allowed to approve purchases of $1,000 or less, a manager still was required to approve any expenditure above $1,000. However, since managers were generally located in the same building, obtaining these signatures was not a lengthy process.

From 1993 to 1998, over $5 million was spent on new equipment, including 40 trucks for snow plowing. This equipment, when combined with the new operating procedures, allowed DPW to remain competitive with private contractors. Prior to the implementation of ABC and the partnership,

---

Side Agreements

The Side Agreements, reached jointly by AFSCME and the City of Indianapolis between March 1995 and October 1998, were reduced to writing, signed by both parties, and were considered supplements to their regular collective bargaining contract. These are a few examples of their 23 Side Agreements:

Issue	Agreement
Black Expo	To promote community awareness, DPW agrees to allow employees to attend Black Expo luncheons, set up Black Expo booths on city time, and be compensated at their regular wage.
Accountability	DPW management will be held to a higher level of accountability than will bargaining unit employees.
Accidents	All accidents will go before the union-management accident review board. If the board determines that the accident was preventable, the employee will be required to attend a defensive-driving training class.
Paycheck Privacy	All paychecks will be placed in a sealed envelope, done by the payroll coordinators, prior to checks being picked up by the employees' area representatives.
Compensatory Pay	Bargaining unit members may use compensatory time in the same week it is earned, but compensatory time cannot be used prior to it being earned.

half of the snow removal responsibilities were contracted out. DPW has since regained all snow removal contracts, thanks to the many improvements realized with the help of the employees.

As these examples demonstrate, the partnership clearly improved the delivery of public services by generating a more efficient and cohesive team of workers. The union also benefited. Typically, union meetings used to be held off-the-clock and were attended by only four or five workers. That changed dramatically when monthly meetings were held on-site and on-the-clock, and attendance rose to between 50 and 80 workers. The meetings ran in an orderly fashion by following a posted agenda so that all labor issues were addressed. In addition, the union now had its own office and vehicles, while previously it simply had "access" to these resources. By providing the union time to organize and meet with its members, management has been able to respond better to employees' needs.

The union, better to meet the needs of its members, shifted its focus. Previously, it had spent large amounts of time and money defending those 5 percent of its members who did a poor job. Now the partnership enabled the union to focus on securing improvements for the other 95 percent who did their job well. These improvements included an incentive program that put $1 of every $4 saved into the pockets of city workers. "Our folks have averaged 5 to 6 percent raises per year," Steve Fantauzzo said. "I'd challenge you to find any place in the country to match." In addition, the gains that the union achieved have spilled over to nonunion employees. Quick said he did not mind the spillover, since "we're all in this together."

The relationship between labor and management that originated during the partnership also impacted Mayor Goldsmith's competition plans. As the employees demonstrated that they could best complete the work, the percentage of the DPW budget that was bid out significantly decreased. In 1993, 20 percent of the DPW budget was bid out, with this percentage dropping to 3 percent by 1998. Within DPW, consensus was reached about what the department was good at and what would be better left to private contractors. In addition, contracts that DPW typically won were no longer bid out each year, but instead had longer contractual intervals to ensure continued efficiency.

Management also benefited from the partnership in other ways. Formal grievances declined significantly in number, freeing up both time and resources. Approximately 250 grievances were filed in 1993, while only one was filed in both 1997 and 1998. Issues still arose between workers and management, but these were resolved within DPW, often informally. In other cases, concerns were resolved by negotiating Side Agreements, supplemental documents agreed to by labor and management that specified DPW policy. These Side Agreements allowed for the immediate resolution of those problems that typically were handled only during regular contract negotiations,

---

such as policy for tardy workers. Between March 1995 and October 1998, 23 such Side Agreements were signed.

The influence of the partnership also improved the collective bargaining process. During the 1998 contract negotiations, the City of Indianapolis brought in an outside labor negotiator accustomed to the traditional, adversarial labor-management relationship. During an initial meeting, the negotiator's uncompromising stance prompted Quick to explain, "That's not the way we do things here. This is a partnership." Quick then called Mayor Goldsmith, who contacted the city's negotiator. At the next meeting, the negotiator apologized and maintained a low profile throughout the remainder of the negotiations, allowing Snyder, Quick, and others familiar with the partnership to work through the contract. Participants estimated that the entire contract was negotiated in 40 hours, much faster than the usual month-long, six-hours-per-day process.

The uniqueness of the partnership that developed in the City of Indianapolis has been acknowledged in many ways. Since the introduction of competition into the delivery of public services and the establishment of the partnership, Indianapolis has served as a model for other municipalities looking to achieve similar gains. The City of Indianapolis has been recognized through numerous awards, including the Kennedy School Innovations in American Government Award from Harvard University in 1995. Of the 1,500 applicants, only 15 awards are given each year. The City of Indianapolis submitted a joint labor-management application, the only application of its kind in 1995. When Vice President Al Gore presented the award, Mayor Goldsmith waited for Steve Quick to reach the podium before accepting the award. Mayor Goldsmith's actions emphasized that the receipt of the award, as well as the existence of the partnership, was in large part due to the willingness of both city management and the union members to break from their traditional adversarial roles and foster a new working relationship.

Findings and Recommendations

While our case study of the Indianapolis labor-management partnership reveals a number of lessons for those organizations interested in implementing collaborative management, it is only through a structured qualitative and quantitative analysis that a complete set of recommendations and findings can emerge. We conducted a qualitative analysis by interpreting the Indianapolis case study with respect to a conceptual model of labor-management collaboration. This model (presented in detail in Appendix II) is based on the underlying principle that collaboration will exist as a supplement to, not a replacement for, traditional collective bargaining and is predicated on this continuing labor-management relationship.

The model identifies the major components of successful collaboration and is comprised of five stages: impetus, initiation, implementation, integration, and institutionalization. First, for collaborative management to be effective, the present collective bargaining process must prove inadequate to address the increasing internal and external pressures on both parties. This constitutes the *impetus* stage. Second, the *initiation* stage is reached when both labor and management develop shared objectives to address these pressures without infringing on their traditional collective bargaining relationship. Third, the *implementation* stage occurs when collaboration develops in conjunction with, not in opposition to, the collective bargaining process. Fourth, the *integration* stage is reached when both the representatives and their constituents are fully committed to collaboration. And, fifth, for collaborative management to be successful over the long term, it must be formalized as a supplement to the collective bargaining process and addressed in the labor-management contract, thus comprising the *institutionalization* stage.

In addition to the qualitative analysis of the case study, we conducted a quantitative analysis utilizing survey research and multivariate regression. This quantitative assessment (which is presented in detail in Appendix III) was used to validate and extend the qualitative results. Through the use of data collected from a survey completed by both labor and management, the model of collaboration was applied to determine those underlying factors that contributed to the success of the partnership. The results provide statistical confirmation of the partnership's success and identify the antecedents of that success.

Based on both the qualitative and quantitative analyses, one of the most fundamental determinants of successful labor-management collaboration is the infrastructure of an existing collective bargaining relationship. Because cooperation is historically counter-intuitive for labor unions, the competition of collective bargaining is critical for their survival. Unionism in government continues to grow throughout the United States and, therefore, any initiative to "reinvent government" must recognize and accept this fact. Any reform in the delivery of public services must be based on the traditional collective bargaining relationship, which in turn becomes the infrastructure for the parallel process of collaboration. Collective bargaining traditionally addresses wages, hours, and working conditions; building upon this infrastructure, labor-management partnerships address the higher-level concerns of both parties. The implication for organizations interested in a collaborative relationship with labor is not to change the collective bargaining process, but to ensure a parallel process for dealing with those issues outside the traditional scope of wages, hours, and working conditions.

Findings

Finding 1: Initiating collaboration requires a defining event for which traditional collective bargaining is inadequate.

This event or situation must generate sufficient internal and external pressure on both parties to force them to recognize that their traditional way of dealing with each other (collective bargaining) is inadequate. In Indianapolis, this event was the mayor's campaign platform to privatize the delivery of city services and the potential loss of union jobs. Simultaneously, racial tensions within city departments had reached critical levels, and collective bargaining had not been adequate to resolve them.

Finding 2: Organizations that are interested in exploring collaborative approaches, without external and internal pressures, need to separate collaboration from collective bargaining.

In terms of a hierarchy, collective bargaining addresses one set of organizational needs, while collaboration addresses another. By protecting the collective bargaining process, the risk of collaboration to labor and management is reduced and the probability of successful collaboration is increased. Moreover, the infrastructure upon which their collaboration is built will be sustained.

Finding 3: Both parties must perceive significant benefits from their collaboration before they will be willing to engage in a joint partnership.

While labor and management may have different reasons to collaborate, both parties must share a common goal for their collaboration to be successful. For example, this shared goal in Indianapolis was the protection of city services and the simultaneous protection of city jobs. Organizations interested in fostering collaboration cannot do so unless *both* labor and management recognize the advantages of cooperation.

Finding 4: Training is a critical factor in implementing collaborative management.

This does not necessarily refer just to training on process skills (e.g., effective listening), but rather to training, as well, on content skills (e.g., cost estimation). In Indianapolis, this took the form of workshops on such topics as bid preparation and budgeting. Since the voice of employees is through their union, collaboration will not occur without the active support of both the local labor union and its affiliate. Thus, an organization wishing to bring about such collaboration must recognize that the collaboration is with the union, not with individual employees. Moreover, based on the importance of parallelism, collaboration must remain a distinct and separate decision-making process from that of collective bargaining, yet can take place concurrently.

Finding 5: Commitment to the partnership and diffusion of this commitment throughout the constituencies of both labor and management are the most critical factors in the success of collaborative management.
This commitment must not be restricted solely to the leadership, but must pervade both organizations. Without the commitment of both parties and acceptance within both organizations, the Indianapolis collaboration effort would have been thwarted, and the traditional adversarial relationship would have recurred. In Indianapolis, both labor and management repeatedly demonstrated this commitment, thus increasing the level of trust between the participants. This suggests that those organizations wanting to emulate the Indianapolis partnership must have a continuing and sustained commitment to the collaborative process from both labor and management.

Finding 6: Individual personalities play an important role in any organizational reform.
The continuing importance of both trust and open communication emerged consistently throughout our research interviews. The initial willingness to explore alternative ways to deliver municipal services incurred significant political risk for Steve Goldsmith, Chuck Snyder, Steve Quick, and Jerry Richmond. But for their personal and sustained commitment to trust and open communication on behalf of their constituents, the Indianapolis partnership would not be the exemplar of success that it has become.

Finding 7: Once collaboration is established, it must be incorporated into the day-to-day operations of the organization.
Even though individual personalities did play a dominant role in the creation and success of the Indianapolis partnership, the process of collaboration, once established, must not remain dependent on individuals. Therefore, we strongly urge those organizations that want to pursue collaboration between labor and management to institutionalize this process by incorporating it within their labor agreement. This not only legitimizes and strengthens the collaborative process, but also assures its survival.

Recommendations

Recommendation 1: Don't force collaboration.
The *impetus* for collaboration should emerge naturally when both labor and management recognize that their traditional collective bargaining process is not able to address those internal and external pressures demanding change. Artificially forcing collaboration, without legitimate threats perceived by both parties, is unlikely to result in a self-sustaining process.

Recommendation 2: Make sure that both labor and management share the primary reason for collaboration.

The primary reason to *initiate* joint collaboration must be clear and accepted by both sides. However, each side can have other, secondary reasons to collaborate, and both parties must accept these different agendas.

Recommendation 3: Ensure that the traditional collective bargaining process is protected.

The process of collaboration must remain separate from the collective bargaining process. Yet collaboration also must involve the same parties, since the union already is the designated representative of the workforce. Additionally, training becomes critical in both collaboration skills (e.g., effective listening) and problem-solving skills (e.g., Activity Based Costing) to help labor and management *implement* this parallel decision-making process.

Recommendation 4: Treat collaboration and collective bargaining as separate but equally important processes.

Since the collective bargaining process already is well *integrated* in government, labor and management also must commit to collaboration and develop this commitment throughout their constituencies. This is critical so that collaboration also becomes well *integrated* in government.

Recommendation 5: Tie collaboration to the collective bargaining agreement.

In order to *institutionalize* and sustain collaboration, labor and management must link collaboration to collective bargaining by incorporating it in their contract. Failure to do this is likely to place the collaborative process at great risk from changes in politics and personality.

Appendix I:
Labor Relations in the Federal Government

Key Events

1962   Executive Order 10988 was signed by President John F. Kennedy. The E.O. recognized the rights of federal employees to join unions, granted recognition to those unions, and allowed limited bargaining rights.

1970   The Postal Reorganizations Act was passed allowing postal workers to come under the National Labor Relations Act.

1978   The Civil Service Reform Act replaced previous executive orders concerning federal employee bargaining rights. Title VII of that act established the Federal Labor Relations Authority (NLRA) and modeled bargaining rights in the federal government after the NLRA.

1993   Executive Order 12871 was enacted by President Bill Clinton as part of the reinvention initiative, creating a National Partnership Council to change the way management and unions relate in the public sector.

Background

In 1962, President John F. Kennedy signed Executive Order 10988, which recognized the rights of federal employees to join or to refrain from joining labor organizations, granted recognition to those labor organizations, and detailed bargaining subjects. Before 1962, only 26 union or association units in the executive branch of the federal government had union shops, and they represented only 19,000 workers. Six years after the Kennedy order, there were 2,305 bargaining units, with a total membership of 1.4 million employees. A number of different unions represented federal workers, the largest being the American Federation of Government Employees (AFGE).

Currently, federal employee labor relations are governed by the provisions of Title VII of the Civil Service Reform Act of 1978. Title VII, Federal Service Labor-Management Relations, is modeled after the National Labor Relations Act. Central authority was placed in a three-member panel, the

Federal Labor Relations Authority. This panel oversees labor-management relations within the federal government; its three members are appointed by the president of the United States. The president also appoints a general counsel empowered to investigate alleged unfair labor practices and to file and prosecute complaints.

The Federal Labor Relations Authority oversees creation of bargaining units, conducts elections, decides representation cases, determines unfair labor practices, and seeks enforcement of its decisions in the federal courts. The Federal Service Impasse Panel was continued by the act and provides assistance in resolving negotiation impasses. Unlike private sector labor laws, Title VII mandates inclusion of a grievance procedure with binding arbitration as a final step in all federal collective bargaining agreements.

In 1993, President Bill Clinton enacted Executive Order 12871 as part of his reinvention initiative. It was hailed as a significant and fundamental change in federal sector labor-management relations. The goal was to change the relationship and alter the process by which the managers and unions reached decisions. A team of federal managers and union representatives worked on the plan. It created a National Partnership Council (NPC) to advise the president on labor-management issues. The NPC is made up of union leaders, representatives from the Federal Labor Relations Board, the Federal Mediation and Conciliation Service, and executive branch directors. The order directs each agency to establish labor-management partnerships at appropriate levels to change the way government operates.

Carrell, M. R. and C. Heavrin, Labor Relations and Collective Bargaining *(6E), 2001. Upper Saddle River, N.J.: Prentice Hall (pp. 34-37).*

Appendix II:
Labor-Management Collaboration—
A Qualitative Model*

Organizational behavior can be viewed as aggregated individual behavior. Therefore, understanding an individual's motivation can be useful in understanding organizational behavior. Motivation theory historically has centered on the notion of a needs hierarchy. Maslow, for example, argued that individuals satisfy lower-order needs before focusing their attention on higher-order needs. Adlerfer reconfigured this notion of a hierarchy into three clusters: existence, relatedness, and growth, and applied his theory to groups as well as to individuals.

Recent theorists provide a link between motivation and the relationship between collective bargaining and collaboration. For example, Trist defined the extrinsic characteristics of work as a desire for fair wages, job security, and safe working conditions, which are analogous to those needs satisfied through collective bargaining. He further defined the intrinsic characteristics of work as a desire for autonomy and professional discretion, which are analogous to those needs satisfied through collaboration. Cutcher-Gershenfeld observed that traditional collective bargaining addresses the lower-order concerns by routinely dealing with issues of wages, hours, and working conditions. Similarly, Lawler and Herrick cited the higher-order concerns of control, competence, and achievement as those usually satisfied by collaboration.

If traditional collective bargaining, as described by the classic Walton-McKersie framework of distributive bargaining, is a precondition for collaboration, any model that predicts success in collaborative management must incorporate the principle that collaboration will exist as a supplement to, not a replacement for, traditional collective bargaining. Consequently, the success of collaborative management will be dependent upon the effectiveness of the collective bargaining relationship.

The model utilized in this research demonstrates how collaborative management structures are implemented. It is predicated on a preexisting collective bargaining relationship between labor and management, identifies the major components of successful collaboration, and encompasses five critical stages. First, for collaborative management to be effective, the present collective bargaining process must prove inadequate to address the increasing internal and external pressures on both parties. Second, both labor and management must develop shared objectives to address these pressures without infringing on their traditional collective bargaining relationship. Third, successful collaboration must develop in conjunction with, not in opposition to, their collective bargaining process. Fourth, successful collaboration requires a full commitment by both the representatives and their constituents. And, fifth, for collaborative management to be successful over the long term, it must be formalized as a supplement to the collective bargaining process and addressed in the labor-management contract.

These five stages contain 11 variables that are used to measure the success of collaborative management. The stages represent the development of collaborative management and describe the antecedents that must exist when implementing a labor-management partnership. The variables within these stages are those dimensions that shape the process. Table 8.1 summarizes the variables that lie within each stage and provides a brief description of each variable.

Impetus Stage

External and internal pressures force employees and managers to seek resolutions. If both parties can reach reasonable solutions through traditional collective bargaining, they will continue to invest in the process. However, if collective bargaining proves to be inadequate, the parties will seek alternative solutions through other mechanisms. Thus, for collaborative management to be explored within an organization, the present collective bargaining process must prove to be inadequate to address the increasing internal and external pressures on both parties. The impetus stage contains three variables: external pressure, internal pressure, and collective bargaining adequacy.

Initiation Stage

Represented employees and their managers must develop congruent organizational objectives to work together effectively. While there must be agreement regarding joint objectives, a simultaneous differentiation of goals must also exist to satisfy both parties' respective constituencies. Successful collaboration requires the congruence of goals only as far as such agreement relates to relieving those individual pressures identified in the impetus stage. Both labor and management must develop shared goals to address the pressures placed upon them without jeopardizing their continuing collective bargaining process. The initiation stage contains two variables: goal congruence and goal differentiation.

Implementation Stage

During the developmental stages of collaborative management, union representation provides credibility to organizational change by encouraging

Table 8.1: Stages and Variables for a Model of Labor-Management Collaboration

Stage	Variable	Description
Impetus	External pressure	External pressure includes demands for change from the business and civic communities, regulatory offices, the courts, or other interest groups.
	Internal pressure	Internal pressure is defined as intraorganizational demands from labor union constituents or management officials desiring change.
	Collective bargaining adequacy	The existing means of joint decision making must be found inadequate before labor and management will explore alternative problem-solving methods.
Initiation	Goal congruence	The need for shared goals to address initial pressures requires a clarification of the shared goals and mutual agreements to achieve them.
	Goal differentiation	Both respective parties must have enough goal differentiation to maintain their credibility and cooperate with each other while dutifully representing their constituencies.
Implementation	Need for representation	Unions serve as a unifying mechanism that provide credibility to the collaborative management process by encouraging labor's participation while continuing to offer the benefits of union membership.
	Parallelism	Parallelism describes the degree to which the collaboration process operates simultaneously with collective bargaining.
	Training	Training is the amount of educational programs and skills development for labor representatives and management.

continued on next page

Table 8.1: Stages and Variables for a Model of Labor-Management Collaboration (continued)

Stage	Variable	Description
Integration	Commitment	Mutual commitment to change is required from both labor and management to achieve collaboration while maintaining their established collective bargaining relationship.
	Diffusion	Diffusion is the capacity of labor and management to spread its commitment to collaboration throughout their constituencies.
Institutionalization	Collective bargaining linkage	The collective bargaining linkage refers to the direct tie between collaborative management and the collective bargaining agreement.

employee participation while continuing to offer the protection of union membership. This protection allows the collaborative management process to develop in conjunction with, not in opposition to, the current collective bargaining process. As the collaborative management process continues to develop, training programs for both employees and their managers become necessary to sustain the change. The implementation stage contains three variables: need for representation, parallelism of collaboration to collective bargaining, and need for training.

Integration Stage

Once the leadership of both labor and management have agreed to implement collaborative management strategies, there must be a commitment to, and a diffusion of, collaboration throughout both organizations. Without the support of both labor and management, participative decision making is likely to fail. To increase the level of commitment, labor and management must foster support for the collaborative management programs within their respective memberships. Sustaining high levels of both commitment and diffusion is critical for full implementation to occur. This stage contains two independent variables: commitment and diffusion.

Institutionalization Stage

Institutionalization is the process of formally negotiating collaborative management into the union contract as an integral component of the traditional collective bargaining relationship. The Dunlop Commission found that the way in which labor leaders view future power relationships determines their willingness to participate in collaborative decision making. Therefore, formalization of collaborative management is required to provide a concrete statement of both labor and management's long-term commitment to collaboration. While collaboration remains a separate and parallel process to collective bargaining, it nevertheless should be formalized and included in the labor-management contract. In this stage, the variable is the collective bargaining linkage.

* This section is adapted from "Successful Collaborative Management and Collective Bargaining in the Public Sector: An Empirical Analysis," that appeared in Vol. 22, No. 4 (1999), of *Public Productivity and Management Review*, pp. 517-536.

Appendix III:
The Indianapolis Partnership—
A Quantitative Analysis**

Together, the case study and our model of collaboration provide a qualitative approach to understand the City of Indianapolis' labor-management partnership. In addition, a quantitative analysis, utilizing survey research and a multivariate regression, was used to validate and extend these qualitative results. Through the use of data collected from a survey completed by both labor and management in the Department of Public Works, the model of collaboration was applied to determine those underlying factors that contributed to the success of the partnership. The following provides a detailed description of the results of this analysis and its statistical support of the model of labor-management collaboration.

The 11 independent variables, sorted among the five developmental stages, provide a quantitative method to analyze the success of the Indianapolis labor-management partnership. To gather data for this largely attitudinal analysis, focus groups and interviews were conducted to refine the survey questionnaire. The resulting five-page questionnaire was distributed to all 445 DPW employees, including both labor and management. Of these 445 workers, 330 were in the bargaining unit and were represented by AFSCME. The others were managers, supervisors, or clerical staff. The questionnaire had a 53 percent response rate, with 237 surveys returned. By eliminating the incomplete or perfunctorily completed surveys, and surveys from individuals with less than a high school education, 110 questionnaires were available for the final data set.

This final data set was analyzed using multiple linear regression. Regression analysis indicates whether or not each independent variable is statistically related to the dependent variable, and provides information on the nature and extent of these relationships. A statistical significance level of 0.05 was established as the minimum to retain independent variables in the regression equation.

The qualitative analysis addressed the historical perspective of the partnership and supported all five stages and the 11 variables of the model. However, the data collection occurred recently, and therefore, the quantitative analysis did not reflect the significance of the impetus stage (external pressure, internal pressure, and bargaining adequacy). In addition, since training on Activity Based Costing took place early in the partnership's development, the training variable also did not prove significant. And, because of the partnership's maturity at the time data were collected, commitment and diffusion were so organizationally entrenched that these variables emerged

as a single, combined variable. This combined variable was a stronger statistical indicator than the two variables separately, and also was consistent
with the evolutionary stage of the Indianapolis partnership during which the
survey was administered. Thus, the final quantitative model incorporated six
independent variables representing the four stages from initiation through
institutionalization.

An F-statistic and an adjusted R-Squared value are generally utilized
with regression analysis to establish the statistical validity of the entire equation, as well as the strength of the relationship between the dependent and
independent variables. The F-statistic and its p-value give the overall statistical significance of all of the independent variables acting simultaneously on
the success of the partnership. The adjusted R-Square value indicates how
much of the total change in the dependent variable can be explained by or
associated with the independent variables as causal factors.

Table 8.2 presents the detailed regression analysis results. For this
regression equation, an F-statistic of 127.9 and an adjusted R-Squared of
0.872 were obtained. This unusually high F-statistic unequivocally indicates
a very strong statistical relationship between the success of the partnership
and the independent variables. The p-value of .0001 indicates the probability that this relationship is a chance result is less than 1 in 10,000. The
adjusted R-Square value indicates that 87.2 percent of the success of the
partnership is attributed to these independent variables.

The regression results are summarized below by presenting the regression equation using standardized coefficients or multipliers for each of the
independent variables. They show the relative importance of each of the
independent variables, while holding the effects of the other independent
variables constant. The higher the standardized parameter estimate, the
greater will be the relative impact of the respective independent variable
on the partnership. The single asterisks in this equation indicate those variables that have the highest degree of statistical confidence, whereas the
double asterisk shows a slightly lower but still very strong degree of statistical confidence.

The final regression equation resulting from the quantitative analysis was:

Success of the Partnership =
   0.06 + 0.24 *Goal Congruence*[+]
   - 0.13 *Goal Differentiation*[+] + 0.20 *Need for Representation*[+]
   + 0.12 *Parallelism*[++] + 0.26 *Commitment/Diffusion*[+]
   + 0.25 *Collective Bargaining Linkage*[+]

With respect to the detailed presentation of the final regression model
in Table 8.2, high t-statistics (generally in excess of 2.0) and low p-values
(generally lower than 0.05) indicate high statistical significance and the
presence of a relationship that is unlikely to occur by chance. All six variables proved to be statistically significant at the 0.05 level, with five of the

Table 8.2: Multiple Regression Analysis of Conceptual Variables Estimating Success of the Indianapolis Labor-Management Partnership

Independent Variables	Parameter Estimate	Standardized Estimate	t-statistic	Prob > | t |
Goal Congruence[†]	0.6887	0.2357	2.923	0.0042
Goal Differentiation[†]	-1.0433	-0.1287	-3.619	0.0005
Need for Representation[†]	1.1175	0.2013	3.390	0.0010
Parallelism[††]	0.9217	0.1245	2.423	0.0171
Commitment/Diffusion[†]	0.4406	0.2619	3.424	0.0009
Collective Bargaining Linkage[†]	1.1864	0.2497	4.624	0.0001
Intercept	0.0570	0.0000	0.019	0.9850

F-Value	127.936
Probability > F	0.0001
R ß Square	0.8787
Adjusted R-Square	0.8718

[†]   Denotes statistical significance at the 0.01 level or better.
[††] Denotes statistical significance at the 0.05 level or better.

six significant at the 0.01 level or better. These are excellent statistical results that verify both strong relationships between the independent variables and the success of the partnership, as well as the validity of the conceptual model of collaborative management.

In summary, the regression results indicate that five of the six independent variables are highly significant and have the expected sign. These variables are *goal congruence*, which represents the initiation stage of the model; *parallelism* and the *need for representation*, which together represent the implementation stage; *commitment/diffusion*, which represents the Integration Stage; and *collective bargaining linkage*, which represents the institutionalization stage. The negative sign on *goal differentiation* is not surprising given that seven years had elapsed between the formation of the partnership and the administration of the survey.

These results are consistent with the conceptual model of collaboration, provide statistical confirmation of the partnership's success, and identify the antecedents of that success. These antecedents are *commitment/ diffusion, collective bargaining linkage, goal congruence,* the *need for representation, parallelism,* and *goal differentiation.* All of these variables are identified within the regression equation as highly significant, and each has a major impact on the partnership. This analysis, coupled with the case study, provides critical insight into how successful labor-management collaboration evolves in the public sector.

** This section is adapted "A Heuristic Model of Collaboration Within Labor-Management Relations: Part II, The Indianapolis Experience," that appeared in Vol. 29, No. 2 (2000), of *Journal of Collective Negotiations in the Public Sector,* pp. 139-151.

Endnotes

1. We gratefully acknowledge the contributions of Michael Armstrong, Sandy Bate, Monica Boyd, and Aaron Sampson. We are especially grateful for the significant contribution of Courtney Sullivan. We also thank The PricewaterhouseCoopers Endowment for The Business of Government for its support of this study. And, we are deeply indebted to all the management of the City of Indianapolis (especially Mayor Stephen Goldsmith and Chuck Snyder) and all its employees represented by the American Federation of State, County and Municipal Employees (especially Steve Quick and Jerry Richmond).

2. Bureau of Labor Statistics. *Union Affiliation of Employed Wage and Salary Workers by Occupation and Industry*. Jan. 19, 2001. (http://stats.bls.gov/news.release/union2.t03.htm)

3. The conceptual model and quantitative analysis are described in the two appendices.

Bibliography

Adlerfer, C. P. "An Empirical Test of a New Theory of Human Needs." *Organizational Behavior and Human Performance*, 4 (1969): 142-175.

Allen, R. E. and K. L. Van Norman. "Employee Involvement Programs: The Noninvolvement of Unions Revisited." *Journal of Labor Research*, 17(3) (1996): 479-495.

Bennett, J. T. and J. T. Delaney. "Research Unions: Some Subjects in Need of Scholars." *Journal of Labor Research*, 14(2) (1993): 95-110.

Bullock, R. J., B. A. Macy, and P. H. Mirvis. "Assessing Unions and Union-Management Collaboration in Organizational Change." In S. E. Seashore, E. E. Lawler, P. H. Mirvis, and C. Camman (Eds.), *Assessing Organizational Change*. 1983. New York: John Wiley.

Collins, D., L. Hatcher, and T. L. Ross. "The Decision to Implement Gainsharing: The Role of Climate, Expected Outcomes, and Union Status." *Personnel Psychology*, 46 (1993): 77-104.

Cooke, W. N. (a). "Factors Influencing the Effect of Joint Union-Management Programs on Employee-Supervisor Relations." *Industrial and Labor Relations Review*, 43 (1990): 587-603.

Cooke, W. N. (b). *Labor-Management Cooperation*. 1990. Kalamazoo, Mich.: Upjohn.

Cooke, W. N. "Employee Participation Programs, Group-Based Activities and Company Performance: A Union-Nonunion Comparison." *Industrial and Labor Relations Review*, 47 (1994): 594-609.

Cooke, W. N. and D. G. Meyer. "Structural and Market Predictors of Corporate Labor Relations Strategies." *Industrial and Labor Relations Review*, 43 (1990): 280-293.

Cutcher-Gershenfeld, J. "Bargaining Over Fundamental Changes in Industrial Relations." *Arbitration Quarterly of the Northwest*, 11(1) (1990): 11-18.

Delaney, J. T. "Workplace Cooperation: Current Problems, New Approaches." *Journal of Labor Research*, 17(1) (1996): 45-61.

Dunlop Commission. *Fact-Finding Report of the Commission of the Future of Worker-Management Relations*. 1994. Washington, D.C.: U.S. Department of Labor, U.S. Department of Commerce.

Herrick, N. *Joint Management and Employee Participation*. 1990. San Francisco: Jossey-Bass.

Kearney, R. C. "Managing Relations with Organized Employees." In J. L. Perry (Ed.), *Handbook of Public Administration*. 1996. San Francisco: Jossey-Bass.

Kearney, R. C., and S. W. Hays. "Labor-Management Relations and Participative Decision Making: Toward a New Paradigm." *Public Administration Review*, 54(1) (1994): 44-51.

Kimberley, J. R. "Appraising Organizational Design Theories." In A. Van DeVen and W. F. Joyce (Eds.), *Perspectives on Organizational Design and Behavior*. 1981. New York: John Wiley.

Kochan, T. A. and L. Dyer. "A Model of Organizational Change in the Context of Union-Management Relations." *Journal of Applied Behavioral Science*, 12(1) (1976): 59-78.

Kohler, T. C. "The Overlooked Middle." In M. W. Franklin (Ed.), *The Legal Future of Employee Representation*. 1994. Ithaca, N.Y.: H. R. Press.

Lawler, E. E. "Foundations of Work Motivation." In B. M. Staw (Ed.), *Psychological Foundations of Organizational Behavior*. 1983. Glenview, Ill.: Scott, Foresman.

Lawler, E. E. and J. A. Drexler, "The Dynamics of Establishing Cooperative Quality-of-Worklife Projects." *Monthly Labor Review*, 10(3) (1978): 23-28.

Levine, D. I. *Re-inventing the Workplace: How Business and Employees Can Both Win*. 1995. Washington, D.C.: Brookings Institute.

Lewin, D. "The Future of Employee Involvement/ Participation in the United States." *Proceedings of the 1984 Spring Meeting of the Industrial Relations Research Association*. 1989. Anaheim, Calf.: Industrial Relations Research Association.

Maslow, A. H. "A Theory of Human Motivation." *Psychological Review*, 50(3) (1943): 370-396.

McLaughlin, M. W. "The RAND Change Agent Study Revisited: Macro Perspectives and Micro Realities." *Educational Researcher*, 19(9) (1990): 11-16.

Mitchell, D. E., F. I. Ortiz, and T. K. Mitchell. *Work Orientation and Job Performance: The Cultural Basis of Teaching Rewards and Incentives*. 1987. Albany: State University of New York Press.

Osterman, P. "How Common Is Workplace Transition and How Can We Explain Who Adopts It: Results from a National Survey." *Industrial and Labor Relations Review*, 47 (1994): 173-188.

Peterson, K. D. and R. Brietske. *Building Collaborative Cultures: Seeking Ways to Reshape Urban Schools*, (North Central Regional Educational Laboratory Urban Monograph Series). 1994. Oak Brook, Ill.: North Central Regional Educational Laboratory.

Steimel, E. L. *Shared Decision-Making with Collective Bargaining*, (Document No. ED381882). 1995. Springfield, Va.: ERIC Document Reproduction Service.

Trist, E. L. "The Sociotechnical Systems as a Conceptual Framework and as an Action Research Program." In A. Van DeVen and W. F. Joyce (Eds.), *Perspectives on Organization Design and Behavior*. 1981. New York: John Wiley.

CHAPTER NINE

A Changing Workforce:
Understanding Diversity Programs
in the Federal Government

Katherine C. Naff
Assistant Professor of Public Administration
Department of Public Administration
San Francisco State University

J. Edward Kellough
Associate Professor of Public and International Affairs
Department of Political Science
University of Georgia

This report was originally published in December 2001.

Introduction

Two reports written by the Hudson Institute in the late 1980s forecasted major demographic changes in the American workforce over the next decade. The reports' predictions spawned the development of an industry of consultants who set about advising employers in how to adapt their management practices to a workforce that was becoming increasingly diverse in terms of race, ethnicity, gender, and other characteristics. The fear was that established practices, traditionally favoring the advancement of white men, would undermine the recruitment, retention, and advancement of women, minorities, and others "outside the mainstream."

A significant body of literature now describes and assesses the practices that are encapsulated under the rubric of what has come to be called "valuing" or "managing" this increasingly diverse workforce. The bulk of that literature, however, is focused on the private sector, even though the need to ascertain such activity in the federal sector is arguably greater, given the important role the federal government plays as the nation's largest employer and as a chief formulator and enforcer of equal employment opportunity policy.

The purpose of this chapter is to address that void in the literature by describing federal government agencies' diversity policies and programs. We begin by providing some background as to the genesis and meaning of the managing diversity enterprise. We then draw on a 1999 survey to describe the activities that federal agencies have utilized to more effectively manage their diverse workforces. We find that agencies span the gamut from doing very little in this regard to pursuing a wide variety of measures. Our discussion then turns to an in-depth description of the state of diversity programs in seven federal agencies, selected in part, on the basis of their distinct approaches to managing diversity. We discuss the need for and demonstrate a means by which the success of diversity programs in federal agencies can be evaluated. This last component of the chapter is particularly important given the financial and political capital that agencies are investing in these efforts.

The Diversity Management Movement

The Hudson Institute reports are often cited as important catalysts to the managing diversity movement. The first, entitled *Workforce 2000*, was released in 1987 and addressed transformations in the civilian labor force (Johnston and Packer 1987). This report drew significant criticism because it appeared to overstate the extent to which white men would shrink as a portion of the labor force (Mishel and Teixera 1991, U.S. General Accounting Office 1992, U.S. Merit Systems Protection Board 1993). Nevertheless, as can be seen in Figure 9.1, the workforce is becoming more diverse. The second Hudson Institute report, *Civil Service 2000*, completed a year later, focused specifically on federal employment and reached similar conclusions (Johnson et al. 1988).

Figure 9.1: Female and Minority Share of the Civilian Labor Force, 1980–1998 and Projected to 2025

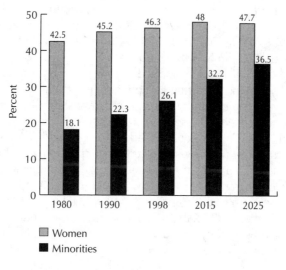

Source: *Fullerton 1999, 10.*

These reports generated significant attention, in part, because they presented a number of observations in a rather ominous fashion. Of particular interest were the Institute's predictions that workplaces oriented toward men working and women staying at home would not accommodate the growing proportion of employed women, and that "[minorities] may have language, attitude, and cultural problems that prevent them from taking advantage of the jobs that will exist" (Johnston and Packer 1987, xxvi). These predictions induced a flurry of consulting activity and the emergence of a variety of books, videos, and other materials designed to sensitize employers to the different perspectives and needs of a more diverse workforce.

This was not the only catalyst boosting the managing diversity movement, however. At the same time, the political and legal climate was growing increasingly intolerant of affirmative action, a vehicle that had been used for providing access to employment and promotions for women and minorities for two decades. The Reagan administration made opposition to affirmative action a core component of its electoral strategy. Following the election, the administration reduced the budgets of agencies with key enforcement responsibilities and filed lawsuits to challenge affirmative action agreements in local governments (Edsall and Edsall 1991). It has been argued that while the subsequent George H. W. Bush administration had promised a "kinder, gentler" approach, Bush was even more conservative on racial issues than his predecessor (Shull 1993).

The courts were also taking a conservative stand toward affirmative action in the late 1980s. In *Richmond v. J.A. Croson Company* (488 U.S. 489, 1989) the Supreme Court invalidated a minority set-aside program in the city of Richmond, Virginia. Justice O'Connor, writing for the Court, said that in the future the Court would apply a standard of "strict scrutiny" to such programs. The Court had historically applied a more lenient standard to federal race-conscious programs, deferring to Congress' judgment as to when such measures serve governmental objectives, but that position was undermined by Croson and completely reversed in a 1995 decision. In *Adarand v. Peña* (115 S. Ct. 2097) the Court ruled that federal programs, like those of state and local governments, must be subjected to strict scrutiny. Following that decision, the Justice Department mandated that all federal agencies review their policies and programs to ensure they would meet this stricter test.

Affirmative action has always been a controversial topic. In a 1996 poll by the Roper Center, for example, respondents were equally divided between those who said they support affirmative action programs that give preference to women, blacks, and other minorities (47 percent) and those that oppose those programs (49 percent). With a legal and political climate that was also making it more difficult to defend those programs, it is perhaps not surprising that organizations concerned about ensuring that minorities and women had equal access to jobs and promotions would look for other means to make that possible. That is what the managing diversity literature has promised to do.

Themes in the Emerging Literature

The first use of the phrase "managing diversity" is often attributed to former Harvard Business School Professor R. Roosevelt Thomas. His 1990 article in the *Harvard Business Review* began with the prediction: "Sooner or later, affirmative action will die a natural death. Its achievements have been stupendous, but if we look at the premises that underlie it, we find assumptions and priorities that look increasingly shopworn" (Thomas 1990, 107). Instead, Thomas argued, "The goal is to manage diversity in such a

The Legal Framework

The Civil Rights Act of 1964: Title VII is the major federal statute that prohibits discrimination in employment. Under the law, employers may not fail or refuse to hire, or discharge any individual, or otherwise discriminate against any individual with respect to compensation, terms, conditions, or privileges of employment on the basis of race, color, gender, religion, or national origin. In 1972, the law was extended to cover federal and other public sector employees.

Age Discrimination in Employment Act of 1967: Employers are prohibited from discriminating based on age.

The Rehabilitation Act of 1973: Federal employers are prohibited from discriminating on the basis of disability.

way as to get from a diverse workforce the same productivity we once got from a homogenous workforce, and do it without artificial programs, standards—or barriers" (Thomas 1990,112). Moreover, Thomas contended, diversity is not just about race, ethnicity, and gender. Rather, it includes other ways in which people differ from one another, including age, background, education, work role, and personality. Table 9.1, taken from the National Institutes of Health (NIH) Workplace Diversity Initiative home page illustrates the distinction that is often made between equal employment opportunity/affirmative action (EEO/AA) and managing diversity.

Thomas's notion that "diversity" is defined not just in terms of characteristics such as gender, race, and ethnicity, but rather encompasses all the ways people differ from one another is echoed in the expanding literature on diversity management (Thomas 1990, 1991; Norton and Fox 1997; Fernandez 1999; Slack 1997; Wilson 1997). The hope is that those who oppose affirmative action based on a belief that it benefits women and minorities at the expense of nonminority men will embrace diversity management efforts because they do not focus attention on simply race/ethnicity and gender. Note that under "Managing Diversity" in Table 9.1, the NIH emphasizes its focus on "all elements of diversity." NASA's Equal Opportunity and Diversity Management Plan provides another example of this viewpoint. It defines cultural diversity as "simply that NASA employees are diverse because they bring a variety of different backgrounds, customs, beliefs, religions, languages, knowledge, superstitions, values, social characteristics, etc., with them to the workplace.... [In addition to racial and ethnic cultural groups] there are also class cultures, age cultures, gender

Table 9.1: National Institutes of Health Definitions of EEO/Affirmative Action and Managing Diversity

EEO/Affirmative Action	Managing Diversity
Mandatory	Voluntary
Legal, social, moral justification	Productivity, efficiency, and quality
Focuses on race, gender, ethnicity	Focuses on all elements of diversity
Changes the mix of people	Changes the systems/operations
Perception of preference	Perception of equality
Short-term and limited	Long-term and ongoing
Grounded in assimilation	Grounded in individuality

Source: National Institutes of Health Diversity home page at
http://oeo.od.nih.gov/diversity/managing_diversity.asp

cultures, and regional cultures to name a few" (NASA 1994, 3). By defining diversity so broadly, organizations such as NASA hope that all employees will support the program, rather than feel excluded from or offended by it.

Not all of the contributors to this literature embrace this expanded focus, however. Morrison (1992, 9) warns, for example, "The most frightening aspect of moving too hurriedly from affirmative action for targeted groups to promoting the diversity in everyone is that this becomes an excuse for avoiding the continuing problems in achieving equity for people of color and white women" (see also Caudron and Hayes 1997).

More recently, Thomas has stepped out in the forefront again by suggesting that even "managing diversity" is no longer relevant. He argues that despite their best efforts, American businesses are "little better equipped today to deal with the fragile threats of a multicultural workforce than they were in earlier days of overt racism. We have changed our vocabulary but not our behavior," says Thomas (1996, xii). His solution is to develop an even broader definition of diversity: "any mixture of items characterized by differences and similarities" (Thomas 1996, 5).

In addition, in case the notion that organizations should accept that all employees are different from one another in some ways is not enough, this literature also goes to great lengths to state the "business case" for managing diversity. Note that the NIH chart (see Table 9.1) distinguishes the reasons for managing diversity from those in which EEO/AA were grounded. EEO/AA were justified on legal, social, and moral grounds. Managing diversity is justified based on grounds such as increasing productivity, efficiency, and quality.

In short, the focus of policies intended to create more equitable employment environments has shifted in many organizations in two fundamental ways since the late 1980s. First, an emphasis on legally mandated EEO and affirmative action programs has frequently been replaced or supplemented by voluntary efforts to "manage diversity" to promote equity. Second, the diversity management movement has defined itself as a strategy that includes everyone. The question now before us is to what extent have federal agencies actually embraced the diversity management movement. In order to address that question, we must first develop a fuller understanding of the specific strategies recommended by the managing diversity literature.

What Does It Mean to Manage Diversity?

The extensive literature on managing diversity takes a variety of forms, including empirical descriptions of organizations that are considered to be models in workforce diversity, summaries of "lessons learned" about managing diversity based on case studies or surveys of human resource professionals, and strategies for managing diversity advocated by consultants in the field. We draw from this literature in order to identify the explicit and implicit recommendations for steps organizations should take to create better climates for diversity. Those recommendations most commonly found in the literature include the broad suggestions displayed in Table 9.2.

It should be readily apparent that while those prescriptions share some of the tenets of traditional EEO and affirmative action programs, they also move beyond such efforts. Traditional EEO programs are primarily oriented toward protecting employees from legally proscribed discrimination and affording them the opportunity for redress should an action meeting the legal definition of discrimination take place. Traditional affirmative action programs are designed to increase the representation of underrepresented groups in various occupations and grade levels.

Managing diversity programs transcend those parameters by attempting to ferret out practices that work to the disadvantage of underrepresented groups whether those practices meet legally actionable definitions of discrimination or not. Examples of such practices might include "attitudinal and organizational barriers" such as the incommensurate access to developmental practices and credential-building experiences and narrow recruitment practices the Department of Labor (1991) identified in its report on the glass ceiling. As noted above, the diversity management literature calls for the organization to proactively examine selection, promotion, performance appraisal criteria, and career development programs for potential bias and, where necessary, to revamp them. Another example is that unlike traditional EEO programs that address discriminatory behaviors, proponents of diversity

Table 9.2: Common Recommendations for Diversity Programs

Ensure management accountability	Management officials' performance ratings and compensation should depend in part on their success in achieving diversity-related goals (Morrison 1992, Cox 1994, Fernandez 1999, Wilson 1997, CAPS 1996, Dobbs 1996).
Reexamine the organization's structure, culture, and management systems	Selection, promotion, performance appraisal criteria, and career development programs should be examined for potential bias, and where necessary, be revamped (Norton and Fox 1997, Thomas 1996, Mathews 1998, Wilson 1997, Morrison 1992, Cox 1994, Fernandez 1999, Dugan et al. 1993, CAPS 1996, Fine 1995).
Pay attention to numbers	The representation of groups in various levels and occupations in the organization should be closely monitored (Morrison 1992, Norton and Fox 1997, Cox 1994, CAPS 1996, Thomas 1996). Wilson (1997) and Morrison (1992) also emphasize the importance of monitoring employees' perceptions of the organizational environment.
Provide training	Organizations should ensure that employees are taught about the importance of diversity goals and the skills required to work effectively in a diverse workforce (Cox 1994, Thomas 1996, Fernandez 1999, Chambers and Riccucci 1997, Wilson 1997, Hudson and Hines-Hudson 1996, CAPS 1996, Mathews 1998, Gardenswartz and Rowe 1993).
Develop mentoring programs	Mentors should be made available to employees as they can serve an important role in communicating organizational expectations to employees who are interested in advancement (Morrison 1992, Fernandez 1999, Cox 1994, Thomas and Gabarro 1999, Wilson 1997, CAPS 1996, Dugan et al 1993, Fine 1995).
Promote internal identity or advocacy groups	Organizations should encourage the development of formally or informally constituted groups representing specific categories of nontraditional employees such as women, African Americans, or gays and lesbians. Such representation can help mitigate the potential isolation of members of these groups and may provide leadership in resolving conflicts (Morrison 1992, Cox 1994, Thomas and Gabarro 1999, Dobbs 1996, Digh 1997; see Norton and Fox 1997 for disagreement with this approach). A variant of this approach is to establish "advisory" groups that include representatives from many distinct groups in the workforce (Wilson 1997, CAPS 1996, Fine 1995).

Continued on next page

Table 9.2: Common Recommendations for Diversity Programs *(continued)*

Emphasize shared values among employees, customers, and stakeholders	Organizations should recognize that, in many cases, their culture and structure reflect the orientation of Euro-American men, and they should work proactively to create a more inclusive climate, linking diversity to their business strategy (Fernandez 1999, Thomas and Gabarro 1999, Wilson 1997, CAPS 1996, Norton and Fox 1997).

management programs also stress the importance of employee perceptions of organizational fairness. Finally, many managing diversity programs address demographic characteristics not addressed by traditional EEO/AA programs, such as language, geographic origin, and/or work style.

Diversity Management in the Federal Government

Civil Service 2000, the Hudson Institute report projecting the future for federal employment, suggested that the federal government also needed to take steps to be able to compete for its "fair share of the best qualified members of [the] changing workforce" (Johnson et al. 1988, 32). However, federal agencies were apparently slower to jump on the diversity bandwagon than their private sector counterparts. The U.S. Merit Systems Protection Board (MSPB) summarized its findings in a 1993 report on federal agencies by saying that overall, they "did not report any significant resource commitment or personnel program changes intended solely to address the changing demographic projections" (MSPB 1993, x). That most federal agencies did not heed the call to manage diversity until the mid-1990s may have been a function of not feeling the pressure to do so until the *Adarand* decision raised the standard under which federal affirmative action programs would be permitted. Moreover, by that time diversity management was widely acknowledged as a subfield of human resources management, and dozens of consultants were marketing their services (Kelly and Dobbin 2001).

A Survey of Federal Agencies

By 1999, however, agencies had become much more active with respect to diversity programs. That year, the Diversity Task Force established by Vice President Gore's National Partnership for Reinventing Government (NPR) administered a survey to 160 federal agencies and departments. The survey asked federal organizations about the components of, and resources devoted to, any diversity initiatives they might have. Responses, in the form of usable returned questionnaires, were obtained from 137 or 86 percent of the organizations surveyed. These included components from the 23 largest departments and agencies, as well as the U.S. Postal Service and many of the smaller agencies. Collectively, these organizations employ more than 80 percent of the federal government's civilian workforce. The collection of data at the subagency level is particularly fortunate. Many examinations of differences among federal agencies on various dimensions previously have had to rely on information aggregated at the full agency or department level, necessarily overlooking the dissimilarities among subagencies within larger departments. As it turns out, there is quite a bit of variation in federal agency approaches to meeting the needs of a changing workforce.

The NPR survey began by asking the EEO directors and other officials completing the survey whether their agencies had undertaken a diversity initiative. More than 88 percent, or 120, of the 137 agencies answered "yes," indicating, as expected, that an overwhelming proportion of federal organizations had such efforts—at least in some form. Perhaps it is more interesting to note, however, that after years of attention given to the issue of diversity, 16 organizations, or nearly 12 percent of the total, reported that they had not undertaken a diversity initiative. (One agency didn't respond to the question.) Four of those 16 indicated that they were planning to develop a program within the year.

The NPR survey asked those agencies with diversity initiatives whether their diversity programs differed from their internal EEO/AA programs "in that [they addressed] workplace diversity issues previously not addressed in the organization's EEO/AEP (affirmative employment programs)." The purpose of this question was to determine the extent to which agencies may have simply relabeled or renamed their EEO/AA programs in an effort to embrace the diversity movement. Interestingly, one-fourth (26 percent) indicated that those programs *did* primarily consist of their former EEO/AA efforts. Apparently those agencies were continuing efforts that had been in place for some time under the rubric of EEO/AA, but at the time of the survey those activities were simply referred to as "diversity initiatives." The remaining 70 percent[1] of the organizations with diversity programs, however, indicated that their diversity initiatives were broader in scope than their EEO/AA programs, in that they addressed workplace issues that had not received significant attention earlier. Previously unaddressed issues could include a focus on nontraditional demographic attributes such as organizational role or geographic origin, or the development of advocacy groups such as a diversity council.

The bulk of the survey asked federal agencies specific questions about the content, organization, and structure of their diversity programs (assuming they had one in place). Table 9.3 displays the proportion of organizations reporting that various characteristics were in place.

A number of interesting observations can be made regarding the presence of these various programmatic elements. For example, the program characteristics that are most frequently included in federal agency efforts are those that address "traditional" dimensions of diversity. More than 90 percent of agencies report that their programs specifically address race/color, ethnicity/national origin and/or gender. Eighty-six percent also address disability status and 73 percent address religion. Discrimination based on these characteristics is explicitly prohibited by statute, and so they have been the focus of EEO efforts for many years.

What is obviously most remarkable here is not that large majorities of agencies' diversity initiatives address these dimensions of diversity, but rather that some agencies apparently *do not* speak to these issues. It is surprising that even 5 percent failed to include racial differences, and nearly 10 percent failed to include ethnicity/national origins on their list of demographic attributes addressed by their diversity programs. One is left to wonder how effective diversity programs could possibly be implemented under such circumstances. More than one-quarter (28 percent) of the responding organizations report that they do not address religious differences, and almost 15 percent apparently fail to address disability status. Alternatively, a very large proportion (82 percent) address one or more nontraditional demographic characteristics; that is, attributes that are not the subject of protective legislation such as language, work style, or experience. Clearly, there are substantial and important differences among these organizations in the nature of their diversity initiatives.

As noted previously, a popular component of many diversity programs is the provision of training (Cox 1994, Thomas 1996, Fernandez 1999, Chambers and Riccucci 1997, Wilson 1997, Hudson and Hines-Hudson 1996, CAPS 1996, Mathews 1998, Gardenswartz and Rowe 1993). When the U.S. Merit Systems Protection Board surveyed federal agencies in 1991/1992 about their diversity programs, 20 of the 33 agencies that responded reported they provide diversity-related training. Many agencies said they *required* it of all of their employees or at least all of those enrolled in supervisory development programs (U.S. MSPB 1993). A substantial proportion (85 percent) of the responding organizations examined in the present study also indicated that they include "diversity training" for employees as a component of their diversity initiatives. But as before, what is more remarkable is that as many as 15 percent of the organizations which claim to have diversity programs in place apparently have chosen not to provide diversity training for their employees as part of their efforts.

Table 9.3: Responses to Specific Items on the Diversity Survey (NPR Survey, 1999)

Item	Proportion of Agencies with Characteristic (percent)
Diversity initiative specifically addresses race	95.0
Diversity initiative specifically addresses ethnicity/ national origin	90.8
Diversity initiative specifically addresses gender	89.2
Diversity initiative specifically addresses disability status	85.8
Diversity training is provided for employees	85.0
Diversity initiative specifically addresses one or more nontraditional demographic characteristics*	81.7
Diversity initiative specifically addresses age	80.0
Other employees, such as a diversity council or diversity trainers, perform significant duties related to the diversity initiative in addition to any single individual with day-to-day operational responsibility	79.2
Diversity training is designed to accomplish specific objectives	78.3
The agency evaluates the effectiveness of diversity training provided to employees	74.2
Training objectives are communicated to employees	73.3
Diversity initiative specifically addresses religion	72.5
Diversity initiative is linked to the organization's strategic plan or performance plan	72.5
Diversity initiative specifically addresses sexual orientation	68.3
Diversity is an element in performance plans of supervisors and managers	67.5
Diversity is an element in performance plans for members of the Senior Executive Service	66.7
Diversity awareness material is available	60.0

* Nontraditional demographic characteristics included such attributes as communication style, economic status, family status, first language, geographic origin, military experience, organizational role, work experience, and work style.

Continued on next page

Table 9.3: Responses to Specific Items on the Diversity Survey (NPR Survey, 1999 *(continued)*

Item	Proportion of Agencies with Characteristic (percent)
Diversity initiative implementation plan exists	56.7
Organization uses measures (such as productivity and performance) to assess the effectiveness of the diversity initiative	55.0
Accomplishment or status report exists	54.2
Head of the organization has key leadership responsibility for diversity	51.7
Diversity policy, directive, or administrative order exists	49.2
Internship program used	48.3
Diversity initiative is incorporated into the organization's vision or mission statement	46.7
The agency has conducted an organizational culture/diversity audit or survey in designing or implementing diversity plan	46.7
Program includes awards and incentives	45.8
Diversity council/group charter in place	44.2
Diversity newsletter or other similar communication in place	43.3
A specific identifiable amount is designated in the organization's budget for the diversity initiative	35.8
Formal mentoring program in place	34.2
Informal mentoring program in place	31.7
Organization requires employees to attend additional diversity training beyond an initial course	31.7
There is a specific person who has overall primary day-to-day operational responsibility for the diversity initiative	26.7
Diversity resource center or reading room is available	25.0
Diversity is an element in performance plans of nonsupervisory employees	11.7

Most of the other program characteristics reported in Table 9.3 are present in the initiatives of relatively fewer organizations. Many of those items are embraced by only about 40 to 50 percent of the federal organizations with diversity programs. For example, only 47 percent of those organizations report that their diversity initiative is incorporated into their organizational vision or mission statement, and only 49 percent have a diversity policy, directive, or administrative order. Thus, there is no clear uniformity in the presence of items thought to be important to diversity initiative success or development.

In fact, some of the items listed in Table 9.3 are found in only a distinct minority of the organizations studied. Fewer than 32 percent require employees to attend diversity training beyond an initial course, and less than 27 percent report that they employ a specific person who has day-to-day operational responsibility for the organization's diversity initiative. The program characteristic found in the smallest number of organizations (nearly 12 percent) is the inclusion of a diversity-related element in the performance plans of nonsupervisory employees.

In summary, by 1999 most federal agencies appear to have heeded the call to develop a program to better manage the increasingly diverse workforce. While many had adopted most of the components that the literature prescribes, there is wide variation in that respect. Some had done little more than rename their traditional EEO efforts while others expanded the demographic characteristics recognized by the program, linked diversity with the organization's strategic plan, and/or issued specific diversity policies or orders.

A Closer Look at Agency Programs

To explore in greater detail what agencies with diversity programs at various stages of development are doing, we examined activities in seven specific agencies. We chose three agencies whose responses to the NPR survey indicated that they had well-developed diversity management programs. These were the National Institutes of Health (NIH), the National Institute of Standards and Technology (NIST), and the Bureau of Land Management (BLM). We also looked at two agencies that had more moderately developed diversity programs. They were the Substance Abuse and Mental Health Services Administration (SAMHSA) and the Mine Safety and Health Administration (MSHA). Finally, we examined two small agencies that reported not having a diversity program at all to see whether, even absent the title "diversity program," they might have similar activities in place. These were the Economic Development Administration (EDA) within the Department of Commerce and the National Agricultural Statistics Service (NASS). In each case we conducted in-person interviews with officials in charge of these efforts at their offices in the Washington D.C., metropolitan area, followed up with telephone interviews, if necessary, and reviewed relevant documents. Table 9.4 provides data on the representation of minorities in these agencies.

Table 9.4: Representation of Minorities in Seven Agencies: GS White Collar Employment (Percentages)

	Asian/Pacific Islander	African American	Native American	Hispanic	White	Total GS Workforce
BLM	2	4	2	6	86	7,764
EDA	3	27	0	4	65	244
MSHA	0	5	0	3	92	2,133
NASS	2	15	1	3	80	1,073
NIST	6	8	0	2	84	2,552
NIH	6	22	0	2	68	10,959
SAMHSA	2	27	1	4	66	505

National Institutes of Health (NIH)

The National Institutes of Health is one of eight agencies of the Public Health Service that, in turn, is part of the U.S. Department of Health and Human Services (HHS). The organization, which is comprised of 27 separate institutes and centers, is one of the world's most prominent medical research operations. Its main location is a 300-acre site with 75 buildings in Bethesda, Maryland, but the NIH also has facilities around the nation and the world. The agency has approximately 14,000 career employees (white collar and blue collar) plus approximately 8,000 individuals holding special appointments for a total workforce of about 22,000.

According to information on the NIH website (www.nih.gov), the mission of the agency is to uncover new knowledge that will lead to better health. The NIH works toward that mission by conducting research; supporting research through grant funding to scientists in universities, medical schools, hospitals, and other research institutions; assisting in the training of research investigators; and promoting the communication of medical information. Stated most simply, the goal of the NIH is to generate knowledge to help "prevent, detect, diagnose, and treat disease and disability, from the rarest genetic disorder to the common cold."

Background

The diversity program at the NIH (called the Workforce Diversity Initiative or WDI) was introduced at a forum in May 1995. Following that forum, a Diversity Congress was convened to facilitate the development of strategies and a structure for implementing the WDI throughout the agency. NIH's efforts in this regard began before those of their parent department, the Department of Health and Human Services, leaving them free to set up a program without direction from the department level.

Several grounds were cited for the development of NIH's interest in undertaking a diversity effort. Naomi Churchill-Earp, director of NIH's Office of Equal Opportunity (OEO) at the time the initiative was undertaken, saw the establishment of the WDI as a means to streamline the various special emphasis programs at the agency.[2] She also recognized the difficulty of dealing with the wide array of separate employee advocacy groups—some of which were engaged in quite vocal protests at the time—that in many cases shared the same concerns. The development of a Diversity Council would serve as a means for better coordinating OEO's work with them. The current acting OEO deputy director, Joan Brogan, suggested that the initiative came about because managing diversity was being promoted in the public and private sectors as a better business model for improving the workplace environment. In fact, a number of other agencies were getting on board already. Another impetus for the development of the diversity effort was the U. S. Department of Justice's guidance on affirmative action in employment, issued in 1996 following the Supreme Court's *Adarand* decision. The HHS Office of General Counsel required the NIH to review their affirmative action plans. There was concern and interest in ensuring that these plans furthered compelling governmental interests and were narrowly tailored, as required by the Court. Some people suggested that even if affirmative action programs became constrained as a result of increasing legal challenges, a diversity effort, with its distinct goals and strategies, could continue. The NIH diversity guide for practitioners notes that "as legal restrictions on affirmative action programs continue to tighten … long-term change strategies [such as the WDI] will become essential."

Nature of the Program

The agency's definition of managing diversity is taken from R. Roosevelt Thomas:

> Managing diversity is the process of creating and maintaining an environment that enables all participants to contribute to their full potential in pursuit of organizational objectives.

To this, the NIH adds:

> Managing diversity is a long-term change strategy enabling the NIH to examine its fundamental values and culture to determine whether all

employees are reaching their full potential and making maximum contributions to the mission of the NIH. Effective management of diversity proactively promotes productivity and respect for the differences and similarities each person brings to the workplace.

The agency's strategic plan for diversity management states: "It is the policy of the National Institutes of Health to manage the diversity of our employees by building an inclusive workforce, fostering an environment that respects the individual, and offering opportunities for all persons to develop to their full potential in support of science."

An important feature of the WDI is its emphasis on the distinction between EEO/affirmative action and managing diversity. The differences are outlined in table form (see Table 9.1 in this chapter) on the WDI website and in its brochure.

As noted in the table, a key distinction is that diversity initiatives are voluntary; that is, laws or executive orders do not drive them. Brogan noted that the agency has made some progress in minority and female representation within its workforce (with the exception of Hispanics, Native Americans, and minority women). Because there is a fair amount of diversity already, the NIH needed to *manage* its diversity at the same time as it continued to enforce EEO program objectives. For example, there are disputes that may arise from cultural differences, occupational status perceptions, or between scientists and nonscientists. An EEO program would not recognize conflict arising from such differences to be unlawful discrimination. The agency's Center for Cooperative Resolution resolves such disputes at the NIH and in this respect is viewed as complementing the WDI. The Complaint Management and Adjudication Branch of the OEO handles illegal discrimination complaint allegations.

In addition, affirmative action is not endorsed as a strategy under the rubric of the NIH managing diversity initiative. Affirmative action certainly complements the overall objectives of a diversity initiative, but affirmative action planning has been in place within the EEO function since 1972. Workplace initiatives such as flexible work schedules or telecommuting are not included in the WDI portfolio either; those are part of the Quality of Work Life program that is housed in the human resource management function at NIH.

Structure and Resources

The WDI and traditional EEO functions are housed together in the Office of Equal Opportunity, and more specifically, within the branch that also has responsibility for EEO programs (including the affirmative recruitment activities). Within this branch, there are three diversity program managers, each of whom works with a set of institutes and centers on their diversity programs. OEO has a staff of 26 full-time employees.

In addition to the three diversity program managers, each institute and center has a person who has been assigned by its director to be a "diversity catalyst." This is not conceived of as a full-time position, although some institute and center directors appoint their EEO directors to the position of catalyst. Directors are asked to allow catalysts at least 20 percent of official duty time for diversity program responsibilities. During their tenure, catalysts are the champions of the diversity initiative within their institute or center, and serve as OEO's partner and point of contact. Catalysts are responsible for disseminating information to the organizations they represent and for initiating the progress evaluation of the initiative. Institutes and centers are also encouraged, but not required, to set up diversity committees or councils.

The other major component of the NIH WDI is the Diversity Council, whose role is to provide the NIH director and staff with advice on OEO policies and programs. Membership on the Council is designed to represent diverse communities within NIH such as scientific, administrative, and blue-collar staff, as well as employees of different ages, races, genders, sexual orientations, physical abilities, and ethnic backgrounds. Council members are appointed by the NIH director after either being nominated by their institute or center, or asked to serve in that capacity. The Council, which consists of 18 voting council members and three ex-officio members (the NIH deputy director, the director of OEO and a former Council member), now reports directly to the NIH director and deputy director.

Training and Awareness

Special observance events (e.g., commemorating Black History Month) take place, but are not the responsibility of the diversity program managers—volunteers from the various institutes organize them with guidance provided by OEO staff. These events are explicitly not to be considered substitutes for diversity training.

OEO has occasionally offered NIH-wide training featuring a recognized expert such as R. Roosevelt Thomas, Samuel Betances, or Trevor Wilson. For example, in April of 2001, OEO sponsored a diversity forum called "Diversity in the New Millennium." Beyond that, whether diversity training is mandated or even offered is left up to the institute and center directors. OEO also has developed online diversity modules, which they will make available to interns and other short-term employees. The catalysts and Council members all receive diversity training.

OEO facilitates the provision of training by making available reading materials and audiovisuals, as well as a list of contractors that provide training. Diversity program managers also provide advice about the content of the training. The list of topics they recommend include managing change in the workplace, evaluating and assessing the workplace environment, cross-cultural communication, coaching and mentoring, dispute resolution, and changing organizational culture. Diversity training does not focus on employees' legal rights and responsibilities with respect to EEO—that is covered by EEO training.

Catalysts and other NIH employees are encouraged to promote diversity in more subtle and informal ways as well. For example, a list of "50 ways to respect diversity and positively impact the work environment" includes the following:

- Take a personal stand against harassment in all forms.
- Develop a technique to let persons know when they refer to women as "girls," or when a team of men and women is referred to as "you guys."
- Encourage conference and lecture planners to consider diversity when arranging for speakers and lecturers.
- Refuse to excuse or tacitly approve of inappropriate behavior because it is committed by a brilliant scientist.
- Develop a management style that allows for healthy disagreements.
- Practice effective listening or take a course on how to listen effectively to others.
- Study another language.

Accountability

There is an EEO and diversity critical element in all executives' performance plans, as mandated by the Public Health Service. EEO and diversity are also included in all managers' and supervisors' performance plans, although it is sometimes included in an element addressing broader human resource concerns. The executive performance element requires managers to "routinely support the NIH EEO program, affirmative action program, Workplace Diversity Initiative, and EEO complaint resolution program." Evidence of support includes such activities as:

- Demonstrating a commitment to recruit, hire, and promote from representative pools of candidates
- Attending conferences and seminars to promote networking and outreach for underrepresented communities
- Developing and implementing strategies that promote the potential of all employees by [doing such things as] establishing multicultural work teams and providing career development opportunities for all employees
- Working to educate employees regarding their rights and responsibilities in open communication sessions
- Providing reasonable accommodation to individuals with disabilities

In addition, an objective within NIH's draft strategic plan calls specifically for establishing "a trans-NIH system of accountability for the implementation of the Workplace Diversity Initiative." This is to be accomplished by:

- Having the Diversity Program managers track results of WDI implementation efforts
- Monitoring and tracking WDI initiatives and statistics using appropriate measurement instruments and tools to assess managers' performance
- Holding at least quarterly meetings of agency leadership to review progress

Evaluation

When asked what has changed as a result of the diversity initiative, Brogan noted that there is a greater awareness of the value of differences among people. No formal accomplishment report has been written to date, although progress is monitored informally through such mechanisms as focus groups of catalysts or annual status reports. There are plans now under way to develop a means for evaluating the effectiveness of the WDI based on Trevor Wilson's model, which combines data on the representation of various groups by occupational category with measures of employees' perceptions through focus groups, interviews, and/or a written survey (see *Diversity at Work* by Trevor Wilson, John Wiley and Sons, 1997).

National Institute for Standards and Technology (NIST)

The National Institute for Standards and Technology is an agency located within the U.S. Department of Commerce. With a total workforce of about 3,000, its mission, as specified on its web page, is to "develop and promote measurement standards and technology to enhance productivity, facilitate trade, and improve the quality of life" (www.nist.gov). In essence, NIST is a physical science research facility dedicated to developing technology needed by industry to "continually improve products and services." The agency employs scientists, engineers, technicians, business specialists, and administrative personnel. Approximately 1,600 guest researchers supplement the permanent staff.

Background

NIST's initial diversity strategy was established in 1993 by then-Director John Lyons, who was concerned about the lack of diversity in the agency's workforce. At that time, a study examining underrepresentation of women and minorities was undertaken and various recommendations were implemented. Support for the initiative was strong both at the departmental and agency levels. A Diversity Advisory Board (DAB) was established, which subsequently proposed that an Office of Diversity be created with a full-time staff person hired to direct the agency's diversity management activities. A search was conducted and Sol de Ande Eaton was selected. More recently, Naomi Churchill-Earp was recruited from the National Institutes of Health to temporarily advise management on program development.

In 1998, the NIST director expanded the DAB's mandate to make it responsible for "providing advice to the director of NIST on diversity-related plans, policies, and programs, and serving as an advocate for diversity and mentoring issues at NIST." Since then, a final draft of a diversity strategic plan was completed, and the DAB chair is working to incorporate it into the management strategic plan for 2010.

One of the significant challenges NIST and other science agencies face is how to get many in the scientific and technical community to support and understand the need for diversity programs. Churchill-Earp commented that in many cases it is difficult to get line employees thinking about diversity or anything not directly mission-related work.

Nature of the Program

The five-year diversity strategic plan developed in October 2000 provides the following vision statement for NIST:

> NIST is committed to maintaining its stature as a premier science agency by building an inclusive workforce, fostering an environment that respects the individual, promoting mentoring, and offering an opportunity for each person to develop their potential in support of the NIST mission.

Eaton and Churchill-Earp acknowledge differences between EEO and diversity. For example, they note a diversity program might seek to address issues of perceived differences between scientific and nonscientific staff. An EEO program probably would not be concerned with such issues because that basis for perceived different treatment is not a protected class under Title VII. Moreover, Churchill-Earp stated, "While EEO ensures everyone is treated the same, managing diversity speaks to treating everyone the same or differently to the extent it is necessary to accomplish the mission. EEO would say if one employee asks for a pencil, a pencil should be provided to everyone. Diversity says if one employee asks for a pencil, give that person a pencil to do the job and ask what others need. Their need could be for a pencil, pen, or crayon. EEO focuses on a class of people and diversity focuses on the individual." Another difference is the statutory mandate for an EEO program, while diversity is based on a business imperative. Although the two programs can complement each other, there is a potential for built-in tension between their objectives.

Certainly, the diversity effort at NIST goes beyond race, gender, and ethnicity, as indicated by the following definition:

> Diversity is the contributions and uniqueness employees bring to fulfilling the mission and global vision of NIST. On an individual level, diversity includes understanding, respecting and valuing physical, cultural and social differences.

Churchill-Earp has an expressed preference for R. Roosevelt Thomas's perspective that organizations should look at how business processes can be changed to better accommodate a diverse workforce. An example might be ensuring that qualification requirements are current and relevant. Another might be to provide formal and informal mentoring. This is where the distinction between EEO and diversity is limited. Those who work in diversity at NIST tend to see underrepresentation of minorities and women as an EEO issue, outside of their jurisdiction, and yet both functions are concerned with increasing the pool of applicants for jobs. Eaton participates in many job fairs during the year to recruit a diverse applicant pool, a traditional EEO function. Despite overlapping responsibilities, diversity and EEO work very cooperatively and strive for good communication between the offices.

Community outreach is another strong component of the diversity program. NIST's Diversity Program Office works in local schools to provide information about ongoing opportunities in the fields of engineering, science, mathematics, and technology. The agency holds a number of events each year to challenge student preparation for careers as scientists, engineers, and in advanced technologies. Scientists visit local schools to make the work of the agency more visible to the diverse population of students in the area and to demystify scientific research as a career option.

Another major component of the NIST diversity program is the Diversity Advisory Board, which plays a key role in lending credibility to the diversity effort. The board reports to the director of NIST. It meets six times a year and holds an annual retreat to discuss its work plan and priorities. The board must endorse any major diversity-related initiatives or policy mandates. The board consists of one member from each organizational unit appointed by that unit's director. Each member is given authority to speak for his/her director on diversity-related matters. Because the focus is on a board that is representative of each operational unit (rather than, for example, occupational or interest groups), there are currently no clerical or blue-collar workers on the board. This lack of job-series diversity will be addressed as board members complete their terms and new members are added. The diversity program staff engages in other efforts to maintain contact with groups not represented on the board to ensure that their views are given consideration.

NIST also has developed a mentoring program for the administrative, clerical, and support personnel, and is in the process of developing a mentoring process for the professional staff. There is also a Self-Improvement and Mentoring Resource Center on the Gaithersburg, Maryland, campus that provides tools for employees to assess and improve their skills. NIST clearly considers the facilitation of mentoring to be an important part of its diversity program, as indicated by its inclusion as one of the "guiding principles" of the agency's diversity program: "Each person at NIST must be mentored to some degree and allowed to contribute to NIST excellence." Conflict management is not a formal component of the diversity program, but Eaton meets with people on an informal basis should diversity-related conflict arise. The Diversity Program Office also coordinates "quality of work-life" programs and activities, in conjunction with the Human Resources Management Division and others.

Structure and Resources

When the diversity program at NIST was started, it was decided that the effort should be kept separate from the agency's traditional equal employment opportunity and affirmative employment programs. Formally, the traditional EEO responsibilities are housed within the Office of Civil Rights, which reports to the director of NIST. The Diversity Advisory Board also reports to the director. The Diversity Program Office reports to the director of administration and chief financial officer, and is one level removed from the director. Informally, there is much collaboration between the Diversity Program Office and the Office of Civil Rights. One example is the online training for the prevention of sexual harassment that they co-sponsor.

The Diversity Program Office employs three full-time staff members. The Diversity Advisory Board is comprised of 15 members who serve in that capacity on a collateral-duty basis. There is also one collateral-duty staff member in the agency's Boulder, Colorado, office.

The existence of at least two separate offices interested in recruitment (the Office of Civil Rights and the Diversity Program Office) and many separate entities (including employee advocacy groups) concerned with raising awareness and training can sometimes result in problems with duplication of effort, communication, and coordination among them. While the Office of Civil Rights is responsible for overseeing special emphasis programs, in practice Eaton has responded to the Department of Commerce Special Diversity Recruitment Initiative by doing most of the recruitment of, and outreach to, Hispanics and other groups. On the other hand, the Diversity Program Office considers the maintenance of two separate entities important for reinforcing that one office is statutory and the other is based on good business practices.

Training and Awareness

Another important aspect of the diversity program at NIST is the training that is provided to managers. Eaton developed a three-part training program with content that builds on each successive course. Specifically, the preferred training starts with a basic introduction to managing diversity. Next there is a session on cross-cultural communication. The third aspect of the training is a class on cultural competence. All new managers are encouraged—but not required—to participate in a one-day diversity training program. The exception is members of the Senior Executive Service, who are required to attend diversity training. The decision to mandate diversity training for all managers and supervisors was rethought after a vendor seemed to do more harm than good with some training techniques. This occurred prior to the establishment of the Diversity Program Office. NIST has found the strategy of required training for executives and encouraged attendance for others to be effective. The heads of each unit are also encouraged to provide their own diversity training, and the Diversity Program Office provides videos and other training materials to assist the organizational units in doing so.

Contractors provide all diversity training for NIST and generally do not address rights and responsibilities under Title VII to any great extent, as the Civil Rights Office covers this subject in depth. The Diversity Program Office also owns several diversity-related videos, which operating units often check out and include as part of staff meetings.

In addition to the events sponsored by the Diversity Program Office, there are seven active employee groups at NIST—representing black, Latino, women, Asian, disabled, and gay and lesbian employees, and one representing guest researchers. These groups also sponsor awareness events.

Other aspects of the agency's diversity educational effort that were specifically mentioned by program staff members include a newsletter, web page, special emphasis programs, lecture series, and a student internship program. The Diversity Program Office also provides books and other literature to directors and members of the advisory board, and the office maintains a resource center.

Accountability

In December 1999, then-Secretary of Commerce William M. Daley issued a department-wide memorandum requiring that the performance plan for each manager and supervisor include a critical element promoting diversity, assigned a weight of at least 15 percent. The element requires managers to "consider equal opportunity and diversity principles in all aspects of program and personnel decisions." It provides a list of suggested "major activities." Activities are suggested rather than stipulated as they don't all apply to all supervisors. Among these are the following:

- Recruit, hire, and train staff based on principles of EEO. To the extent resources are available, provide on an equal opportunity basis training and learning/growth experiences for staff; e.g., details, rotational assignments, cross-training, and other developmental activities.
- Participate in and support staff involvement in outreach efforts of the organization; e.g., participation in minority and disabled recruitment, and cultural observance programs.

- Attend and actively promote training that supports diversity and EEO programs.
- Actively promote and encourage the use of mediation, facilitation, or other appropriate forms of alternative dispute resolution to address workplace conflicts.
- Promote and encourage the use of family-friendly workplace options.

Evaluation

Officially, the Five Year Strategic Plan for Managing Diversity, which covers October 2000 to September 2005, commits the agency to assessing organizational unit progress annually and the overall success of the initiative at the end of the five-year period. The agency is to develop measurable performance goals that provide a basis for comparing actual results with expected results. Staff has also developed a detailed implementation plan for achieving their goals that includes completion dates, resources needed, and measures of success. The implementation plan indicates that a Diversity Tracking System will be developed to share trend information with management on such employment actions as accessions, separations, promotions, personal development, and reassignments.

Churchill-Earp acknowledged that there are problems in finding good measures of the effectiveness of a diversity program. A stable or increased EEO complaint caseload, for example, could be evidence of heightened awareness and confidence in filing complaints rather than an increase in behavior that is perceived as discriminatory. She is considering working with the Employee Assistance Program to assess whether a change in the number and kinds of ailments reported to that program might be suggestive of an improved climate for diversity. She also believes that anecdotal evidence about the environment and retention rates for minorities and women are good measures of the impact of a diversity program on the organizational climate.

Two employee surveys (conducted in 1999 and 2000) revealed the presence of some negative attitudes toward diversity. NIST has seen some improvement and has plans to readminister the survey in late 2002 or early 2003 in order to assess whether the diversity program has helped to lessen some of those attitudes or raise awareness.

Bureau of Land Management (BLM)

The Bureau of Land Management is an agency located within the U.S. Department of the Interior. It administers 264 million acres of public land located primarily in 12 western states and Alaska. The areas of BLM responsibility include "extensive grasslands, forests, high mountains, arctic tundra, and deserts" (www.blm.gov). As noted on the BLM web page, the agency and its workforce of approximately 7,800 employees manage a wide variety of resources and uses including "energy and minerals, timber, forage, wild horse and burro populations, fish and wildlife habitat, wilderness areas, archaeological, paleontological, and historic sites" (www.blm.gov). The BLM is charged with sustaining the "health, diversity, and productivity of public lands for the use and enjoyment of present and future generations" (www.blm.gov).

Background

Historically, the BLM, like its parent department, has found it difficult to recruit sufficient minorities and women. As a result, by the early 1990s equal employment opportunity and diversity-related issues were a focus of concern. During the Clinton years, a number of top agency and departmental officials were dedicated to changing the agency's profile and worked aggressively to do so. The diversity program, implemented in 1996, was an outgrowth of that effort.

Nature of the Program

The agency's diversity effort is broader in orientation than traditional affirmative employment activities, according to Gloria Innis, director of the EEO Group. Traditional affirmative employment programs (AEP) are specified in law and tied to specific formulas, and so "under that orientation, once you achieve parity, the effort should end," she explained. By contrast, the diversity program at the BLM focuses on additional issues not covered by Title VII of the 1964 Civil Rights Act, such as sexual orientation and geographic origin, and it includes flexibilities to accommodate single mothers or people who have large distances to commute to work. There is a Diversity Committee at the agency comprised of representatives of various offices and groups, providing a forum for the discussion of diversity-related issues and guidance for the program.

Despite recognition of the ways in which a diversity program may be distinct from traditional EEO/AEP, much of what is included within the diversity effort at the BLM bears considerable similarity to conventional EEO. In fact, Innis reported that the principal goals of the agency's diversity program were recruitment (primarily through visits to colleges and universities) and retention of underrepresented groups. Indeed, the first goal listed in the agency's written Work Force Diversity Program Plan from 1997 is to "recruit a workforce that reflects the diversity of the nation's population." Specific items included in that plan are expansion of the agency's affirmative employment program, further development of targeted recruitment strategies to increase minority and female representation in specified job categories, an annual assessment of those strategies, and a review of position requirements to ensure that stated requirements are appropriate and applicable. The agency also conducts exit interviews to identify ways to improve minority and female retention. All of these "diversity" efforts are consistent with traditional EEO/AEP activities.

Structure and Resources

Organizationally, the diversity program at the BLM falls under the responsibility of the agency's EEO Group and is implemented through the efforts of two full-time staff members. The EEO Group also performs traditional EEO-related activities such as handling EEO complaints and developing affirmative recruitment plans.

Training and Awareness

In addition to the emphasis on recruitment, the diversity program at the BLM is also oriented toward changing the agency's culture to make it more supportive of individuals from diverse backgrounds. That goal is reflected in the agency's written diversity plan that stresses the importance of efforts to "educate managers and employees regarding diversity" and calls for "mandatory diversity training for supervisors and managers." The training is to focus on "general diversity in organizations, preventing and resolving interpersonal conflict in the workplace, accessibility and reasonable accommodation issues (for the disabled), and preventing and dealing with sexual harassment." Similar training is part of the orientation process for all new employees. Innis stressed that the training effort is intended to prevent conflict and facilitate the resolution of problems before they escalate into major disputes. It is hoped that as a result, conflict among employees and between employees and their supervisors would be reduced as they learn strategies for dealing with interpersonal differences.

Accountability

To help ensure accountability, a diversity element is included within the performance plans of Senior Executives and all managers and supervisors, requiring them to support the diversity program and its implementation.

Evaluation

There has been no significant effort to measure the effectiveness of the diversity program at the BLM. Indeed, Innis noted that it would be extremely difficult to make such an assessment because it would require measuring changes in the organizational culture over time. An employee attitude survey—intended, in part, to assess the extent to which employees believe that the organizational culture was supportive of people from different backgrounds—was administered in 1999. There is discussion of administering that survey again sometime in the future, but Innis points out many factors affect employees' views of the organization's climate besides the diversity program.

Substance Abuse and Mental Health Services Administration (SAMHSA)

The Substance Abuse and Mental Health Services Administration is an agency within the U.S. Department of Health and Human Services. Established by Public Law 102-321 on October 1, 1992, the agency's mission is to "strengthen the nation's health care capacity to provide prevention, diagnosis, and treatment services for substance abuse and mental illness" (www.samhsa.gov). SAMHSA works with states, communities, and private organizations to address the needs of people with substance abuse problems and to help assess community risk factors. The agency conducts its work primarily through the administration of a series of federal block grant programs intended to enhance substance abuse and mental health services. Targeted Capacity Expansion grants give local communities resources for the early identification and management of emerging substance abuse and mental health service needs. SAMHSA's more than 500 employees are organized into three units: the Center for Mental Health Services, the Center for Substance Abuse Prevention, and the Center for Substance Abuse Treatment (see www.samhsa.gov).

Background

According to Sharon Lynn Holmes, director of the Office of EEO and Civil Rights at SAMHSA, the diversity program was developed in 1995 by a former director of the Office of EEO, in conjunction with the agency's administrator.

Nature of the Program

Holmes stressed that the EEO and diversity programs are distinct, with the latter encompassing more dimensions than race and sex. The program's current focus is on a concept she referred to as "cultural competence," which involves the promotion of attitudes respectful of people from diverse cultural backgrounds. Holmes noted that the focus in EEO is on complaints resolution, and while the diversity program staff at SAMHSA try to reduce the number of discrimination complaints through their education and training efforts, their primary focus is on recruitment. As the agency's work involves dispensing services to the public in the form of grants, they want to ensure their staff includes people who understand the needs of diverse communities. Presumably, they see "cultural competence" as a way to make the agency a more attractive employer to minorities, so that the agency can be responsive to the diverse communities it serves. Since women already comprise 70 percent of the workforce, they are interested in increasing the representation of men of color, especially those under 30 years of age. Last year they concentrated on the recruitment of Hispanic men. They work closely with the agency's Human Resources Department in developing outreach efforts to minority communities. SAMHSA's diversity program also includes a mentoring program focused on opening opportunities to employees in lower grade levels.

The programmatic orientation at SAMHSA appears to fit well within the traditional EEO paradigm, rather than extending to the broader diversity management framework, as it is focused largely on recruitment and upward mobility. When asked for documents regarding their diversity program, Holmes provided copies of the agency's *Affirmative Employment Program Plan for Minorities and Women* (for fiscal year 2001) and their *Affirmative Action Program for People With Disabilities* (for 2001). Both examine levels of representation of specified groups; review the previous year's accomplishments in increasing representation; and identify objectives for complaint processing, recruitment and hiring, employee development, and upward mobility for the coming year—all traditional EEO/AA concerns.

Structure and Resources

As would be expected, given the nature of the agency's program, the diversity effort is housed within the Office of EEO and Civil Rights. That office employs five full-time staff persons, 20 to 25 collateral-duty EEO counselors, and 20 EEO advisors.

Training and Awareness

Diversity training for agency managers is provided by the directors of the three centers (Substance Abuse Treatment, Substance Abuse Prevention, and Mental Health Services), but the training is not mandatory. The agency has developed online, self-training modules as well as literature explaining rules and responsibilities with respect to EEO. They also conduct team-building exercises that include a diversity component.

Accountability

There are no diversity elements included in the performance plans of managers and supervisors, with the exception of members of the Senior Executive Service and agency division directors.

Evaluation

There are no efforts to evaluate the effectiveness of the diversity program at SAMHSA.

Mine Safety and Health Administration (MSHA)

The Mine Safety and Health Administration, with a workforce of about 2,400, is an agency within the U.S. Department of Labor (DOL). Its mission is to "enforce compliance with mandatory safety and health standards" at all mining and mineral processing operations (www.msha.gov). MSHA inspectors examine each surface mine at least twice a year and each underground mine at least four times a year (although seasonal or intermittent operations are inspected less frequently) to identify imminent danger and compliance with standards. MSHA also investigates "mine accidents, complaints of retaliatory discrimination filed by miners [and] hazardous conditions complaints" (www.msha.gov). The agency's other services include assisting mine operators in meeting legal requirements and improving their employee education and training programs.

Background

Michael Thompson, director of the Office of Diversity, Outreach, and Employee Safety, has emphasized the importance of the concepts of diversity and inclusion since he became director in 1982, although the use of the term "diversity" did not arise until many years later. In March of 1996, Assistant Secretary for Mine Safety and Health J. Davitt McAteer issued a policy statement on the subject of EEO and workforce diversity. The letter stated MSHA's diversity policy as follows:

> Implementation of MSHA's workforce diversity and equal opportunity program involves all MSHA employees, as well as individual employees who are assigned specific program responsibilities. Indeed, the challenge for employees today and in the future is how to work more effectively with a workforce that is becoming more diverse and aware of culture, race, religion, language, ethnicity, and sexual orientation. Workforce diversity and understanding people's differences are crucial to our continued success as a highly professional organization. I encourage and welcome the support of every employee in MSHA to strengthen our commitment to achieving equal opportunity and workforce diversity by working with managers, supervisors, employees, and the MSHA Office of Equal Opportunity in a concentrated effort to support workforce diversity and equal opportunity.

The letter went on to state that the Secretary of Labor had instructed all of its agencies to establish a comprehensive EEO and workforce diversity program. Officially, the diversity program at MSHA began with the development of a diversity action plan in 1998. The impetus for development of the action plan, which covers 1998 to 2003, was the convening of a department-wide Diversity Task Force by then-Secretary of Labor Alexis Herman.

The MSHA has always faced a particularly difficult challenge in meeting EEO targets because of the nature of its labor force. Mine inspectors, for example, must have five years of experience in the mining industry, in which women and minorities are severely underrepresented. MSHA's Diversity Action Plan (signed in 1998) states that minorities comprise only 15 percent, and women 6 percent, of nontraditional positions in the mining industry.

Nature of the Program

MSHA defines diversity as follows:

> Diversity refers to differences in ethnic identification, cultural background, gender, age, sexual orientation, physical ability, family status, experience level, and religious and political beliefs. It is about differences across individuals or groups of individuals.

Despite the diversity policy and action plan, the main focus of MSHA's effort appears to be on traditional EEO activities. For example, because of the poor representation of women and minorities for the reasons stated above, they have recently created a new position—outreach manager—to focus on increasing the diversity of the candidate pool. Action items in MSHA's Diversity Action Plan for 1998-2003 include:

- Identifying the current characteristics of the mining workforce and seeking to use that information to establish diversity benchmarks.
- "Applying diversity initiatives" to increase minority representation.
- Continuing to update and endorse the diversity and EEO policies and procedures.
- Developing a videotape communicating top leadership's commitment to diversity.
- Developing a schedule of special emphasis programs.
- Providing mandatory diversity and EEO training as well as training for managers on the merit staffing and rating processes.
- Revising performance standards for all MSHA managers and supervisors to hold them accountable for diversity.
- Expanding career opportunities for employees via such mechanisms as the Career Enhancement program, bridges, and upward mobility.
- Developing a mentoring program.
- Recruiting job candidates more aggressively and broadly.

Conflict management, while originally included as part of the diversity training, is officially under the purview of the employee and labor relations function in the Human Resource office. It was de-emphasized as a diversity issue in order to make it clear to managers that any advice they need about problems with employees should be directed to the agency's employee relations specialists. Similarly, initiatives such as telecommuting and flexible scheduling are the responsibility of Human Resources. There are plans to create a diversity council in the coming year.

Structure and Resources

The diversity program, housed within the Office of Diversity, Outreach, and Employee Safety, has a staff of five full-time employees. These employees are EEO specialists with diversity-related work included in their job description—there are no employees assigned solely to diversity efforts. The director reports directly to the director of administration; the office is independent of the human resources function.

Training and Awareness

As noted above, the MSHA provides mandatory diversity training to all managers, supervisors, and employees, which often includes a film by Morris Massey that addresses improving communication among diverse groups. The training emphasizes how diversity is broader than traditional EEO and affirmative employment programs and that the rights of all groups (defined broadly) must be protected.

Thompson noted that when he speaks to employees about the importance of diversity, he emphasizes that "you can have diversity even if the workforce is all white men because of differences in religion, age, and other factors." He believes the goal for a diversity program should be the inclusion of everyone. Special emphasis program functions are also an important component of MSHA's diversity effort.

Accountability

Managers' and supervisors' performance management plans include a critical element that requires them to demonstrate effective management of people by:

- Fostering an inclusive working environment which encourages all employees to be participants in achieving organizational goals.
- Supporting recruitment/outreach to achieve a diverse workforce.
- Demonstrating fairness in selecting, assigning work to, and developing staff, basing decisions on merit and encouraging employee self-development.
- Taking steps to address issues of discrimination on the basis of race, color, religion, sex, age, national origin, disability, or sexual orientation that are observed or brought to his/her attention.
- Periodically reviewing DOL EEO policy and workplace values with staff.
- Providing frequent and constructive fact-based performance information to staff and good performance solutions to performance issues.
- Helping staff to set ambitious goals that stretch the capacity of the individual and organization and encouraging the staff to go further towards achieving more than what traditionally would be expected.

The action plan also calls for the development of a "workplace values" performance appraisal element for nonsupervisory employees, following consultation between the department's Human Resource Center and the unions. That objective has not been accomplished yet.

Evaluation

When asked how the diversity program had improved the environment at MSHA, an EEO staff member replied, "People are getting more training in their rights and responsibilities." The agency conducts no formal evaluation of the impact of its diversity initiatives, but they do ask training participants to complete an evaluation form immediately following the session. The form consists of three open-ended questions inquiring as to the usefulness of the session, its anticipated impact on the trainees' work in a diversified environment, and suggestions for improving the course.

The agency does submit yearly status reports to the Department of Labor on the completion of items included in the 1998 Diversity Action Plan. The 1999 report submitted at the end of the first year showed that most items were "on target" or had been given revised completion dates.

Economic Development Administration (EDA)

The Economic Development Administration is located within the U.S. Department of Commerce. Its purpose is to help "generate jobs, help retain existing jobs, and stimulate industrial and commercial growth in economically distressed areas of the United States" (www.doc.gov/eda). The EDA has a workforce of approximately 270 employees who work in partnership with state and local governments, regional economic development districts, and nonprofit organizations to address problems associated with "long-term economic distress, as well as sudden and severe economic dislocations including recovering from the economic impacts of natural disasters, the closure of military installations and other federal facilities, changing trade patterns, and the depletion of natural resources" (www.doc.gov/eda). The EDA provides grants for infrastructure and business development so that distressed areas can develop their own locally based comprehensive economic development strategies.

Background

In completing the 1999 NPR survey, the EDA reported that it had no diversity program in place, and that remains largely true two years later. Gerald R. Lucas, EDA's deputy chief financial and chief administrative officer, is also responsible for EEO and diversity issues. According to Lucas, the Clinton administration's first Secretary of Commerce, the late Ron Brown, pushed strenuously for greater effort to be made throughout the department in the areas of EEO and diversity. Lucas found Secretary Brown's charismatic approach very effective. The Secretary established a department-wide Diversity Council and required all operating units (such as the EDA) to establish councils as well. Succeeding secretaries kept the initiative in place. In 1998, Secretary William Daley issued a memorandum to all Commerce Department employees stressing the department's commitment to the concepts of diversity and equal opportunity, and urging the creation of "an organizational culture that embodies mutual acceptance, inclusion and empowerment, and firmly rejects all forms of discrimination and harassment."

Nature of the Program

Although the EDA does not have an official diversity program, it promotes diversity through intern and mentoring programs, family-friendly workplace practices, and efforts to resolve workplace disputes at the lowest possible organizational level. The agency's Diversity Council is comprised of representatives from each division, and meets periodically to advise EDA top management on diversity-related matters. Currently, it is in the process of developing a diversity action plan, which presumably will form the basis for a more formal diversity program. The action plan is expected to recognize that diversity management includes issues associated with sensitivity, participation, respect for cultural differences, and an acknowledgment that people differ from one another in more ways than by race, ethnicity, and gender.

Structure and Resources

The EDA's EEO program and activities designed to promote diversity are housed in the Office of Finance and Administration, under Lucas's direction. Prior to assuming this position, he served as the director of the Office of Civil Rights for the Commerce Department from 1982 to 1994. Lucas's diversity-related responsibilities in EDA are primarily to ensure that the agency meets the department's objectives regarding minority and female employment, which are determined by the department's Office of Civil Rights. Consistent with those objectives, the EDA focuses on establishing specific hiring goals for minorities and women and conducting recruitment and outreach efforts to attract them as potential employees.

Training and Awareness

Relatively little has been done at the EDA in terms of diversity training, although all Senior Executives received such training in early 2001. In the fall of 2001, all managers and supervisors will also receive diversity training as part of a broader training effort. The focus for the training is on understanding and valuing differences among people and managing conflict within the workplace.

Accountability

As noted earlier in the discussion of NIST, former Secretary Daley sent a memorandum to all secretarial officers and heads of operating units and departmental offices in 1999 mandating that a critical element reflecting the promotion of diversity be included in the performance plans of all Senior Executives, managers, and supervisors (see this chapter's section on NIST for a list of associated activities). Lucas indicates that inclusion of the diversity element in the performance appraisal process forces managers to be conscious of diversity and accountable for it, thus helping the agency move forward. Nonsupervisory employees at EDA are also rated with respect to diversity, but the objective is much more broadly defined in those cases.

Evaluation

When asked about the impact of the EDA's diversity efforts, Lucas responded that its accomplishments have included a greater awareness among employees of the importance of diversity and an increased commitment by management to the concept. He also suggested that employee attitudes have changed and employee expectations have grown. "Some managers have gone through a metamorphosis from a traditional view to a much more tolerant view," Lucas reported. No formal evaluation of the EDA's efforts has taken place, however, other than through monitoring compliance with the diversity element in the performance appraisal process.

National Agricultural Statistics Service (NASS)

Located within the U. S. Department of Agriculture, the National Agricultural Statistics Service is charged with providing timely, accurate, and useful statistics in service to the American agricultural community. They discharge their responsibility by conducting the agricultural census, administering numerous surveys, and preparing hundreds of reports each year covering virtually every facet of agriculture in the United States. The agency's approximately 1,100 employees address subjects ranging from agricultural production and the supply of food to prices paid to farmers, the level of farm wages, and the labor market within agriculture. NASS reports examine issues associated with traditional crops, such as corn and wheat, but also address specialties such as mushrooms and flowers (www.usda.gov/nass).

Background

NASS has no formal diversity management program. The agency employs one full-time EEO and civil rights officer (Rafael Sanchez), with other employees assigned on a collateral-duty basis to ensure attention is paid to specific groups (e.g., women, Asian/Pacific Islanders). Sanchez and Linda M. Raudenbush, a human resources and organizational development specialist with the agency, report that NASS makes no distinction between EEO and diversity. The agency's efforts focus primarily on traditional EEO concerns including minority and female recruitment, the processing of discrimination complaints, and employee career development.

Training and Awareness

NASS has provided training on the concept of diversity since 1995 to all staff and managers, and since 1997 that training has been mandatory. In that year, an internal study described a history of civil rights problems within the Department of Agriculture, which helped to spur the requirement for diversity training. The instruction addresses the importance of valuing differences among people and supervisory skills needed to better manage diverse employees. Since 1997 the agency has also included diversity training in its orientation process for new employees.

Summing Up: Similarities and Differences Among Agencies

Table 9.5 compares all seven of the agencies studied on a number of programmatic dimensions. It is clear from these case studies that regardless of the size or scope of the agency or its diversity programs, there are some common elements. These include the premise that a diversity program is meant to be broader than a traditional EEO/AA program in that it focuses on differences that are not addressed by those programs, such as work style or occupational differences. This is reflected in the definitions of diversity that some of these agencies have developed. As MSHA puts it, diversity is "about differences across individuals or groups of individuals."

While all but two (NASS and EDA) claim to have a diversity program in place, only the efforts of NIH and NIST really appear to extend into arenas beyond the traditional EEO/AA activities that focused on recruitment and complaint processing. These two have chosen to incorporate distinct elements into their approaches. NIST's diversity program emphasizes community outreach and the development of mentoring programs, while NIH has created a new position called a "diversity catalyst" and encourages employees to "show respect for diversity and positively impact the work environment" in many everyday ways such as by practicing effective listening or studying another language. NIST, like BLM, includes flexible working arrangements within the rubric of its workforce diversity program, while NIH and MSHA have assigned management of those programs to their human resource offices.

While most of the seven agencies have programs that are more aligned with traditional EEO/AA than the newer managing diversity model, an exception is in the area of training. All of the seven offer training (and half require it) that is broader than the traditional EEO training focusing on legal rights and responsibilities. This training generally stresses the importance of valuing differences among people and sometimes more general topics such as effective communication and negotiation.

Even while emphasizing the differences between EEO/AA and diversity, most of these agencies house their diversity efforts within their EEO offices and have no staff solely dedicated to diversity. Even though NIH has devoted considerable attention to emphasizing the distinction between EEO

Table 9.5: Summary of Agency Program Characteristics

Diversity Program Component	BLM	EDA	MSHA	NASS	NIH	NIST	SAMHSA
Date of initiation of formal diversity program	1996	*	1998	*	1995	1997/98	1995
Housed within EEO office	Yes	*	Yes	*	Yes	No	Yes
Number of full-time staff	2	0	5	1	26	3	5
Diversity defined as more than sex, race, and other traditional EEO categories	Yes	Yes	Yes	Yes	Yes	Yes	Yes
Have diversity action or strategic plan	Yes	No**	Yes	No**	Yes	Yes	No
Major focus on recruitment	Yes	Yes	Yes	Yes	Yes	Yes	Yes
Includes awareness events (e.g., special emphasis functions)	Yes	Yes	Yes	Yes	No	Yes	Yes
Includes flexible scheduling, telecommuting, etc.	Yes	Yes	No	Yes	No	Yes	Yes
Includes a diversity council	Yes	Yes	No	No***	Yes	Yes	No
Includes focus on conflict management	Yes	Yes	No	No	Yes	No	No
Diversity training required for managers and supervisors	Yes	Yes	Yes	Yes	No	Yes****	No
Diversity training included in employee orientation	Yes	Yes	Yes	Yes	No	Yes	No
Measure effectiveness	No	No	No	No	Yes	Yes	No
Have administered attitude survey as part of assessment	Yes	No	No	Yes	No	Yes	No
Diversity element in supervisors/managers performance plans	Yes	Yes	Yes	Yes	Yes	Yes	Yes

   * These agencies don't have a formal diversity program.

   ** There is an agency affirmative action plan that includes discussion of diversity-related issues.

   *** NASS has a Civil Rights Advisory Committee that provides guidance on issues related to civil rights, EEO, and affirmative employment plans.

   **** Diversity training is required for executives, recommended for others.

and diversity, the diversity program resides in the Office of Equal Opportunity, and diversity program managers also perform EEO functions. The exception is NIST, in which the decision was made to separate the two completely. Yet even NIST's diversity program staff is involved in some traditional EEO functions such as targeted recruitment of underrepresented groups. EDA has no staff assigned full-time to EEO or diversity, and NASS has only a single EEO officer responsible for all efforts in that regard. Size of staff is not necessarily a function of agency size; SAMHSA has half the workforce that NASS does, but five full-time staff members.

There has been little effort to systematically assess the effectiveness of these diversity programs. Only NIH has begun a process, prescribed by Trevor Wilson (1997), to do so. The final sections of this chapter provide our recommendations for how such an evaluation could be carried out.

The Importance of Measuring Effectiveness

It is useful to know what activities comprise federal agency diversity programs, but even more essential to assess whether these programs are accomplishing their intended purpose of creating a more equitable work environment than may have existed in the past. This is particularly timely in light of the federal government's recent emphasis on measuring performance in order to ensure the public is attaining the most return for the tax dollars and other resources they invest in government.

This is the purpose served by impact analysis, which involves the application of social science methodology to questions of whether and to what extent the objectives or goals of public programs have been met. It requires the identification of appropriate measures of goal achievement, the utilization of appropriate research designs, data collection, and analysis to determine whether the program has had the desired impact. Only under such circumstances can reasonably valid conclusions necessary for fair evaluation be reached.

Given the disputes that sometimes emerge regarding organizational diversity programs, it would seem all the more imperative that there be a systematic impact evaluation of those efforts within federal agencies. In its most recent report on the demographics of the American labor force, even the Hudson Institute denounced the "diversity craze" that was launched by its 1987 analysis and the response from "diversity entrepreneurs" who "misread" *Workforce 2000* (Judy and D'Amico 1997, xiv-xv). Frederick Lynch has criticized the "diversity machine" as one that "indiscriminately blends social science and ideology, [and] serious substance with silly platitudes" (1997a, 17-18; see also Lynch 1997b). Some argue that diversity training, in particular, has been not just ineffective, it has been harmful, creating such a backlash that new firms have been created to "mop up" the messes made by other diversity trainers (Lubove 1997, Flynn 1999, Hemphill and Haines 1997). Others have expressed the concern that broadly focused diversity programs have diluted the still-needed focus on ensuring the continuance of traditional equal employment opportunity and affirmative action for women and people of color (Morrison 1992, Caudron and Hayes 1997). Another view agrees with the importance of organizational restructuring to create a more inclusive environment, but argues that the managing diversity approaches that emphasize identity consciousness will not achieve the desired results (Krefting and Kirby 1997).

Federal diversity programs are not immune from this criticism. A 1994 article in the *Washington Times* lampooned the Department of Housing and Urban Development for including "cultural diversity" in the performance standards for managers and supervisors (Price 1994). Near the end of her period in office, Environmental Protection Agency Administrator Carol Browner found herself defending her agency's diversity initiatives before the House Science Subcommittee (Lunney 2000).

It is perhaps, then, quite reasonable for Ivancevich and Gilbert to argue: "Demography-is-destiny speeches and statements by advocates must be replaced with bottom-line data and proof that diversity management adds value to the organization and its employees." Wise and Tschirhart (2000, 389) agree: "The lack of empirical research on the organizational-level outcomes is troubling, given the emphasis in the literature on the organizational-level benefits of the managing for diversity approach." Even while arguing against an identity-conscious approach to managing diversity, Krefting and Kirby (1997) contend that the demographic effects of human resource practices should be tracked to ensure those practices are not having an adverse impact on some groups of employees in a way that would suggest they are not identity-blind.

Indicators of Success

The first step in an analysis of impact is to identify appropriate measures to serve as indicators of whether a program is accomplishing its intended objectives. As is the case with many other public endeavors, reasonable goals for agency diversity management programs might be specified in a number of ways. Based on the literature summarized early in this chapter, however, one would expect that diversity management programs would be intended to ensure that the climate within public organizations is such that people of diverse backgrounds would find those organizations comfortable and attractive places to work and would be able to progress within them as far as their abilities were able to take them. It also would be expected that diversity programs would help to educate managers and supervisors about biases (often unconscious) that might hamper their willingness to provide all employees with equal opportunities for fulfilling work and advancement.

Of course, diversity may be defined in terms of a broad number of factors, but in the context of American public agencies, race, ethnicity, and gender are among the most salient demographic variables. Inequities that manifest themselves along racial, ethnic, and gender lines are still common. It is, undoubtedly, for this reason that when agencies are asked to describe their measures of effectiveness for their programs, many refer to measures that traditionally are used in EEO/AA programs such as a comparison of agency workforce demographics with the civilian labor force. However, given the slow nature of employment progress for women and minorities, it can take a long time to change significantly the composition of an organization in those terms. As a result, such a comparison may not be the best gauge for assessing the effectiveness of a diversity program in the short term.

It has been suggested that employee perceptions as to whether they find their work environment to be equitable similarly would provide a good measure of diversity program effectiveness (see, for example, Wilson 1997). The difficulty with this measure is that stable or increased dissatisfaction with the work environment may also reflect expectations that have been heightened as a result of the diversity initiative. Moreover, many other factors can affect employee perceptions of their work environment, including a potential or imminent reduction in force, or adverse publicity in the press resulting from employee advocacy groups' efforts to draw attention to perceived inequities.

Because diversity programs are intended to have a broader impact on the work environment than traditional EEO programs, it would seem that more dynamic measures are required to assess their success. We recommend that agencies examine various types of personnel actions and their effects on women and minorities. In particular, for the reasons described below, it seems appropriate to focus on promotions, dismissals, and voluntary turnover.

Promotions

The distribution of promotions among various groups is an important indicator of equity. In its studies of the federal workforce, the Merit Systems Protection Board (MSPB) found that women and minorities are promoted proportionately less than men and nonminorities from entry- or lower-level jobs (e.g., grades GS-7 or GS-9) in professional and administrative occupations. The MSPB suggested that among the reasons for these restricted opportunities were negative stereotypes, which are often unconscious and seldom intended. For example, women are often presumed to be more interested in their families than in their careers, and Asian/Pacific Islanders are typecast as more capable of performing technical than managerial work (MSPB 1992, 1996; see also Naff 2001). One expectation of a diversity program is that it would provide training that would make managers aware of the tendency to stereotype so they could make a conscious effort to avoid it.

The MSPB also noted that women were sometimes hampered by formal and informal criteria for advancement, such as the number of geographic relocations or hours worked each week. For most jobs, these are not valid indicators of job performance or promotion potential and tend to have an adverse impact on women. Much of the diversity literature recommends a reexamination of the organization's promotion and performance appraisal criteria to identify potential bias and, where necessary, to revamp them (see Table 9.1). One would expect, then, that a successful diversity program would create greater promotion opportunities for minorities and women.

Because the MSPB determined that minorities and women faced lower rates of promotion in lower-graded jobs, it would seem important to focus on promotions at these levels. However, many professional and administrative positions have career ladders where an incumbent can expect to be promoted to a journey-level grade of GS-12 without competition. It would seem wise, then, also to examine promotions from GS-12 to GS-13, where incumbents are more likely to face competitive promotion decisions.

Most analyses using aggregate data to determine whether men and women or minorities and nonminorities have equal promotion opportunities rely on a comparison of simple promotion rates (see, for example, MSPB 1992, 1996). Such a rate could be calculated by dividing the number of women or minorities promoted by the number of women or minorities present at a given grade level. Under this approach, if one quarter of the women and one quarter of the white men are promoted from GS-9 positions in a particular organization, the assumption is that an equitable distribution of promotions has occurred in that women are promoted at the same "rate" as white men.

However, this measure overlooks a critical factor. Where a group is few in number in an organization, fewer promotions of members of that group might be required to achieve equitable or even superior promotion rates compared to other groups. For example, assume that in a particular organization there are 100 white men and 10 minorities. Promoting 10 white men yields a promotion rate of 10 percent. To achieve an equivalent promotion rate for minorities, the organization need promote only one minority. Promoting two minorities, for a promotion rate of 20 percent, suggests that minorities enjoy a much greater opportunity to be promoted than white men, but in fact far fewer minorities than white men are actually promoted.

To minimize this difficulty, we recommend a measure that is based on the assumption that minorities and women should be promoted at least in approximately the same proportions as their numbers in the relevant workforce. For example, if minorities represent 10 percent of the workforce, they should be expected to receive no fewer than 10 percent of the promotions, if, in fact, there is an equitable environment within the organization. Essentially then, our measure consists of the minority (or female) share of total promotions in the year 1999 (from GS-9 and GS-12 positions) relative to the minority (or female) share of the relevant workforces in that same year calculated as follows for minority group members:

$$\frac{\text{Number of Minority Promotions}}{\text{Total Number of Promotions}}$$

$$\frac{\text{Number of Minorities}}{\text{Total Number of Positions}}$$

A quotient of 1.0 or greater means that minorities and women are being promoted in proportion to their representation in the workforce or better.

Dismissals

A second possible indicator of success of agency diversity programs is a measure of the extent to which African Americans are discharged from their jobs at rates disproportionate to their presence in the workforce. We focus in this case on African Americans because of the long history of disparity in adverse actions for that group (U.S. Office of Personnel Management 1995, Zwerling and Silver 1992, Halloran 1988, Harmon, Vaughn, and Cromwell 1987, National EEO Task Force Report 1991, 1993). In the mid 1990s, the Office of Personnel Management conducted an extensive study of the disparity in federal firing rates and ruled out differences in education, experience, performance appraisal ratings, or other such factors as the sole cause of the disparity. Instead, they suggested that "actual bias or lack of cultural awareness" was an explanation (OPM 1995, ii).

Such attitudes are precisely the kind of discord that managing diversity programs are meant to address (Soni 2000). Diversity training programs are often designed to root out bias and increase cultural awareness. The literature also suggests that organizations provide training in the skills required to work in a diverse workforce. Among the important skills are effective communication and conflict resolution. Greater proficiency in these areas could certainly reduce the likelihood that poor communication and conflict between supervisors and employees would ultimately lead to a dismissal action. The diversity literature also stresses the importance of holding managers accountable for success in achieving diversity-related goals. One such diversity goal could be, as is the case at MSHA, the requirement that they provide frequent fact-based performance information and solutions to staff, a practice that should also reduce performance problems that ultimately result in a dismissal.

Therefore, it seems appropriate to look at whether an agency's diversity program has achieved a more equitable distribution of dismissals between African Americans and other employees. This would be calculated in the same fashion as our promotion ratio discussed above. In this case, a positive outcome would be a quotient of less than or equal to 1.0, indicating that African Americans are dismissed in numbers less than or equal to their proportion of the workforce.

Voluntary Turnover

A third measure of the success of an agency's diversity efforts is based on the frequency of voluntary separations by women or minorities. It is well established that unwanted turnover can have severe consequences for organizations (Abbasi and Hollman 2000). Indeed, in the late 1980s the National Commission on the Public Service (1989; known more commonly as the Volcker Commission), the National Academy of Public Administration (Levine 1986), and others referred to a "quiet crisis" in the federal government (see also GAO 1990) that would result when the federal government would be unable to retain its fair share of the "best and brightest." Voluntary turnover can result from dissatisfaction with the job (Cotton and Tuttle 1986) and perceptions of unfairness in decisions regarding work-related outcomes (e.g., promotions) (Rutte and Messick 1995).

Some of the diversity literature encourages organizations to facilitate the development of groups representing specific categories of employees such as Latinos, women, or African Americans. These groups may help to reduce the isolation of members of these groups, which presumably would increase their willingness to remain on the job. It is also suggested that organizations work proactively to change an organizational culture that reflects the orientation of nonminority men to create a more inclusive environment. Diversity training is also expected to positively affect the culture by making people more aware of, and receptive to, cultural differences. It is expected that these activities would result in minorities feeling greater acceptance so they would be less likely to voluntarily leave their jobs. Therefore, we would expect that the female and minority share of voluntary quits in such circumstances would be equal to or less than their share of the workforce. The measure is constructed in a fashion similar to that used for our promotion and discharge ratios, but with the desired outcome being a quotient of less than or equal to 1.0. Once these measures are constructed, one need only examine whether the ratios improved following the implementation of the diversity program.

For example, Figure 9.2 shows promotion rates for women and minorities by year at NIH. (Recall that NIH has a very well developed diversity program). As can be seen, women, in general, have been promoted at a rate that is in proportion to their representation in the NIH workforce, or slightly better. These promotions exhibit a relatively stable pattern across the entire period of time analyzed, before and after the implementation of the diversity program. With respect to minority promotion ratios, a generally upward trend prior to the beginning of the program was reversed in the years following the program—although the ratio remained at 1.0 or better. It may be that the diversity program actually had the effect of distributing promotions more equitably across the entire workforce, admittedly not necessarily a positive outcome from the minority perspective.

Figure 9.3 shows dismissal and quit ratios computed for African Americans over the same period of time. In all the years examined, the firing ratio has been above 1.0, meaning that, as is the case government-wide, African Americans at NIH have been fired at rates disproportionate to their representation in the NIH workforce. The ratio has fluctuated rather wildly during the period analyzed, although there was a downward trend following the implementation of the program and a noticeable decline in the last year analyzed. If that trend continues, it may suggest that the diversity program is having a positive effect with respect to this measure. African-American quit behavior appears to be very stable across the entire series of years examined, hovering at about 1.0. This means that African Americans are leaving their jobs at NIH in about the same proportion as their representation in the workforce.

This kind of visual analysis, then, is useful for assessing whether a diversity program is successfully creating a more equitable work environment for women and minorities. It can be supplemented with interrupted time-series regression analysis, which provides quantitative estimates of the impact of the program at the time it was implemented and during the years following. An explanation of this method is provided in the Appendix to this chapter.

Concluding Observations and Recommendations

Observations

Since the early 1990s, employers across the country have developed programs to create better work environments for their increasingly diverse workforces. While much has been written about these efforts in the private sector, few have commented on the work of federal agencies. Yet, diversity efforts in the federal sector are arguably even more important than private

Figure 9.2: Minority and Female Promotion Ratios at the NIH (promotions in GS grades 9 and 12)

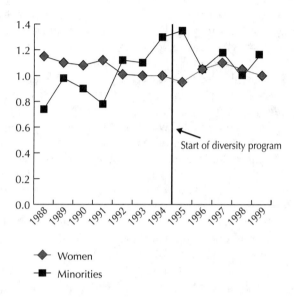

Figure 9.3: African-American Firing and Quit Ratios at the NIH

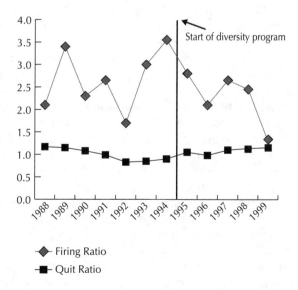

sector ones, because of the government's vital and visible role as the nation's largest employer and enforcer of equal employment opportunity laws.

We found that by 1999, the majority of federal agencies reported having a diversity program in place. Survey results show, however, that the activities they employ vary widely, spanning the range from continuing to do little more than what was expected of traditional EEO/AA programs to extending significantly beyond those parameters. This finding was confirmed by our in-depth case study analysis of seven federal agencies, whose programs matched this pattern. For example, NIST has chosen to completely separate its diversity program from EEO and to emphasize mentoring as an important component, while NIH has chosen to keep its program within the EEO office, but to establish diversity "catalysts" within each of its institutes and centers. BLM and MSHA focus, understandably, on recruitment since their white- collar workforces are the least diverse of the seven, while SAMHSA maintains that its program has shifted its focus from diversity to "cultural competence."

There has been very little effort to systematically evaluate the impact of federal agency programs despite the fact that public sector agencies are increasingly being called upon to show they are meeting their objectives by measuring performance and documenting improvements. Diversity programs should not be excepted from this expectation, particularly because they oftentimes have been subject to sharp criticism in Congress, the media, and elsewhere.

We suggested some measures that would serve as viable indicators of the success of diversity programs. These include ratios that assess whether women or minorities (or potentially any other category of employees) are promoted, dismissed from, or voluntarily leave their jobs in proportions commensurate with their representation in the workforce. These measures would show, for example, whether the mentoring or career advancement programs that are characteristic of many diversity programs are helping to ensure equitable promotion opportunities for all groups within the workplace. They would also show whether training in communication and conflict negotiation has helped to ameliorate the dynamics that have resulted in the disparate dismissal rate of some minority groups. An examination of turnover patterns would suggest whether the diversity program has created a more inclusive organizational climate, in which minorities and women believe they are respected and have commensurate access to consequential work assignments and advancement opportunities.

The collection and analysis of these data also highlight the problem areas that the diversity program should seek to address. In a particular agency, promotions of women vis-à-vis their representation at particular grade levels may indeed be a problem, in which case that agency might want to direct its attention to identifying potential barriers to their advancement, and/or developing a mentoring program for women. Another agency might find that the quit ratio for Latinos, for example, is greater than one would expect, and so that agency might develop initiatives specifically focused on Latino retention. The advantage of a diversity program is that it is not defined by laws and regulations that require specific activities, such as an EEO program might be, and therefore it can be tailored to an agency's unique circumstances.

In the example included in the previous section, promotion opportunities for women and voluntary quits by African Americans at NIH appear to be unaffected by the implementation of the diversity program. However, these numbers also show that female promotions and voluntary separations of African Americans were not a problem that needed to be addressed. These numbers were in proportion to their representation in the workforce before the diversity program was implemented. Minority promotions exhibited a slight downturn, but the effect of the diversity program may have been to begin to smooth out what had been an uneven trend. Prior to implementation of the program, minorities were, at times, promoted significantly less than and, at times, greater than their representation in those grades. The diversity program appears to have had a positive impact on the disproportionate dismissal rate of African Americans.

Recommendations

Federal agencies have largely come around to believe that diversity programs are important, and they are devoting varying levels of resources to their development. The range of activities differs among them, appropriately so, given their differing missions, workforces, and other circumstances. They should be encouraged to continue to develop their own agency-specific programs. However, they should also be encouraged to collect and analyze empirical data to discover where disparities may be greatest, as well as to evaluate the impact of their programs. We offer the following specific recommendations for federal agencies and their managers.

Recommendation One: All federal agencies should develop and implement diversity management programs consistent with their resources, mission, and unique needs.

It is clear that the American workforce is becoming increasingly diverse and its full potential will not be tapped by an organizational structure and culture that developed in an era when the workforce was largely white and male. The underlying purpose of diversity management programs should be to promote environments in which all employees are given the opportunity to succeed to the fullest extent possible, given their abilities and skills. The climate should facilitate the recruitment and retention of underrepresented groups. In this fashion, diversity programs will complement traditional equal employment opportunity recruitment efforts.

Each agency should be cognizant that its circumstances regarding diversity may be unique, and that the program it develops should be adapted to meet its particular concerns. A well-developed diversity program would include some or all of the following elements:

1. *Diversity training.* Ideally this training should confront the challenging issues of stereotypes and discrimination and the organizational structures that sustain them. Training should also focus on developing skills such as communication and conflict resolution. Some organizations require such training of all employees, or of all supervisors and managers, while others prefer to make attendance voluntary. Unfortunately, poorly conceived diversity training can (and has) caused more harm than good by increasing employee alienation and distrust of the organization. For that reason, agencies should take great care in developing training content and/or choosing contractors to provide it. Until an agency can be sure that the training will achieve its goals, it should not be made mandatory.

2. *Diversity council or board.* Whether representative of the agency by organizational component (as at NIST), or by occupational or interest group (as at NIH), a council can be a forum for airing and resolving diversity-related issues and for making recommendations to the agency head. It will provide a unifying mechanism through which employee concerns can be identified and potential resolutions recommended. Its representative nature will add to the credibility of the policies it endorses for adoption by the agency head.

3. *Critical element in the performance plans of managers and supervisors.* All managers and supervisors should be held accountable for achieving diversity-related objectives. The objectives should not be as amorphous as, for example "fostering an inclusive environment." Rather, they should be measurable and/or observable. In some cases, it may be appropriate to expect a manager to achieve an improvement in the ratio measures described in the previous section. In other cases, it may be enough to expect managers to undertake specific projects such as developing a career development or mentoring program, creating multicultural work teams, or engaging in the active recruitment of underrepresented groups.

4. *Mentoring opportunities.* Many employees who are successful in organizations identify and associate themselves with mentors who provide advice and guidance on career development. For some employees, this works best when they identify mentors who informally provide information and guidance. Others require a more formal and structured program. Regardless of approach, the agency should facilitate the

establishment of these relationships for employees who want them, so that all employees enjoy access to career-enhancing information, advice, networks, and work-related opportunities.

5. *Reexamination of job qualifications, performance, and promotion criteria.* Agencies should critically assess qualification standards and promotion criteria to ensure that they don't contain elements that may have been put in place some time ago and are no longer relevant. This is particularly important when these criteria have an adverse impact on particular groups of employees, such as minorities and women. An example might be requiring a specific degree such as a Ph.D. for a position when that is not really necessary for the effective performance of the job. Informal criteria, such as perceived availability to work overtime or relocate, should also be reexamined in this light.

Recommendation Two: Agencies should make a clear distinction between diversity management and traditional EEO and affirmative action programs.

Traditional EEO and affirmative action programs are mandated by law and are targeted toward preventing and overcoming discrimination directed toward women, racial and ethnic minorities, and the disabled. As such, agencies should continue to provide them with sufficient autonomy and resources to pursue these objectives and their unfaltering focus on the continued inequities confronting these groups. Diversity programs should complement them, not replace them. Diversity programs often have much broader objectives and are not mandated by law. As such, they should be flexible enough to allow agencies to create and experiment with strategies aimed at addressing subtle barriers or obstacles that confront people from diverse backgrounds. In many cases, these barriers do not constitute legally proscribed forms of discrimination, and so would not be within the purview of an EEO program. This distinctive nature of diversity management may be best maintained when the EEO program and the diversity program have separate organizational identities, as at NIST. Even if housed in the same office, they should be seen as distinct programmatic efforts that have different general purposes and methods, even while sharing some common goals. Clearly, mechanisms should be established to enhance their cooperation and ensure they don't step on each other's toes in pursuing their highly related objectives.

Recommendation Three: Agencies should gather baseline data to guide diversity program efforts and to serve as a means for continuous evaluation of the impact of their diversity programs.

As discussed in some detail in this chapter, a well-developed diversity management program should produce identifiable outcomes that reflect the existence of an open and equitable work environment. In the previous section, we suggested that such outcomes should include equitable prospects for minority and female promotions from middle- and higher-level grades as well as reductions in disproportionate numbers of voluntary separations and discharges of African-Americans. Agencies should collect and maintain the data necessary for construction of the promotion, quit, and discharge ratios proposed earlier. Early collection of these data will provide a basis for identifying problem areas requiring focused attention. These ratios should be tracked across time to determine if the diversity program is having its intended impact.

Diversity programs in federal agencies have come a long way from the scant attention they received in the early 1990s. Now most agencies are involved in an array of activities under the rubric of managing diversity. This chapter is intended to inform other agencies or public sector organizations interested in launching a diversity effort about how such efforts differ from traditional EEO and affirmative action, and the components they commonly include. We believe this information and the recommendations presented here can help agencies ensure their programs achieve a maximum return on their investment.

Appendix:
A Time-Series Regression Model for the NIH

The interrupted time-series regression model provides an appropriate method for the analysis of data collected to assess the impact of agency diversity programs. In the model, the dependent variable (minority or female promotion ratios or black quit or dismissal ratios) is regressed on a time trend variable coded 0 (zero) at the point of the initiation of the program with negative values prior to the program and positive values afterwards. Additional independent variables are then added to the model to assess the short- and long-term impacts of the program.

The model is estimated using the following equation:

Dependent Variable = $a + b_1X_1 + b_2X_2 + b_3X_3 + e$

Where: Dependent Variable = Minority Promotion Ratio
                                 or
                                 Female Promotion Ratio
                                 or
                                 Black Quit Ratio
                                 or
                                 Black Dismissal Ratio

a = the constant; i.e., it provides an estimated value of the dependent variable at the point where all independent variables are equal to zero (the year 1995 in this case) based on the preprogram trend.

X_1 = A counter for time, coded -7 for 1988, -6 for 1989, -5 for 1990 through 0 for 1995 (the year the program began), 1 for 1996, 2 for 1997, etc.

X_2 = An intervention variable coded 0 for years prior to the program (1988-1995) and 1 for years after the beginning of the program (1996-1999). This variable measures any change in the intercept at the time of the beginning of the program.

X_3 = An intervention variable coded 0 for years prior to the program (1988-95) and 1 for 1996, 2 for 1997, 3 for 1998, and 4 for 1999. This variable measures any change in the slope during the years following the program.

In the model, the parameter "a" is the estimated level of the dependent variable for the year 1995 based on the trend that occurred prior to the program. The coefficient b_1 provides the slope or rate of change in the dependent variable before the program. The parameter b_3 adjusts that slope as necessary to account for change that occurred following the program. Thus, the estimated slope for the postprogram years is given by $b_1 + b_3$. The coefficient b_2 estimates any change in the intercept at the point of the initiation of the program that would indicate an immediate increase or decrease in the dependent variable.

The equation for the black dismissal ratio is:

$$\text{Black Dismissal Ratio} = 2.997 + .085X_1 - .256X_2 - .344X_3$$

These results indicate that prior to the diversity program at NIH, the black employees' share of dismissals relative to their share of the workforce was increasing (on average) by the amount of .085 per year. After the program began, however, there was an immediate decline in the black dismissal ratio (indicated by the coefficient on the variable X_2 of -.256) and the ratio continued to decline across time from 1996 to 1999, as illustrated by the coefficient of -.344 on the variable X_3. Thus, we have a quantitative estimate of the extent to which the diversity program had the effect of ameliorating the problem of high dismissal rates for black employees.

Endnotes

1. Approximately 4.2 percent of the organizations with diversity programs had no useful response to this question.

2. Special emphasis programs focus on specific demographic groups such as Hispanics or women.

Bibliography

Abbasi, Sami M. and Kenneth W. Hollman. 2000. "Turnover: The Real Bottom Line," *Public Personnel Management* 29(3): 333-342.

Bowen, William G. and Derek Bok. 1998. *The Shape of the River*. Princeton, N.J.: Princeton University Press.

Caudron, Shari and Cassandra Hayes. 1997. "Are Diversity Programs Benefiting African Americans?" *Black Enterprise*. February, 121-124.

Chambers, Tamu and Norma Riccucci. 1997. "Models of Excellence in Workplace Diversity." In Carolyn Ban and Norma Riccucci (eds.) *Public Personnel Management: Current Concerns, Future Challenges*. New York: Longman, pp. 73-90.

Chicago Area Partnerships (CAPS). 1996. "Pathways and Progress: Corporate Best Practices to Shatter the Glass Ceiling." Chicago: Chicago Area Partnerships. April.

Cotton, John L. and Jeffrey M. Tuttle. 1986. "Employee Turnover: A Meta-Analysis and Review with Implications for Research," *Academy of Management Review* 11: 55-70.

Cox, Taylor Jr. 1994. *Cultural Diversity in Organizations*. San Francisco: Berrett-Koehler.

Digh, Patricia. 1997. "Well-Managed Employee Networks and Business Value," *HR Magazine*. August, 67-72.

Dobbs, Matti. 1996. "Managing Diversity: Lessons From the Private Sector," *Public Personnel Management* 25(3): 351-367.

Dugan, Beverly A., et al. 1993. "The Glass Ceiling: Potential Causes and Possible Solutions." Alexandria, Va.: Human Resources Research Organization. July.

Edsall, Thomas B. and Mary D. Edsall. 1991. *Chain Reaction*. New York: W.W. Norton and Company.

Fernandez, John P. 1999. *Race, Gender and Rhetoric*. New York: McGraw Hill.

Fine, Marlene G. 1995. *Building Successful Multicultural Organizations*. Westport, Conn.: Quorum Books.

Flynn, Gillian. 1999. "White Males See Diversity's Other Side," *Workforce* 78(2): 52-56.

Gardenswartz, Lee and Anita Rowe. 1993. *Managing Diversity: A Complete Desk Reference and Planning Guide*. New York: Irwin.

Halloran, Richard. 1988. "Navy is Studying Bias in Promotions," *New York Times*. July 24, 14.

Harmon, Gloria, Walter Vaughn and Martin F. Cromwell. 1987. *Review of Disciplinary Actions in State Service*. Sacramento: State Personnel Board. June 2.

Hemphill, Hellen and Ray Haines. 1997. *Discrimination, Harassment and the Failure of Diversity Training*. Westport, Conn.: Quorum Books.

Hudson, J. Blaine and Bonetta M. Hines-Hudson. 1999. "A Study of Contemporary Racial Attitudes of Whites and African Americans," *The Western Journal of Black Studies* 23,1. Spring, 22-34.

Johnston, William B. and Arnold E. Packer. 1987. *Workforce 2000: Work and Workers for the 21st Century*. Indianapolis: Hudson Institute.

Johnston, William B., et al. 1988. *Civil Service 2000*. Washington, D.C.: U.S. Office of Personnel Management.

Judy, Richard W. and Carol D'Amico. 1997. *Workforce 2020*. Indianapolis, Ind.: Hudson Institute.

Kelly, Erin and Frank Dobbin. 2001. "How Affirmative Action Became Diversity Management: Employer Response to Antidiscrimination Law, 1991-1996." In John David Skrentny (ed.) *Color Lines: Affirmative Action, Immigration and Civil Rights Options for America*. Chicago: University of Chicago Press.

Krefting, Linda A. and Susan L. Kirby. 1997. "Managing Diversity as a Proxy for Requisite Variety," *Journal of Management Inquiry* 6(4): 376-390.

Levine, Charles. 1986. *The Quiet Crisis of the Civil Service: The Federal Personnel System at the Crossroads*. Washington, D.C.: National Academy of Public Administration (December).

Lubove, Seth. 1997. "Damned if You Do, Damned if You Don't," *Forbes* 160(13): 122-126.

Lunney, Kellie. 2000. "EPA Officials Deny Discrimination," *Government Executive*. Available at www.govexec.com/dailyfed (Oct. 5).

Lynch, Frederick R. 1997a. *The Diversity Machine*. New York: The Free Press.

_____. 1997b. "Managing Diversity," *National Review* 49(19): 56-60.

Mathews, Audrey. 1998. "Diversity: A Principle of Human Resource Management," *Public Personnel Management* 27(2), 175-186.

Mishel, Lawrence and Ruy A. Teixera, 1991. *The Myth of the Coming Labor Shortage: Jobs, Skills, and Incomes of America's Workforce 2000*. Washington, D.C.: Economic Policy Institute.

Morrison, Ann M. 1992. *The New Leaders: Guidelines on Leadership Diversity in America*. San Francisco: Jossey-Bass.

Naff, Katherine C. 2001. *To Look Like America*. Boulder, Colo.: Westview Press.

National Aeronautics and Space Administration (NASA). 1994. "Equal Opportunity and Diversity Management Plan." Washington, D.C.: NASA. May 1.

National Commission on the Public Service. 1989. *Leadership for America: Rebuilding the Public Service*. Lexington, Mass.: D.C. Heath and Company.

National EEO Task Force Report. 1991. Washington, D.C.: National Treasury Employees Union and U.S. Internal Revenue Service. April.

_____. 1993. Washington, D.C.: National Treasury Employees Union and U.S. Internal Revenue Service. April.

Norton, J. Renae and Ronald E. Fox. 1997. *The Change Equation: Capitalizing on Diversity for Effective Organizational Change.* Washington, D.C.: American Psychological Association.

Price, Joyce. 1994. "Cultural Diversity Required at HUD," *The Washington Times* (Feb. 11).

Rutte, Christel G. and David M. Messick. 1995. "An Integrated Model of Perceived Unfairness in Organizations," *Social Justice Research* 8(3): 239-261.

Shull, Steven A. 1993. *A Kinder, Gentler Racism?* Armonk, N.Y.: M.E. Sharpe.

Slack, James D. 1997. "From Affirmative Action to Full-Spectrum Diversity in the American Workplace," *Review of Public Personnel Administration* 17(41): 75-87.

Soni, Vidu. 2000. "A Twenty-First-Century Reception for Diversity in the Public Sector: A Case Study," *Public Administration Review* 60(5): 395-408.

Thomas, David A. and John J. Gabarro. 1999. *Breaking Through: The Making of Minority Executives in Corporate America.* Boston: Harvard University Press.

Thomas, R. Roosevelt Jr. 1990. "From Affirmative Action to Affirming Diversity," *Harvard Business Review* 68(2): 107-117.

_____. 1991. Beyond Race and Gender: *Unleashing the Power of Your Total Work Force by Managing Diversity.* New York: Amacom.

_____. 1996. *Redefining Diversity.* New York: Amacom.

U.S. General Accounting Office. 1992. *The Changing Workforce: Demographic Issues Facing the Federal Government.* Washington, D.C.: U.S. General Accounting Office, GAO/GGD-92-38 March.

U.S. Office of Personnel Management. 1995. *Minority/Non-Minority Disparate Discharge Rates.* Washington, D.C.: U.S. Office of Personnel Management. April.

Wilson, Trevor. 1997. *Diversity at Work: The Business Case for Equity.* Toronto: John Wiley and Sons.

Wise, Lois R. and Mary Tschirhart. 2000. "Examining Empirical Evidence on Diversity Effects: How Useful is Diversity Research for Public-Sector Managers?" *Public Administration Review* 60(5): 386-394.

Zwerling, C. and H. Silver. 1992. "Race and Job Dismissals in a Federal Bureaucracy," *American Sociological Review* 57, 651-60.

About the Contributors

Mark A. Abramson is executive director of The PricewaterhouseCoopers Endowment for The Business of Government, a position he has held since July 1998. Prior to the Endowment, he was chairman of Leadership Inc. From 1983 to 1994, Mr. Abramson served as the first president of the Council for Excellence in Government. Previously, Mr. Abramson served as a senior program evaluator in the Office of the Assistant Secretary for Planning and Evaluation, U.S. Department of Health and Human Services.

He is a Fellow of the National Academy of Public Administration. In 1995, he served as president of the National Capital Area Chapter of the American Society for Public Administration. Mr. Abramson has taught at George Mason University and the Federal Executive Institute in Charlottesville, Virginia.

Mr. Abramson is the co-editor of *Transforming Organizations, Managing for Results 2002, E-Government 2001,* and *Innovation.* He also recently edited *Memos to the President: Management Advice from the Nation's Top Public Administrators* and *Toward a 21st Century Public Service: Reports from Four Forums.* He is also the co-editor (with Joseph S. Wholey and Christopher Bellavita) of *Performance and Credibility: Developing Excellence in Public and Nonprofit Organizations,* and the author of *The Federal Funding of Social Knowledge Production and Application.*

He received his Bachelor of Arts degree from Florida State University. He received a Master of Arts degree in history from New York University and a Master of Arts degree in political science from the Maxwell School of Citizenship and Public Affairs, Syracuse University.

Ray Blunt primarily focuses on helping to grow public service leaders, on organizational succession, and on change management initiatives as a coach, teacher, and mentor. In addition to currently working with several individual government organizations, he has been affiliated as a leadership coach and instructor with the Council for Excellence in Government Fellows. He also works with the Federal Executive Institute and the Leadership Development Academy of The Graduate School as a leadership coach and instructor. He formerly served as a senior consultant with the Center for Human Resources Management of the National Academy of Public Administration (NAPA).

Mr. Blunt frequently speaks to a variety of forums in the public sector on leadership and strategic thinking issues as well as on the use of story-telling in leadership. He also works with nonprofit organizations on strategic planning and board management.

Mr. Blunt served 35 years in public service in the Air Force and the Department of Veterans Affairs—the last 17 of those years as a Senior Executive. He has successfully led a number of significant change initiatives and has headed organizations involved in strategic and human resources planning and policy and organizational analysis.

He is a 1964 graduate of the U.S. Air Force Academy and holds a master's degree in economics from Central Missouri State University. He has done extensive post-graduate studies in management and theology.

His publications include *Leaders Growing Leaders: Preparing the Next Generation of Public Service Executives* (The PricewaterhouseCoopers Endowment for The Business of Government, May 2000); "Leaders and Stories: Growing the Next Generation, Conveying Values, and Shaping Character," *The Public Manager* (Spring 2001); *Managing Succession and Developing Leadership: Growing the Next Generation of Public Service Leaders* (The National Academy of Public Administration, September 1997); "Filling Executive Shoes," *The Government Executive* (October 1997); and "Growing Public Service Leaders," with Hugh Clark, *The Public Manager* (Summer 1997).

Carol Chetkovich is Assistant Professor of Public Policy at Harvard University's John F. Kennedy School of Government, where she is affiliated with the Malcolm Wiener Center for Social Policy. She teaches courses on public management, diversity in the workplace, and research methods.

Professor Chetkovich is the author of *Real Heat: Gender and Race in the Urban Fire Service,* a study of occupational culture and workforce diversity in the Oakland (California) Fire Department. *Real Heat,* a winner of *Choice's* Outstanding Academic Book award, tells the story of a class of firefighter recruits from their academy training through their 18-month probation, exploring the ways in which race and gender diversity affect the entry of newcomers into the traditional culture.

Her current research project, part of which is reported here, examines the occupational culture of policy professionals. The project is motivated by questions about both the movement of policy students away from government and the relevance of race and gender in student experience.

Professor Chetkovich has conducted policy research for state and federal government agencies in a number of social service areas, and she served for several years as the vice president of a nonprofit medical clinic. Before joining the Kennedy School, she taught at the University of California, Berkeley, and Mills College.

Professor Chetkovich is a graduate of Stanford University (1970) and holds an M.P.P. (1987) and Ph.D. (1994) from the Graduate School of Public Policy at the University of California, Berkeley.

Ruby Butler DeMesme is Director, PwC Consulting in the Human Capital Solutions and Defense practice. Prior to joining PwC Consulting, she was Assistant Secretary for Manpower, Reserve Affairs, Installations and Environment, the most senior personnel official in the Air Force, responsible for recruiting, training, and the well-being of active duty, reserve component, and civilian employees. During 32 years as a public servant, her career has spanned from classroom instructor, social work administrator, and human resource manager, as well as U.S. Senate staff advisor.

She serves on the boards of the University of North Carolina School of Social Work and Andrews Federal Credit Union. She has received numerous awards including the Exceptional Civilian Service Medal and is a member of various Who's Who rosters.

Mrs. DeMesme holds a B.A. in English from St. Augustine's College and a Master of Social Work from the University of North Carolina at Chapel Hill. She has published many articles and speeches within the military community.

Nicole Willenz Gardner is a Partner, PwC Consulting and guides the Learning Solutions Group's team of dedicated learning and education professionals. She is also the business unit leader for PwC Consulting's Human Capital Solutions practice in the public sector.

As a recognized industry leader, Ms. Gardner chairs an executive advisory board to the Kogod School of Business at American University. She is a popular speaker and has presented on the latest trends in learning to such groups as the American Society for Training and Development (ASTD) and The Conference Board.

Ms. Gardner holds a B.A. in economics from Boston University and co-authored the *Price Waterhouse EDI Handbook* and contributed to *Better Change*. She has published numerous articles on e-business, change management and organizational best practices.

J. Edward Kellough is Associate Professor in the School of Public and International Affairs and Director of the Doctoral Program in Public Administration at the University of Georgia. Professor Kellough teaches courses in Public Personnel Administration/Human Resources Management, Program Evaluation, Public Administration and Democracy, and other topics. His principal research interests are in the area of public personnel management. He has focused recently on employee turnover in the public service, alternative pay structures including pay for performance, civil service reform, the reinventing government movement, equal employment opportunity/affirmative action in the public sector, and the concept of representative bureaucracy.

Dr. Kellough has published in numerous scholarly journals including *Public Administration Review, American Journal of Political Science, Review of Public Personnel Administration, Public Personnel Management, Social Science Quarterly, The American Review of Public Administration, Public Administration Quarterly,* and others. He is also the author of *Federal Equal Employment Opportunity Policy and Numerical Goals and Timetables: An Impact Assessment.* Professor Kellough serves on the editorial review board of the *Review of Public Personnel Administration,* and has completed terms on the editorial board of the *Public Administration Review* and the *Journal of Public Administration Education.* He has consulted with federal, state, and local government organizations in the United States and has provided training in conjunction with the University of Georgia, Carl Vinson Institute of Government in public management to Ukrainian local government officials at Uzhgorad State University, Uzhgorad, Ukraine, and to regional government officials in Shanghai and Beijing, China.

Katherine C. Naff is Assistant Professor of Public Administration at San Francisco State University and Senior Evaluation Coordinator for the University's Public Research Institute. Among the courses she teaches are Research Methods, Human Resource Management, Program Evaluation, and Diversity Issues in Public Administration. Professor Naff's research focuses on public sector human resource management, civil service reform, equal employment opportunity and affirmative action, and representative bureaucracy.

She recently published a book entitled *To Look Like America,* which examines barriers to the participation and advancement of women and people of color in the federal government. Professor Naff has also published in *Public Administration Review, Political Research Quarterly, Public Personnel Management,* and *Policy Studies Journal,* among others. Her articles published in *Policy Studies Review* (1994) and the *Review of Public Personnel Administration* (2000) won awards for the best articles appearing in those journals that year, and she received the Distinguished Researcher award from the Section on Women in Public Administration, American Society for Public Administration in 2000. Professor Naff has served as a consultant to the National Performance Review's Diversity Task Force and the U.S. Customs Service.

Hal G. Rainey is Alumni Foundation Distinguished Professor of Political Science and Public Administration at the University of Georgia. His research concentrates on management in the public sector, with emphasis on leadership, incentives, change, and performance. He also conducts research on comparisons of the public and private sectors, and on the privatization of public services.

His most recent book is *Advancing Public Management* (Georgetown University Press, 2000, co-edited with Jeffrey Brudney and Laurence O'Toole). He is preparing a third edition of his book *Understanding and Managing Public Organizations,* which won the Best Book Award of the Public and Nonprofit Sector Division of the Academy of Management.

In 1995, he received the Levine Award for excellence in research, teaching, and service, conferred jointly by the American Society for Public Administration and the National Association of Schools of Public Affairs and Administration. He has served as chair of the Public and Nonprofit Sector Division of the Academy of Management, and as chairperson of the Public Administration Section of the American Political Science Association.

Professor Rainey's recent research projects include participation with a research team evaluating the Department of Energy's contracting out of the management of the National Laboratories. He is also working with a team of researchers on a study of the reforms and changes under way at the U.S. Internal Revenue Service.

In 1991, he served on the Governor's Commission on Effectiveness and Economy in Government of the State of Georgia. As a commissioner, he served on the Task Force on Privatization. In 1996 he served on the Athens-Clarke County (Georgia) Consolidation Charter Overview Commission. Before entering university teaching and research, he served as an officer in the U.S. Navy and as a VISTA volunteer.

He holds a B.A. from the University of North Carolina at Chapel Hill, and an M.A. (psychology) and Ph.D. (public administration) from the Ohio State University.

Barry M. Rubin is a Professor in the School of Public and Environmental Affairs (SPEA) at Indiana University in Bloomington. He has been a member of the School's faculty since 1979. His B.S. degree is from the Florida State University, and his M.A. and Ph.D. degrees are from the University of Wisconsin – Madison.

Professor Rubin's research has focused on public and environmental policy issues at local and regional levels, and on the application of statistical and quantitative analysis tools to policy and management. He has done extensive work on the effectiveness of urban enterprise zones as local and regional economic development tools, on the regional economic development impacts of global climate change, and on the effectiveness of strategic planning and management in local government. Over the past five years, his research has turned to the question of applying quantitative tools to assess and improve the delivery of local public services through new management structures. His work has been published in *Public Administration Review*, the *Journal of the American Planning Association, Public Productivity and Management Review*, the *Journal of Collective Negotiations in the Public Sector, Urban Affairs, Economic Development Quarterly*, the *Transportation Journal, Land Economics*, and the *Journal of Regional Science*, among others.

Professor Rubin teaches in the areas of statistics and quantitative methods, management information systems, urban economic development, urban policy, and strategic planning and management. While at Indiana University, he has also served as a consultant to several private firms and to a number of local, state, and federal government agencies.

Richard S. Rubin is a Professor in the School of Public and Environmental Affairs (SPEA) at Indiana University in Bloomington. Before joining the SPEA faculty in 1973, he was Senior Extension Associate in the School of Industrial and Labor Relations at Cornell University in Ithaca, New York. While there, his efforts were directed toward training both government officials and labor leaders in the newly developing area of labor-management relations in the public sector. His A.B. degree is from Middlebury College, and both his M.I.L.R. and Ph.D. degrees are from Cornell University.

Professor Rubin's teaching and research center on labor-management relations in the public sector with a particular focus on conflict resolution and labor-management cooperation. His current research interest is in labor-management cooperation strategies for unionized public employees and their governmental employers. Much of his work is based on applied research and has been published in the *Industrial and Labor Relations Review, Public Administration Review, Public Productivity and Management Review, Employee Relations Law Journal*, and *Journal of Collective Negotiations in the Public Sector*.

In addition to teaching and research, Professor Rubin regularly serves as a mediator, fact finder, and arbitrator in collective bargaining disputes between public employee unions and government, specializing in state and local disputes. He has served as the neutral chair of several joint labor-management committees.

Michael Serlin led the financial management team for the National Performance Review (Reinventing Government) Task Force, most of whose recommendations were incorporated into the Government Management Reform Act of 1994. The law included requiring audited financial statements for all major agencies and introduced franchising—competitive cross-servicing of agency administrative support.

A former Senior Executive Service Presidential Rank award winner, and a former president of the Federal Executive Institute Alumni Association, Mr. Serlin worked for three departments (Treasury, Post Office, and Navy) and two independent agencies (Federal Deposit Insurance Corporation and Federal Home Loan Bank Board) in his federal career.

He is a Principal with The Council for Excellence in Government and currently serves on the boards of directors of three nonprofit organizations— The International Institute of Business Technologies, the Treasury Historical Association, and the Arlington (Virginia) Retirement Housing Corporation. He has contributed frequent articles on entrepreneurial government and other government change efforts to magazines and professional journals.

Barry Sugarman is currently involved in a partnership between the Society for Organizational Learning and several federal government agencies. He is the author of four books and numerous articles. He earned a Ph.D. from Princeton University in sociology and anthropology, an M.A. from Southern Illinois University, and a B.A. from the University of Exeter, England.

Dr. Sugarman has been a professor of management at Lesley University in Cambridge, Massachusetts, since 1979. He is now a research associate at the Veterans Evidence-based Research, Dissemination and Implementation Center (VERDICT), supported by the Veterans Health Administration at the University of Texas, San Antonio, to study and improve the dissemination of new medical knowledge.

Formerly a research associate at the Center for Organizational Learning at the MIT Sloan School of Management, Dr. Sugarman is conducting a 20-case, comparative study of change initiatives in business and government organizations that emphasize participation and a learning-based approach to change leadership. Among the topics being investigated are the roles of formal and informal leaders in introducing new ways of learning in the workplace; the shifting of shared understandings about the boundary between "work" and "learning"; and ways of more effectively creating, refining, and sharing knowledge in work groups, communities of practice, and other social networks.

The first five years of Dr. Sugarman's career were spent at Oxford University, England, and focused on the sociology of learning. Towards the end of that period he became deeply interested in what was then the radically new model of the therapeutic community for addiction recovery. He was one of the first to study and assist those therapeutic communities in the early 1970s and published several pieces in this area. That interest led to several years of working outside the academy, gaining experience in both the nonprofit sector and county government. In Dayton, Ohio, he developed an accountability system for all the nonprofit agencies that contracted with the county board of mental health and mental retardation.

At Lesley University Graduate School, he taught mid-career professionals in health services and general management areas. He also designed and directed the unique master's degree program in management of substance abuse services.

Dr. Sugarman grew up in London, England, and began to explore the United States as a graduate student. He is now a U.S. citizen. He has been a consultant to a variety of organizations on strategic management, program assessment, and the improvement of learning systems. He is now teaching a course on organizations in the Internet economy at the Harvard University Extension School.

About The PricewaterhouseCoopers Endowment for The Business of Government

Through grants for research, The PricewaterhouseCoopers Endowment for The Business of Government stimulates research and facilitates discussion of new approaches to improving the effectiveness of government at the federal, state, local, and international levels.

Research grants of $15,000 are awarded competitively to outstanding scholars in academic and nonprofit institutions across the United States. Each grantee is expected to produce a 30- to 40-page research report in one of the areas presented on pages 421-423. Grant reports will be published and disseminated by The Endowment. All the chapters presented in this book were originally prepared as grant reports to The Endowment.

Founded in 1998 by PricewaterhouseCoopers, The Endowment is one of the ways that PricewaterhouseCoopers seeks to advance knowledge on how to improve public sector effectiveness. The PricewaterhouseCoopers Endowment focuses on the future of the operations and management of the public sector.

Who is Eligible?
Individuals working in:
- Universities
- Nonprofit organizations
- Journalism

Description of Grant

Individuals receiving grants will be responsible for producing a 30- to 40-page research report in one of the areas presented on pages 421-423. The research paper should be completed within a six-month period from the start of the project. Grantees select the start and end dates of the research project.

Size of Grant

$15,000 for each research paper

Who Receives the Grant

Individuals will receive the grant, not the institution in which they are located.

Application Process

Interested individuals should submit:
- A three-page description of the proposed research
- A résumé, including list of publications

Application Deadlines

There are three funding cycles annually, with deadlines of:
- The last day of February
- The last day of June
- The last day of October

Applications must be postmarked or received online by the above dates.

Submitting Applications

Hard copy:

> Mark A. Abramson
> Executive Director
> The PricewaterhouseCoopers Endowment for The Business of Government
> 1616 North Fort Myer Drive
> Arlington, VA 22209

Online:

> endowment.pwcglobal.com/apply

Program Areas

E-Government

The Endowment is seeking proposals that examine the implementation of e-government in the following areas: (1) Government to Business (G2B); (2) Government to Citizen (G2C); (3) Government to Employee (G2E); and (4) Government to Government (G2G). The Endowment is especially interested in innovative approaches to providing information so citizens can make their own choices, complete service transactions electronically, hold government more accountable for results, and offer feedback.

Examples of previous grants in this area:
- The Auction Model: How the Public Sector Can Leverage the Power of E-Commerce Through Dynamic Pricing *by David Wyld*
- Commerce Comes to Government on the Desktop: E-Commerce Applications in the Public Sector *by Genie N. L. Stowers*
- The Use of the Internet in Government Service Delivery *by Steven Cohen and William B. Eimicke*

Financial Management

The Endowment is seeking proposals that examine specific financial management issues, such as cost accounting and management, financial and resource analysis, financial risk management and modeling, internal controls, operational and systems risk management, financial auditing, contract management, reconciliation, and overpayment recovery. The Endowment is especially interested in full costs and budgeting approaches for support services and capital assets, retirement, and other employee benefits, and other nondirect costs associated with delivering program services.

Examples of previous grants in this area:
- Audited Financial Statements: Getting and Sustaining "Clean" Opinions *by Douglas A. Brook*
- Credit Scoring and Loan Scoring: Tools for Improved Management of Federal Credit Programs *by Thomas H. Stanton*
- Using Activity-Based Costing to Manage More Effectively *by Michael H. Granof, David E. Platt, and Igor Vaysman*

Human Capital

The Endowment is seeking proposals that examine human capital issues related to public service. Human capital consists of the knowledge, skills, abilities, attitudes, and experience required to accomplish an organization's mission. It also includes an organization's ability to recruit and retain employees, as well as to undertake workforce planning and analysis.

Examples of previous grants in this area:
- Leaders Growing Leaders: Preparing the Next Generation of Public Service Executives *by Ray Blunt*
- Reflections on Mobility: Case Studies of Six Federal Executives *by Michael D. Serlin*
- Winning the Best and Brightest: Increasing the Attraction of Public Service *by Carol Chetkovich*

Managing for Results

The Endowment is seeking proposals that examine how organizations align their processes—such as budgeting, workforce, and business processes—around their strategic goals. This area also focuses on how organizations use performance and results information to make policy, management, and resource allocation decisions. The Endowment is especially interested in how different organizations work collaboratively to achieve common outcomes. The Endowment is also interested in case studies of the use of balanced scorecards, including the measurement of customer service.

Examples of previous grants in this area:
- The Challenge of Developing Cross-Agency Measures: A Case Study of the Office of National Drug Control Policy *by Patrick Murphy and John Carnevale*
- Using Performance Data for Accountability: The New York City Police Department's CompStat Model of Police Management *by Paul O'Connell*
- Using Evaluation to Support Performance Management: A Guide for Federal Executives *by Kathryn E. Newcomer and Mary Ann Scheirer*

New Ways to Manage

The Endowment is seeking proposals that examine specific instances of new ways of delivering programs and services to the public, including contracting out, competition, outsourcing, privatization, and public-private partnerships. The Endowment is also interested in innovations in the way public organizations are managed.

Examples of previous grants in this area:
- Entrepreneurial Government: Bureaucrats as Businesspeople *by Anne Laurent*
- San Diego County's Innovation Program: Using Competition and a Whole Lot More to Improve Public Services *by William B. Eimicke*
- The Challenge of Innovating in Government *by Sandford Borins*

Transforming Organizations

The Endowment is seeking proposals that examine how specific public sector organizations have been transformed with new values, changed cultures, and enhanced performance. This area also includes studies of outstanding public sector leaders.

Examples of previous grants in this area:
- Transforming Government: The Renewal and Revitalization of the Federal Emergency Management Agency *by R. Steven Daniels and Carolyn L. Clark-Daniels*
- Transforming Government: The Revitalization of the Veterans Health Administration *by Gary J. Young*
- Transforming Government: Dan Goldin and the Remaking of NASA *by W. Henry Lambright*

For more information about The Endowment

Visit our website at: endowment.pwcglobal.com
Send an e-mail to: endowment@us.pwcglobal.com
Call: (703) 741-1077

About PricewaterhouseCoopers

The Management Consulting Services practice of PricewaterhouseCoopers helps clients maximize their business performance by integrating strategic change, performance improvement, and technology solutions. Through a worldwide network of skills and resources, consultants manage complex projects with global capabilities and local knowledge, from strategy through implementation. PricewaterhouseCoopers (www.pwcglobal.com) is the world's largest professional services organization. Drawing on the knowledge and skills of more than 150,000 people in 150 countries, the practice helps clients solve complex business problems and measurably enhance their ability to build value, manage risk, and improve performance in an Internet-enabled world. PricewaterhouseCoopers refers to the member firms of the worldwide PricewaterhouseCoopers organization.